The Gospel according to
ST JOHN
11 - 21
and
The First Epistle of John

CALVIN'S COMMENTARIES

CALVIN'S COMMENTARIES

The Gospel according to
ST JOHN

11 — 21
and
The First Epistle of John

Translator
T. H. L. PARKER

Editors
DAVID W. TORRANCE
THOMAS F. TORRANCE

Wm. B. Eerdmans Publishing Company
Grand Rapids, Michigan

Published *1959*
Published *1961*
Reprinted *1979*

ISBN 0-8028-2044-1

CHAPTER ELEVEN

Now a certain man was sick, Lazarus of Bethany, of the village of Mary and her sister Martha. And it was that Mary which anointed the Lord with ointment, and wiped his feet with her hair, whose brother Lazarus was sick. The sisters therefore sent unto him, saying, Lord, behold, he whom thou lovest is sick. But when Jesus heard it, he said, This sickness is not unto death, but for the glory of God, that the Son of God may be glorified thereby. Now Jesus loved Martha, and her sister, and Lazarus. When therefore he heard that he was sick, he abode at that time two days in the place where he was. Then after this he saith to the disciples, Let us go into Judaea again. The disciples say unto him, Rabbi, the Jews were but now seeking to stone thee; and goest thou thither again? Jesus answered, Are there not twelve hours in the day? If a man walk in the day, he stumbleth not, because he seeth the light of this world. But if a man walk in the night, he stumbleth, because the light is not in him. (1-10)

1. *Now a certain man was sick.* The Evangelist now goes on to another story, which relates a specially remarkable miracle. For besides putting forth a wonderful example of His divine power by raising Lazarus, Christ also set before our eyes a lively image of our future resurrection. And this was almost the last and final act, since the time of His death was drawing near. Therefore it is not surprising that He showed His glory especially in this work, for He wanted the memory of it to be fixed in the minds of His own, that it might be a kind of seal of everything that had happened before. Christ had raised others from the dead; but now He shows His power upon a rotted corpse. But we shall notice in their proper place the circumstances that bring praise to God's glory in this miracle.

Lazarus is said to be of Bethany, the village of Mary and Martha, probably because he was less well known among the faithful than his sisters. For those holy women used to welcome Christ to their home, as appears in Luke 10.38. It was a very silly idea of the monks and such like cheapjacks of the Papacy to make of this village (*castellum*)— that is to say, a little town or a country village—a castle.

They are also ignorant when they think that this Mary, Lazarus' sister, was the woman of evil repute and life mentioned in Luke 7.37. The anointing led them astray, as if it were not certain that Christ was anointed more than once and in different places. The woman who was a sinner anointed Christ, according to Luke, at Jerusalem, where she lived. But Mary of Bethany did the same things later on in her village. And the perfect tense which the Evangelist uses should not be referred to the time when these things happened but to the time when they were written about—as if he were saying, 'This is Mary, who afterwards poured on Him the ointment and made the disciples murmur' (Matt. 26.7f).

3. *Behold, he whom thou lovest is sick.* It is only a short message, but Christ could easily gather from it what the two sisters wanted. For under their lament they modestly introduce their prayers that He will help them. It is true that we are not forbidden a longer form of prayer; but the chief thing is to cast our cares and whatever troubles us into the bosom of God, that He may supply the remedy. This is how those women act towards Christ. They explain their trouble to Him intimately and look for relief from Him. It must also be noted that from Christ's love they conceive a trust to receive help. And this is a perpetual rule of true prayer; for where there is God's love, there is sure and present salvation. He does not love and forsake.

4. *But when Jesus heard it.* By this reply He wanted to set His disciples free from worry and vexation at seeing Him so careless of His friend's danger. Lest they should be anxious for Lazarus' life, He says that the sickness is not mortal and promises that it will afford fresh material for His glory. Moreover, although Lazarus did in fact die, yet because Christ restored him to life shortly afterwards, He has an eye to this outcome when He says that the sickness was not unto death.

The other clause, *for the glory of God,* is not opposed to this in such a way as to make it a generally valid argument; for we know that although the reprobate perish, the glory of God shines no less clearly in their destruction than in the salvation of the godly. But in this place Christ is properly pointing to the glory of God which was joined with His office. Moreover, the power of God in Christ's miracles was not threatening, but kind and sweet. Therefore, by His denial that Lazarus was in danger of death when He wanted to manifest His own and the Father's glory, we must consider wherefore and to what end He was sent by the Father: to save and not to destroy.

This expression *for the glory of God that the Son of man may be glorified,* is very important. From it we gather that God wants to be known in the person of His Son in such a way that whatever honour He demands for Himself may be paid to the Son. Therefore we find in chapter 5.23, 'He that honoureth not the Son honoureth not the Father.' The Turks and Jews pretend to worship God, but their

2

insolence against Christ means that they are trying to tear God from Himself.

5. *Now Jesus loved Martha.* At first it seems inconsistent that Christ remained for two days beyond Jordan as if He did not care about Lazarus' life, and yet that He is said to love him and his sisters. Love brings forth care; and He should have run to him at once. As Christ is the unique mirror of the divine grace, we are taught by His delay that we must not reckon the love of God by the present state of things. Often He delays His help when asked—either that He may sharpen our zeal in praying, or that He may exercise our patience and at the same time get us used to obedience. Therefore believers must so pray for God's help as to learn to suspend their own wishes if He undertakes their help more slowly than their need seems to demand. Although He may delay, He never sleeps, nor is forgetful of His own. And let us be quite sure that He wishes all whom He loves to be saved.

7. *Then after this he saith.* And now at last, when His disciples thought that He had forgotten Lazarus, or at least was putting other things before his life, He shows that He does care for him. Therefore He tells them to cross the Jordan and make for Judaea.

8. *Rabbi, the Jews were but now seeking.* The disciples try to scare Him off, not so much for His sake as for their own; each of them is afraid for himself, since the danger is common to all. Therefore, when they evade the cross and are ashamed to confess it, they put forward the more specious pretence that they are anxious for their Master. The same thing happens daily with many. Those who turn aside from their duty from fear of the cross look everywhere for excuses to cover up their weakness, lest they should seem to defraud God of due obedience without just cause.

9. *Are there not twelve hours?* There are various explanations of this verse. Those who think the words teach that men's minds are changeable, so that every hour they have a new and different purpose, are far from Christ's meaning. Indeed, I should not have troubled to refer to this if it had not become a common proverb. Let us be content with the real and simple meaning. First, Christ takes a metaphor from night and day. If anyone journeys in the dark, it is not surprising if he often knocks into things or goes astray or falls over. But in daytime the sunlight shows the way and there is no danger. Now the calling of God is like the daylight, which does not suffer us to err or stumble. Therefore, whoever obeys the Word of God and undertakes nothing save at His command will also have Him as leader and guide from heaven and in this confidence can go safely and boldly on his way. For, as Psalm 91.11 puts it, whoever walks in His ways has guardian angels and is safe with them leading him, so that he will not dash his

3

foot against a stone. Christ therefore relies on this help and goes courageously into Judaea without being frightened that He will be stoned. For there is no danger of going astray when God is a sun to shine on us and direct our way. We are taught by these words that whenever a man gives himself up to his own counsels without the calling of God, his whole life is nothing but a wandering and straying. And those who seem to themselves very wise and do not inquire at the mouth of God or have His Spirit as the ruler of all their actions are just blind men wandering in the darkness. The one right way is when we are well aware of the divine calling and always have God going before us. Sure confidence in a successful outcome will follow this rule of ordering our lives aright, because God cannot but govern us well. And this knowledge is more than necessary to us, for believers can scarcely move a foot to follow Him without Satan immediately heaping up a thousand obstacles, putting various dangers everywhere and in every way scheming to block our paths. But when the Lord as it were kindles His light and invites us to advance, we must go forward with a stout heart, though many deaths lie in our path. He never orders us to advance without encouraging us with a promise, so that we may be convinced that whatever we undertake at His command will turn out well and happily for us. This is our chariot. Whoever enters it will never faint from tiredness. Nay! if the obstacles are too difficult for us to travel just by the chariot, yet if we are furnished with these wings we shall always find a way out until we reach our goal—not that believers encounter no opposition, but the oppositions become helps to their salvation. The sum of it is that God's eyes will always be attentive to keep those who are attentive to His will. Hence again we gather that whenever men allow themselves to neglect and overlook God's Word and undertake what they please, the whole course of their life is accursed by God and vengeance on their rashness and blind passion is always imminent.

Here Christ is dividing the day into twelve hours, according to the manner of the ancients. For although the day varied in summer and winter, they always had twelve hours of the day and twelve of the night.

These things spake he: and after this he saith unto them, Our friend Lazarus is fallen asleep; but I go, that I may awake him out of sleep. The disciples therefore said unto him, Lord, if he is fallen asleep, he will recover. Now Jesus had spoken of his death: but they thought that he spake of taking rest in sleep. Then Jesus therefore said unto them plainly, Lazarus is dead. And I am glad for your sakes that I was not there, to the intent ye may believe; nevertheless let us go unto him.

4

Thomas therefore, who is called Didymus, said unto his fellow-disciples, Let us also go, that we may die with him. So when Jesus came, he found that he had been in the tomb four days already. (11-17)

11. *Our friend Lazarus is fallen asleep.* Before this He had said that the sickness was not mortal. But now, lest they should be too distressed at an unexpected shock, He tells them that Lazarus is dead, and gives hope of his resurrection. But their ignorance is amazing when they take Christ's word as meaning sleep. For although this is a metaphor, it is so frequent and common in Scripture that it should have been well known to all the Jews.

12. *If he is fallen asleep, he will recover.* When they make the point that sleep will be good for Lazarus, they are indirectly aiming at dissuading Christ from going there. And yet it is not as if they craftily turn Christ's word to their own ends; but when they think He spoke about sleep, they gladly seize the opportunity of fleeing from danger. Augustine and many after him speculate subtly about the word 'sleep'. They say that it is applied to death because it is as easy for God to raise the dead to life as it is for us to awaken the sleeping. But we may infer from its constant use in Scripture that Christ had nothing of this sort in mind. Indeed, since even in secular writers this same application is common, it is certain that it came into use merely because a lifeless corpse lies insensible just like the body of a man fast asleep. This is why sleep is quite appropriately called 'the image of death', and Homer calls it κασίγνητος θανάτου, death's brother. What is more, the word denotes only the sleep of the body, and it is too absurd for some fanatics to apply it to souls, as if they too were subject to death by being deprived of understanding.

Now, Christ commends His power when He says that He will come to waken Lazarus. For though, as has been said, the easiness of the resurrection is not expressed in the word 'sleep', Christ shows that He is the Lord of death by saying that He wakens those whom He restores to life.

14. *Then he therefore said unto them plainly.* Christ's kindness in putting up with such stupidity in the disciples was remarkable. Indeed, the reason why He temporarily delayed giving them the fuller grace of the Spirit was to heighten the miracle of restoring them in a moment.

When he says, *And I am glad for your sakes,* He means that it was good for them that He was not there, since His power would have been less obvious if He had helped Lazarus at once. The more nearly God's works approximate to the ordinary course of nature, the more are they despised and the less obvious is their glory. And this we experience daily. For if He stretches out His hand at once we are not

conscious that He is helping us. Therefore, for the disciples to acknowledge the resurrection of Lazarus as a truly divine work, it had to be
delayed, so that it might be very different from a human remedy.

But, as I have pointed out before, we should remember that in the
person of Christ there is here represented God's fatherly kindness
towards us. When God permits us to be overwhelmed and to faint
under ills a long time, let us know that in this way He is thinking of
our salvation. At such times, of course, we groan in anxiety and
sadness, but the Lord rejoices for our good; and a twofold kindness
shows in His not only pardoning our sins, but joyfully devising
means to correct them.

To the intent ye may believe. He does not mean that this was the
very beginning of faith in them, but that it was the confirmation of
faith already begun though still very meagre and weak. Yet He hints
that if the hand of God had not been openly displayed, they would
not have believed.

16. *Thomas therefore.* So far the disciples had tried to dissuade
Christ. Thomas is now ready to follow, but without any confidence.
Or at any rate, he does not fortify himself with Christ's promise and
follow Him cheerfully and calmly.

Let us go, that we may die is the language of despair. They ought to
have been sure of their lives. The relative phrase *with him* can be
explained either of Lazarus or of Christ. If you expound it as referring
to Lazarus, it will be ironical, as if he said, 'What is the point of going
there?—unless the only way we can do our duty as friends is to die
with him!' But I prefer the other meaning—Thomas does not refuse
to die with Christ. Nevertheless, as I have said, this arises from
thoughtless enthusiasm. He should rather have taken heart from faith
in the promise.

*Now Bethany was nigh unto Jerusalem, about fifteen furlongs off; and
many of the Jews had come to Martha and Mary, to console them
concerning their brother. Martha therefore, when she heard that Jesus
was coming, went and met him: but Mary still sat in the house. Martha
therefore said unto Jesus, Lord, if thou hadst been here, my brother had
not died. And even now I know that, whatsoever thou shalt ask of
God, God will give it thee. Jesus saith unto her, Thy brother shall
rise again. Martha saith unto him, I know that he shall rise again in
the resurrection at the last day. Jesus said unto her, I am the resurrection,
and the life: he that believeth on me, though he die, yet shall he live:
and whosoever liveth and believeth on me shall never die. Believest
thou this? She said unto him, Yea, Lord: I believe that thou art the
Christ, the Son of God, even he that cometh into the world.* (18-27)

Now Bethany. The Evangelist carefully describes everything that contributes to the certainty of the story. He relates how near Jerusalem was to the village of Bethany, lest anyone should be surprised that many friends came to comfort the sisters from there, whom God meant to be witnesses of the miracle. For although they were moved by neighbourly duty, they were really assembled there by the secret counsel of God for another purpose—that Lazarus' resurrection might not be obscure or that the witnesses might not be only his own family. And this convicts the malignant ingratitude of the nation, that this shining demonstration of Divine power at a well-known place, before a vast crowd and near the city gates—as if it were performed in a theatre—instantly vanishes from everyone's eyes. More, the Jews maliciously shut their eyes and refuse to see what is before them. Nor is it new or uncommon that men who too incessantly gape after miracles are quite dull and stupid in thinking about them.

The distance between the two places was less than two miles. For the *stadium* or furlong is six hundred feet, that is, one hundred and twenty-five Roman yards.

19. *To console them concerning their brother.* This was their purpose; but God had another aim, as we have said. It is clear from this that the house of Lazarus and his sisters was greatly respected and honoured. Again, as it is natural that the death of their own folk should bring grief and mourning to men, this duty that the Evangelist mentions, is not to be blamed, except in that sinful excess, which prevails in this as in other parts of life, corrupts what is not in itself sinful.

20. *Martha therefore, when she heard.* Martha goes outside the village, as we shall see later, not only, perhaps, because of her reverence for Christ, but that she might meet Him more secretly. For His danger was fresh in her mind; the rage of His enemies, though it had cooled off a little at His departure into Galilee, had not really died down, but might break out again more violently when they heard of His arrival.

21. *Lord, if thou hadst been here.* She begins with a lament, although in it she also modestly makes her wish known. It is as if she had said, 'You could, by your presence, have saved my brother from death; and even now you can do it, for God will not deny you anything.' But by speaking like this, she rather gives way to her feelings than restrains them under the rule of faith. I acknowledge that her words came from faith partly; but I say that disorderly passions were mixed with them and carried her beyond proper bounds. For when she tells herself that her brother would not have died had Christ been present, what grounds has she for her confidence? It was not conceived from any promise of Christ. It remains, therefore, that she

thoughtlessly yields to her own wishes instead of subjecting herself to Christ. Her ascribing to Christ power and supreme goodness proceeds from faith; but when she persuades herself of more than she had heard Christ declare, it is foreign to faith. We must always hold the mutual concord between the Word and faith, lest any should fabricate anything for himself apart from the Word of God. Moreover, Martha adhered too closely to Christ's corporeal presence. Therefore her faith, mixed up and entangled with unregulated desires, and even not completely free from superstition, could not shine with full brightness. And so only sparks of it gleam in these words.

23. *Thy brother shall rise again.* Christ's friendliness is wonderful. He forgives those faults of Martha that we have mentioned and of His own accord promises her more than she had dared to ask plainly and directly.

24. *I know that he shall rise again.* Here Martha's excessive timidity shows itself; she weakens what Christ had said. We said that she went further than she had a right to do when she fabricated for herself a hope out of her own thoughts. She now slips into the opposite fault of standing still, as if she were alarmed, when Christ holds out His hand. We ought to guard against both these. We must not, without God's Word, drink in empty and as it were windy hopes. Nor, when the Lord speaks must He find our hearts blocked up or shut too tight. Again, in her reply Martha wanted to ascertain more than she dared hope from Christ's words; as if she said, 'If you mean the last resurrection, I do not doubt that my brother will be raised again at the last day, and I comfort myself with this trust. But I do not know if you are pointing me to something greater.'

25. *I am the resurrection and the life.* Christ first proclaims that He is the resurrection and the life. Then He explains each clause of the statement separately and distinctly. First, He calls Himself the resurrection; for restoration from death to life precedes the state of life. But the whole human race is plunged in death. Therefore, no man will possess life unless he is first risen from the dead. Hence Christ teaches that He is the beginning of life. Afterwards He adds that the continuity of life is also the work of His grace.

The explanation which follows shows plainly that He is speaking of spiritual life: 'He that believeth on me, though he die, yet shall he live.' In what way, then, is Christ the resurrection? In that by His Spirit He regenerates the sons of Adam, who by their sin were alienated from God, so that they begin to live a new life. I have treated this subject more fully in chapter 5.21 and 24. Paul is the best interpreter of this passage in Eph. 2.5 and 5.8. Away with those who prate about men being prepared for the reception of God's grace by

8

the movement of nature! They might just as well say that the dead walk. For since no part or faculty of the soul is not corrupted and turned aside from what is right, the fact that men live and breathe and are endowed with sense, understanding and will tends to their destruction. Thus it is that death reigns everywhere. For the death of the soul is alienation from God. Therefore those who believe in Christ, although they had before been dead, begin to live; for faith is a spiritual resurrection of the soul, and as it were quickens the soul, that it may live unto God. As it is said in that passage, 'The dead shall hear the voice of the Son of God; and they that hear shall live' (John 5.25). This is indeed a bright commendation of faith, that it transfuses to us the life of Christ and thus liberates us from death.

26. *And whosoever liveth and believeth on me.* He expounds the second clause, on how Christ is the life—because He will never allow the life to be lost which He has once given, but keeps it unto the end. What would become of men, flesh being so frail, if when they have obtained life they are left to themselves thereafter? The continual state of life must therefore also be founded on the power of Christ, so that He may finish what He has begun.

Believers are said never to die because their souls, in that they are born again of incorruptible seed, have Christ dwelling in them, by whom they are continually quickened. For although the body is subject to death because of sin, the Spirit is life because of righteousness (Rom. 8.10). The fact that day by day the outward man decays in them, so far from detracting anything from their true life, in fact aids its progress, since the inward man is renewed day by day (II Cor. 4.16). More, death is itself a sort of liberating from the bondage of death.

Believest thou this? At first it seems as if Christ is conversing about spiritual life to take Martha's mind off her present desire. Martha wanted her brother to be restored to life. Christ replies that He is the author of a better life; because He quickens the souls of believers with a heavenly power. Yet I do not doubt that He meant to include a twofold grace. So He describes in general that spiritual life which He bestows on all His own; but He also wants to offer her a taste of the power which He was soon after to show in raising Lazarus.

27. *Yea, Lord.* To prove that she believes what she had heard about Christ—that He is the resurrection and the life—Martha replies that she believes He is the Christ and the Son of God. And this knowledge embraces the sum of all blessings, for we must always remember the purpose for which the Messiah was promised and the office the prophets ascribe to Him. When Martha confesses that He was the one who was to come into the world, she fortifies her faith by the

predictions of the prophets. It follows from this that the full restoration of all things as well as perfect happiness are to be looked for from Him, and in short that He was sent to set up and prepare the true and complete state of the kingdom of God.

And when she had said this, she went away, and called Mary her sister secretly, saying, The Master is here, and calleth thee. And she, when she heard it, arose quickly, and went unto him. (Now Jesus was not yet come into the village, but was still in the place where Martha met him.) The Jews then which were with her in the house, and were comforting her, when they saw Mary, that she rose up quickly and went out, followed her, supposing that she was going unto the tomb to weep there. Mary therefore, when she came where Jesus was, and saw him, fell down at his feet, saying unto him, Lord, if thou hadst been here, my brother had not died. When Jesus therefore saw her weeping, and the Jews also weeping which came with her, he groaned in the spirit, and was troubled, and said, Where have ye laid him? They say unto him, Lord, come and see. Jesus wept. The Jews therefore said, Behold how he loved him! But some of them said, Could not this man, which opened the eyes of him that was blind, have caused that this man also should not die? Jesus therefore again groaning in himself cometh to the tomb. Now it was a cave, and a stone lay against it. (28-38)

28. *And called her sister.* It was probably at Martha's request that Christ stayed outside the village and did not enter into a great crowd of men. She was afraid of the danger, since He had only recently barely escaped from the midst of death Accordingly she tells her sister privately, so that the news of His arrival should not spread.

The Master is here. The word *Master* shows the place those godly ladies gave to Christ. Although they had so far profited less than they should have done, it was a great thing that they were entirely devoted to Him as His disciples. Mary's hasty departure to go and meet Him is testimony of no ordinary reverence.

31. *The Jews then which were with her.* Although Martha was allowed by Christ to go home to withdraw her sister from the big crowd, Christ had also another purpose—that the Jews might be witnesses of the miracle. They themselves have no idea at all about this; but it was not new that men should be led as in darkness by the secret providence of God whither they did not intend. They think that Mary is going to the tomb, as is customary with those who seek to excite their grief. For this is a common disease, that husbands deprived of their wives, parents bereft of their children, and on the other hand, wives bereft of their husbands, and children deprived of

their parents or other relatives or friends, eagerly increase their grief by every possible means. It is also customary to seek various contrivances for this purpose. The affections of men are already disordered enough; but they excite them with new stimuli, so as to rush against God with greater force and violence. It was their duty to dissuade Mary, lest the sight of the tomb should minister to her grief. But they do not dare to apply so harsh a remedy, but even nourish the excess of her grief by accompanying her. Thus it often happens that the comforting of those who treat their friends too gently does little good.

32. *She fell down at his feet.* From the fact that she fell down at His feet we gather that He was honoured in that house beyond the ordinary custom of men. For although they used to throw themselves on the ground before kings and leaders, yet, since Christ had, so far as the flesh was concerned, nothing royal or magnificent in Himself, Mary fell down at His feet for a different reason. She would not have done so had she not been persuaded that He was the Son of God.

Lord, if thou hadst been here. She seems to be speaking reverently to Christ, but we have just shown what is wrong with her words. She ought not to have limited Christ's power, which filled heaven and earth, to His bodily presence.

33. *He groaned in the spirit.* Had Christ not been sorry for their unhappiness, He would have kept an unmoved face. But when He voluntarily conforms with them, even to tears, He shows His συμπάθεια. For to my mind the Evangelist expresses the reason for this emotion when he says that He saw Mary and the others weeping. Yet I do not doubt that He was looking higher, namely, at the common misery of the human race. For He remembered what He had been commanded by the Father and why He had been sent into the world —to free us from all ills. This very thing He has done, and He wants to show us that He has done it with earnestness and feeling. Accordingly, when He is about to raise Lazarus, before He grants the cure or help, He shows by His groaning in spirit, by a strong emotion of grief and by tears, that He is as much affected by our ills as if He had suffered them in Himself.

But how do groaning and trouble of mind belong to the person of the Son of God? It seems absurd to some when we say that Christ, as one among men, was subject to human passions; and they think that the only way He sorrowed or rejoiced was by taking into Himself those emotions, when He thought fit, by some secret dispensation. Augustine thinks that the Evangelist says this in the sense that He troubled Himself, whereas others are carried away by their feelings, which dominate or rather tyrannize their minds with trouble. There-

fore he thinks the meaning is that Christ, otherwise calm and free
from all passion, summoned groaning and grief of His own accord.
But it will, to my mind, be more agreeable to Scripture if we make
the simple statement that when the Son of God put on our flesh He
also of His own accord put on human feelings, so that He differed in
nothing from His brethren, sin only excepted. In this way we detract
nothing from the glory of Christ when we say that it was only a
voluntary submission, by which it came to pass that He was like us
in the emotions of the soul. Moreover, since He was submissive from
the beginning, we must not imagine that He was free and exempt
from them. Herein He proved Himself to be our brother, so that
we might know that we have a Mediator who willingly excuses
and is ready to help those infirmities which He has experienced in
Himself.

If any object that men's passions are sinful and that therefore it is
inconsistent that they should be shared by the Son of God, I reply
that there is a wide difference between Christ and us. Our feelings
are sinful because they rush on unrestrainedly and immoderately; but
in Christ they were composed and regulated in obedience to God and
were completely free from sin. Indeed, men's feelings are vicious and
perverse in two ways; first, because they are carried away in wild
confusion and are not ordered by the true rule of modesty; and
secondly, because they do not always arise from a legitimate cause,
or at least are not directed to a legitimate end. I say that there is
excess because none rejoices or grieves only sufficiently or as God
permits, and many even shake off the bridle altogether. The vanity
of our mind makes us sorrow or grieve over trifles, or for no reason
at all, because we are too much devoted to the world. Nothing like
this was to be found in Christ. No passion of His ever went beyond
its proper bounds. He had none that was not right and founded on
reason and sound judgment.

To make this still clearer, it is important for us to distinguish
between man's first nature, as it was composed by God, and this
degenerate nature which is corrupted by sin. When God created man,
He implanted emotions in him, but emotions which were obedient
and submissive to reason. The fact that those emotions are now disorderly and rebellious is an accidental fault. But Christ took upon
Him human emotions, yet without ἀταξία. For he who obeys the
passions of the flesh is not obedient to God. Christ indeed troubled
Himself and was strongly agitated; but in such a way that He kept
Himself under the will of the Father. In short, if you compare His
passions with ours, they are as different as pure, clear water flowing
in a gentle course from muddy and thick foam.

Christ's example alone should be sufficient for rejecting the unbending hardness of the Stoics; for where should we seek for the rule of supreme perfection but in Him? We ought to try to correct and tame that obstinacy implicit in our emotions on account of the sin of Adam, that we may follow Christ as our leader and He may bring us to order. Thus Paul does not demand of us a stony numbness, but tells us to grieve in moderation, and not abandon ourselves to grief like unbelievers who have no hope (I Thess. 4.13). For Christ also took our emotions into Himself, so that by His power we may subdue whatever is sinful in them.

36. *Behold how he loved him!* John here describes to us two different judgments on Christ. The first people, who said 'Behold how he loved him!' think less highly of Christ than they ought to have done, for they ascribe to Him nothing but what is human. Nevertheless, they speak of Him with greater frankness and modesty than the others, who maliciously decry Him for not having delivered Lazarus from dying. For although they applaud Christ's power, about which the former are silent, yet in doing so they reproach Him. It is clear enough from this that the miracles which Christ had done were not unknown to them. But the baser is their ingratitude that they do not hesitate to grumble because now on this single occasion He abstained. Men have always been ungrateful to God in this way, and continue to be so. If He does not satisfy all our wishes, we immediately break out into complaints: 'He has been accustomed to help me hitherto; why does He now forsake and disappoint me?' Here is a twofold disease. We thoughtlessly desire what is not expedient for us, and want to subject God to the perverse desires of our flesh. Again, we press importunately for an answer and the ardour of our impatience carries us untimely forward.

38. *Jesus therefore again groaning in himself.* Christ does not come to the sepulchre as an idle spectator, but like a wrestler preparing for the contest. Therefore no wonder that He groans again, for the violent tyranny of death which He had to overcome stands before His eyes. Some explain this groan as arising from indignation and offence at the unbelief we have spoken of. But another reason seems far more apt to me—that He was thinking of the event itself rather than the people. Various details follow, displaying more fully the power of Christ in raising Lazarus. They are the time of four days, during which the tomb had been closed by a stone, which Christ commands to be removed in the sight of them all.

Jesus saith, Take ye away the stone. Martha, the sister of him that was dead, saith unto him, Lord, by this time he stinketh: for he hath been dead four days. Jesus saith unto her, Said I not unto thee, that, if thou believedst, thou shouldest see the glory of God? So they took away the stone from the place where he that was dead lay. And Jesus lifted up his eyes, and said, Father, I thank thee that thou heardest me. And I knew that thou hearest me always: but because of the multitude which standeth around I said it, that they may believe that thou didst send me. And when he had thus spoken, he cried with a loud voice, Lazarus, come forth. He that was dead came forth, bound hand and foot with grave-clothes; and his face was bound about with a napkin. Jesus saith unto them, Loose him, and let him go. (39-44)

39. *Lord, by this time he stinketh.* This is a sign of distrust, for she expects less from the power of Christ than she should have done. The root of the evil lies in her measuring God's infinite and incomprehensible power by her carnal sense. Since there is nothing less accordant with life than putrefaction and stench, Martha infers that there is no place for a remedy. When our minds are ruled by irregular thoughts we so to say banish God from us so that He cannot accomplish His work in us. Certainly it was no thanks to Martha that her brother did not lie for ever in the grave, for she cuts off the hope of life for him and at the same time tries to hinder Christ from raising him, even though nothing was further from her mind. The weakness of faith causes this. Pulled in this way and that, we fight with ourselves, and while we stretch out the one hand to ask assistance from God, we push away that readily offered assistance with the other hand. True, Martha was not lying when she said, 'I know that whatsoever thou shalt ask of God, He will give it thee;' but a confused and implicit faith avails little unless it is put to use when we come to a concrete situation.

Moreover, we can see in Martha how many defects there are in the faith of even the best people. She was the first to come and meet Christ—no ordinary example of piety. And yet she keeps on putting difficulties in His way. Hence, that the grace of God may have an entrance into us, let us learn to ascribe to it far greater power than our senses can grasp. And if the first and single promise of God is not strong enough for us, let us at any rate, like Martha, acquiesce when He confirms us a second and third time.

40. *Said I not unto thee?* He reproves Martha's distrust in not conceiving enough hope from the promise she had heard. It is clear from this passage that something more was said to Martha than John expressed in words; though, as I have suggested, this is what Christ meant when He called Himself the resurrection and the life. Martha is therefore condemned for not expecting a divine work.

14

If thou believedst. This is said, not only because faith opens our eyes to be able to see God's glory shining in His works, but because our faith smoothes the way for God's power and goodness to be displayed towards us; as Psalm 81.10 has it, 'Open thy mouth wide, and I will fill it.' Again, unbelief blocks God's way, and as it were keeps His hands shut. For this reason it is said elsewhere, 'Jesus could not perform any sign there because of their unbelief' (Matt. 13.58). Not that God's power is bound by the will of men, but because, as far as they can, their malice opposes it and therefore they do not deserve it to be manifested to them. It often happens that God overcomes such obstacles. But whenever He withdraws His hand and does not help unbelievers, it is because they are enclosed within the straits of their unbelief and will not give it entrance.

Thou shouldest see the glory of God. Observe: a miracle is called the glory of God, because God, by displaying in it the power of His hand, glorifies His name. Martha, satisfied with Christ's second declaration, allows the stone to be removed. As yet she sees nothing; but when she hears the Son of God with a good reason give this order, she willingly depends on His command alone.

41. *And Jesus lifted up his eyes.* The sign of a mind truly prepared for prayer. For anyone to call on God aright, he must be joined with Him and this cannot be done unless he is raised above the earth and ascends to heaven. True, this is not always visible. Hypocrites, plunged in the deep filth of their flesh, seem to bring heaven down to them by their serious looks. But what they pretend, the children of God must do sincerely. And yet he who raises his eyes to heaven must not mentally shut God up in heaven, for He is diffused everywhere and fills heaven and earth. But since men's minds can never break free from gross imaginations and thinking something low and earthy about God unless they are raised above the world, Scripture calls them thither and declares that heaven is God's throne.

So far as lifting up the eyes is concerned, it is not a perpetual ceremony without which prayer is not legitimate. For the publican, praying with his face cast down to the ground still reaches heaven by his faith. Yet it is a useful practice, for by it men are stirred up to seek God. Moreover, the fervour of prayer often affects the body in such a way that the body unwittingly follows the mind of its own accord. We certainly cannot doubt that when Christ raised His eyes to heaven He was carried thither with extraordinary vehemence. Besides, as He was entirely with the Father, He wanted to bring others to the Father with Himself.

I thank thee. Although He has not asked for anything, He begins with thanksgiving. In fact, there can be no doubt that although the

Evangelist does not relate that He had prayed in formal words, a prayer had preceded this, for otherwise it could not have been heard. Probably He prayed in the midst of those groanings which the Evangelist mentions. For nothing could be more inconsistent than that He was violently agitated within Himself, as stupid men are wont to be. Having gained Lazarus' life, He now thanks the Father. By saying that He has received this power from the Father and not claiming it for Himself, He merely acknowledges that He is the minister of the Father. By accommodating Himself to men's capacity, He will at one time assert His divinity and claim for Himself what is of God, and at another time will be satisfied with bearing a human character and give the whole glory of divinity to the Father. The Evangelist brings together both sides admirably in one word when he says that Christ was heard by the Father, but that He gives thanks that men may know that He was sent by the Father and acknowledge Him to be the Son of God. Since Christ's majesty could not be perceived in its loftiness, the power of God, which was manifest in His flesh, gradually raised men's gross and slow senses to that height. For he wished to be wholly ours and we need not be surprised if He accommodates Himself to us in various ways. If He even allowed Himself to be emptied for us, there is no absurdity in saying that He abases Himself on our account.

42. *And I knew that always.* This is to forestall anyone thinking that He did not stand so high in the Father's favour as to be able to perform as many miracles as He chose. Hence He means that there is so much agreement between Him and the Father that the Father denies Him nothing; even that He had no need to pray, since He only performed what He knew the Father had commanded Him. But He called on the name of the Father so that men should be more fully assured that this is truly a divine work. If any object, 'Why then, did He not raise all the dead?' the reply is easy. By the counsel of God there was assigned to miracles a certain measure, which He knew to be sufficient for confirming the Gospel.

43. *He cried with a loud voice.* His divine power is the better shown by the fact that He did not touch with the hand but only cried with His voice. At the same time He commends to us the secret and wonderful efficacy of His Word. For how did Christ restore life to the dead by His Word? Therefore, in raising Lazarus He exhibited a visible sign of His spiritual grace which we daily experience by the perception of faith, when He shows that His voice is quickening.

44. *Bound with grave-clothes.* The Evangelist takes care to refer to the napkin and grave-clothes, to tell us that Lazarus came out of the tomb just as he had been laid in it. This method of burying is still

used by the Jews. They cover the body with linen and wrap the head separately in a kerchief.

Loose him. To magnify the glory of the miracle, all that remained was that the Jews should touch with their hands the divine work which they had seen with their eyes. For Christ might have shaken off the grave-clothes binding Lazarus or made them give way of themselves. But He meant to use the hands of the bystanders as His witnesses. The Papists are extremely ridiculous when they infer auricular confession from this. They say: 'When Christ had restored Lazarus to life, He wished His disciples to loose Him. Therefore, it is not sufficient for us to be reconciled to God, unless the Church also pardons our sins.' But how do they guess that it was the disciples who were told to loose Lazarus? On the contrary, we gather that the order was given to the Jews, to take from them every trace of doubt.

Many therefore of the Jews, which came to Mary and beheld that which he did, believed on him. But some of them went away to the Pharisees, and told them the things which Jesus had done. The chief priests therefore and the Pharisees gathered a council, and said, What do we? for this man doeth many signs. If we let him thus alone, all men will believe on him: and the Romans will come and will take away both our place and our nation. But a certain one of them, Caiaphas, being high priest that year, said unto them, Ye know nothing at all, nor do ye take account that it is expedient for us that one man should die for the people, and that the whole nation perish not. Now this he said not of himself: but being high priest that year, he prophesied that Jesus should die for the nation; and not for the nation only, but that he might also gather together into one the children of God that are scattered abroad.
(45-52)

45. *Many therefore.* Christ did not let the miracle He had done remain fruitless, but by means of it drew some to faith. We must understand that miracles have a twofold use. Either they prepare us for faith or confirm us in faith. Here the Evangelist points to the former. He means that those of whom He speaks admired and revered Christ's divine power, so that they submitted to Him as His disciples. Otherwise the bare miracle would not have been sufficient to produce faith. Hence, by the word *believe* we must only suppose he means a teachableness in embracing Christ's teaching.

In others, who accuse Christ, appears a detestable ingratitude, or rather horrible rage, which betrays the madness and blindness of their ungodliness. The resurrection of Lazarus ought certainly to have softened even hearts of stone. But ungodliness will infect and corrupt any work of God with its bitter poison. So before men can profit

17

from miracles, their hearts must be purified; for those in whom dwells no fear or reverence of God, even though they saw heaven and earth mingled, will always reject sound doctrine through their obstinate ingratitude. In our own day you will see many enemies of the Gospel fighting fanatically against the open and visible hand of God. They demand miracles from us, but only to show that they are monsters of men in their stubborn resistance. Christ was reported to the Pharisees because they, in proportion to their hypocrisy, were the more fierce in opposing the Gospel. For the same reason the Evangelist soon after mentions them expressly when he relates that the council was assembled. They were a part of the priesthood; but he named them particularly because they were, so to say, the bellows to kindle the anger of the whole council.

47. *The chief priests therefore and the Pharisees gathered.* The priests' blindness, described here, is no less monstrous. If they had not been quite stupid and brutish, they would have been touched with at least some reverence for Christ after such a remarkable demonstration of His divine power. They meet together now for the deliberate and intentional purpose of burying God's glory, which they could not help being astonished at. True, they do not openly boast that they want to make war on God. But since they cannot extinguish Christ without overturning God's power, they are fighting against it openly and undoubtedly by their presumptuous sacrilege. Unbelief is always proud and a despiser of God; but it does not always break out into open conflict with God. But when men have been struggling against God for a long time their final action is to try, without any dread of the Divinity, to ascend above heaven like the Titans. They acknowledge that Christ did many signs. Where does His great power come from? They therefore openly make ready to crush God's power shining in Christ's miracles. Yet God is not slack. Although He ignores them at the time, He laughs at their foolish arrogance until the time for executing His wrath comes, as Psalm 2.12 says.

What do we? They blame their sloth with these words, as if they were saying that it is because of their inactivity that Christ makes gradual headway, and if they actively exerted themselves they could stop His progress. This is the confidence of wicked men, claiming everything for themselves, as if it were in their power to do what they like, and as if even the result of the work depended on their will. If anyone ponders this aright, they are opposing their own industry to the divine power, as if by persevering they could turn out stronger than God.

48. *If we let him thus alone.* What if they do not let Him alone? Then, as has already been said, they have no doubt that it is in their

18

power to block up Christ's path and prevent His progress if only they strive hard against Him. If Christ had been an impostor it would indeed have been their duty to interfere, lest He should lead the sheep away from the Lord's flock. But when they acknowledge His miracles, they make it quite plain that they care nothing for God, whose power they so boldly and disdainfully despise.

The Romans will come. A specious disguise cloaks their wickedness —zeal for the public good. Their chief worry and fear was that their tyranny would be destroyed; but they pretend to be anxious about the Temple and the worship of God, about the reputation of their nation and the condition of the people. And why all this? They are not seeking these sort of pretences so as to deceive anyone. They are not addressing the people, but are deliberating *in camera* among themselves. They are all aware of their common treachery. Why do they not bring forward their plans and ideas frankly? Because impiety, however gross and manifest, is almost always accompanied by hypocrisy. So it wraps itself up in indirect evasions or shadows, to deceive under the appearance of virtue. Their main object was, indeed, to show something like gravity, moderation and prudence, so as to practise deception upon others. But it is probable that when they pretended to have a just cause for persecuting Christ, they were themselves deceived by that empty mask. Hypocrites may be inwardly reproved by their consciences, but they are afterwards intoxicated by vain imaginations, and when they sin, seem to be innocent. Yet they plainly contradict themselves. At first they confessed that Christ did many miracles. Now they are afraid of the Romans, as if there were not more than enough protection in God's power, which showed itself present in these signs.

The Romans will come. The Evangelist means that the main object of their deliberation was to guard against the danger that threatened. They are saying: 'If the Romans knew that any changes were being made in public affairs they would, we fear, send an army to destroy our nation along with the Temple and the worship of God.' But it is wicked to deliberate about guarding against dangers which we can avoid only by deciding to depart from the right path. We should first ask what God commands and wants to be done. Whatever the outcome for us, that must stand firm. These men, on the contrary, determine to remove Christ so that no trouble shall ensue from letting Him continue as He began. But what if He has been sent by God? Shall they reject a prophet of God, so as to buy peace with the Romans? These are the counsels of men who do not truly and sincerely fear God; they are indifferent about what is lawful and right, for they are only interested in the consequences.

But the only godly and holy way to consider it is this. We should first inquire what is pleasing to God. Then we should follow boldly whatever He commands, and not be discouraged by any fear, though we are beset by a thousand deaths. Our actions must not be directed by any gust of wind, but constantly by the Word of God alone. He who boldly despises dangers, or at least, rises above the fear of them and simply obeys God, will be successful in the end. For against all expectation, God blesses the constancy which is founded on obedience to His Word. Unbelievers, on the contrary, are so far from benefiting from their caution, that the more timid they are, the more snares do they get entangled in.

In this story there is graphically portrayed for us the form of our own age. Those who want to be regarded as prudent and circumspect continually have this same song in their mouths about caring for public quiet and that the renovation we are attempting is not without many dangers. After they have raised this unfair odium against us, they can find no better way to counteract disturbances than by burying Christ. As if such ungodly contempt for God's grace could really be successful when they work out the remedy of abolishing the doctrine of salvation so as to allay disturbances. On the contrary, the dread of the ungodly will come to pass. Even if they get what they want, it is a most unworthy reward, to appease the world by offending God.

Our place. It is not clear whether they mean the Temple or the land. They thought their salvation depended on both. For if the Temple were destroyed, sacrifices and the public worship of God and calling on His name would cease. So they could not help being anxious about the Temple if they had any care for religion. It was also of great importance for maintaining the state of the Church, that they should not be led away into exile again. They still remembered the Babylonian captivity, which was a most severe vengeance of God. They also had a common proverb, frequently found in the Law, that it was a kind of disowning if the Lord cast them out of that land. They therefore conclude that the Church will not be safe unless Christ is destroyed.

49. *One of them, Caiaphas.* Their deliberations were brief, for Caiaphas did not let them hesitate long. He shows only one way of purchasing safety—the slaying of an innocent man. What wickedness men break out into when, without any fear of God, they plan according to the judgment of the flesh and not to the Word of God, and are confident that what the Author of all good does not allow is nevertheless good for them! For it is as if Caiaphas were saying that they had to provoke the wrath of God if they were to do well and prosper. Therefore, let us learn never to separate what is useful from what is

lawful, since we must not expect anything good or pleasing but from God's blessing—and that is promised, not to the ungodly and rebels, who ask the devil to help them, but to believers, who sincerely walk in His ways. And yet this argument had some plausibility, for the public good should always be put first. But, as I have said, a people is no better guarded by the unjust death of an innocent man than the whole body of a man is guarded when you only cut his throat or run his breast through with a sword.

Being high priest. He does not call him the high priest of that year as if the office were only annual, but because it was venal and was conveyed to various men against the commands of the Law. God meant this dignity to be terminated only by death, but when things were troubled and confused, the Romans frequently changed the priests at will.

When the Evangelist says that Caiaphas *said not this of himself,* he does not mean that Caiaphas, like a madman or a fanatic, uttered what he did not understand, for he voiced his own opinion. The Evangelist means that something greater incited his tongue, because God intended to testify by his mouth something higher than came into his mind. Caiaphas was then, as it were, two-tongued. He vomited out the ungodly and cruel design of killing Christ which he had conceived in his own mind; but God turned his tongue to a different purpose, so that under ambiguous words he at the same time proclaimed a prophecy. God meant the heavenly oracle to flow from the high priest's throne, that the Jews might have the less excuse. For although in the whole assembly none was touched in his conscience, yet afterwards they saw that their insensibility did not deserve pardon. Nor did Caiaphas' wickedness prevent his tongue from being the organ of the Holy Spirit, for God had regard to the priesthood instituted by Himself rather than this man's person. And this was the reason I hinted at, that a voice uttered from a lofty place would be more clearly heard and have greater reverence and authority. In the same way, He wished to bless His people by the mouth of Balaam, to whom He had given the Spirit of prophecy.

But it is quite ridiculous for the Papists to infer from this that we should regard as an oracle whatever the Roman pontiff sees fit to pronounce. First, even granting (which is not true) that the high priest is always a prophet, they still have to prove that the Roman pontiff is created by the command of God. For the priesthood was abolished by the advent of the one man Christ, and we nowhere read that God later enjoined that any one man should rule the whole Church. Granting them secondly that the right and dignity of high priest was transferred to the Bishop of Rome, we must see what good it did the priests to embrace Caiaphas' prophecy. In agreement with his judgment, they conspire to put Christ to death. But far be it from us to have the sort of obedience that drives us into the horrible apostasy of denying the Son of God. With the one voice Caiaphas blasphemes and prophesies. Those who follow his declaration despise the prophecy and adopt the blasphemy. We must take care the same thing does not happen to us if we listen to the Caiaphas of Rome; else would the comparison be defective. Moreover, I ask, because Caiaphas prophesied once, is every word uttered by the high priest always a prophecy? Soon after, he condemned as blasphemy the highest and chief Head of our faith. Therefore we conclude that what the Evangelist now relates is extraordinary and that it would be foolish to treat it as an example.

That Jesus should die. First, the Evangelist shows that the whole of our salvation consists in Christ's bringing us into one flock (*in unum aggreget*); for it is thus that He reconciles us to the Father, within whom is the fountain of life. From this we also gather that the human race is dispersed and alienated from God, until God's children are united under Christ their Head. The communion of saints is therefore a preparation for eternal life, since all whom Christ does not gather to the Father remain in death, as we shall see again in chapter 17. This is also why Paul teaches in Eph. 1.10 that Christ was sent to gather together all things in heaven and earth. And so, to enjoy the salvation brought by Christ, discord has to be removed, and we must become one with God and the angels and among ourselves. The cause and the pledg of this unity was Christ's death, by which He drew all things unto Himself; and we are gathered into Christ's fold daily by the Gospel.

52. *And not for the nation only.* The Evangelist means that the reconciliation effected by Christ is extended to the Gentiles also. But how is it that they are called the children of God who, because they were miserably scattered and wandering, became God's enemies? I reply, as has been said already, that there were in the heart (*pectus*) of God children who in themselves were wandering and lost sheep, or rather, were not sheep at all, but rather wolves and wild beasts. Hence it is by election that he reckons as God's children, even before they are called, those who at last begin to be manifested to themselves and others.

So from that day forth they took counsel that they might put him to death. Jesus therefore walked no more openly among the Jews, but departed thence into the country near to the wilderness, into a city called Ephraim; and there he tarried with the disciples. Now the pass-

over of the Jews was at hand: and many went up to Jerusalem out of
the country before the passover, to purify themselves. They sought
therefore for Jesus, and spake one with another, as they stood in the
temple, What think ye? That he will not come to the feast? Now the
chief priests and the Pharisees had given commandment, that, if any
man knew where he was, he should shew it, that they might take him.
(53-57)

53. *They took counsel that they might put him to death.* The Evangelist
relates that Christ fled again, knowing that His enemies were seeking
for Him in their rage. Yet we must remember that He did not fly so
as to withdraw from His Father's calling. His only intention was to
offer Himself to undergo a voluntary death at the divinely appointed
time. The counsel that the Evangelist mentions was not so much for
slaying Christ as to find some way of putting Him down. They had
already determined to do away with Him. It only remained to decide
how they could carry their resolution into effect.

54. *Called Ephraim.* As to the name of the town which we read
here, I think it was either pronounced corruptly then or was quite
new. For we know how much the language changed after the Babylonian exile, and also how different the country looked. So it is not
surprising that some places are mentioned which were unknown to
antiquity.

He names the disciples of Christ, not those who had received His
teaching, but His constant companions, who used to live with Him
in the same house.

55. *Many went up, etc.* There was no precise injunction that they
should purify themselves before sacrificing the passover. So the
Evangelist does not say that all, but only many, came. No one unclean, of course, was allowed to eat it; but I say that this sanctification
was undertaken voluntarily and from personal inclination. Others
were not forbidden to eat, even though they had not been prepared
by such a ceremony before the feast day.

Moreover, the Evangelist's purpose is to show how well-known
Christ was throughout Judaea; for those who assemble in the Temple,
wherever they come from, are chiefly intent on seeking Christ and
arguing among themselves about Him. True, they seek Him in a
human way; but yet, by seeking Him, they show that it is the priest's
tyranny which prevents Him from appearing openly.

23

CHAPTER TWELVE

Jesus therefore six days before the passover came to Bethany, where Lazarus was, who had been dead, whom Jesus raised from the dead. So they made him a supper there: and Martha served; but Lazarus was one of them that sat at meat with him. Mary therefore took a pound of ointment of spikenard, very precious, and anointed the feet of Jesus, and wiped his feet with her hair: and the house was filled with the odour of the ointment. But Judas Iscariot, the son of Simon, one of his disciples, which should betray him, saith, Why was not this ointment sold for three hundred pence, and given to the poor? Now this he said, not because he cared for the poor; but because he was a thief, and having the bag, took away what was put therein. Jesus therefore said, Let her alone; against the day of my burial she hath kept it. For the poor ye have always with you; but me ye have not always. (1-8)

1. *Jesus came to Bethany.* We see that those who thought that Christ would not go to the feast were judging too hastily. This warns us not to be rash, but to wait patiently and quietly until the proper time, which is unknown to us, comes. Now Christ came to Bethany first, that He might go on from there to Jerusalem three days later. Meanwhile, He wanted to give Judas a suitable time and place to betray Him—so that He might present Himself, a victim prepared for the sacrifice, at the appointed hour. He is not ignorant of what is to happen, but comes to His sacrificing voluntarily.

As He had come to Bethany six days before the passover, it can be gathered from Matthew and Mark that He remained there four days. John does not say on which day the supper was made for Him, when He was anointed by Mary. But it seems likely that it was not long after His arrival. Those who think that the anointing mentioned by Mark and Matthew is different from this one are mistaken. The time factor has misled them; for the two Evangelists mention two days before relating that Christ was anointed. But the solution is easy and may be given in two ways. John does not say that Christ was anointed on the first day of His arrival; so it could have taken place even when He was preparing to depart. Yet, as I have said, the other conjecture is the more probable, that He was anointed at least one or two days before His departure. Judas had certainly made a bargain with the priests, before Christ sent two of His disciples to prepare the passover. Now, at least one day must have elapsed between these two events. The Evangelists add that he sought a convenient time to betray Christ after he had received the bribe. And so when, after mentioning two days they add the story of the anointing, they narrate last what happened first. The reason is that when they have related the words of Christ, 'Ye know that after two days the Son of man shall be betrayed,' they now put in what they had omitted—the manner and the occasion on which He was betrayed by His disciple. There is thus sufficient agreement that He was anointed at Bethany.

Matthew and Mark say that on this occasion He was dining with Simon the leper. John does not name the house, but hints plainly enough that He was not dining in the house of Lazarus and Martha, for he makes *Lazarus one of them that sat at meat with Him*—a fellow guest of Christ's. Nor indeed is there any contradiction in Matthew and Mark relating that Christ's *head* was anointed, while our author says it was His feet. Anointing was usually of the head, and for this reason Pliny regards it as extravagant when some anointed the ankles. The three agree that Mary did not anoint Him sparingly but poured a large quantity of ointment on Him. John's reference to His feet is equivalent to his saying that Christ's whole body was anointed down to the feet. The word feet amplifies the sense, as appears better in what follows, when he adds that Mary wiped His feet with her hair.

And the house was filled with the odour. It was not a simple liquid extracted from nard, but a compound of many scented substances. It is not surprising that the whole house was filled with the odour.

4. *But one of his disciples saith.* There follows Judas' grumbling, which Matthew ascribes to the disciples in general and Mark to some of them. But it is common in Scripture to use synecdoche and apply to many what is true of only one or a few. Yet I think it likely that the murmuring originated with Judas and that the rest were moved to support him, as murmurings are like bellows, to kindle in us all sorts of dispositions, and especially as we are too prone to unfavourable judgments, disparagement finds a place in us. But the credulity which God's Spirit reproves in the apostles is a warning to us not to be too facile and credulous in listening to malicious words.

5. *Why was not this ointment sold for three hundred pence?* Pliny tells us that a pound of common ointment cost not more than ten *denarii*. But he also says that the highest price of the best ointment was three hundred and ten *denarii*. The Evangelists agree that this was very expensive ointment, and Judas is correct in valuing a pound of it at three hundred *denarii*. (This, according to Budaeus' reckoning, comes to fifty French *livres*.) Moreover, since almost all luxuries involve excess and superfluity, the greater the expense the more plausible

reason Judas had for grumbling. It was as if he said, 'If Mary had spent only a little, she would have had some excuse. But she has wasted a vast sum of money for nothing; has she not done harm to the poor, who might have been greatly helped with such a sum? Therefore her action is unpardonable.'

6. *Because he was a thief.* The rest of the apostles condemn Mary thoughtlessly and not from any evil will. But Judas takes up a plausible position for his wickedness when he puts forward the poor, for whom he cared nothing. From this we learn what a repulsive monster cupidity is. It is the loss which Judas thinks he has sustained by this chance of stealing being taken away that stirs him to such a rage that he does not hesitate to betray Christ. And probably he was not only lying to others about the poor having been defrauded, but was even flattering himself inwardly, as hypocrites do, as if the betrayal of Christ were a trivial fault, by which he wanted to compensate for his loss. He really had only one reason for betraying Christ—to regain somehow the loot which had slipped out of his fingers. It was indignation over his lost gains that drove him to the design of betraying Christ.

It is surprising that Christ should have chosen as treasurer a man whom He knew to be a thief. For what was it but giving him a rope to hang himself with? Mortal man's only reply can be that the judgments of God are a profound abyss. Yet Christ's action should not be made an ordinary rule for committing the care of the poor or any sacred fund to a worthless and wicked man. God has laid down a law as to who ought to be called to the government of the Church and other offices; and it is not lawful to break this law. It was different with Christ: as the eternal Wisdom of God He gave a place for His secret predestination in the person of Judas.

7. *Let her alone.* When Christ tells them to leave Mary alone He is showing that they act wickedly and unjustly who disturb their neighbours without a cause and start up quarrels about nothing. In the other Evangelists, Christ's reply is longer, though the substance is the same. The anointing which Judas blames is defended on the ground that it is for His burial. Christ therefore does not approve of it as an ordinary service or one which should be commonly used in the Church; for if He had wanted some office of this sort to be performed daily, He could have said something else instead of relating it to His burial. God certainly does not care for external display. On the contrary, He sees that man's mind is too prone to carnal observances and frequently commands us to be sparing and sober in the use of them. They are absurd interpreters, therefore, who infer from Christ's reply that costly and splendid worship is pleasing to God. In fact He

excuses Mary on the grounds that she had rendered Him an extra-ordinary office which should not be regarded as a perpetual norm for the worship of God.

Against the day of my burying, etc. When He says that the ointment had been kept, He means that it was not poured out at the wrong time but at the proper time. For a thing is said to be kept when it is held in store to be brought out appropriately and opportunely. It is certain that if anyone earlier had loaded Him with costly delicacies, He would not have allowed it. But He says that Mary did this, not as something ordinary, but as her last duty towards Him. Moreover, the anointing of bodies was a spiritual symbol then, not an empty rite. It set before them the hope of resurrection. The promises were still obscure and Christ, rightly called 'the first-fruits of them that rise' (I Cor. 15.20) was not yet risen. Therefore believers needed such aids, which directed them to Christ who was still absent. Accordingly, the anointing of Christ was not superfluous then; for He was soon to be buried, and was anointed as if to be laid in the tomb. The disciples did not know this yet; and undoubtedly Mary was suddenly moved by the directing of the Spirit to do something she had not thought of before. But Christ applies what they disapproved to the hope of His resurrection, so that this use of it might recall them from their wicked bad temper. God wanted the childhood of His ancient people to be ruled by such exercises; but it would be foolish to try to do the same thing today—and indeed, it could not be done without injury to Christ, who has dispelled such shadows by the brightness of His coming. Since, however, His resurrection had not yet brought the end of the shadows of the Law, His burial had to be adorned with an outward ceremony. The scent of His resurrection is now strong enough of itself to quicken the whole world, without spikenard and ointments. And let us remember that when we judge men's actions we must abide by Christ's verdict alone, for we must one day stand before His judgment seat.

8. *For the poor ye have always with you.* We must keep to what I have already pointed out—that a distinction is expressly drawn here between Mary's extraordinary action and the daily service due to Christ. They who want to worship Christ with splendid and costly trappings are apes, not imitators. Christ approved what was done that once, but forbade its repetition.

His saying that He would not always be with His disciples should be referred to the kind of presence to which carnal worship and extravagant honours are suitable. His presence with us by the grace and power of His Spirit, His dwelling in us and His feeding us with His flesh and blood, have nothing to do with bodily observances.

Hence all the pomp that the Papists have invented for the worship of
Christ is offered to Him in vain, for He openly rejects it. When He
says that the poor will be with us always He is, it is true, reproving
the hypocrisy of Judas[1] but we may learn from it the valuable lesson
that alms for relieving the needs of the poor are sacrifices and of a
sweet savour to God, and that any other expense in the worship of
God is out of place.

*Then a great multitude of the Jews learned that he was there: and they
came, not for Jesus' sake only, but that they might see Lazarus also,
whom he had raised from the dead. But the chief priests took counsel
that they might put Lazarus also to death; because that by reason of
him many of the Jews went away, and believed on Jesus. On the
morrow a great multitude that had come to the feast, when they heard
that Jesus was coming to Jerusalem, took the branches of the palm trees,
and went forth to meet him, and cried out, Hosanna: Blessed is he that
cometh in the name of the Lord, even the King of Israel. And Jesus,
having found a young ass, sat thereon; as it is written, Fear not,
daughter of Zion: behold, thy King cometh, sitting on an ass's colt.*
(9-15)

9. *Then a great multitude knew.* The nearer the time of Christ's
death approached, the more necessary was it that His name should
be made known everywhere, as a preparation for a fuller faith after
His death. In particular, the Evangelist relates that the recent miracle
of the resurrection of Lazarus became very widely known. Since
Christ had shown in it a striking proof of His divinity, God wanted
it to have many witnesses. When he says that they came, not only
because of Jesus, but also on account of Lazarus, he does not mean
that they came as an act of courtesy to Lazarus, as if they were honouring him in particular, but that they might see the wonderful example
of Christ's power in Lazarus.

10. *But the chief priests took counsel.* What insane fury, to try to kill
someone who had manifestly been raised from the dead by divine
power! But Satan torments the wicked with such a spirit of giddiness
that their madness is unending, even though God should set heaven
and earth and sea against them. For this wicked council meeting is
described in this way to show us that Christ's enemies were brought
to their great obstinacy, not by error or folly but by furious wickedness, so that they were not even afraid to make war on God. It also
tells us that God's power in the raising of Lazarus was not obscure;

[1] All copies I have seen have *Judaeorum*—of the Jews. But as this passage does
not refer to the Jews, and Jesus' reproof is aimed at Judas (whose hypocrisy is
pointed to under v. 6), we ought no doubt to read *Judae*.

for the only way in which ungodliness could wipe it out was by basely and shockingly doing away with an innocent man. Moreover, Satan tries his hardest to bury altogether, or to some extent to obscure, the works of God, and therefore it is our duty to devote ourselves diligently to continual meditation on them.

12. *On the morrow a great multitude.* Christ's entry is related more fully by the other Evangelists; but here our author gives a complete summary. In the first place, we must remember Christ's purpose. He came to Jerusalem of His own accord to offer Himself up to death. For it was necessary that His death should be voluntary, since the wrath of God against us could be appeased only by a sacrifice of obedience. And the outcome was not hidden from Him. But before He is dragged to the Cross, He wants to be received by the people as their King in a solemn ceremony. Nay, He openly acknowledges that His reign is inaugurated by His marching to death. But though His arrival was acclaimed by a great crowd of people, He remained unknown to His enemies until He proved that He was the true Messiah by fulfilling the prophecies, as we shall see later. He did not want to omit anything that would help to confirm our faith substantially.

A great multitude, that had come to the feast. Foreigners were far more ready to pay homage to the Son of God than were the citizens of Jerusalem, who should have been an example to everyone else. They had daily sacrifices; the Temple was ever before them, and should have kindled in their hearts a desire to seek God; the chief teachers of the Church were there, and there, too, was the sanctuary of the divine light. Their ingratitude was therefore utterly base; they had been steeped in these practices from their childhood, and yet they reject and neglect the Redeemer promised to them. But it is a fault common to nearly every age that the closer and more familiarly God has showed Himself to men, the more audaciously have they despised Him. There was a much greater zeal in these others who had left their own lands and come together to celebrate the feast. They eagerly ask about Christ, and when they hear that He is coming to the city, go out and rejoice with Him. But there is no doubt they were aroused by a secret impulse of the Spirit to go to Him. We do not read of this being done before. But as earthly princes summon their subjects by the sound of a trumpet or the voice of a herald when they enter into possession of their kingdom, so Christ assembled this people by the moving of His Spirit to acclaim Him as king. When the crowds wanted to make Him king in the wilderness He withdrew into the mountain in secret; for the only kingdom they thought of then was one in which they could be well fattened like cattle. Christ could not allow and agree with their foolish and absurd desire without denying Himself and renouncing the office enjoined Him by the Father. But now He claims for Himself the kind of kingdom which He received from the Father. I confess that the people who went out to meet Him did not really understand the nature of this kingdom. But Christ looked to the future. In the meanwhile He did not allow anything to be done that was inconsistent with His spiritual kingdom.

13. *Took the branches of the palm trees.* The palm was a symbol of victory and peace in antiquity. But it was also customary to use branches of palm trees when they conferred kingship on anyone or when they humbly asked pardon of a conqueror. But these men seem to have taken up branches of palm trees as a sign of joyfulness and festivity at welcoming a new king.

Cried out, Hosanna. By using this expression they showed that they recognized Christ as the Messiah promised of old to the fathers and from whom redemption and salvation were to be looked for. Psalm 118.25-26, from which the acclamation is taken, was written about the Messiah so that all the saints might ardently long for His coming with an unceasing desire and, when He was manifested, welcome Him most reverently. It is therefore likely, in fact it can be inferred with certainty, that this prayer was common among all the Jews and therefore was on everyone's lips. So the Spirit of God supplied words for these men to wish Christ well; and He chose them as heralds to bear witness that the Messiah had come.

The word Hosanna is made up of two Hebrew words, and is equivalent to 'Save!' or 'Make safe, I pray you!' The Hebrews pronounce it differently: Hosiah-na. But it is quite usual for pronunciation to be corrupted when words are taken over into a foreign language. Although the Evangelists wrote in Greek, they purposely kept the Hebrew word, the better to express that the multitude used the established form of prayer, first delivered by David and from age to age uninterruptedly received among the people of God and specially consecrated to blessing the kingdom of Christ. To the same purpose is what immediately follows: 'Blessed is he that cometh in the name of the Lord.' This is a joyful prayer for the happiness and prosperity of that kingdom on which the restoration and blessedness of the Church of God depended.

But David seems to speak of himself rather than Christ in that psalm. This difficulty must therefore be solved first. And the solution is not hard. We know that the kingdom was given to David and his line to be a kind of prelude of the eternal kingdom which was to be manifested in its own time. Nor did it behove David to keep to himself, for the Lord often through His prophets directs the eyes of all the godly to another. Thus all that David sang about himself is rightly referred to the King who, it was promised, should spring from his seed as the Redeemer.

We must derive a useful lesson from this. If we are members of the Church, the Lord stirs us up today to cherish the same desire in common with believers under the Law. We ought to desire wholeheartedly Christ's kingdom to flourish and prosper; and moreover, our prayers should show this. We should note that He dictates the words to us so that there might be more spirit in our praying. Woe to our laziness if by our coldness we extinguish, or by our lukewarmness we quench, that heat which God kindles! But let us know that the prayers we conceive by the leading and teaching of God will not be in vain. If only we are not lazy or become weary in asking, He will be a faithful guardian of His kingdom and defend it by His invincible power and protection. It is true that even if we remain slack, His majesty will continue to stand. But as often as it does not flourish as magnificently as it should, or even collapses—as we see today a terrible scattering and desolation—this definitely happens through our fault. And when the restoration is small, or negligible, or at least is slow in advancing, let us blame our own sluggishness. Daily we pray God that His kingdom may come, but hardly one in a hundred with seriousness. We are justly deprived of that blessing of God which it is too much trouble for us to ask.

By this word we are also taught that it is God alone who saves and defends the Church. For He does not claim for Himself or command us to render Him anything but His own. Therefore, in our speech, shaped by Him, we pray that He may save Christ's kingdom and we acknowledge that God is the only author of the safety that keeps this kingdom firm. He uses the activities of men for this end, but they are men whom His own hand has prepared. Moreover, He makes use of men for advancing or upholding the kingdom of Christ in such a way that He alone begins and completes everything through them by the power of His Spirit.

That cometh in the name of the Lord. We must first understand the meaning of 'to come in the name of the Lord.' He comes in God's name who does not rashly thrust himself forward or falsely assume the honour, but, because he is properly called, has God as the leader and author of his actions. The title belongs to all true ministers of God. A prophet comes in God's name who, directed by the Holy Spirit, honestly delivers to men the teaching he has received from heaven. A king comes in the same name by whose hand God governs His people. But because the Spirit of the Lord rested on Christ and He is the Head of all things, so that all who have ever been ordained to rule the Church are under His command—or rather, are streams flowing from the fountain—He is properly said to have come in the name of God. And it is not only that He surpasses all others in the exaltedness of His kingship; but God manifests Himself to us fully in Him, for 'in Him dwelleth all the fulness of the Godhead bodily', as Paul says (Col. 2.9), and He is the lively image of God and, in short, the true Emmanuel. Therefore by special right He is said to have come in the name of the Lord, since by Him God has manifested Himself completely and not partially as formerly in the prophets. We ought therefore to start out from Him as the Head when we want to bless the servants of God.

Now, since false prophets arrogantly claim the name of God and advertise themselves under this false pretence (although in fact they are carried away by the impulse of the devil to destroy the Church), we should supply the antithesis, that the Lord may scatter and annihilate them. Thus we cannot bless Christ without at the same time cursing the Pope and the sacrilegious tyranny he has erected against Christ. He hurls his anathemas at us with great violence like thunderbolts; but we can despise them safely as mere bombast. But here the Holy Spirit dictates an awful anathema to us to sink the Pope with all his splendour and pomp to the depths of hell. Nor is any pontiff needed to pronounce the curse against him; for Christ once gave this power to children when He approved their shouting, as the other Evangelists relate.

14. *And Jesus, having found a young ass.* The other Evangelists narrate this part of the story in greater detail. They tell us that Christ sent two of His disciples to fetch an ass. John, writing last of all, thought it sufficient to note briefly the substance of what the others had said. This is why he omits many details. An apparent contradiction which worries many is very easily resolved. When Matthew says that Christ sat on a she-ass and her foal, we should take it as synecdoche. Some imagine that He sat first on the ass and then on the foal. From this conjecture they make up an allegory, that He sat first on the Jewish people who had long ago been broken in by bearing the yoke of the Law, and afterwards tamed the Gentiles like a wild and fresh colt. But the simple truth is that Christ rode on an ass which had been brought with its mother. And this agrees with the words of the Prophet who expressed the same thing twice in different words by a repetition common enough among the Hebrews. *On an ass*, he says, *and on its colt which was under the yoke.* Our Evangelist, who tries to be brief, leaves out the former clause, quoting only the latter.

The Jews are forced to explain the prophecy of Zechariah (9.9) which was then fulfilled, of the Messiah. But at the same time they laugh at us for being deceived by a mere trifle[1] into giving the honour of Messiah to the son of Mary. But our faith rests on very different testimonies. When we say that Jesus is the Christ, we do not start out from His entry into Jerusalem sitting on an ass. For in Him such a glory as belonged to the Son of God was visible, as we have seen in chapter 1 of this Gospel. But it was in His resurrection that His divine power especially shone forth. Yet we should not despise this confirmation, that by His wonderful providence God showed in that entry, as in a theatre, the fulfilment of Zechariah's prophecy.

Fear not. In the prophet's statement, as the Evangelist quotes it, we ought to observe that our minds are quietly calm, and fear and trembling are banished from them only when we know that Christ reigns among us. The prophet's actual words are different. He exhorts believers to joy and jubilation. But our Evangelist expressed how our minds exult with true joy. It is when that fear is removed with which all must be tormented until they are reconciled to God and obtain the peace which is born of faith (Rom. 5.1). Therefore, we receive through Christ the benefit that, freed from the tyranny of Satan, the yoke of sin broken, guilt cancelled and death abolished, we safely glory, relying on the protection of our king, since they who are put under His guardianship need not fear any danger. Not that we are free from fear so long as we live in the world; but because the trust which rests on Christ is above all fear. Though Christ was still far away, the prophet told the godly men of that age to be joyful and happy, because He was to come. 'Behold!' he said, 'Your king will come. Therefore, fear not.' Now that He is come for us to enjoy His presence, we ought to fight against fear more boldly, so that, delivered from our enemies, we may peacefully and joyfully honour our king.

The prophet apostrophized Zion in his own age because the habitation and seat of the Church was there. Now God has collected for Himself a Church out of the whole world; but this promise is directed peculiarly to believers who submit to Christ that He may reign in them. When he describes Christ as riding on an ass, he means that His kingdom will be quite different from the pomp, splendour, wealth and power of the world, and it was proper that this should be made known by an outward appearance, so that all should know perfectly that it is spiritual.

These things understood not his disciples at the first: but when Jesus was glorified, then remembered they that these things were written of

---

[1] *asini umbra*, 'the shadow of an ass', from περὶ ὄνου σκιᾶς. Presumably a learned pun.

him, and that they had done these things unto him. The multitude therefore that was with him when he called Lazarus out of the tomb, and raised him from the dead, bare witness. For this cause also the multitude went and met him, for that they heard that he had done this sign, The Pharisees therefore said among themselves, Behold how ye prevail nothing: lo, the world is gone after him. (16-19)

16. *These things understood not.* As the seed does not germinate the moment it is cast into the earth, so the fruit of God's works does not appear immediately. The apostles are God's servants in fulfilling the prophecy; but they do not understand what they are doing. They hear the shout of the multitude as distinctly welcoming Christ the King and not as a confused noise. But yet they do not see the point of it or what it means. To them therefore it is an empty show until the Lord opens their eyes.

When he says that they at last remembered that these things were written of Him, he indicates the cause of such gross ignorance before they come to knowledge. It was because they had not the Scripture as their guide and master to direct their minds to right and pure thinking. For we are blind unless God's Word leads the way. Nor is it even enough that the Word of God should shine upon us, unless the Spirit does not in His turn enlighten our eyes, which would otherwise be blind to the brightest light. Christ honoured His disciples with this grace after His resurrection, because the time was not ripe for the Spirit to pour out His riches as it were with a liberal hand until He was received into the heavenly glory, as we had it in chapter 7.39. Let us be taught by this example to form our judgment of everything that relates to Christ, not by the sense of our flesh, but from the Scriptures. Let us also understand that it is a special grace of the Spirit to educate us gradually out of our dullness in considering God's works.

The clause *that these things were written concerning him, and that they had done these things unto him* I interpret thus: Then, for the first time, it came to the disciples' minds that Christ had not done these things thoughtlessly, and that the men were not just playing a meaningless game, but that the whole affair had been governed by God's providence, because it was necessary to fulfil all that had been written. Understand it, therefore, as, 'they did these things to Him, just as had been written about Him'.

17. *The multitude bare witness.* He again repeats his statement that many had been aroused by the report of such a great miracle to come to meet Christ. They go out in their crowds because the rumour of Lazarus' restoration to life had spread everywhere. They had good

reason therefore for ascribing to the Son of Mary the office of Christ, since His most remarkable power had been made known to them.

19. *Behold how ye prevail nothing.* With these words they urge themselves to greater rage. For it is a sort of reproach of their slothfulness—as if they had said that the reason why the people revolted to Christ was their own excessive slowness and spinelessness. This is how desperate men will talk when they are preparing to make their last effort. And if God's enemies are so pertinacious in evil, it behoves us to be the more firm in a righteous undertaking.

Now there were certain Greeks among those that went up to worship at the feast: these therefore came to Philip, which was of Bethsaida of Galilee, and asked him, saying, Sir, we would see Jesus. Philip cometh and telleth Andrew: Andrew cometh, and Philip, and they tell Jesus. And Jesus answereth them, saying, The hour is come, that the Son of man should be glorified. Verily, verily, I say unto you, Except a grain of wheat fall into the earth and die, it abideth by itself alone: but if it die, it beareth much fruit. He that loveth his life loseth it; and he that hateth his life in this world shall keep it unto life eternal. If any man serve me, let him follow me; and where I am, there shall also my servant be: if any man serve me, him will the Father honour. (20-26)

20. *Now there were certain Greeks.* I do not think that they were Gentiles or uncircumcised, for it follows at once that they had come to worship. Now it was strictly prohibited by Roman law and severely punished by the proconsuls and other magistrates, if any was found to have left the worship of his own land and gone over to Judaism. But Jews who were dispersed throughout Asia and Greece were allowed to cross the sea to offer sacrifices in the Temple. Moreover, the Jews were not allowed to associate with Gentiles in the solemn worship of God, because they thought that they themselves, the Temple and the sacrifices would in that way be defiled. But although they were the descendants of Jews, yet as they lived far across the sea, it is not surprising if the Evangelist introduces them as foreigners and unacquainted with what was then happening in Jerusalem and round about. The significance of this is, therefore, that Christ was welcomed as King, not only by the inhabitants of Judaea, who had come from villages and towns to the feast, but that the report had also gone out to men who lived beyond the sea and who had come from far lands.

To worship. They could have done this in their own country. But John is here describing the ceremonious worship associated with sacrifices. For although religion and godliness were not confined to the Temple, yet they were nowhere else allowed to offer sacrifices to

God, nor had they anywhere else the Ark of the Testimony, the symbol of the divine presence. Every man worshipped God daily at home spiritually. But there was expected also of the saints under the Law an outward profession of worship, such as was prescribed by Moses, by appearing in the Temple in the presence of God. To this end were the feasts ordained. And if those men undertook so long a journey at great expense, with considerable inconvenience and not without risk, so that they should not neglect the outward profession of their piety, what excuse can we offer today unless we show that we worship the true God in our own land? Certainly, the worship of the Law has come to an end. But the Lord has left to His Church baptism, the holy Supper and the rite of public prayer for believers to practise. If we neglect them, it shows that our desire for godliness is very cold.

21. *They came to Philip*. It is a sign of reverence that they do not force themselves on Christ, but wish to obtain access through Philip; for reverence always begets modesty. But when the Papists draw from this the invocation of the dead to be our advocates with Christ and the Father, it is too ridiculous to need refutation. The Greeks speak to Philip who is present. How, I ask you, is this like calling upon the dead from whom one is separated? But such are the fruits of human presumption after it has once let itself wander outside the limits of the Word of God. The Papists have thoughtlessly invented invocation of the saints out of their own brains. And now, to acquire a false warrant from the Word of God, they corrupt and tear up the Scripture and do not hesitate to expose it to unworthy derision.

23. *The hour is come*. Many expound this of His death, inasmuch as it manifested His glory. So, according to them, Christ now declares that the time of His death is at hand. But I refer it rather to the proclamation of the Gospel, as if He had said that soon the knowledge of Him would be spread throughout every region of the world. Thus He wanted to forestall the dismay into which His death might throw the disciples; for He shows that there is no reason why their courage should fail, for the teaching of the Gospel will be proclaimed throughout the whole world. Again, in case this contemplation of His glory should quickly vanish away when He was condemned to death, hung on the cross and then buried, He anticipates and warns them in good time that the ignominy of His death does not obstruct His glory. To this end He uses a very appropriate simile:

Except a grain of wheat shall die or putrefy, it remains dry and sterile, but the death of the seed quickens it so that it bears fruit. So Christ compares His death to sowing, which seems to lead to the destruction of the wheat, but is nevertheless the cause of an abundant increase. Now although this admonition was especially necessary then, it is of continual use in the Church. And first, we ought to begin at the Head. That dreadful appearance of ignominy and malediction which is seen in the death of Christ, not only obscures His glory, but removes it altogether from our sight. We must not, then, hold to His death alone, but must also consider the fruit which His resurrection bears. In this way nothing will prevent His glory from shining everywhere. From Him we must then come to His members. For not only do we think that in death we perish, but even our life is a sort of continual death (Col. 3.3). It is all up with us then unless that consolation which Paul sets up helps us: 'If our outward man is decaying, yet our inward man is renewed day by day' (II Cor. 4.16). The godly are pressed down by various afflictions; they are held tight in hard straits; they suffer hunger or nakedness or disease; they are worried by reproaches; they seem every moment to be almost swallowed up by death. Let this then be their continual meditation, that it is a sowing which will yield fruit in its season.

25. *He that loveth his soul loseth it.* Christ adds an exhortation to His teaching. For if, to bring forth fruit, we must die, we should patiently suffer God to mortify us. But as He contrasts the love and the hatred of life, we must understand what it is to love and to hate life. He who is tied up by an immoderate desire for this present life and cannot leave the world without coercion, is said to love life. But he who despises this life and advances courageously to death, is said to hate life. Not that we should hate life absolutely, for it is justly reckoned among the highest of God's blessings. But believers ought to lay it down cheerfully when it hinders their access to Christ. Just as a man wishing to make haste in any matter would shake a heavy and inconvenient burden from his shoulders. In short, it is not in itself wrong to love this life, provided we only journey in it as foreigners, always intent on our bourne. For the true way to love life is when we remain in it as long as God pleases and are prepared to change our home as soon as He tells us—or, to put it in a word, when we, so to say, carry it in our hands and offer it to God as a sacrifice. Whoever is over-addicted to the present life loses his life; that is, he casts it to everlasting ruin. For to lose does not mean to abandon, or to suffer the loss of something valuable, but to give it over to destruction.

It is quite common for the word 'soul' to be taken for life. Some regard it in this passage as the seat of the affections—as if Christ had said, 'He who over indulges the desires of the flesh loses his soul.' But this is too forced, and the other is more natural: that he who neglects his life is going the best way about enjoying it eternally.

To make the meaning still clearer, the phrase *in this world*, used only once, ought to be repeated, so that the sense may be: Those who love their life in this world do not have its best interests at heart. On the other hand, those who despise their life in this world truly know how to preserve it. And, indeed, whoever is attached to this world deprives himself of his own accord of the heavenly life, of which we can only be heirs by being lodgers and guests in the world. Therefore it is a brutish attitude which reigns in all believers that they desire to exist but confine that existence to this world. Hence the more anxious anyone is about his safety, the further he removes himself from God's kingdom, that is, from the true life.

He that hateth his soul. I have already pointed out that this is said comparatively, in that we ought to despise life so far as it hinders us from living to God. For if meditation on the heavenly life predominated in our hearts, the world would have no power to hold us back. Hence, too, an objection which might be raised is solved. Many, through despair or other reasons, and especially from weariness of life, commit suicide. But we cannot say that they provide for their own safety. Others are swept away to death by ambition, who also throw themselves into ruin. But here Christ is speaking expressly of the hatred or contempt of this fleeting life which believers derive from the feeling of a better life. Consequently, he who does not look to heaven has not yet learned how life is to be saved. Moreover, Christ added this latter clause to terrify those who desire the earthly life too much; for if we are overwhelmed by the love of the world so that it is not easy to forget it, it is impossible for us to advance to heaven. But since Christ arouses us so violently, it would be madness to sleep the sleep of death.

26. *If any man serve me.* That death may be less bitter and disagreeable to us, Christ invites us by His example to submit to it cheerfully. And certainly this makes us ashamed of refusing the honour of being His disciples. But He only admits us into that number on condition we follow the path that He points out. He leads the way before us to encounter death. The bitterness of death is therefore moderated and, in a way, made sweet when we undergo it in common with the Son of God. So far from shrinking from Christ because of the cross, we should rather desire death to please Him. What immediately follows is to the same purpose:

And where I am, there shall also my servant be. For He demands that His servants should not refuse to submit to death, to which they see Him going before them. For it is not right that the servant should have anything separate from his Lord. The future tense in the word *shall be* is put for the imperative, after the custom of Hebrew. Some take it as a consolation, as if Christ had promised to those who were not unwilling to die with Him that they should be partakers of His resurrection. But as I said, the former view is the more probable. For He afterwards adds the consolation, that the Father will not leave Christ's servants unrewarded when they have been His inseparable companions in life and death.

Now is my soul troubled; and what shall I say? Father, save me from this hour. But for this cause came I unto this hour. Father, glorify thy name. There came therefore a voice out of heaven, saying, I have both glorified it, and will glorify it again. The multitude therefore, that stood by, and heard it, said that it had thundered: others said, An angel hath spoken to him. Jesus answered and said, This voice hath not come forth for my sake, but for your sakes. Now is the judgment of this world: now shall the prince of this world be cast out. And I, if I be lifted up from the earth, will draw all men unto myself. But this he said, signifying by what manner of death he should die. (27-33)

27. *Now is my soul.* This statement seems at first to differ widely from His former discourse. He had shown a superlatively heroic courage in exhorting His disciples not only to suffer death but to desire it willingly and eagerly whenever the circumstances demanded. Yet now, by shrinking from death, He confesses His weakness. But we read nothing here that is not perfectly consistent, as every believer knows from his own experience. It is not surprising if scornful men laugh at it, for it can only be understood by practice.

Moreover, it was useful and even necessary for our salvation that the Son of God should be so affected. The chief thing to consider in His death is His expiation, by which He appeased the wrath and curse of God. But He could not have done that without transferring to Himself our guilt. Therefore, the death which He underwent had to be full of horror, since He could not perform the satisfaction for us without apprehending the dreadful judgment of God in His own senses. From this we learn better the enormity of sin, for which the heavenly Father exacted so dreadful a punishment from His only begotten Son. So we must learn that death was no pastime or game to Christ, but that He was cast into the severest torments for our sake.

Nor was it absurd that the Son of God should be troubled like this. For His divinity was hidden, did not put forth its power and, in a sense, rested, that an opportunity might be given for making expiation. But Christ put on not only our flesh but also human feelings. It is true that in Him these feelings were voluntary. For He feared, not because He was forced to, but because of His own accord He had subjected Himself to fear. Yet we must believe that it was not in pretence but in truth that He feared. But He differed from other men

39

in that He kept all His feelings ruled by obedience to God's righteousness, as we have said elsewhere.

This brings us another advantage. If the dread of death had not upset Christ, which of us would have thought that His example concerned us? For it has not been given to us to meet death without sorrow. But when we learn that even He had not an iron hardness within Him, we summon up courage to follow Him, and the weakness of the flesh which is terrified by death does not hinder us from becoming the companions of our Leader in fighting it.

And what shall I say? Here we see, as if it were before our eyes, how much our salvation cost the Son of God, when He was reduced to such straits that He found neither words to express the intensity of His sorrow nor yet decision as a man. He flees to prayer, which alone remains to Him, and asks to be delivered from death. And also, seeing that He has been appointed by the eternal purpose of God to be a sacrifice for sins, He quickly corrects that wish which His great sadness had expressed, and so to say, He puts out His hand to pull Himself back, that He may acquiesce entirely in His Father's will.

In this passage we should note five steps. First stands the complaint which breaks forth out of infinite sorrow. Secondly, He feels that He needs a remedy, and lest He should be overwhelmed by fear He asks Himself what He ought to do. Thirdly, He goes to the Father, and begs Him to deliver Him. Fourthly, He retracts the wish, which He knows to be against His calling, and chooses rather to suffer anything than not to fulfil what His Father had enjoined on Him. Last of all, He is satisfied with the glory of God alone, forgets all the rest and deems them nothing.

But it may seem unbecoming in the Son of God to pour out a wish which He must at once retract to obey His Father. I readily admit that this is the folly of the cross, which is an offence to proud men. But the more the Lord of glory humbled Himself, the plainer proof we have of His infinite love to us. Moreover, we must remember, as I have already said, that the human feelings from which Christ was not immune were in Him pure and free from sin. The reason is that they were composed and regulated to the obedience of God, for there is nothing to prevent Christ having a natural fear of death and yet desiring to obey God—and that in various respects. Hence His correction when He says:

For this cause came I unto this hour. Although He may legitimately dread death, yet when He considers why He was sent and what His office of Mediator demands, He offers to His Father the dread conceived of His natural senses, that it might be subdued—or rather, having subdued it, He prepares freely and willingly to execute God's command. Now, if Christ's feelings, which were completely free from sin, needed to be restrained for Him to be obedient to the Father, how earnest we should be in this, for the numerous affections springing from our flesh are so many inward enemies. We must also observe that we ought to bridle not only those affections which are diametrically opposed to the will of God, but also those which hinder the course of our calling, even though, in other respects, they are not wicked or sinful. To make this clearer, we should put in the first place the will of God. In the second, the pure and entire will of man, such as God gave to Adam and such as was in Christ. Then lastly, our own, which is infected by the contagion of sin. The will of God is the rule to which everything inferior to it should be subjected. Now the pure will of nature will not of itself rebel against God. But man, even if he were wholly formed to righteousness, would encounter many hindrances unless he subjected his affections to God. Christ had only the one battle to fight—to cease fearing what He naturally feared as soon as He knew that God's will was otherwise. But we have a twofold battle, for we have to struggle with the obstinacy of our flesh. Consequently the bravest wrestlers never win without a wound.

Father, save me. The rule we should observe whenever we are either distressed by fear or oppressed with grief is to raise our hearts to God at once. For there is nothing worse or more harmful than inwardly brooding over what torments us. We see a large part of the world gnawed by hidden torments; and it is a just punishment of apathy in all who will not rise up to God that they receive no relief.

28. *Father, glorify thy name.* He testifies by these words that He puts the glory of the Father before everything else and disregards and neglects even His own life. And the true regulating of our desires is so to seek God's glory that all the rest gives place to it. For we should regard it as abundant reward, that we may with a quiet mind bear all that is troublesome and irksome.

I have both glorified it. This is equivalent to His saying: 'I will perfect what I have begun,' for 'God does not leave the work of his hands defective' as Psalm 138.8 says. But since God's purpose was to forestall the offence of the cross, He not only promises that Christ's death will be glorious, but also commends the many ornaments with which He had already adorned it.

29. *That it had thundered.* It was a monstrous thing that the multitude was obtuse to so plain a miracle. Some were deaf, and caught what God had pronounced distinctly only as a confused sound. Others were less dull, but yet detracted greatly from the majesty of the divine voice by pretending that its author was an angel. But the same thing

is common today. God speaks plainly enough in the Gospel, in which there is also displayed a power and energy of the Spirit which should shake heaven and earth. But many are as cold towards the teaching as if it came only from a mortal man, and others think God's Word to be a barbarous stammering, as if it were nothing but thunder.

But it will be asked whether that voice sounded from heaven in vain and without profit. I reply that what the Evangelist here ascribes to the multitude pertained only to a part of it. Besides the apostles there were some who interpreted it more correctly. But the Evangelist wanted to indicate briefly what commonly happens in the world; that the majority, although they hear God speaking clearly and loudly, do not in fact hear Him.

30. *Not for my sake.* Did Christ need no confirmation, or had the Father less care for Him than for us? We must keep to this principle: Because Christ clothed Himself with flesh for our sake, all the blessings He received from the Father were given for our sake. Again, it is true that the voice came from heaven for the people's sake, for He did not need an outward miracle. Moreover, there is a tacit reproof here, that the Jews are stone-deaf to the voice of God, for since God speaks for their sake, their ingratitude in not listening is inexcusable.

31. *Now is the judgment of this world.* As if He had already finished the fight, the Lord now rejoices as the victor, not only over fear but also over death. For He proclaims magnificently the fruit of His death, which might have been a cause of consternation to His disciples. The word *judgment* is taken as 'reformation' by some and 'condemnation' by others. I agree rather with the former, who expound it that the world must be restored to due order. For the Hebrew word מִשְׁפָּט which is translated as *judgment* means a well-ordered constitution (*rectam constitutionem*). Now we know that outside Christ there is nothing but confusion in the world. And although Christ had already begun to set up the kingdom of God, it was His death that was the true beginning of a properly-ordered state and the complete restoration of the world.

We must also notice, however, that this right ordering (*rectitudo*) cannot be set up in the world, until first Satan's kingdom is wiped out and until the flesh and whatever is against God's righteousness is annihilated. Finally, the renewing of the world must be preceded by a mortifying. And so Christ declares that the prince of this world is to be cast out. For confusion and deformity arise because, while Satan exercises his tyranny, iniquity is spread abroad. Therefore, when Satan has been cast out, the world is called back from its revolt to the rule of God. If anyone asks how Satan was cast out by Christ's death, since he does not cease to go on making war, I reply that this casting out is not to be limited to any short time, but is a description of the remarkable effect of Christ's death which appears daily.

32. *If I be lifted up.* Next follows the way in which the judgment is to be decided. When Christ is uplifted on the cross He will gather all men to Himself to raise them from earth to heaven. The Evangelist says that Christ indicated the manner of His death. Therefore, the meaning no doubt is that the cross will be a sort of carriage in which He will exalt all men with Himself to His Father. It might have been thought that He was then carried away from the earth so as to have nothing in common with men any longer. But He proclaims that His departure will be very different, for He will draw up to Himself those who were fixed to the earth. Although He refers to the form of His death, He means in general that it will not be a parting to separate Him from men but a new way of drawing earth up to heaven.

When He says *all* it must be referred to the children of God, who are of His flock. Yet I agree with Chrysostom, who says that Christ used the universal word because the Church was to be gathered from Gentiles and Jews alike, according to the saying, 'There shall be one shepherd and one sheepfold' (John 10.16). The Vulgate has 'I will draw all things to me,' and Augustine maintains that it should be read so. But the consent of all the Greek manuscripts should weigh more with us.

The multitude therefore answered him, We have heard out of the law that the Christ abideth for ever: and how sayest thou, The Son of man must be lifted up? who is this Son of man? Jesus therefore said unto them, Yet a little while is the light among you. Walk while ye have the light, that darkness overtake you not: and he that walketh in the darkness knoweth not whither he goeth. While ye have the light, believe on the light, that ye may become sons of light. These things spake Jesus, and he departed and hid himself from them. (34-36)

34. *We have heard out of the law.* Without doubt they just intended to carp maliciously at Christ's words. And their malice blinds them so that amid clear light they see nothing. They say that Jesus was not to be regarded as the Christ, because He said that He would die, whereas the Law ascribes eternity to the Messiah. As if the Law had not definitely declared both sides—that Christ will die and that His kingdom will flourish to the end of the world. But they seize on the second clause as an excuse for calumny. The source of their error was that they judged the splendour of the Messiah's kingdom from their carnal sense. Hence they reject Christ because He does not correspond to their conception. Under the word *the law* they compre-

hend also the prophets; and the present tense *remaineth* is used for the future, after the Hebrew idiom.

The query *Who is this Son of man?* has mockery in it, as if Christ had been defeated by that little refutation. This shows how arrogant ignorance is. It is as if they said, 'Go on, boast that you are the Christ, when your own confession proves that you have no affinity with him.'

35. *Yet a little while.* In His reply the Lord gently admonishes them, and yet at the same time pricks them sharply. He accuses them of being blind to the light and threatens that the light will soon be taken away from them. When He says that some light remains for a little while, He confirms what He had already said about His death. For although the light does not mean His bodily presence but His Gospel, He nevertheless refers to His departure, as if He were saying, 'I shall not cease to be the light when I have gone away, and so nothing in me will be diminished by your darkness.'

When He says that *the light is with them*, He indirectly reproves them for closing their eyes and shutting out the light. Hence He means that they do not deserve an answer to their objection, because they deliberately look for opportunities to err.

When He says that the light shines on them for only a little while, it is true of all unbelievers. Scripture promises to God's children that the Sun of righteousness will rise and never set. 'The sun shall be no more thy light by day; nor the moon by night: but the Lord shall be unto thee an everlasting light' (Isa. 60.19). But all should walk warily, for darkness will follow on contempt of the light. And the reason why such a thick and murky night lay over the world for many centuries before this was because so few troubled to advance into the brightness of heavenly wisdom. For Christ enlightens us by His Gospel that we may follow the way of salvation which He shows us. Therefore those who make no use of the grace of God, extinguish, as far as they can, the light offered to them.

To strike them with more fear, He warns them how wretched is the state of those who are destitute of the light and do nothing but go astray in the whole direction of their life. For they cannot take one step without the risk of slipping or even falling down. But now Christ declares that we are in darkness unless He shines upon us. From this you can gather what the human mind is worth when it is its own leader and master apart from Christ.

36. *Believe on the light.* He exhorts them to keep possession of the light by faith, for He calls them *the children* of light who as true heirs enjoy it to the end.

These things spake Jesus. It might seem surprising that He withdrew from those who were so eager to welcome Him. But we can easily gather from the other Evangelists that this is a reference to His enemies, who were galled at the godly zeal of these good and sincere men. For the foreigners who had gone out to meet Christ, followed Him to the Temple, where He fell in with the scribes and the town mob.

But though he had done so many signs before them, yet they believed not on him: that the word of Isaiah the prophet might be fulfilled, which he spake, Lord, who hath believed our report? And to whom hath the arm of the Lord been revealed? For this cause they could not believe, for that Isaiah said again, He hath blinded their eyes, and he hardened their heart; lest they should see with their eyes, and perceive with their heart, and should turn, and I should heal them. These things spake Isaiah, because he saw his glory; and he spake of him. (37-41)

37. *But though he had done so many signs.* Lest any should be hindered or disturbed that Christ was despised by the Jews, the Evangelist removes the offence by showing that He was furnished with clear and certain testimonies, which gave authority to Him and His teaching. But God's glory and power, which shone brightly in His miracles, were not displayed to the blind. Therefore we must first understand that it was not Christ's fault that the Jews did not believe in Him. He abundantly testified who He was by many miracles; and therefore it was unjust and extremely unreasonable that their unbelief should detract from Him. But since many might become anxious and worried as to why the Jews were so stupid that the visible power of God did not move them at all, John goes further and says that faith is not begotten of an ordinary human faculty but is a unique and rare gift of God. And it was once foretold of Christ that hardly any would believe the Gospel.

38. *That the word of Isaiah.* John does not mean that this prediction imposed a necessity on the Jews, for Isaiah spoke nothing but what the Lord revealed to him from the secret treasures of His counsel. Indeed, this must have happened, even had the prophet been silent. But as no one would have known what was going to happen if God had not testified by the mouth of the prophet, in the prediction the Evangelist sets before their eyes as in a mirror what otherwise would have been obscure and incredible to men.

Lord, who hath believed? This sentence has two clauses. Isaiah has already begun to speak about Christ, and when he foresees that everything he proclaims about Him and everything that will afterwards be preached by the apostles will be everywhere rejected by the Jews, he first exclaims, as if amazed at some evil monstrosity, 'Lord, who shall believe our report?' In the second clause he acknowledges why they are few—because men do not reach this by their own exertions, and God does not enlighten all indiscriminately, but honours a few with the grace of His Spirit. And if the obstinate unbelief of a few among the Jews should not have been an obstacle to believers, however few they were, the same reason ought to persuade us today not to be ashamed at the Gospel though it has few disciples. But we must first observe the reason added—that it is not their own acumen but the revelation of God which makes believers. The word *arm*, as is well known, denotes power. The prophet declares that God's arm, which is contained in the teaching of the Gospel, is hidden until it is revealed; and at the same time he says that not all are partakers of this revelation indiscriminately. Hence it follows that many are left in their blindness without inward light, because hearing they do not hear.

39. *For this cause they could not believe.* This is somewhat harsher. For as the words sound, the way was shut up against the Jews and the power to believe was taken from them by the prophet dooming them to blindness before they had made a choice either way. I reply that there is no absurdity in this if nothing can happen differently from what God has foreseen. But we must note that the bare foreknowledge of God is not the cause of things. We are, however, not so much concerned with God's foreknowledge here as with His judgment and vengeance. For God declares not what He sees from heaven that men will do, but what He Himself will do; that is, that He will strike the ungodly with stupidity and dizziness that He may take vengeance on their malice. In this passage he points out the near and inferior reason why God intends His Word, by nature salutary, to be destructive and deadly to the Jews. Their malice deserved it.

It was impossible for them to escape this punishment. For God had once determined to give them over to a reprobate mind and to change the light of His Word into darkness for them. This prophecy differs from the former in that there the prophet says that none believe save those whom God of His free grace·enlightens in His own good pleasure, the cause of which does not appear. Since all are equally ruined, God of His mere goodness distinguishes from the rest some as it seems good to Him. But in this passage he speaks of the hardness with which God punished the malice of an ungrateful people. Those who do not notice these degrees confound Scriptural passages of varying meaning.

40. *He hath blinded their heart.* This passage is from Isaiah (6.9-10) where the Lord forewarns the prophet that his labour in teaching will have no other result than to make the people worse. First He says, 'Go and say to this people, Hearing, hear and do not hear;' as if He were saying, 'I send you to speak to the deaf.' He afterwards adds, 'Blind the heart of this people, etc.' By these words He means that

He intends His Word to be a punishment to the reprobate that it may make their blindness worse and plunge them in deeper darkness. It is indeed a terrifying judgment of God when He so overwhelms men's minds by the light of teaching as to deprive them of all understanding; out of their only light He even brings darkness upon them.

We ought to observe, moreover, that it is accidental to the Word of God (*accidentale esse Verbo Dei*) to blind men. For there is nothing less reasonable than that truth should not differ from falsehood, that the bread of life should become a death-dealing poison and that medicine should make a disease worse. But men's malice is to blame, which turns life into death.

Again, we ought to observe that sometimes the Lord of Himself blinds men's minds by depriving them of judgment and understanding —either by Satan and false prophets when through their impostures He sends them out of their minds, or by His ministers when the preaching of salvation is harmful and deadly to them. Yet so long as the prophets devote themselves faithfully to the task of teaching and commit the fruit of their work to the Lord, they ought not to give up or waver, even though the result is less than they hope for. Rather let them be satisfied with knowing that God approves of their labour, though it be useless to men, and that the very savour of the teaching which the ungodly render deadly to themselves, is good and sweet to God, as Paul testifies (II Cor. 2.15).

In Scripture *the heart* is sometimes taken as the seat of the affections. But here, as in many other places, it means the so-called intellectual part of the soul. Moses speaks in the same sense: 'God hath not given you an heart to know (*ad intelligendum*)' (Deut. 29.4).

Lest they should see with their eyes. We must remember that the prophet is speaking of unbelievers, who had already rejected the grace of God. It is certain that all would continue to be so by nature, did not the Lord form to obedience to Himself those whom He has elected. At first, then, the state of men is equal and the same. But when reprobate men have of their own accord and by their own malice rebelled against God, they make room for this vengeance that they may be given over to a reprobate mind and rush ever more and more to their own destruction. It is their own fault if God does not wish to convert them, for they were the authors of their own hopelessness. By these words of the prophet we are also briefly taught what is the beginning of our conversion to God. It is when He enlightens hearts which were necessarily turned from Him so long as they were possessed by the darkness of Satan. Yet such is the power of divine light that it attracts us to itself and transforms us to the image of God.

He adds that *healing* is the result of conversion. By this word the prophet means God's blessing and a prosperous condition as well as deliverance from all the miseries which spring from the wrath of God. Now if this last falls on the reprobate contrary to the nature of the Word, we ought to attend to the antithesis of its opposite use— the purpose for which the Word of God is preached to us is to enlighten us in the true knowledge of God, to turn us to God and to reconcile us to Him that we may be blessed and happy.

41. *These things said Isaiah.* Lest readers should think that the prediction was quoted inaptly, John expressly says that the prophet was not sent as a teacher to one age, but rather the glory of Christ was shown to him that he might witness the things which should occur under His reign. For what other aim had the prophetical revelations than to hand on to others what they had received from God? The Evangelist takes it for granted that Isaiah saw Christ's glory; and from this he infers that Isaiah accommodates his teaching to the future state of Christ's kingdom.

Nevertheless even of the rulers many believed on him; but because of the Pharisees they did not confess it, lest they should be put out of the synagogue: for they loved the glory of men more than the glory of God. And Jesus cried and said, He that believeth on me, believeth not on me, but on him that sent me. And he that beholdeth me beholdeth him that sent me. I am come a light into the world, that whosoever believeth on me may not abide in the darkness. (42–46)

42. *Nevertheless many.* When the Jews in uproar and ferocity rejected Christ so wantonly, it might have seemed that they all conspired against Him to a man. But the Evangelist says that amidst the general madness of the nation many remained sane. A remarkable example indeed of the grace of God; for when ungodliness has once got the upper hand, it is a sort of universal pestilence which infects every part of the body with its contagion. It is therefore a remarkable gift of God that among such a corrupt people some remain untainted. And yet in the world today we see the same grace of God. Although ungodliness and contempt for God abound everywhere and very many strive furiously to exterminate the teaching of the Gospel altogether, it always finds some retreats, so that faith has, as it were, its havens that it may not be banished completely from the world.

The word *even* is emphatic. For in the ranks of the rulers there was such an aggressive and dangerous hatred of the Gospel that it was incredible that a single believer could be found among them. The more wonderful was the power of God's Spirit, which penetrated where no entrance was open. It was not a vice of that age alone that rulers were obstinate and disobedient to Christ. Honour, wealth and rank are usually accompanied by pride. The consequence is that those who are swollen with arrogance and hardly acknowledge that they are men are not easily subdued by voluntary humility. Whoever, then, is exalted in the world will mistrust his rank if he is wise, lest it should be an obstacle to him. When he says that there were *many* it must not be understood as if they were the majority or even half, for compared with the huge crowd of the rest they were few; but they were many, reckoned in themselves.

Because of the Pharisees. He seems to speak incorrectly when he separates faith from confession. 'For with the heart man believeth unto righteousness; and with the mouth confession is made unto salvation' (Rom. 10.10). It is impossible that the faith which has been kindled in the heart shall not produce its flame. I reply that he was showing here how weak faith was in those lukewarm, or rather cold, men. In short, John means that they embraced Christ's teaching because they knew it had come from God. But their faith was neither so lively nor so strong as it should have been. For Christ does not give His own a spirit of fear but of constancy, that they may dare boldly and fearlessly to confess what they have learned from Him. I do not think they were completely silent; but as their confession was not frank, the Evangelist simply, to my mind, denies that they professed their faith. For their true profession would have been to ally themselves openly to Christ. Let no man, therefore, flatter himself who in any way conceals or dissembles his faith lest he should incur men's hatred. For however hateful Christ's name may be, the cowardice is inexcusable which makes us swerve, in even the smallest degree, from confessing Him.

We must also notice, that rulers have less courage and constancy, because ambition almost always reigns in them, and there is nothing more servile than that. To put it in a word, earthly honours may be called golden shackles binding a man so that he cannot freely do his duty. For this reason, obscurer and poorer people ought to bear their lot with greater patience, for they are at least free from many dangerous snares. Yet the great and noble ought to struggle against their fortune, lest it should hinder them from submitting to Christ.

John says that they were afraid of the Pharisees. Not that the other scribes and priests allowed any man with impunity to call himself a disciple of Christ, but because in them cruelty (under the guise of zeal) burned with greater violence. Zeal in defending religion is certainly an excellent virtue. But when hypocrisy is added to it, there is no more dangerous plague. The more, then, should we ask the Lord to guide us by the sure rule of His Spirit.

Lest they should be put out of the synagogue. It was the fear of disgrace that hindered them; for they would have been put out of the synagogue. From this appears the great depravity of men, which not only corrupts and debases the best of God's ordinances but turns them into destructive tyrannies. Excommunication should have been the nerve of holy discipline, that punishment might be prompt if anyone despised the Church. But it was now so used that anyone who confessed that he belonged to Christ was banished from the fellowship of the faithful. Likewise today the Pope, that he may practise the same kind of tyranny, falsely claims the right of excommunication and not only thunders with blind rage against all the godly, but strives to cast down Christ from His heavenly throne. Yet he does not hesitate impudently to claim the title of sacred jurisdiction with which Christ has adorned His Church.

43. *For they loved the glory.* The Evangelist expressly says that these men were not inspired by some superstition, but were only avoiding disgrace among men. For if ambition weighed more with them than the fear of God, it follows that they were free of vain scruples of conscience. Now let readers observe how dishonourably in God's sight is condemned the cowardice of those who from fear of unpopularity dissemble their faith among men. What is more foolish, nay, what is more brutish, than to prefer the paltry approval of men to the judgment of God? But he declares that all who shrink from unpopularity among men when the pure faith ought to be confessed are full of this kind of madness. And justly; for the apostle, when praising the invincible constancy of Moses, says that 'he endured, as if he saw the invisible' (Heb. 11.27). By this he means that when anyone has his eyes fixed on God his resolve will be unbreakable and inflexible.

The softness which makes us give way to treacherous pretence comes from our senses being blunted at the sight of the world. For a true sight of God would immediately scatter all the mists of wealth and honour. Away with those who see the indirect denial of Christ as something trivial, or as they call it, venial! The Spirit declares, on the contrary, that this monstrosity is more horrible than if heaven and earth were confused.

To love the glory of men means in this passage to want to be valued among men. The Evangelist therefore says that they were so devoted to the world that they preferred to please men rather than God. Moreover, when he accuses of this crime those who denied Christ, he shows at the same time that the excommunication which the priests abused, contrary to divine and human law, was empty and worthless. Let us know then, that all the anathemas which the Pope mouths against us today are mere scarecrows when we are aware that all he is trying to do is to lead us away from Christ.

44. *And Jesus cried.* Christ's declaration aims at encouraging His people to a right and unshakeable constancy of faith. But there is also a rebuke here, by which He wanted to correct their perverse fear. The cry suggests vehemence, for it is not a simple lesson but an exhortation to excite them more keenly. The sum of it is that faith in Christ does not rely on any mortal man, but on God; for it finds in Christ nothing but what is divine, or rather, it beholds God in His face. Hence He concludes that it is foolish and unworthy for it to waver doubtfully. For it is impossible to do a greater injustice to God than to be dissatisfied with His truth. He then has duly profited by the Gospel who relies on the confidence of believing, not men, but God, and firmly and quietly stands fast against all the machinations of Satan. Therefore, to pay God His honour, we must learn to stand firm in faith, not only though the world were wavering but even though Satan disturbed and overthrew everything under heaven.

Believers are said not to believe in Christ when they do not stop at His human appearance. For He compares Himself with the Father and tells us to look at God's power; for the weakness of the flesh has no strength in itself. When He later exhorts the disciples to belief in Him, the sense will be different. In that passage God is not contrasted to man, but Christ is put forward with all His gifts, and this should suffice to uphold our faith.

45. *And he that beholdeth me.* 'Behold' here should be taken for 'knowledge'. For that our consciences may be really and profoundly quiet, which otherwise would have been continually liable to all sorts of disturbances, He recalls us to the Father. The stability of faith is sure and secure because it transcends the world. Now, when Christ is truly known, the glory of God shines in Him, so that we may know for certain that our faith in Him does not depend on man, but is founded on the eternal God; for it rises from Christ's flesh to His divinity. Because this is so, it must not only be fixed for ever in our hearts, but also show itself boldly in our tongues when need be.

46. *I am come a light.* To make His disciples bolder and more spirited, He goes further in proclaiming the certainty of faith. First, He testifies that He came into the world to be a light by which men could be delivered from darkness and wanderings. At the same time He shows how we obtain so great a blessing when He says *that whosoever believeth on me etc.* Moreover He accuses of ingratitude all who do not separate themselves from unbelievers, even after they have been taught by the Gospel. For the higher the excellence of this blessing of being called from darkness into light, the less excuse have

51

they who, through indolence or neglect quench the light once kindled
in them.

There is great weight in the words *I am come a light into the world*.
Although Christ was a light from the beginning, He has every reason
to distinguish Himself by the claim that He came to do the work of
light. And that we may keep the various steps distinct He tells us,
first, that He is a light for others rather than for Himself; secondly,
not only for angels but for men also; thirdly, that He was manifested
in the flesh to shine with full brightness.

The universal particle seems to have been put in deliberately, partly
that all believers without exception might enjoy this benefit in common and partly to show that unbelievers perish in darkness because
they flee from the light of their own accord. Now, if all the wisdom of the world were gathered into one, not a spark of true light
would be found in that huge heap. On the contrary, it would be a
formless chaos; for it belongs to Christ alone to deliver us from
darkness.

*And if any man hear my sayings, and keep them not, I judge him not:
for I came not to judge the world, but to save the world. He that rejecteth me, and receiveth not my sayings, hath one that judgeth him:
the word that I spake, the same shall judge him in the last day. For I
spake not from myself; but the Father which sent me, he hath given me
a commandment, what I should say, and what I should speak. And I
know that his commandment is life eternal: the things therefore which I
speak, even as the Father hath said unto me, so I speak.* (47–50)

47. *If any man hear my sayings.* When He had spoken of His grace
and exhorted His disciples to steadfast faith, He now began to pierce
the rebels. Yet even here He softened the severity deserved by the
ungodliness of those who, as it were, set themselves to reject God.
For He delayed pronouncing judgment on them, because He had
come rather for the salvation of all. We must understand that He
was not speaking here of unbelievers in general but of those who
wittingly and voluntarily reject the preaching of the Gospel exhibited
to them. Why then did Christ not wish to condemn them? Because
He had temporarily laid aside the office of judge and offers salvation
to all indiscriminately and stretches out His arms to embrace all, that
all may be the more encouraged to repent. And yet He heightens by
an important detail the crime of rejecting an invitation so kind and
gracious; for it is as if He had said: 'See, I have come to call all; and
forgetting the role of judge, my one aim is to attract and rescue from
destruction those who already seem doubly ruined.' Hence no man
is condemned for despising the Gospel save he who spurns the lovely

news of salvation and deliberately decides to bring destruction on himself.

The word *judge*, as is clear from its antithesis *save*, is here put for 'condemn'. Now this should be referred to the proper and genuine office of Christ. For that unbelievers are the more severely condemned on account of the Gospel is accidental (*accidentale*) and does not spring from its nature, as we have said elsewhere.

48. *He that rejecteth me.* Lest the ungodly should flatter themselves that they can wanton against Christ with impunity, He adds the dreadful threat that, though He were to be quiet, His teaching would suffice of itself to condemn them—as He elsewhere says that no other judge would be needed but Moses in whom they boasted (John 5.45). The meaning therefore is, 'Because I burn with a great desire for your salvation, I refrain from my right of condemning you and am entirely employed in saving what is lost. But do not imagine that you have slipped out of the hands of God; for even should I be altogether silent, the Word which you have despised, is of itself your fit judge.'

And receiveth not my sayings. This is an explanation of the previous clause. Since hypocrisy is innate in men, nothing comes easier to them than to boast in words that they are ready to receive Christ; and we see how common this boasting is, even among the worst men. We must therefore keep to this definition, that we reject Christ when we do not embrace the pure teaching of the Gospel. The Papists shout aloud the name of Christ; but as soon as His pure truth is put forward, nothing is more hateful to them. Such kiss Christ Judas-like. Let us therefore learn to include Him in His Word and to give Him that worship of obedience which He claims alone.

The word that I speak. It is impossible to extoll the authority of the Gospel with a more splendid praise than to grant it the power of judging. For, according to this, the last judgment will be simply the approbation of the teaching of the Gospel. Certainly, Christ will Himself mount the judgment seat, but He declares that He will pronounce judgment from the Word which is now preached. This threat ought to terrify the ungodly, since they cannot escape the judgment of His teaching which they now despise so proudly.

But when Christ mentions the last judgment, He hints that they are now without understanding. He reminds them that the punishment which is now a joke to them will then be made public. On the other hand, it gives the godly an inestimable consolation that however much they may now be condemned by the world, they do not doubt that they are already absolved in heaven. For wherever the faith of the Gospel has its abode, the judgment seat of God is set up for saving. If we rely on this right we need not worry about Papists or their absurd judgments, for our faith rises even above angels.

49. *For I spake not from myself.* Lest the outward appearance of the man should detract from the majesty of God, Christ frequently sends us to the Father. This is why He so often mentions the Father. And indeed, inasmuch as it would be wrong to transfer to another any spark of the divine glory, the Word, to which judgment is granted, must have proceeded from God. Now Christ here distinguishes Himself from the Father, not simply according to His divine person, but according rather to His flesh, lest His teaching should be judged humanly and therefore have less weight. If consciences were subject to human laws and teaching, Christ's argument would not apply. 'My Word,' He says, 'will judge because it has not come from man;' according to the saying, 'One only is the lawgiver, etc.' (Jas. 4.12). From this we may also infer how monstrous the Pope's sacrilege is in daring to bind souls by His inventions. For in this way he claims more than does the Son of God, who declares that He only speaks by commandment of His Father.

50. *And his commandment is life eternal.* He again praises the fruit of His teaching, that all may yield to it the more readily. And it is only fair that the ungodly should feel God's vengeance, whom they now refuse to have as the author of life.

CHAPTER THIRTEEN

Now before the feast of the passover, Jesus knowing that his hour was come that he should depart out of this world unto the Father, having loved his own which were in the world, he loved them unto the end. And after supper, the devil having already put into the heart of Judas Iscariot, Simon's son, to betray him, Jesus knowing that the Father had given all things into his hands, and that he came forth from God, and goeth unto God, riseth from supper, and layeth aside his garments; and he took a towel, and girded himself. Then he poureth water into the bason, and began to wash the disciples' feet, and to wipe them with the towel wherewith he was girded. So he cometh to Simon Peter. He saith unto him, Lord, dost thou wash my feet? Jesus answered and said unto him, What I do thou knowest not now; but thou shalt understand hereafter. (1-7)

1. *Before the feast.* John deliberately omits many things which he knew had been narrated by Matthew and the others. He undertakes to treat what they had left out, like the story of the washing of the feet. And although he will later explain more clearly why Christ washed His disciples' feet, he prefaces this with the saying that He testified by this same sign that the love with which He first embraced them was constant and eternal, so that when they should be deprived of His presence they might still be convinced that even death would not quench this love. This conviction ought now to be fixed in our hearts, too.

It says that Christ *loved his own which were in the world unto the end.* Why this circumlocution to describe the Apostles, unless to tell us that because they, like us, were struggling in a dangerous and difficult warfare, Christ had the more care for them? And therefore, although we seem to be far from Christ, let us know that He is mindful of us, for He loves His own who are in the world. And there is no doubt but that He still bears the same attitude now which He had at the crisis of His death.

That he should depart out of this world unto the Father. This is a noteworthy phrase, for it refers to Christ's knowledge that His death was a passing to the heavenly kingdom of God. And if while He was hurrying there He did not cease to love His own as before, we have no reason to think that His attitude is changed. Now, since He is the firstborn from the dead, this definition of death applies to the whole body of the Church, that it is a passing to God, absent from whom believers now wander.

2. *After supper.* We shall afterwards at the proper place treat more fully Christ's purpose in washing their feet, and the fruit of this story. Let us now attend to the actual words. He says that it was done when Judas had already made up his mind to betray Christ—not only to show the wonderful patience of Christ, that He could bear to wash the feet of such a wicked and treacherous apostate, but also because He purposely chose the time when He was near death for performing what may be regarded as the last action of His life.

When he says that Judas' decision to betray Christ had been motivated by the devil, it is equivalent to showing the enormity of the crime. For it was a dreadful and most tragic wickedness, in which the power of Satan was openly displayed. Certainly, all the wickedness which men do is incited by Satan; but the more revolting and execrable the crime, the more should we see in it the rage of the devil, who drives men forsaken by God hither and thither. But though men's passion (*concupiscentia*) is inflamed by Satan's bellows, it does not cease to be a furnace in itself. It has the fire burning within itself and it greedily receives the draught of the bellows; and so no excuse is left to the ungodly.

3. *Jesus, knowing that the Father had given all things.* I interpret this as put in to tell us the source of Christ's quiet composure of mind. Having already gained the victory over death, He raised His mind to the glorious triumph which should soon follow. Men in the grasp of fear are usually greatly agitated. The Evangelist means that there was no such agitation in Christ, because, although He was soon to be betrayed by Judas, He knew that the Father had given Him all things. If any ask why He was reduced to such a grief that He sweated blood, I reply that both sides were necessary—that He should dread death, and that He should nevertheless fearlessly discharge all the office of the Mediator.

4. *And layeth aside his garments.* Understand that He laid aside His upper garment, not His tunic. For we know that the Orientals wore long garments.

Afterwards follow the words *he began to wash their feet, etc.*, expressing Christ's purpose rather than His outward action; for the Evangelist adds that He began with Peter.

6. *Lord, dost thou wash my feet?* This speech expresses a loathing of something as foolish and unworthy. By asking what Christ was doing, he pushes Him away with his hand, so to say. This modesty would be laudable, were not obedience of greater value in God's sight than any kind of service or honouring; or rather, if it were not the

true and only rule of humility to submit in obedience to God and have all our senses devoted to His good pleasure, so that everything He declares to be agreeable to Him shall also be approved by us, without any argument. We should therefore, above all, keep this rule of serving God aright that we may be always ready to agree without delay, whenever and whatever He commands.

7. *What I do.* These words teach us that we should simply obey Christ even though it is not clear why He wishes this or that to be done. In a well-regulated house the decision rests with one person, the head of the family; and the servants have to employ their hands and feet for him. Thus the man who refuses God's command because he does not know the reason for it is too haughty. But the admonition has an even more extensive meaning. We should not be worried that we are ignorant of the things that God wishes to be hidden from us for a time. This kind of ignorance is more learned than any other kind of knowledge, when we let God be wiser than we are.

Peter saith unto him, Thou shalt never wash my feet. Jesus answered him, If I wash thee not, thou hast no part with me. Simon Peter saith unto him, Lord, not my feet only, but also my hands and my head. Jesus saith to him, He that is bathed needeth not save to wash his feet, but is clean every whit: and ye are clean, but not all. For he knew him that should betray him; therefore said he, Ye are not all clean. (8-11)

8. *Thou shalt never wash.* Hitherto Peter's modesty was excusable, though not entirely blameless. But now he sins more grievously when he has been corrected and yet does not yield. And it is indeed a common fault that obstinacy goes with error. It is, no doubt, a plausible excuse that the refusal arises from reverence, but because he does not simply obey the word, the very desire to honour Christ loses all its goodness. The true wisdom of faith is to approve and embrace with reverence whatever comes from God, as done rightly and properly. Nor, indeed, can His name be sanctified by us in any other way. For if we do not decide that whatever He does is done for the best reason, our flesh, naturally stubborn, will continually grumble and will not render Him His due honour unless it is forced to. In short, until a man renounces his liberty of judging the works of God, however he may strive to honour God, pride will be always latent under the semblance of humility.

If I wash thee not. This reply of Christ does not yet express His purpose in deciding to wash His disciples' feet. But by a comparison drawn from the soul to the body, He shows that in washing the disciples' feet He does nothing new to Himself or foreign to His role. Meanwhile He shows the foolishness of Peter's wisdom. The same thing will always happen to us whenever the Lord begins to dispute with us. So long as He is silent, men do not think that they are rashly differing from Him. But nothing is easier than for Him to refute with a word all their plausible arguments. Since Christ is his Lord and Master, it seems absurd to Peter that He should wash his feet. But in refusing such a service, he rejects the principal part of his own salvation. The statement also contains a general lesson. In the sight of God we are all filthy and polluted until Christ washes away our stains. Now, since He claims the office of washing, let everyone offer himself to be cleansed from his pollution, that he may obtain a place among the children of God.

But before going on, we must understand the meaning of the word *wash*. Some refer it to the free pardon of sins; others to newness of life; others again extend it to both—and this last view I freely admit. For Christ washes us when He wipes out our sins by the expiation of His sacrifice, that they may not come into God's judgment. On the other hand, He washes us when by His Spirit He takes away the depraved and vicious desires of the flesh. But since the context will soon make it clear that He is speaking of the grace of regeneration, I do not absolutely insist that He here included the washing of pardon.

9. *Lord, not my feet only.* When Peter heard that he was lost unless he permitted the cleansing offered him by Christ, the need was at last a master that could tame him. He therefore drops his opposition and gives way, but wishes to be entirely washed, and indeed, acknowledges that for his own part he is by nature altogether covered with pollution and that therefore it is no good for him to be washed only in one part. But even here he errs through thoughtlessness, in treating as valueless the benefit he had already received. For he speaks as if he had not been given any remission of sins, any sanctification of the Spirit. For this reason, Christ justly reproves him, for He reminds him of what He had earlier bestowed on him. And at the same time He tells all His disciples in the person of one man that they should not only remember the grace they had received but also consider what they still need for the future.

First, He says that believers are entirely *clean*. Not that they are pure in every part, so that there no longer remains in them any stain, but because they are cleansed in their chief part, that is, when the reign of sin is destroyed, so that the righteousness of God is in command—just as if we were to say, that a body is altogether healthy because it was not infected in general with any disease. We must declare ourselves to be Christ's disciples by newness of life; for He says that He is the author of purity in all His own.

Moreover, the other comparison was also applied to the present instance, that Peter might not reject the washing of the feet as foolish. For, as Christ washes from head to foot those whom He admits to be His disciples, so the lower part remains to be daily cleansed in those whom He has cleansed. The children of God are not totally regenerated on the first day so that they only live a heavenly life. On the contrary, the remnants of the flesh remain in them, and they have a continual struggle all through their lives *Feet* therefore, is a metaphor for all the passions and cares by which we are brought into contact with the world. For if the Spirit occupied every part of us we should no longer have anything to do with the pollutions of the world. But, as it is in the part in which we are carnal, we crawl on the ground, or at least our feet stick in the mire and we are to that extent unclean. Therefore Christ always finds something in us to cleanse. Moreover, what is spoken of here is not the forgiveness of sins, but the renewal by which Christ gradually and continually delivers His followers completely from the desires of the flesh.

10. *And ye are clean.* This proposition is as it were the minor in the syllogism, and hence it follows that the washing of the feet belongs properly to them. But an exception is added, so that they may all examine themselves, to see if perhaps Judas might be touched with a feeling of repentance. Yet His intention was to fortify the rest of the disciples in time, lest they should be worried by the atrocity of the crime which was soon afterwards manifested. Yet He purposely refrains from naming him, lest He should shut the gate of repentance against him But since he was beyond hope, the warning served only to aggravate his guilt But it was of great advantage to the other disciples, for by means of it Christ's divinity was made known to them more fully, and they also perceived that purity is no common gift of the Spirit.

So when he had washed their feet, and taken his garments, and sat down again, he said unto them, Know ye what I have done to you? Ye call me Master, and Lord: and ye say well; for so I am. If I then, the Lord and the Master, have washed your feet, ye also ought to wash one another's feet. For I have given you an example, that ye also should do as I have done to you. Verily, verily, I say unto you, A servant is not greater than his lord; neither one that is sent greater than he that sent him. If ye know these things, blessed are ye if ye do them. (12-17)

12. *So when, etc.* Now at last Christ explains His intention in washing His disciples' feet; for what He had interjected about spiritual washing was a sort of digression from His aim. Had it not been for Peter's opposition, Christ would not have said a word about it. Now He unfolds the reason for what He had done. He who is the Master

and Lord of all gave an example to be followed by all the godly, that none might think it a burden to stoop to a service, however mean and low, to his brethren and fellows. For the reason why love is despised is that everyone puts himself too high and despises almost everybody else. Nor did He intend merely to teach modesty, but also to lay down this rule of love, that they should serve one another. For there is no love where there is not a willing slavery in assisting a neighbour.

Know ye what I have done? We see that for a little while Christ kept His disciples in the dark so that He might try their obedience; and then at the right time He revealed to them what it had not been expedient for them to know earlier. Nor does He wait until they ask, but anticipates them of His own accord. We shall experience the same thing, provided we let ourselves be guided by His hand, even through unknown ways.

14. *If I then, the Lord.* An argument from the greater to the less. Pride hinders us from fostering the equality which ought to flourish among us. But Christ, who is far exalted above all, humbles Himself that He may shame the proud men who forget their station and rank and exempt themselves from brotherly fellowship. For what does a mortal man think he is, when he refuses to bear his brethren's burdens, to fit in with their customs and, in short, to perform the duties by which the unity of the Church is upheld? Briefly, the man who does not think of associating with weak brethren on the basis of submitting in a kindly and friendly way to services which seem low, claims too much for himself.

It is to be noted also that Christ says that He gave an example. For it is not right to take all His actions indiscriminately as objects of imitation. The Papists boast that they follow Christ's example in keeping the Lenten fast. But we must first see whether or no He intended to put forward an example as a norm for disciples to conform to. We read nothing of this sort. Therefore, the imitation of it is no less wicked than if they tried to fly up into heaven. Besides, whereas they ought to have followed Christ, they were aping rather than imitating Him. Every year they hold a theatrical feet-washing, and when they have discharged this empty and bare ceremony they think they have done their duty finely and are then free to despise their brethren. But more, when they have washed twelve men's feet they cruelly torture all Christ's members and thus spit in the face of Christ Himself. This ceremonial comedy is nothing but a shameful mockery of Christ. At any rate, Christ does not enjoin an annual ceremony here, but tells us to be ready all through our life to wash the feet of our brethren.

16. *Verily, verily, I say unto you.* These are proverbial sayings with a wider reference, though they should also be applied to the present circumstance. In my opinion, they are mistaken who take them generally, as if Christ were now exhorting His disciples to bear the cross. It is more correct to say that He was turning the sayings to His purpose..

He afterwards adds that they are *happy* if they know and do these things. For knowledge does not deserve to be called true unless it leads believers to conform themselves to their Head. On the contrary, to look on Christ and the things that belong to Him as outside ourselves is a vain imagination. Infer from this that until a man has learned to give way to his brethren he does not know whether Christ is his Master. Since no one devotes himself to his brethren in every respect and there are many who are slow and cold in the duties of love, it shows us how far we still are from the full light of faith.

I speak not of you all: I know whom I have chosen: but that the scripture may be fulfilled, He that eateth my bread lifted up his heel against me. From henceforth I tell you before it come to pass, that when it is come to pass, ye may believe that I am. (18-20)

18. *I speak not of you all.* He again declares that among the disciples is one who is in reality anything but a disciple. And He does so, partly on Judas' account, to make him the more inexcusable, and partly for the sake of the others, that they might not be shaken by Judas' downfall. Not only does He encourage them to persevere in their calling in spite of Judas' fall, but because the happiness He mentions is not common to all, He tells them to seek it more eagerly, and remain in it more firmly.

The very fact that they will persevere He ascribes to their election. For the frail strength of men would sway before every breeze and would be laid by the lightest movement did not the Lord uphold it by His hand. But since He guides those whom He has elected, all the stratagems that Satan can use will not stop them persevering to the end with unshaken constancy. And He ascribes to election not only their perseverance but also the beginning of their godliness. What is the cause of one man rather than another devoting himself to the Word of God? Because he has been elected. Again, what is the cause of this man going on, but because the purpose of God is steadfast to complete the work which His hand began? In short, the source of the distinction between the children of God and unbelievers is that the former are drawn to salvation by the Spirit of adoption while the others are carried away to destruction by their flesh, unrestrained by any bridle. Otherwise Christ would have said, 'I know what kind of man each of you will be.' But He sets before them that free election on which they are founded, that they may claim nothing for themselves but, on the contrary, may acknowledge that they differ from Judas by grace alone and not by their own virtue. Let us therefore learn that every part of our salvation depends on this.

When elsewhere[1] He includes Judas in the number of the elect, the expression is different, not contradictory. For there a temporal election is meant, by which God appoints us to any particular work—just like Saul, who was elected king, but yet was reprobate. But here Christ is speaking of the eternal election by which we are made God's children, and by which God predestinated us to life before the creation of the world And indeed, the reprobate are sometimes adorned by God with the gifts of the Spirit, to carry out the office with which He invests them. Thus, regal virtues shone forth for a time in Saul, and Judas also was distinguished by outstanding gifts befitting an apostle of Christ. But this is very different from the sanctification of the Spirit with which the Lord honours only His own children. For He renews them in mind and heart that they may be holy and unblamable in His sight. Besides it has a deep root in them which cannot be torn up, because God does not repent of His adoption. Meanwhile, it is settled that it is the gift of the divine election when, having embraced the teaching of Christ by faith, we also follow it in our life; and that this is the only cause of our happiness by which we are distinguished from the reprobate. They perish miserably, for they are destitute of the grace of the Spirit; but we have Christ for our guardian, guiding us by His hand and upholding us by His power.

Moreover, Christ here gives a clear witness to His divinity: first, by declaring that He does not judge in a human way; and secondly, by making Himself the author of election. For when He says *I know* the knowledge He speaks of is peculiar to God. But the second proof is the more powerful, for He testifies that those who were chosen before the creation of the world were chosen by Himself. Such a remarkable demonstration of His divine power should affect us more deeply than if the Scripture had called Him God a hundred times.

That the scripture may be fulfilled. It might have been thought wrong that a man should be elected to such an honourable position who was not imbued with true piety. It could easily have been objected, Why did not Christ elect one whom He intended to admit as an apostle? Or rather, Why did He appoint a man to be an apostle who, as He well knew, would become so wicked? He says that this must have happened because it was foretold—or at least, it was not new, for David had experienced the same thing. Some think that the pre-

[1] John 6.70.

diction quoted applied properly to Christ. To others it seems merely a comparison; that as David was basely betrayed by an enemy in his own house, so a similar state awaits the Son of God.[1] According to this, the meaning would be, 'The fact that one of my disciples wickedly betrays his Master is not the first treachery to happen in the world. On the contrary, we now experience what Scripture says happened in ancient times.' But since in David there was outlined what was afterwards to be seen more fully in Christ, I readily agree with the former who expound this as strictly the fulfilment of what David had foretold by the Spirit of prophecy (Psalm 41.9). Some think that the words are broken off and need the principal verb supplying. But if you read it continuously, 'That the Scripture may be fulfilled, he that eateth my bread lifted up his heel against me,' there will be nothing lacking.

To lift up the heel is a metaphor meaning to attack anyone treacherously under the pretence of friendship so as to overcome him when he is not ready. Now, what Christ our Head and Pattern suffered, we who are His members should endure patiently. And indeed, it has usually happened in the Church in nearly every age that it has had no enemies more dangerous than its own household. Therefore, lest believers should be troubled by such shamefulness, let them get used to putting up with traitors in good time.

19. *I tell you before it come to pass.* In this statement He tells His disciples that when one reprobate forsakes their company, it is far from being a good reason for them to be discouraged. It ought rather to confirm their faith. For if we did not see before our eyes in the Church what has been foretold about her distresses and struggles, the doubt might rise in our minds, Where are the prophecies? But when the truth of Scripture agrees with our experience, we perceive more clearly that God takes care of us, and that we are guided by His providence.

Moreover, by this phrase, *ye may believe that I am*, He means that He is the promised Messiah. Not that Judas' treachery began to lead the disciples to faith, but because their faith made greater progress when they came to experience what they had heard about before from the mouth of Christ. Now, this can be explained in two ways: either, that He says they will believe after the event, because nothing was hidden from Him; or that there will be nothing lacking in Him of all that the Scripture testifies concerning Christ. As the two interpretations agree well enough, I leave readers free to choose between them.

20. *Verily, verily, I say unto you.* Either he describes a new discourse, which is broken and imperfect, or Christ was forestalling the offence which would arise from the crime of Judas. For the Evangelists do

---

[1] Reading *filium* for *filios*.

not always connect up the discourses of Christ, but sometimes assemble various statements in fragments (*truncatim*). It is more probable, however, that Christ wanted to provide against this offence. It is more than plain that we are very ready to be wounded by bad examples. Thus it is that the failure of one man inflicts a deadly wound on two hundred others, extinguishing their faith, whereas the steadiness of ten or twenty godly men hardly edifies one. This is why, when Christ was setting such a monstrosity before their eyes, it was also necessary that He should stretch out His hand to His disciples, lest, struck by this new thing, they should fall backwards. Nor was He thinking only of them, but also reflected on those who should come after. Otherwise the memory of Judas might even today harm us grievously. When the devil cannot alienate us from Christ by hatred of His teaching, he excites either boredom or else contempt of the ministers.

Now this admonition of Christ shows that it is unjust that the ungodliness of any whose conduct in their office is wicked or criminal should at all detract from the apostolic dignity. The reason is that we ought to consider God, the author of the ministry, in whom we find nothing worthy of contempt. And then we ought to contemplate Christ Himself who, appointed by the Father to be the sole teacher, speaks by His apostles. Whoever, therefore, does not deign to receive the ministers of the Gospel, rejects Christ in them and God in Christ.

The Papists are foolish and absurd when they turn this into applause for themselves, to establish their tyranny. In the first place they prink themselves out with strange and borrowed feathers which have no connexion with Christ's apostles. Secondly, even granting they are apostles, nothing was further from Christ's mind in this passage than to transfer His own right to men—for what else is it to receive those whom Christ sends, but to give to them, that they may fulfil the office committed to them?

When Jesus had thus said, he was troubled in the spirit, and testified, and said, Verily, verily, I say unto you, that one of you shall betray me. The disciples looked one on another, doubting of whom he spake. There was at the table reclining in Jesus' bosom one of his disciples, whom Jesus loved. Simon Peter therefore beckoneth to him, and saith unto him, Tell us who it is of whom he speaketh. He leaning back, as he was, on Jesus' breast, saith unto him, Lord, who is it? Jesus therefore answereth, He it is, for whom I shall dip the sop, and give it him. So when he had dipped the sop, he taketh and giveth it to Judas, the son of Simon Iscariot. And after the sop, then entered Satan into him. Jesus therefore saith unto him, That thou doest, do quickly. Now no man at the table knew for what intent he spake this unto him. For some thought, because Judas had the bag, that Jesus said unto him, Buy what things we have need of for the feast; or, that he should give something to the poor. (21-29)

21. *When Jesus had thus said.* The holiness and excellence of the apostolic office makes Judas' treachery even more base and detestable. Such a hateful monstrosity struck even Christ with horror when He saw the incredible wickedness of one man polluting the sacred order (*sacrum ordinem*) where God's majesty ought to have shone. To the same end the Evangelist adds that *he testified.* He means that the thing was so monstrous that at first hearing it was absolutely unbelievable.

The Evangelist says that Christ *was troubled* in Spirit, so that we should know that He did not merely put on the appearance of being troubled in His face and voice, but that He was deeply moved in His mind.

Spirit here denotes the mind or the soul. I do not agree with those who expound it as if Christ was driven by a violent impulse of the Spirit to break out into these words. I readily acknowledge that all Christ's affections were guided by the Spirit; but the Evangelist means something different, that Christ's suffering was inward and unfeigned. And it is very important for us to know this, for His zeal is held out for our imitation, that we may be deeply horrified by those monstrosities which overturn the sacred order (*sacrum ordinem*) of God and His Church.

22. *The disciples looked one on another.* Those who are unconscious of any evil in themselves are made uneasy by Christ's saying. Judas alone is so senseless in his malice that he is untouched. Christ had such great authority among the disciples that they were quite convinced that He never said anything unthinkingly. But Satan had sifted all reverence from Judas' heart so that it was harder than a rocky cliff and threw back every admonition. And although Christ seems to be unkindly torturing the innocent for a time, this sort of anxiety was profitable to them and Christ did them no harm. It is proper that, when the children of God have heard the judgment on the ungodly, they should also be tortured that they may sift themselves and guard against hypocrisy; for this gives them an opportunity of examining themselves and their life.

The passage also teaches us that we should sometimes not point out the ungodly at once until God has dragged them into the light by His own hand. For it often happens that there are secret diseases in the Church which we must not disguise. And yet the wickedness of the men concerned is not ripe enough for discovery. In such cases we should take this middle path.

23. *Whom Jesus loved.* The special love which Christ had for John plainly testifies that it is not always inconsistent with Christian love (*caritas*) if we love some more than others. But everything depends on our love being directed towards God and on our loving every man the more in proportion as he excels in the gifts of God. Christ never swerved in the slightest from this end. But with us it is a very different matter, for such is the vanity of our mind that there are few who come nearer to God when they love men. But the love of men for one another will never be properly regulated unless it is directed to God.

What John here related, that *he reclined* in Jesus' bosom, might seem improper today. But this was how they sat at meals. They did not sit at a table like we do, but when they had taken off their shoes, they lay half stretched out, leaning on couches.

26. *For whom I shall dip the sop.* If it is asked what the point was in offering the sop to indicate the traitor when Christ could have openly named him if He wanted him to be known, I reply that the indication was such that it made Judas known to one man only and did not immediately expose him to them all. But it was of use for John to witness the fact, so that he might afterwards reveal it to others at the proper time. And Christ intentionally delayed the unmasking of Judas that we may more patiently endure hypocrites being hidden until they are dragged forth to the light. We see Judas sitting among the others and yet condemned by the mouth of the judge. The state of those who have a place among the children of God is no whit better.

27. *Then Satan entered into him.* It is certain that Judas conceived such a crime only by the moving of Satan. Why then is it said only now that Satan entered into him, when he already held rule in his heart? Just as those who are more fully confirmed in the faith which they had before are often said to believe, so that the increase of their faith is called faith, so now that Judas is entirely given up to Satan and is carried away by a wild impetuosity to extremes, Satan is said to have entered into him. For as the saints gradually progress and in proportion as they increase with new gifts are said to be filled with the Holy Spirit; so, in proportion as the ungodly provoke God's anger against themselves by their ingratitude, the Lord strips them of His Spirit, of all light of reason and indeed, of all human feelings and delivers them to Satan. It is a terrifying judgment of God when men are given up to a reprobate mind, so that they are hardly different from the beasts—nay, rush into vices from which the very beasts shrink. Therefore, we must walk carefully in the fear of the Lord, lest, if we overcome His goodness by our evil, He should at last deliver us to Satan.

By offering the sop Christ was not giving a place to Satan. But rather Judas delivered himself entirely to Satan when he had taken the sop. It was the occasion, not the cause. His heart ought to have been softened by Christ's great kindness, but it was harder than iron. And so his desperate and incurable obstinacy deserved that God should, by His righteous judgment, harden his heart still more by Satan. When by kindnesses to our enemies we heap coals of fire on their heads they are, if they are incurable, the rather burnt up to their destruction. And yet our kindness is not to blame, for their hearts should have been influenced to love us.

Augustine was wrong in thinking that this sop was a symbol of Christ's body, for it was given to Judas apart from the celebration of the supper. Moreover those who imagine that the devil entered essentially, as they say, into Judas are absurd. The Evangelist is only speaking of his power and efficacy. By this example we are warned of the dreadful punishment which awaits all those who profane the benefits of the Lord by abusing them.

That thou doest, do quickly. Christ does not address Judas in such a way that He can be regarded as pushing him on. It is rather the language of detestation. Hitherto He had striven to call him back by various methods, but in vain. Now He addresses him as a man beyond hope, 'Perish, since you are determined to perish.' And in this, He executes the office of judge, who condemns to death not those whom he for his part wants to ruin, but those who have already ruined themselves by their own fault. In short, Christ does not lay on Judas the necessity of perishing, but declares him to be what in fact he had been all along.

28. *And no man at the table.* Either John had not yet told the others what he had heard from Christ, or they were so stricken by it that they lost their presence of mind. Indeed, it is probable that John himself was almost out of his mind. But we can often see taking place in the Church what happened then to the disciples—that few believers discern the hypocrites whom the Lord condemns with a clear voice.

29. *Or, that he should give something to the poor.* Christ's great poverty is well known from other places. Yet out of His little He gave something to the poor, so as to lay down a rule for us. For the apostles would not have guessed that He was speaking about the poor unless it had been their custom to help the poor.

He then having received the sop went out straightway: and it was night. When therefore he was gone out, Jesus saith, Now is the Son of man glorified, and God is glorified in him. And if God is glorified

in him, God shall glorify him in himself, and straightway shall he
glorify him. Little children, yet a little while I am with you. Ye shall
seek me: and as I said unto the Jews, Whither I go, ye cannot come;
so now I say unto you. A new commandment I give unto you, that ye
love one another; even as I have loved you, that ye also love one another.
By this shall all men know that ye are my disciples, if ye have love one
to another. (30–35)

31. *Now is the Son of man glorified.* The last hour was at hand.
Christ knew how weak the minds of the disciples were, and He
wanted to support them in every possible way so that they might not
fail. Even today, the very thought of the cross of Christ would make
us tremble were we not at once met by the consolation that on the
cross He triumphed, victorious over Satan, sin and death. What
then might have happened to the apostles when they saw the Lord
soon carried off to the cross, laden with every kind of insult? Might
not a sight so sad and ugly have overwhelmed them a hundred times?
Christ therefore forestalls this danger and recalls them from the
external aspect of His death to its spiritual fruit. So whatever ignominy
appears in the cross which could bewilder believers, Christ testifies
that the same cross is glorious to Him.

The immediately following clause, *And God is glorified in him,* is
put in for confirmation. For it was a paradox that the glory of the
Son of man arose from a death humanly ignominious and even
accursed before God. He shows therefore how He would win glory
from such a death—because He glorifies God the Father. For in the
cross of Christ, as in a splendid theatre, the incomparable goodness of
God is set before the whole world. The glory of God shines, indeed,
in all creatures on high and below, but never more brightly than in
the cross, in which there was a wonderful change of things (*admirabilis*
rerum conversio)—the condemnation of all men was manifested, sin
blotted out, salvation restored to men; in short, the whole world was
renewed and all things restored to order.

Although the preposition *in* is often used for the Hebrew כ, and
in such instances is equivalent to 'through', I have preferred to translate
it simply that 'God is glorified in the Son of man,' because that phrase
seemed more emphatic.

When He says, *And God is glorified,* the copula *and* ought, to my
mind, to be made into a causal particle (*for*).

32. *If God is glorified.* Christ concludes that He will win a glorious
triumph by His death, because His sole aim in it is to glorify His
Father. For the Father did not seek His glory from the death of the
Son without making the Son a partaker of that same glory. Therefore

He promises that when the ignominy which He will endure for a time has been wiped out, a sublime glory will shine in His death. And this was accomplished; for the death of the cross which Christ suffered, so far from obscuring His honour, there shines brightest, since there His incredible love to mankind, His infinite righteousness in atoning for sin and appeasing the wrath of God, His wonderful power in overcoming death, subduing Satan, and, indeed, opening up heaven, put forth its full brightness. This truth is now also extended to all of us; for though the whole world should conspire to disgrace us, yet if we sincerely and honestly strive to promote God's glory, we should not doubt but that He on His side will also glorify us.

Christ increases the consolation by referring to the shortness of the time, promising that it will happen *straightway*. And although this glory began at the day of His resurrection, yet here He especially describes its extension, which straightway followed, when raising the dead by the power of the Gospel and of His Spirit, He created a new people for Himself. For the peculiar glory of the death of Christ is the fruit which sprang from it unto the salvation of men.

33. *Little children, yet a little while.* Because the disciples could not help feeling the profoundest sorrow at their Master's departure, He tells them in good time that He will no longer be with them, at the same time exhorting them to patience. Finally, to remove any untimely eagerness of desire, He says that they cannot immediately follow Him. In calling them, caressingly, *little children*, He teaches them that He is not going away from them because He cares little for their salvation, for He loves them most tenderly. It is true that it was to be our brother that He put on our flesh; but by this other name He expresses the vehemence of His love the more strongly.

When He says that He repeats to them what He had earlier said to the Jews, it is true so far as the words go, but the meaning is different. It is that they may endure patiently His temporary absence that He declares that they cannot follow Him. He so to say puts a check on them, that they may remain at their post until they have finished their earthly warfare. He does not therefore exclude them for ever from God's kingdom, like the Jews, but only tells them to wait quietly until He gathers them to Himself in the kingdom of heaven.

34. *A new commandment I give unto you.* To the consolation He adds this exhortation, that they should love one another. As if He were saying, 'While I am absent from you in body, testify by your mutual love, that you have not been taught by me in vain. Let this be your constant study, your chief meditation.' There is no general agreement on why He calls it a new commandment. Some think it is because, whereas whatever was commanded in the Law about love was literal

and external, Christ inscribed it by His Spirit in the hearts of believers. Thus, according to them, the Law is new because He published it in a new way, that it might be wholly vigorous. But that is in my opinion too forced, and foreign to Christ's meaning. Others expound it that though the Law calls us to love, yet because in it the teaching of love is bound up with so many ceremonies and additions, it does not appear so clearly; whereas on the other hand, perfection in love is set forth in the Gospel without any shadows. I myself, without rejecting this interpretation out of hand, consider Christ's meaning to be more simple. We know that laws are kept more carefully at the beginning but gradually slip out of men's minds until at last they become obsolete. Therefore, the better to fix the doctrine of love in His disciples' minds, Christ commends it as new. As if He said, 'I wish you to remember this commandment always, as if it were a law recently made.'

In short, we see that Christ's purpose in this passage was to exhort His disciples to love, that they might never let themselves be drawn away from the pursuit of it, or the truth of it to slip away from them. How necessary this admonition was we learn from daily experience. Since it is hard to keep to love, men lay it aside and contrive for themselves new methods of worshipping God, and Satan suggests many ways in which they may occupy themselves. Thus, by their own affairs it comes about that they vainly try to mock God, but they deceive themselves. Let this name of newness, therefore, stir us up to cultivate love. Meanwhile, let us know that it is not called new because it now first began to please God, since elsewhere it is called the fulfilling of the Law.

That ye love one another. Love is, indeed, extended to those outside, for we are all of the same flesh and are all created in the image of God. But because the image of God shines more brightly in the regenerate, it is proper that the bond of love should be much closer among the disciples of Christ. Love seeks its cause in God; from Him it has its root; to Him it is directed. Thus, as it recognizes anyone as a child of God, it embraces him with the greater zeal and warmth. Moreover, the mutual attitude of love can only exist in those who are ruled by the same Spirit. Christ here speaks of the highest degree of love; but we ought to believe on the other hand that, just as the goodness of God extends to and is shed upon the whole world, so we ought to love all, even those who hate us. And Christ holds out His own example —not because we can attain it, for He is infinitely in advance of us, but that we may at any rate aim at the same mark.

35. *By this shall all men know.* Christ again confirms His earlier saying that those who love one another have not been taught in His school in vain. As if He said, 'Not only will you know that you are

my disciples, but your profession will also be approved by others as true.' Since by this mark Christ distinguishes His own from strangers, those who discard love and adopt new and fabricated worship, labour in vain—a kind of vanity which today prevails in the Papacy. Nor is it superfluous that Christ insists on this so earnestly. The love of ourselves and of our neighbour no more agree than do fire and water. Self-love keeps all our senses bound in such a way that love is altogether banished. And yet all the time we think that we have acquitted ourselves well. For Satan has many attractions to deceive us with. Whoever then, desires truly to belong to Christ and to be acknowledged by God must form and direct his whole life to loving the brethren and stir himself up to this diligently.

Simon Peter saith unto him, Lord, whither goest thou? Jesus answered, Whither I go, thou canst not follow me now; but thou shalt follow afterwards. Peter saith unto him, Lord, why cannot I follow thee even now? I will lay down my life for thee. Jesus answereth, Wilt thou lay down thy life for me? Verily, verily, I say unto thee, The cock shall not crow, till thou hast denied me thrice. (36-38)

36. *Lord, whither goest thou?* This question depends on Christ's saying, 'As I said unto the Jews, etc.' It is clear from this how ignorant Peter was. After he had been so frequently warned about Christ's departure, he was as worried as if it were news to him. But we are too like him in this. We hear daily from the mouth of Christ all that is fitted for the conduct of life and all that is needful to be known; but when we come to it we are as surprised as newcomers (*novitii*), to whom nothing had been told. Peter also shows that he is held by an immoderate desire for Christ's bodily presence, for he regards it as unthinkable that he shall remain and Christ go elsewhere.

Whither I go. With these words Christ restrains Peter's unsuitable desire. He speaks briefly, as becomes a teacher, but immediately softens the severity of His statement. He says that He will be separated from His own temporarily. This passage teaches us to subject all our desires to God, that they may not go beyond their bounds; and if ever they wanton, let us at least submit to be held in by this bridle. Besides, lest we should be disheartened, a consolation is immediately put in to help us, when Christ promises that we shall one day be gathered to Him.

He means that Peter is not yet ripe for bearing the cross, but, like corn still in the blade, must be formed and strengthened by the passing of time, so that he may follow. We must therefore pray to God that He will increase and improve what He has begun in us. Meanwhile we must crawl until it is given to us to run more swiftly. Now as

Christ bears with us while we are soft and tender, so let us learn not to despise the weak brethren, who are still very far from the goal. It is, of course, to be desired that all should run with the greatest eagerness, and we all ought to be speeded up; but if there are any who proceed more slowly, we ought to hope the best of them, so long as they keep to the way.

37. *Why cannot I follow thee even now?* Peter declares by these words that he was dissatisfied with Christ's answer. He understands that he has been warned of his own weakness and therefore concludes that he is to blame for not following Christ immediately. Yet he remains unconvinced. For men are by nature puffed up with confidence in their own strength. Peter's expression reflects our innate opinion, in attributing too much to our own strength. Consequently, those who are powerless venture to attempt everything without imploring God's help.

38. *Wilt thou lay down thy life for me?* Christ did not choose to argue with Peter, but wanted him to grow wise by his own experience, like fools who never become wise until they have undergone some misfortune. Peter promises unshaken constancy, and indeed speaks from a sincere conviction; but his confidence is full of rashness, for he does not consider what has been given him. Now since this example applies to us, let each one examine his own defects, that he may not be swollen with a vain confidence. We cannot promise too much about the grace of God; but what is reproved here is the careless presumption of the flesh—faith produces fear and anxiety.

The cock shall not crow. Since temerity and rashness come from self-ignorance, Peter is accused of being a vigorous soldier while he is out of range; for he had not yet tried his strength, and thinks he can do anything. Later, he was punished for his arrogance as he deserved. Let us learn to distrust our own strength and betake ourselves early to the Lord, that He may support us by His power.

CHAPTER FOURTEEN

Let not your heart be troubled: ye believe in God, believe also in me. In my Father's house are many mansions; if it were not so, I would have told you; for I go to prepare a place for you. And if I go and prepare a place for you, I will come again, and will receive you unto myself; that where I am, there ye may be also. And whither I go ye know, and the way ye know. Thomas saith unto him, Lord, we know not whither thou goest; how know we the way? Jesus saith unto him, I am the way, and the truth, and the life: no one cometh unto the Father, but by me. If ye had known me, ye would have known my Father also: from henceforth ye know him, and have seen him. (1-7)

1. *Let not your heart be troubled.* Christ speaks at length to confirm His disciples, and not without reason; for an arduous and terrible struggle lay before them. For it was an extraordinary temptation that soon they would see Him hanging on the cross, a sight that would cause them nothing but despair. The hour of deepest distress was at hand, and so He shows them the remedy, that they may not be vanquished and overwhelmed. He does not simply encourage them to steadfastness by exhortation, but teaches them where they must seek for courage—that is, in faith, when He who has in Himself sufficient strength to uphold the salvation of His followers is acknowledged to be the Son of God.

We must always notice the time when these words were spoken; Christ wanted His disciples to stand bravely and courageously when everything seemed in utter confusion. And so we ought to use the same shield to ward off such attacks. It is, of course, impossible for us to avoid feeling these various tumults; but though we may be shaken, we must not fall. Thus it is said that believers are not troubled, because, although they are pressed down by very great difficulties, yet, relying on the Word of God, they hold their ground, upright and steady.

Ye believe in God. This could also be read in the imperative: 'Believe in God and believe in me.' But the former fits in better and is the more commonly received. Here, as I have already said, He points out the way to stand fast—by our faith resting on Christ and only regarding Him as present and stretching out His hand to help us. But it is surprising that faith in the Father is here put first. For He ought rather to have told His disciples that they should believe in God because they had believed in Christ. For, since Christ is the express image of the Father, we ought first to look to Him. And this is also why He descends to us, so that our faith may begin with Him and rise to God. But Christ had a different object. All acknowledge that we should believe in God; it is, indeed, a settled axiom to which all assent without contradiction. But there is scarcely one in a hundred who really believes; not only because the naked majesty of God is too distant from us, but also because Satan interposes all sorts of clouds to block our sight of God. In consequence, our faith, seeking God in His heavenly glory and inaccessible light, comes to nothing. Moreover, the flesh suggests of its own accord a thousand imaginings which turn us away from the right view of God. Therefore, Christ holds out Himself as the object to which our faith, if it is directed, will easily find where it may rest. For He is the true Emmanuel who, as soon as He is sought by faith, responds within us (*intus nobis respondet*). It is one of the leading articles of our belief, that our faith should be directed to Christ alone and not wander through round-about ways; and that it should be fixed in Him, that it may not waver in temptations. And the true proof of faith is when we never let ourselves be torn away from Christ and from the promises given in Him. When the Papist divines dispute (or rather, prattle) about the object of faith, they make a bare mention of God only and have no interest in Christ. Those who have a taste for their notions must be shaken by the slightest breath of a breeze. Proud men are ashamed of Christ's humiliation and therefore fly to God's incomprehensible divinity. But faith will never reach heaven unless it submits to Christ who appears as the God lowly in aspect; nor will it be firm unless it seeks a foundation in the weakness of Christ.

2. *In my Father's house.* Because Christ's absence caused them grief, He declares that He is not going away in such a manner as to remain separate from them, since there is a place for them also in the heavenly kingdom. He had to remove the idea that when He ascended to the Father He left His disciples neglected on earth. This passage has been interpreted in another sense and erroneously, as if Christ taught that there were different degrees of honour in the heavenly kingdom. He says that the mansions are many, not that they are different or unlike, but that there are sufficient for a great number; as if He said that there is room there, not only for Himself, but also for all His disciples.

If it were not so, I would have told you. Commentators differ on this. Some read it as a single context: 'If the dwellings had not been prepared for you already, I would have said that I go before to prepare them.' But I agree rather with the opinions of others who interpret it thus: 'If the heavenly glory had awaited me only, I would not have deceived you. I would have told you that there was no place for anyone but myself in my Father's house. But the fact is quite different. I go before to prepare a place for you.' The context, to my mind, demands that we read it like this, for there immediately follows, 'If I go and prepare a place for you.' By these words Christ signifies that the purpose of His departure was to prepare a place for His own. In a word, Christ did not ascend to heaven privately for Himself, to dwell there alone, but rather that it might be the common inheritance of all the godly, and that in this way the Head might be united to the members.

But the question arises as to the state of the fathers after death, before Christ ascended to heaven. For it is commonly inferred that believing souls were shut up in limbo, because Christ says that by His ascension into heaven the place will be prepared. But the answer is easy. This place is said to be prepared for the day of resurrection. By nature the human race is banished from the kingdom of God; but the Son, who is the unique Inheritor of heaven, took possession of it in their name, that through Him we also might enter. For in His person we already possess heaven by hope, as Paul teaches in Eph. 1.3. Yet we shall not enjoy this great blessing until He appears again in the sky. The state of the fathers after death therefore is not distinguished from ours here. Christ has prepared a place both for them and us, into which He will receive all at the last day. Before reconciliation was made, believing souls were, so to say, placed on a watch-tower, peering for the promised redemption; and now they enjoy a blessed rest until the redemption is completed.

3. *And if I go.* The conditional particle should be interpreted as an adverb of time, as if He said, 'After I have gone, I will return to you again.' This return is not to be understood of the Holy Spirit, as if Christ manifested to the disciples a new presence of Himself in the Spirit. It is indeed true that Christ dwells with us and in us by His Spirit. But He is here speaking of the last day of judgment, when He will finally come to gather His own. And indeed, if we consider the whole body of the Church, He prepares a place for us every day. Whence it follows that the proper day for our entrance into heaven is not yet come.

4. *And whither I go ye know.* Because we need an extraordinary fortitude to endure patiently our long separation from Christ, He adds another confirmation—that the disciples know that His death is not an annihilation but a passing to the Father; and that they know the way they must follow to arrive at the communion of the same glory. Both clauses should be carefully noticed. First, we must see Christ by the eyes of faith in His heavenly glory and blessed im-

mortality. Secondly, we must understand that He is the first-fruits of our life, and that He has opened up the way which was closed against us.

5. *Thomas saith unto him.* Although Thomas' reply seems at first to contradict what Christ had said, he did not mean to disbelieve his Master. But it may be asked how he denies what Christ asserted. I reply, knowledge is sometimes confused among the saints by their not understanding the manner or the reason of things that are certain and have been explained to them. Thus, the prophets foretold the calling of the Gentiles with a true perception of faith, and yet Paul declares that it was a mystery hidden from them. Therefore, when the apostles believed that Christ was departing to the Father, and yet did not know how He would acquire the kingdom, Thomas justly points out that they do not know where He is going. Hence he concludes that the way is even more obscure; for before we start on a course, we must know where we are going to.

6. *I am the way.* Christ does not reply directly to the question, but He omits nothing that is useful to know. Thomas' curiosity had to be curbed, and so Christ does not explain what His future with the Father would be but emphasizes a more necessary subject. Thomas would have liked to have heard what Christ was going to do in heaven, as we never weary of these subtle speculations. But it behoves us rather to place our study and labour elsewhere—how we may become partakers of the blessed resurrection. His saying comes to this, that whoever obtains Christ wants nothing, and hence that whoever is not satisfied with Him alone strives after something beyond perfection.

Now, He sets out three degrees, as if saying that He is the beginning, the middle and the end. From this it follows that we should begin with Him, continue in Him and end in Him. We must certainly not seek for higher wisdom than that which leads us to eternal life. He declares that this is to be found in Him. Now the way to obtain life is to become new creatures. He says that we must not seek it elsewhere. At the same time He tells us that He is the way by which alone we can reach it. That He may not fail us in any respect, He stretches out His hand to those going astray and humbles Himself even to guide the sucking child. Presenting Himself as the leader, He does not leave His people in the middle of the race, but makes them partakers of the truth. Finally He makes them enjoy the fruit of it, than which nothing more excellent and delightful can be imagined. Because Christ is the way, the weak and ignorant have no cause to complain that they are forsaken by Him. As He is the truth and the life He possesses in Himself what will satisfy even the most perfect.

In short, Christ now declares about blessedness what I recently said about the object of faith. All think and confess that man's blessedness resides in God alone. But they thereupon go wrong in that, seeking God elsewhere than in Christ, they so to say tear Him from His true and substantial divinity.

The truth is supposed by some to signify the saving light of heavenly wisdom, by others the substance of life and of all spiritual blessings, which is contrasted to shadows and figures, as it says in chapter 1, 'grace and truth came by Jesus Christ.' To me it seems that *the truth* is to be taken as the perfection of faith, just as *the way* for its beginning and rudiments. The sum of it is this: If any man turns aside from Christ he can do nothing but go astray. If any man does not rest on Him, he will feed elsewhere on nothing but wind and vanity. If any aims beyond Him, he will find death instead of life.

No one cometh unto the Father. This explains the former statement. He is the way because He leads us to the Father. He is the truth and the life because in Him we apprehend the Father. In regard to calling on God it can be said with truth that no prayers are heard but through the advocacy of Christ. But Christ is not treating of prayer here, and so simply understand it as saying that men invent mere labyrinths for themselves whenever they try to come to God after forsaking Christ. For Christ proves that He is the life, inasmuch as God, with whom is the fountain of life, can be possessed in no other way than in Him. Therefore all theology separated from Christ is not only confused and empty but also mad, deceiving and counterfeit. For although the philosophers sometimes utter splendid words, they contain nothing but what is ephemeral and even entangled with perverse errors.

7. *If ye had known me.* He confirms what we have just said, that it is a foolish and noxious curiosity when men are not satisfied with Him but aspire to God by indirect paths. They admit that there is nothing better than the knowledge of God; but when He is close to them and comes to them intimately, they wander through their own speculations and seek above the clouds Him whom they do not deign to acknowledge when He is present. Christ therefore blames the disciples for not acknowledging that the fulness of the Godhead was manifested in Him. He says, 'I see that you have hitherto not known Me rightly and properly, because you do not yet know the lively image of the Father which is expressed in Me.'

From henceforth. He adds this, not only to soften the severity of the rebuke, but also to accuse them of ingratitude and laziness if they do not consider and ponder what has been given to them, for He said this in commendation of His teaching rather than to extoll their faith. The meaning therefore is that God is now plainly exhibited to them

F   77

if they only open their eyes. The word *see* expresses the certainty of faith.

> *Philip saith unto him, Lord, shew us the Father, and it sufficeth us. Jesus saith unto him, Have I been so long time with you, and dost thou not know me, Philip? he that hath seen me hath seen the Father; how sayest thou, Shew us the Father? Believest thou not that I am in the Father, and the Father in me? the words that I say unto you I speak not from myself: but the Father abiding in me doeth his works. Believe me that I am in the Father, and the Father in me: or else believe me for the very works' sake. Verily, verily, I say unto you, He that believeth on me, the works that I do shall he do also; and greater works than these shall he do; because I go unto the Father. And whatsoever ye shall ask in my name, that will I do, that the Father may be glorified in the Son. If ye shall ask me anything in my name, that will I do.* (8-14)

8. *Shew us the Father.* It seems quite absurd that the apostles should continually argue with the Lord. For why did He speak at all except to teach them what Philip was asking about? Yet there is not one of their faults described here that we do not share with them. We profess to be enthusiastic in seeking God. Yet when He presents Himself before our eyes, we are blind.

9. *Have I been so long time with you?* Christ rightly reproves Philip that he has not the clear eyes of faith. He had God present in Christ; yet he did not see Him. What prevented him but his own ingratitude? So today, those who, because they are not satisfied with Christ alone, are carried away into wandering speculations to seek God, progress badly in the Gospel. This foolish desire is bred from contempt of Christ's lowliness, and it is a very great injustice, for in that aspect He represents the infinite goodness of the Father.

10. *That I am in the Father, and the Father in me.* I do not refer these words to Christ's divine essence, but to the mode of the revelation. For Christ, so far as His secret divinity is concerned, is no better known to us than is the Father. But He is said to be the express image of God, because in Him God has entirely revealed Himself, inasmuch as His infinite goodness, wisdom and power appear in Him substantially. And yet the ancients are not at fault when they take it as a testimony for defending Christ's divinity. But as Christ does not simply declare what He is in Himself, but what we should acknowledge Him to be, it records His power rather than His essence. Therefore, the Father is said to be in Christ because in Him full divinity dwells and displays its power. And Christ, in His turn, is said to be in the Father,

because by His divine power He shows that He is one with the Father. *The words that I say unto you.* From the effect He proves that God must not be sought anywhere else than in Him. For He states that His teaching, which is heavenly and truly divine, is a testimony and bright mirror of God's presence. If it be objected that all the prophets should be accounted Son of God because they speak divinely by the inspiration of the Spirit and have God as the author of their teaching, the answer is easy—we must consider what their teaching contains. For the prophets send their disciples away to another, but Christ keeps them to Himself. Besides, we should remember what the apostle declares in the first chapter of Hebrews, that now God has spoken from heaven by the mouth of His Son, whereas He spoke by Moses from the earth, as it were.

I speak not from myself, He says. That is, only as a man, or humanly. For the Father, putting forth the power of His Spirit in what was taught, wants His divinity to be recognized in Him.

When He says, *the Father doeth the works,* it should not be restricted to miracles. Rather, it continues the former statement that in His teaching is clearly exhibited the majesty of God; as if He said that this is truly a work of God, from which it may be determined with certainty that God dwells in Him. Therefore I understand by 'the works' an example of God's power.

11. *Believe me that I.* He first demands of the disciples that they believe in His testimony when He asserts that He is the Son of God. But as they hitherto had been too slow, He indirectly reproves their indolence. He says, 'If my statement does not produce faith, and if you think so meanly of me that you do not reckon you should believe my words, yet at any rate consider that power which is the visible image of the presence of God.' It is very absurd of them not to rely entirely on the words of Christ, for they should have embraced without hesitation everything that He said, every single word. But here Christ reproves His disciples for making so little progress in spite of receiving so many lessons on this same subject. He does not explain the nature of faith to them, but declares that He possesses what is sufficient for convincing unbelievers.

It is not superfluous that He again insists: *I am in the Father, and the Father in me.* For we know well enough by experience that our nature pricks us to empty curiosity. As soon as we have gone outside Christ we have nothing but the idols we have formed. But in Christ is nothing but what is divine and keeps us in God.

12. *Verily, verily, I say unto you.* All that He had so far told His disciples about Himself, so far as it was relevant to them, was temporary. The consolation would therefore not have been complete

without His adding this clause—especially since our memory is so short in considering God's benefits. On this there is no need for outside examples. When God has loaded us with every kind of blessing, we imagine He is no longer alive if He rests for a fortnight. This is why Christ not only mentions His present power, which the apostles then beheld with their eyes, but promises a continual sense of it in the future. And indeed, His divinity was not only attested while He lived on earth, but believers experienced vivid instances of it after He had gone to the Father. But our stupidity or our malice prevents us considering God in His works and Christ in God's works.

It perplexes many that He said that the apostles *would do greater works than he had done*. I pass by the other and usual answers and will be content with just one thing. First, we have to understand what Christ means. The power by which He proves Himself the Son of God is so far from being bound to His bodily presence that it must shine forth in more and greater examples when He is absent. Now Christ's ascension was soon followed by the wonderful conversion of the world (*admirabilis conversio mundi*), in which His divinity was displayed more powerfully than when He lived among men. Thus we see that the proof of His divinity was not confined to the person of Christ but was diffused through the whole body of the Church. Again, this *doing* of which He spoke was not peculiar to the apostles alone, nor to a few of the godly, but related to the whole body of the Church.

Because I go unto the Father. The reason why the disciples will do greater things than Christ is that when He has entered into possession of His kingdom, He will demonstrate His power more fully from heaven. It is therefore clear that His glory is no way diminished; for after His departure the apostles, His mere instruments, did more excellent works. Moreover, from this it was plain that He sits at the right hand of the Father, that every knee may bow before Him. And a little later He Himself plainly declares that He will be the author of everything that will be done by the hands of the apostles.

13. *And whatsoever ye shall ask in my name, that will I do*, He says. But it may be asked whether He was not even then the Mediator in whose name men had to pray to the Father. I reply that He discharged the office of Mediator more clearly after He entered into the heavenly sanctuary, as will be said again at the proper place.

That he may be glorified. This passage agrees with what Paul says: 'That every tongue should confess that Jesus is Christ, to the glory of God the Father' (Phil. 2.11). The aim of everything is the sanctifying of God's name. But here is declared the true way to sanctify it—in the Son and by the Son. For although the majesty of God is in itself hidden from us, it shines in Christ; although His hand is concealed, we have it visible in Christ. Accordingly, in the benefits which the Father bestows on us, we have no right to separate the Son from Him, as it is said, 'He that honoureth not the Son, honoureth not the Father.'

14. *If ye shall ask me anything, etc.* This is no mere repetition. All perceive and feel that they are unworthy to approach God, and yet the majority burst forward as if they were frantic, and rashly and arrogantly address God. Afterwards, when they remember the unworthiness I have mentioned, everyone invents various means for himself. But when God invites us to Himself He sets before us one Mediator, by whom He is entreated and gracious. But here again the wickedness of the human mind runs riot, for most do not cease to forsake the road and to go by tortuous and round-about ways. They do this because they have a weak and mean idea of the power and goodness of God in Christ. A second error is joined to this. We do not consider that we are justly debarred from approaching God until He calls us, and that we are called only through the Son. And if the one passage carries insufficient weight for us, let us know that when Christ says a second time that we must pray to the Father in His name He, as it were, lays His hand on us that we may not waste our effort in vainly seeking other intercessors.

If ye love me, ye will keep my commandments. And I will pray the Father, and he shall give you another Comforter, that he may be with you for ever, even the Spirit of truth: whom the world cannot receive; for it beholdeth him not, neither knoweth him: ye know him; for he abideth with you, and shall be in you. I will not leave you orphans: I come unto you. (15-18)

15. *If ye love me.* The love of the disciples for Christ was true and sincere; and yet there was something superstitious mixed with it, as is often so with us. For it was ridiculous of them to want to keep Him in the world. To correct this fault, He tells them to re-orientate their love—that is, to occupy themselves in keeping the commandments He had given them. This is indeed useful teaching, for very few of those who seem to love Christ honour Him aright. On the contrary, when they have performed mere trifles, they flatter themselves in self-satisfaction. But the true love of Christ is determined by keeping His teaching as the unique rule. But we are also warned how sinful our affections are, since even our love for Christ is not faultless unless it is joined to pure obedience.

16. *And I will pray the Father.* He gave this as a remedy, to soothe the grief that they would feel at His absence. At the same time Christ promises to give them strength to keep His commandments; for other-

wise the exhortation would have had little power. So He loses no time in telling them that although He will be absent in body He will never let them be without help, for He will be present with them by His Spirit.

Here He calls the Spirit 'the gift of the Father'—but a gift which He will obtain by His prayers. Elsewhere He promises that He Himself will give the Spirit. Both statements are true and appropriate, for inasmuch as Christ is our Mediator and Intercessor, He obtains from the Father the grace of the Spirit; but inasmuch as He is God, He bestows that grace from Himself. Therefore the passage means: The Father gave Me to you as a Comforter, but only temporarily. Now that I have discharged my office, I will pray Him to give another Comforter, not just for a little while but who will remain with you for ever.

The word *Comforter (Paracletus)* is here applied to both Christ and the Spirit; and justly, for it is an office common to both to comfort and exhort and guard us by their patronage. Christ was the Patron of His own so long as He lived in the world. Afterwards He committed them to the protection and guardianship of the Spirit. If it is asked whether we today are not still under the patronage of Christ (*sub Christi clientela*), the answer is easy. Christ is a continual Patron, but not in a visible manner. While He dwelt in the world, He openly manifested Himself as their Patron. Now He guards us by His Spirit.

He calls Him *another* because of the difference in the blessings we obtain from each. Christ's proper work was to appease the wrath of God by atoning for the sins of the world, to redeem men from death and to procure righteousness and life. That of the Spirit is to make us partakers not only of Christ Himself, but of all His blessings. And yet it would not be amiss to infer from this a distinction of persons, for there must be some property in which the Spirit differs from the Son so as to be another.

17. *The Spirit of truth.* Christ gives the Spirit another title—that He is the Teacher of truth (*magister veritatis*). From this it follows that until we have been inwardly taught by Him all our minds are held by vanity and falsehood.

Whom the world cannot receive. This contrast heightens the excellence of the grace with which God honours only His elect, for He means that it is no ordinary gift that the world is deprived of. In this sense too, Isa. 60.2 says: 'Behold, darkness shall cover the earth, and gross darkness the people: but the Lord shall arise upon thee.' For God's mercy towards the Church deserves the more praise when He exalts her by a unique privilege above the whole world. And yet Christ exhorts the disciples not to be puffed up (as the world usually is by the

outlook of the flesh) and thus drive from themselves the grace of the
Spirit. All that Scripture declares about the Holy Spirit is only a
dream to earthly men, because they rely on their own reason and
despise heavenly illumination. Although this pride, which extinguishes
so far as it can the light of the Holy Spirit, abounds everywhere, yet
we ought to be conscious of our own poverty and to know that whatever belongs to sound understanding flows from no other source.
But Christ's words show that nothing relating to the Holy Spirit can
be learned by human reason, but that He is known only by the experience of faith.

The world, He says, *is not capable of the Spirit, for it does not know
Him; but you know Him because He dwells with you.* Hence it is the
Spirit alone who, by dwelling in us, makes Himself to be known.
Otherwise He is unknown and incomprehensible.

18. *I will not leave you orphans.* This passage teaches what men are
and can do without the protection of the Spirit. They are orphans,
exposed to every sort of trickery and injustice, unequal to governing
themselves, and in brief, unfit to do anything of themselves. The
only remedy for such a great weakness is for Christ to rule us by His
Spirit, which He promises to do. First, then, the disciples are reminded
of their weakness, that they may distrust themselves and rely only on
the protection of Christ. Secondly, He promises them a remedy and
so rouses them to hope; for He says that He will never leave them.
When He says, *I will come unto you*, He shows the manner in which
He dwells in His people and fills all things—by the power of His
Spirit. It is therefore clear that the grace of the Spirit is a striking
testimony to His divinity.

*Yet a little while, and the world beholdeth me no more; but ye behold
me: because I live, ye shall live also. In that day ye shall know that I
am in my Father, and ye in me, and I in you.* (19-20)

19. *Yet a little while.* He continues to commend this special grace,
which should have been sufficient to lighten and even remove altogether the grief of the disciples. He says, 'When I have withdrawn
from the sight of the world, I shall none the less be present with you.'
But, if we are to enjoy this secret sight of Christ, we must not judge
His presence or absence by carnal perception, but must look diligently
at His power with the eyes of faith. In this way believers always have
Christ present by His Spirit and see Him although they are physically
distant from Him.

Because I live. This can have a twofold meaning. Either it is a
confirmation of the former clause, or it may be read separately, that
believers will live because Christ lives. I willingly embrace the former

sense; though we may infer the other doctrine from it, that Christ's life is the cause of ours. First He points out the reason for the distinction, why He should be seen by His disciples and not the world. It is because Christ can be seen only according to the spiritual life, which the world lacks. The world does not see Christ; but this is not surprising, for death-dealing blindness (*mors caecitatis*) is the cause. But as soon as a man begins to live by the Spirit, he is at once given eyes to see Christ. And this is because our life is conjoined with Christ's and flows from it as a well. In ourselves we are dead, and the life we flatter ourselves we have is the worst death. Therefore, when it is a question of obtaining life, our eyes must be directed to Christ and His life must be transferred to us by faith, so that our consciences may be surely convinced that while Christ lives we are free from all danger of destruction. For it is an immutable fact that His life would be nothing if His members were dead.

20. *In that day.* Many refer this to the day of Pentecost; but it rather denotes what we might call the uninterrupted course of the one day from the time when Christ put forth the power of His Spirit until the last resurrection. They then began to know; but it was, so to say, weak and elementary, because the Spirit had not yet wrought so powerfully in them. For the drift of these words is that we cannot know by idle speculation what is the sacred and mystic union between us and Him and again between Him and the Father, but that the only way to know it is when He pours His life into us by the secret efficacy of the Spirit. And this is the experience of faith, which I mentioned just now.

The Arians abused this testimony to prove that Christ is God only by participation and grace. But it is easy to refute their quibbling. Christ is not speaking merely of His eternal essence but commending that divine power which was manifested in Him. As the Father has placed in the Son all the fulness of blessings, so on the other hand the Son has given Himself entirely to us. We are said *to be in him* because, grafted into His body, we are partakers of all His righteousness and all His blessings. He is said to be in us because He plainly shows by the efficacy of His Spirit that He is the author and cause of our life.

He that hath my commandments, and keepeth them, he it is that loveth me: and he that loveth me shall be loved of my Father, and I will love him, and will manifest myself unto him. Judas (not Iscariot) saith unto him, Lord, why is it that thou wilt manifest thyself unto us, and not unto the world? Jesus answered and said unto him, If a man love me, he will keep my word: and my Father will love him, and we will come unto him, and make our abode with him. He that loveth me not keepeth not my words: and the word which ye hear is not mine, but the Father's who sent me. (21-24)

21. *He that hath my commandments.* He repeats His earlier statement that the sure proof of our love to Him lies in keeping His commandments; and He reminds the disciples of this so often, lest they should turn aside from this object. For we are most of all prone to slip into a carnal attitude and love something other than Christ under the name of Christ. This is also what St Paul's saying means in II Cor. 5.16-17: 'Though we have known Christ after the flesh, yet now we know him so no more. Let us therefore be a new creature.' *To have his commandments* means to be properly instructed in them. *To keep* them is to fashion ourselves and our lives to their rule.

He that loveth me. Christ speaks as if men forestalled God in love. This is absurd, for 'while we were enemies, he reconciled us to himself' (Rom. 5.10). And John's words are well known, 'Not that we first loved him, but he first loved us' (I John 4.10). But this is not an argument about cause and effect; and therefore it is a false inference that the love we have for Christ precedes the love of God towards us. Christ only meant that all who love Him will be blessed because they in their turn will be loved by Him and the Father. Not that God begins to love them then, but because they have a testimony of His Fatherly love engraven on their hearts.

The clause which immediately follows has the same intention: *And will manifest myself unto him.* Knowledge undoubtedly precedes love; but Christ meant that He would grant to those who keep His teaching purely, to progress in faith from day to day; that is, 'I will make them to approach closer and more intimately to Me.' Infer from this that the fruit of godliness is progress in the knowledge of Christ. For He who promises that He will give to him who has, rejects hypocrites and causes to progress in faith all those who wholeheartedly embrace the teaching of the Gospel and fashion themselves entirely in obedience to it. And this is why many fall away, and why we see scarcely one in ten proceed on the right course. The greater part do not deserve Christ to manifest Himself to them. It must also be noted that here a fuller knowledge of Christ is represented as an extraordinary reward of our love to Christ. From this it follows that it is an inestimable treasure.

22. *Judas (not Iscariot) saith unto him.* He asks, not unreasonably, why Christ confines His light to only a few; for He is the Sun of righteousness, by whom the whole world should be enlightened. It therefore seems inconsistent that He should shine on only a few and not shed His brightness everywhere indiscriminately. Christ's reply does

not solve the whole problem, for it makes no mention of the first cause why Christ, manifesting Himself to a few, hides Himself from the most of men. For certainly He finds all men alike at first, that is, utterly alienated from Him. Therefore, He cannot choose anyone who loves Him, but chooses from His enemies those whose hearts He bends to love Him. But just now He did not intend to treat of that distinction, which was far from His object. His purpose was to exhort His disciples to the earnest study of godliness, that they might make greater progress in faith. He is therefore content to distinguish them from the world by this mark of keeping the teaching of the Gospel.

Now this mark follows the beginning of faith, for it is the effect of their calling. Elsewhere Christ told the disciples that they were called by grace. Later He will remind them of it. But now He only commands them to keep in His teaching and to apply themselves to godliness. By these words Christ shows how the Gospel is rightly obeyed—when our duties and outward actions proceed from love of Him. For the arms, the feet and the whole body labour in vain unless the love of God reigns in the heart to govern the outward members. And since it is certain that we keep Christ's commandments only in so far as we love Him, it follows that a perfect love of Him can be found nowhere in the world, since there is no man who keeps His commandments perfectly. But God is pleased with the obedience of those who make a real effort to reach this end.

23. *And my Father will love him.* We have already explained that the love of God is not put in the second place, as if it followed our godliness as the cause of our love, but that believers may be fully convinced that their obedience to the Gospel is pleasing to God, and that they may continually expect from Him new and increasing gifts.

And we will come unto him who loves me; that is, he will feel that God's grace dwells in him and will daily increase more and more in the gifts of God. He is therefore speaking, not of the eternal love which He had for us before we were born and even before the world was created, but that which He seals on our hearts when He makes us partakers of His adoption. Moreover, He does not mean the first illumination, but those degrees of faith by which believers must continually advance, according to the saying, 'Whosoever hath, to him shall be given.'

The Papists are therefore wrong in inferring from this passage that our love for God is twofold. They imagine that we love God naturally before He regenerates us by His Spirit, and also that by this preparation we merit the grace of regeneration. As if Scripture did not everywhere teach, and experience also proclaim, that we are altogether turned away from God and infected and filled with a hatred of Him until He change our hearts. We must therefore keep to Christ's meaning, that He and the Father will come to establish believers in continual trust in His grace.

24. *He that loveth me not.* Since believers are mixed with unbelievers in the world and must be agitated by all sorts of storms as in a rough sea, Christ again confirms them with this admonition, lest they should be led astray by bad examples. It is as if He had said, 'Do not look to the world and depend on it. There will always be those who despise Me and My teaching. For your part, keep steadfastly to the end the grace you have once received.' Yet He also suggests that the world is justly punished for its ingratitude, when it perishes in its blindness; for, by despising true righteousness, it shows an ungodly hatred against Christ.

And the word which ye hear. Lest the disciples should be discouraged or waver because of the wilfulness of the world, He again claims authority for His teaching by testifying that it is from God and was not of human or earthly invention. The steadiness of our faith consists in knowing that God is our Leader and that we are founded on His eternal truth alone. Therefore, however the world may rage in its shamelessness, let us follow the teaching of Christ which transcends heaven and earth. When He says that the Word is not His, He accommodates Himself to the disciples. It is as if He said that it is not human, for He faithfully hands on what the Father has given Him. Yet we know that, inasmuch as He is the eternal Wisdom of God, He is the only fount of all doctrine and that all the prophets who have been from the beginning spoke by His Spirit.

These things have I spoken unto you, while yet abiding with you. But the Comforter, even the Holy Spirit, whom the Father will send in my name, he shall teach you all things, and bring to your remembrance all that I said unto you. Peace I leave with you; my peace I give unto you: not as the world giveth, give I unto you. Let not your heart be troubled, neither let it be fearful. Ye heard how I said unto you, I go away, and I come unto you. If ye loved me, ye would have rejoiced, because I go unto the Father: for the Father is greater than I. (25-28)

25. *These things have I spoken unto you.* He adds this that they might not at any rate despair, even though perhaps they profited less than they should have done. He sowed a seed of doctrine then which for a while lay in the disciples hidden and smothered. So He exhorts them to have a good hope until the doctrine, which might now seem useless, should yield fruit. In short, He tells them that in the teaching they have heard they have an abundance of consolation and that they should not seek it elsewhere. And if this is not immediately plain to

them He bids them be of good courage until the Spirit, the inward Teacher (*interior magister*) shall speak the same thing in their hearts. This admonition is very useful to everyone; for if we do not understand at once what Christ teaches, pride overcomes us and we cannot be bothered to spend unprofitable labour on what is obscure. But we must bring a ready teachableness; we must listen hard and pay attention if we want to progress properly in the school of God. Most of all, we need patience until the Spirit makes plain what we seemed to have often read or heard in vain.

That the zeal for learning may not grow weak in us or that we may not slip into despair when we do not immediately perceive the meaning of what Christ says, let us know that this is spoken to us all: *The Spirit will* at last *bring to your remembrance* what I have said. Isaiah threatened unbelievers with the punishment that the Word of God would be like a closed book to them. But the Lord frequently humbles His people also in this way. We must therefore wait patiently and calmly for the time of revelation and not reject the Word on that account. Again, when Christ declares that it is the peculiar office of the Holy Spirit to teach the apostles what they had already learned from His own mouth, it follows that outward preaching will be useless and vain unless the teaching of the Spirit is added to it. So God has two ways of teaching. He sounds in our ears by the mouth of men; and He addresses us inwardly by His Spirit. These He does simultaneously or at different times, as He thinks fit.

But observe what all these things are which He promises that the Spirit will teach. He says that He will suggest, or bring to your remembrance *all that I have said*. Hence it follows that He will not be a constructor of new revelations. By this one word we may refute all the inventions which Satan has brought into the Church from the beginning under the pretended authority of the Spirit. Mohammed and the Pope have this religious principle in common, that Scripture does not contain the perfection of doctrine, but that something higher has been revealed by the Spirit. The Anabaptists and Libertines have in our own day drawn their madness from the same ditch. But the spirit which introduces any invention foreign to the Gospel is a deceiver and not of Christ; for Christ promises the Spirit who will confirm the teaching of the Gospel, as if He were signing it. I have already explained what is meant by the Spirit being sent by the Father in Christ's name.

27. *Peace I leave with you.* By the word 'peace' He means prosperity, which men are accustomed to wish one another when they meet or part. For this is what the word 'peace' means in Hebrew. He is therefore alluding to the ordinary custom of His country, as if He

were saying, 'I leave you my farewell.' But He at once adds that this peace is far more than usually exists among men, who for the most part have the word 'peace' on their lips only as a cold politeness, or, even if they sincerely wish peace to anyone, cannot give the reality of it. But Christ tells them that His peace does not consist in a bare and empty wish but is conjoined with its effect. In short, He says that He is going away from them in body, but that His peace remains with the disciples. In other words, they will always be happy with His blessing.

Let not your heart be troubled. He again corrects the disciples' alarm at His departure. He says that there is no reason for alarm, for they lack only His bodily presence, but will enjoy His true presence through the Spirit. Let us also learn to be satisfied with this kind of presence and not yield to the flesh, which always binds God with its outward inventions.

28. *If ye loved me.* The disciples undoubtedly loved Christ, but not as they should have done. There was something carnal mixed with it, so that they could not bear to be separated from Him. If they had loved Him spiritually, they would have desired nothing more than His return to the Father.

For the Father is greater than I. This passage has been twisted in various ways. The Arians, to prove that Christ is some sort of inferior God argued that He is less than the Father. To remove any excuse for such a calumny, the orthodox fathers said that this should be referred to His human nature. But although the Arians had wickedly abused this testimony, the solution of the fathers was neither correct nor applicable. For Christ is not speaking here either of His human nature or of His eternal divinity, but for the sake of our weakness interposes Himself between God and us. And indeed, as it is not given to us to reach the height of God, Christ descended to us to raise us to it. He says, 'You should have rejoiced because I return to the Father. For this is the ultimate goal to which you should strive.' In these words He shows, not in what respect He differs in Himself from the Father, but why He descended to us; which was, to unite us to God. For, until we have reached that point, we stand so to say in mid-course. We also imagine only a semi-Christ and a mutilated Christ unless He leads us to God.

Paul has a similar passage in I Cor. 15.24, where he says that Christ 'will deliver up the kingdom to God, even the Father, that God may be all in all.' Christ indeed reigns, not only in His human nature, but as He is God manifested in the flesh. In what way, therefore, will He lay aside the kingdom? Because the divinity which is now beheld in Christ's face alone, will then be openly visible in Him. The only difference is that Paul there describes the highest perfection of the divine brightness whose rays began to shine from the time when Christ ascended into heaven. To make the matter clearer, we must speak even more bluntly. Christ is not here drawing a comparison between the divinity of the Father and of Himself, nor between His own human nature and the divine essence of the Father, but rather between His present state and the heavenly glory to which He was shortly to be received. It is as if He said, 'You desire to keep me in the world, but it is better that I should ascend to heaven.' Let us therefore learn to view Christ humbled in the flesh, that He may lead us to the fount of blessed immortality. For He was not appointed our leader just to draw us to the sphere of the moon or the sun, but to make us one with God the Father.

And now I have told you before it come to pass, that, when it is come to pass, ye may believe. I will no more speak much with you, for the prince of the world cometh: and he hath nothing in me; but that the world may know that I love the Father, and as the Father gave me commandment, even so I do. Arise, let us go hence. (29-31)

29. *And now I have told you.* The disciples had to be warned about this frequently; for it was a secret far above all human grasp. He declares that He foretells what shall happen, that when it has happened, they may believe. It was a valuable confirmation of their faith when they remembered Christ's predictions and saw the things they had heard from His own mouth accomplished before their eyes. But it seems to be a kind of concession; as if Christ had said, 'Because you are not yet capable of such a profound mystery I will excuse you until after the event, which will be an interpreter to explain this teaching.' Although at the time He seemed to be singing to the deaf, it afterwards appeared that His words were not sown in the air, so to say, but were a seed cast into the ground. Now as Christ here speaks about His Word and the accomplishment of events, so His death, resurrection and ascension to heaven are combined and united with His teaching to produce faith in us.

30. *I will no more speak much with you.* With this word He wanted to turn the disciples' attention to Himself and fix His teaching more deeply in their minds. Satiety usually brings distaste, and we long more eagerly for what we do not possess and grasp more avidly what is going to be taken away at once. Therefore, to make them more desirous of hearing His teaching, He announces that He will shortly go away. Although Christ does not cease to teach us in the whole course of our lives, this statement can also be applied to our use. For since our lives are short, we must use our opportunities.

For the prince of this world cometh. He could have said straight out that He was soon to die, that the hour of His death was at hand. But He uses a paraphrase, to fortify their minds beforehand, lest they should be terrified by a death so hideous and terrible and become faint. For to believe in Him crucified is simply to seek life in hell. First, He says that this power will be given to Satan; and then He adds that He will go away, not because He is forced to of necessity, but to obey the Father.

The devil is called the prince of this world, not because he has some kingdom distinct from God (as the Manichees imagined), but because by God's permission he exercises his tyranny in the world. Therefore, when we hear this title applied to the devil, let us be ashamed of our miserable lot. For however proud men may be, they are the possession of the devil until they are regenerated by the Spirit of Christ. For in the word *world* is here embraced the whole human race. And there is but one Saviour who rescues and saves us from this dreadful slavery. Now, since this punishment was inflicted for the sin of the first man, and since it daily grows worse because of new sins, let us learn to hate both ourselves and our sins. But we are held captive under Satan's rule in such a way that this slavery (which is voluntary) does nevertheless not excuse us from blame. It must also be observed that the activities of ungodly men are here ascribed to the devil; for since they are motivated by Satan, all that they do is justly reckoned his work.

And he hath nothing in me. Satan holds the kingdom of death because of the sin of Adam. Therefore he could not touch Christ, who is free from all fault, without His voluntarily subjecting Himself. Yet I think these words have a wider meaning than they are usually given. For the expositors speak like this: Satan found nothing in Christ, for there is in Him no cause of death, since He is free from every blemish of sin. But in my judgment, Christ not only asserts His purity, but also His divine power, which was not subject to death. For it was proper to declare to the disciples that He did not yield through weakness, lest their belief in His power should suffer. But in this general statement the former one is also included, that He was not coerced by Satan to undergo death. From this we infer that it was in our place that He submitted to death.

31. *But that the world may know.* Some read these words as a single sentence: 'That the world may know . . . arise, let us go hence,' to complete the speech. Others read the words separately and think that something is missing. It is not very important for the meaning and I leave it undecided for you to choose between the two. What is specially to be noticed is that God's decree is here put in the highest

place, lest we should imagine that Christ was dragged to death by the
violence of Satan, in such a way that anything happened to Him
contrary to God's plan. For it was God who appointed His Son to be
the Reconciler and determined that the sins of the world should be
expiated by His death. To accomplish this He permitted Satan to
triumph over Him for a little while, as if victorious. Therefore, that
He may obey His Father's decree, Christ offers no resistance to Satan
and can thus offer His obedience as the ransom (*pretium*) for our
righteousness.

Arise, let us go hence. Some think that after saying these things,
Christ left that place, so that what follows was spoken as they were
walking along. But, as John afterwards adds that Christ went out
with His disciples, it seems more reasonable that He wanted to exhort
them to give God the same obedience of which they saw such an outstanding example in Him, and not that He led them away at that
moment.

CHAPTER FIFTEEN

I am the true vine, and my Father is the husbandman. Every branch in me that beareth not fruit, he taketh it away: and every branch that beareth fruit, he cleanseth it, that it may bear more fruit. Already ye are clean because of the word which I have spoken unto you. Abide in me, and I in you. As the branch cannot bear fruit of itself, except it abide in the vine; so neither can ye, except ye abide in me. I am the vine, ye are the branches: he that abideth in me, and I in him, the same beareth much fruit: for apart from me ye can do nothing. If a man abide not in me, he is cast forth as a branch, and is withered; and they gather them, and cast them into the fire, and they are burned. (1-6)

1. *I am the true vine.* The heart of this comparison is that by nature we are barren and dry save in so far as we have been engrafted into Christ, and draw a new and extraneous power from Him. I have followed others in translating ἄμπελος by *vitis* (vine) and κλήματα by *palmites* (branches). Now *vitis* is properly the plant itself and not a field set with vines, which they call *vinea*—though it is sometimes used for *vinea*, as when Cicero groups together *pauperum agellos et viticulas* —'the poor folks' crofts and little vineyards'.[1] *Palmites* are the arms of the tree which it sends out above ground. But as the Greek word κλῆμα sometimes means *vitis* and ἄμπελος *vinea*, I incline to the opinion that Christ compares Himself to a field planted with *vites* and us to the plants themselves. I will not quarrel with anyone about this however. I only want to advise the reader to follow what seems the more probable from the context.

First comes to mind the rule which is to be observed in all parables. We should not investigate every single property of the vine, but only consider in general the object to which Christ applies the comparison. And there are three chief parts. First, we have no power to do good save what comes from Himself. Secondly, when we have our root in Him, the Father cultivates us by pruning. Thirdly, He removes unfruitful branches, so that they can be thrown into the fire and burned.

Almost everyone is ashamed to deny that all the good he has comes from God. But then they imagine that a universal grace (*universalem gratiam*) has been given them, as if it had been implanted in them naturally. But Christ insists chiefly on this, that the vital sap flows

---

[1] *De deorum natura* 3.86.

from Himself alone. It follows that man's nature is unfruitful and destitute of all good. For no man has the nature of the vine until he is implanted in Him. But this is given by special grace (*speciali gratia*) to the elect alone. So the Father is the first Author of all blessings, planting us with His hand. But the beginning of life is in Christ, in that we begin to take root in Him.

When He calls Himself the true vine, it is as if He were saying, 'I am truly the vine; and therefore men toil in vain when seeking strength elsewhere. Useful fruit will proceed from none but the branches produced by Me.'

2. *Every branch.* When He declares that all unfruitful branches will be taken away from the vine, Christ is arousing anxiety; for some corrupt God's grace, some suppress it maliciously and others choke it by laziness. But it may be asked whether anyone engrafted in Christ can be fruitless. I reply that many are reckoned by men's opinions to be in the vine who in fact have no root in the vine. Thus in the prophets the Lord calls the people of Israel His vine because by outward profession they had the name of the Church.

And every branch that beareth fruit. In these words He teaches that believers need continual cultivating lest they should degenerate, and that they produce nothing good unless God is continually at work. For it is not enough to have been made partakers of adoption once, unless God continues the progress of His grace in us. He speaks of pruning because our flesh abounds in superfluities and harmful vices and is too fertile in them, and because they grow and shoot forth endlessly unless we are cleansed by the hand of God. When He says that vines are pruned that they may bear fruit more abundantly, He tells us what the progress of the godly in the course of godliness ought to be.

3. *Already ye are clean because of the word.* He reminds them that they have already experienced in themselves what He said. They have been planted in Him and also cleansed. He indicates the method of cleansing, namely, teaching. He is undoubtedly speaking of outward preaching, for He expressly mentions the Word which they had heard from His mouth. Not that the voice coming from a man's mouth has so much efficacy in itself, but it is because Christ works in the heart by the Spirit; the voice itself is the instrument of cleansing. Yet Christ does not mean that the apostles are free from all sin, but sets their experience before them that from it they may learn how necessary is the continuance of grace. He also commends to them the teaching of the Gospel from its fruit, that they may be the more stirred to meditate on it continually, since it is like the vine-dresser's knife to cleanse what is unclean.

4. *Abide in me.* He again exhorts them to be diligent and careful in keeping the grace with which they were endowed. For the security of the flesh can never be stirred up enough. And indeed, Christ's only purpose is to keep us as a hen keeps her chicks under her wings, lest we should be carried away by our carelessness and fly to our destruction. Therefore, to prove that He did not begin the work of our salvation only to interrupt it in mid-course, He promises that His Spirit will always be efficacious in us so long as we do not prevent Him. 'Abide in me; for I am prepared to abide in you,' He says. And again, 'He that abideth in me, the same beareth much fruit.' With these words He declares that all who have a living root in Him are fruitful branches.

5. *Apart from me ye can do nothing.* This is the conclusion and application of the whole parable. So long as we are outside Him, we bear no fruit good and pleasing to God, for we are quite unfit to do anything good. The Papists not only weaken this statement, but exhaust it completely, and indeed, they avoid it altogether. For although they acknowledge in words that we can do nothing without Christ, they dream that we have a certain faculty, not indeed sufficient in itself, but which, aided by God's grace, co-operates with it. For they cannot bear man to be so emptied that he can contribute nothing from himself. But Christ's words are too plain to be evaded as easily as that. The Papist invention is that we can do nothing without Christ but that when we are helped by Him we have something of ourselves in addition to His grace. Christ, on the contrary, declares that we can do nothing of ourselves. 'The branch bears no fruit of itself,' He says. Therefore, He does not merely extol the assistance of His grace in co-operating, but deprives us completely of all power except what He supplies. Hence this phrase *without me* must be explained as meaning 'except from me'.

There is another quibble. They argue that the branch has something from nature; for if an unfruitful scion is grafted into the vine it will produce nothing. But this is easily answered. Christ is not concerned with what the branch has by nature before it is joined to the vine, but means rather that we begin to become branches when we are united to Him. Indeed, Scripture shows us elsewhere that we are useless and dry wood before we are in Him.

6. *If a man abide not in me.* He again draws their attention to the punishment of ingratitude and so arouses and stimulates them to perseverance. This last is indeed a gift from God, but the exhortation to fear is not unnecessary, for our rioting flesh can uproot us.

It is those who are cut off from Christ who are said to *wither* like a dead faggot. For, just as the commencement of strength comes from

Him, so also its uninterrupted continuance. Not that any one of the elect is in fact ever cut off. But there are many hypocrites who apparently flourish and are green for a time, but who afterwards, when they should yield fruit, disappoint the Lord's hope.

If ye abide in me, and my words abide in you, ask whatsoever ye will, and it shall be done unto you. Herein is my Father glorified, that ye bear much fruit; and so shall ye be my disciples. Even as the Father hath loved me, I also have loved you: abide ye in my love. If ye keep my commandments, ye shall abide in my love; even as I have kept my Father's commandments, and abide in His love. These things have I spoken unto you, that my joy may remain in you, and that your joy may be fulfilled. (7-11)

7. *If ye abide in me.* Believers often feel starved and very far from that rich fatness which will yield abundant fruit. This is why it is expressly added, 'Whatever those in Christ may lack, there is relief ready for their poverty, so soon as they seek it from God. This is a very useful admonition, for the Lord often lets us go hungry to train us to earnestness in prayer. If we fly to Him we shall never lack what we ask, but He will supply us from His inexhaustible abundance with all that we need (I Cor. 1.5).

When He says, *If my words abide in you,* He means that we take root in Him by faith. As soon as we depart from the teaching of the Gospel, we seek Christ outside Himself.

When He promises to grant whatever we wish, He does not permit us undisciplined asking. God would have a poor care for our salvation if He gave way to us so easily and indulgently; for we know how men wanton in foolish desires to the extreme. Here He limits His people's wishes to that principle of praying aright which subjects all our affections to the will of God. This is confirmed by the context, for He means that His own do not *will* riches or honours or the like, which the flesh foolishly desires, but the vital sap of the Holy Spirit, by which they bear fruit.

8. *Herein is my Father glorified.* Here is a confirmation of the preceding sentence. For He shows that we must not doubt that God will listen to the prayers of His people when they long to be made fruitful, for this greatly glorifies Him. But by this end or effect He also kindles in them the desire to do good, since there is nothing we should prize more highly than that God's name may be glorified by us.

The latter clause is to the same effect: *and so shall ye be my disciples.* For He declares that He has none in His flock who does not bear fruit to the glory of God.

9. *Even as the Father hath loved me.* He wanted to express something

far greater than is usually thought. Those who imagine that He here speaks of the secret love of God the Father which He always had towards the Son, philosophize beside the point. Rather, it was Christ's design to place, so to say, in our bosom a sure pledge of the divine love towards us. Therefore that subtlety as to how the Father always loved Himself in the Son has nothing to do with this passage. The love mentioned here must be referred to us, because Christ declares that the Father loves Him as the Head of the Church—a thing extremely necessary for us. For he who seeks to be loved by God without the Mediator gets imbrangled in a labyrinth in which he will find neither the right path nor the way out. We should therefore direct our gaze to Christ, in whom will be found the pledge of the divine love. For the love of God was poured out on Him completely, that it might flow from Him to His members. He was marked out by this title, that He was the beloved Son in whom the Father's will is satisfied. But we must notice the end—that in Him God may look upon us as pleasing. Thus in Him, as in a mirror, we may behold God's fatherly love towards us all, since He is not loved separately, or for His own private advantage, but that He may unite us along with Himself to the Father.

Abide ye in my love. Some expound this that Christ demands from His disciples love in return. Others are better, who take it actively as Christ's love. He wants us continually to enjoy the love with which He once embraced us and accordingly warns us to beware not to deprive ourselves of it. Many reject the grace offered to them and many throw away what they once had in their hands. Therefore, once we have been received into Christ's grace, we must see that we do not fall from it by our own fault.

Some quite foolishly infer from these words that there is no efficacy in the grace of God unless it is helped by our steadfastness. I do not allow that the Spirit demands from us only what we are capable of. Rather, He shows us what we ought to do, so that if we have no strength we may seek it elsewhere. Likewise, when Christ here exhorts us to perseverance, we must not rely on our own efforts and activity, but pray to Him who commands us, to confirm us in His love.

10. *If ye keep my commandments.* He shows us how we persevere by following where He calls. For, as Paul says, 'They which are in Christ walk not after the flesh, but after the Spirit' (Rom. 8.1). For these two things are always joined: the faith which apprehends the free love of Christ; and a good conscience and newness of life. Indeed, Christ does not reconcile believers to the Father that they may wanton with impunity, but that by governing them by His Spirit, He may

keep them under the hand and rule of His Father. Whence it follows that Christ's love is rejected except by those who prove by true obedience that they are His disciples.

If any object that this is making the security of our salvation depend on ourselves, I reply that it is wrong to put this construction on Christ's words. The obedience which believers render Him is not so much the cause of His continuing His love towards them as the effect of His love. For whence comes it that they respond to their calling, but because they are activated by the Spirit of free adoption?

But it may seem that the condition imposed on us is too hard: that we should keep Christ's commandments, which contain the precise perfection of righteousness, far exceeding our capacity. For it would follow from this that the love of Christ will be useless unless we are endued with angelical purity. The solution is easy. When Christ treats of the desire to live a good and holy life, He does not at all exclude the chief article in His teaching, namely, the free imputation of righteousness, by which through the kindness of forgiveness our duties are pleasing to God, although in themselves they deserve to be rejected as imperfect and impure. Therefore, believers are regarded as keeping Christ's commandments when they apply themselves to them, though they be far distant from their mark. For they are released from that rigour of the Law, 'Cursed be everyone that fulfilleth not all' etc.

Even as I have kept my Father's commandments. As we have been elected in Christ, so in Him the living image of our calling is exhibited to us. And so He justly puts Himself forward here as a pattern, to the imitation of which all the godly may be conformed. He says, 'In Me shines the similitude of what I demand from you; for you see how sincerely I am devoted to obedience to My Father and keep on in this course. He too has loved Me; not for a moment or for a little while, but His love towards Me is an uninterrupted continuation.' We must always keep this conformity between the Head and the members before our eyes, not only that believers may endeavour to form themselves to the pattern of Christ, but that they may trust to be reformed daily for the better by His Spirit so that they may walk unto the end in newness of life.

11. *These things have I spoken unto you.* He adds that His love is not at all unknown to the godly but that it is perceived by the sense of faith, so that they enjoy the blessed peace of conscience. For the joy he mentions is bred from that peace which all who are justified freely have with God. Therefore, as often as God's fatherly love towards us is proclaimed, let us know that we are given ground for true joy, that with quiet consciences we may be sure of our salvation.

Moreover, it is called Christ's *joy* and ours in different respects. It is Christ's because He gives it to us; for He is both its author and cause. I say that He is its cause inasmuch as we were freed from guilt when the correction of our peace was put on Him. I called Him also its author, since by His Spirit He destroys fear and anxiety in our hearts, and from this arises that tranquil gaiety. It is called ours for a different reason. We enjoy it because it has been given to us. Now, as Christ declares that He spoke these things that the disciples might have joy, we conclude that all who have duly profited by this speech have something to rest in.

By the word *remain* He means that it is not a fleeting or temporary joy of which He speaks, but one which will never perish or pass away. Therefore, let us learn that we musk seek the assurance of salvation in the teaching of Christ, which flourishes both in life and in death.

That your joy may be fulfilled. He adds that this joy will be substantial and full. Not that believers will be completely free from all sadness, but that the ground for joy will be far the greater; so that no fear, no anxiety, no grief, will ever swallow them up. For those to whom it has been given to glory in Christ will not be prevented by life or by death or by any miseries from triumphing over sadness.

This is my commandment, that ye love one another, even as I have loved you. Greater love hath no man than this, that a man lay down his life for his friends. Ye are my friends, if ye do the things which I command you. No longer do I call you servants; for the servant knoweth not what his Lord doeth: but I have called you friends; for all things that I heard from my Father I have made known unto you. (12-15).

12. *This is my commandment.* Since it is right that we should direct our life according to the commandment of Christ, we must first understand what He wills or commands. Therefore He now repeats what He had said before; that above all He wishes believers to cultivate mutual love among themselves. Love and reverence for God certainly come first in order, but, as the genuine proof of it is love toward our neighbours, He dwells specially on this point. Besides, as He previously held Himself out as a pattern for keeping the general teaching, so He does now in a particular instance for us to follow. For He cared for all His own that they might love one another. Why in this passage He prescribes nothing expressly about loving unbelievers, we have said in chapter 14.

13. *Greater love than this.* Christ sometimes commends the greatness of His love to us the better to establish assurance of our salvation. But now He goes further, to inflame us by His example to love the brethren.

Yet He joins the two together. For He wants us to perceive by faith the infinite sweetness of His goodness; and then He persuades us for this reason to strive after love. Thus Paul writes in Eph. 5.2: 'Walk in love, as Christ also loved us, and gave himself up for us, an offering and sacrifice to God for an odour of a sweet smell.' God could have redeemed us by a word or a wish, save that another way seemed to Him best for our sakes: that by not sparing His own and only-begotten Son He might testify in His person how much He cares for our salvation. And those hearts must be harder than iron or stone which are not softened by the incomparable sweetness of the divine love.

But it may be asked how Christ died for His friends, since we were enemies before He reconciled us. For, having expiated our sins through the sacrifice of His death, He abolished the enmity between God and us. The answer to this will be found in chapter 3, where we said that in reference to us there is discord between us and God until our sins are blotted out by the death of Christ; but that the cause of this grace which was manifested in Christ was the everlasting love of God, with which He loved even His enemies. In the same way, Christ laid down His life for strangers, yet He already loved them; otherwise He would not have died for them.

14. *Ye are my friends.* He does not mean that we obtain such a great honour by any merit of our own, but only reminds them of the condition on which He receives us into favour and deigns to reckon us among His friends. As He said earlier, 'If ye keep my commandments, ye shall abide in my love.' 'For the grace of God our Saviour hath appeared, instructing us to the intent that, denying ungodliness and worldly lusts, we should live soberly and righteously and godly in this present world' (Titus 2.11). But ungodly men who, through wicked contempt of the Gospel wanton against Christ, renounce His friendship.

15. *No longer do I call you servants.* He shows His love for the disciples by another argument, in that He opens His heart and mind fully to them, as intimate communication takes place among friends. He says, 'I have deferred far more to you than a mortal man usually does with his servants. Let it be, therefore, a pledge of My love toward you that I have in a kind and friendly way explained to you the secrets of heavenly wisdom which I heard from the Father.' It is indeed a wonderful commendation of the Gospel that we have the heart of Christ as it were opened in it, so that His love is not doubtful to us or obscure. We need not want to rise above the clouds or to penetrate down through the deep to seek the certainty of our salvation. Let us be content with the testimony of His love toward us which is contained in the Gospel, for it will never deceive us. Moses said to

the people of old, 'What nation under Heaven is so favoured as to have God nigh unto them as God talketh with you this day?' (Deut. 4.7). But far higher is our distinction, that God has entirely given Himself to us in His Son. So much the greater is the ingratitude and perversity of those who, not satisfied with the wonderful wisdom of the Gospel, fly away with the eagerness of pride to new speculations.

All things that I heard. The disciples certainly did not know all that Christ knew; and, indeed, they could not attain to such a height. And since God's wisdom is incomprehensible, He distributed to each of them a certain measure of knowledge, as much as was sufficient. Why then does He say that He revealed all things? I reply: This is restricted to the person and office of the Mediator. He sets Himself between God and us; for He has received from God's secret sanctuary those things which He was to deliver to us from hand to hand, as they say. Christ did not fail to teach His disciples one of those things which related to our salvation and which it was to our advantage to know. Thus, inasmuch as He was appointed to be the unique Master and Teacher of the Church, He heard nothing from the Father which He did not faithfully teach His people. Let us just have a humble desire and readiness to learn and we shall feel that Paul had good reason to call the Gospel the wisdom that makes men perfect (Col. 1.28).

Ye did not choose me, but I chose you, and appointed you, that ye should go and bear fruit, and that your fruit should abide: that whatsoever ye shall ask of the Father in my name, he may give it you. These things I command you, that ye may love one another. If the world hateth you, ye know that it hath hated me before it hated you. If ye were of the world, the world would love its own: but because ye are not of the world, but I chose you out of the world, therefore the world hateth you. Remember the word that I said unto you, A servant is not greater than His lord. If they persecuted me, they will also persecute you; if they kept my word, they will keep yours also. But all these things will they do unto you for my name's sake, because they know not him that sent me. (16-21)

16. *Ye did not choose me.* He expresses even more clearly that it is to be ascribed to His grace, and not to their own merit, that they have attained so great an honour. For when He says that they did not choose Him, it is as good as saying that they did not obtain by their own skill or industry whatever they have. It is commonly thought that there is a certain mutual combination between the grace of God and the human will, but that contrast, 'I chose you; I was not chosen by you,' claims completely (*in solidum*) for Christ alone what is usually divided between Him and man. As if He had said that a man

is not moved of his own accord to seek Christ until he has been sought by Him.

True, this does not treat of the common election of believers, by which they are adopted to be God's children, but of that special election by which He appointed His disciples to the office of preaching the Gospel. But all the same, if they were elected to the apostolic office freely and by no merit of their own, much more is it certain that the election is free by which, from being the children of wrath and an accursed seed, we are made His eternal heirs. Moreover, in this place Christ so commends His grace, by which they had been chosen to be apostles, as to join with it that earlier election, by which they had been engrafted into the body of the Church. Indeed, He includes in these words all the dignity which He had conferred on them. Yet I acknowledge that He treats expressly of the apostolate. For Christ's design is to stir up the disciples to do their duty actively.

As the basis of His exhortation, He takes the free favour with which He had honoured them. For the more we owe to the Lord, the more fervent should we be in performing the duties He demands of us. Otherwise we cannot escape the charge of base ingratitude. It is therefore clear that there is nothing which should more keenly kindle in us a striving for holy and godly living than when we acknowledge that we owe everything to God and that we have nothing of our own, that both the beginning of our salvation and all the parts which follow from it flow from His free mercy. Besides, the truth of this statement of Christ's may be clearly seen from the fact that He chose as apostles those who might have seemed the most unfit of all. Yet in their person He wanted to set up for all time a monument of His grace; for, as Paul says, who among men shall be found fit to discharge the embassy by which God reconciles mankind to Himself? (II Cor. 2.16). Or rather, what mortal is able to represent God's person? It is Christ alone who makes them fit by His election. Hence Paul derives his apostleship from grace (Rom. 1.5). Again, he declares that he had been separated even from his mother's womb (Gal. 1.15). More, since we are altogether unprofitable servants, those who seem the most excellent of all will not be equal to the lowest calling till they have been chosen. But the higher the degree of honour to which anyone has been raised, let him remember that he owes the more to God.

And appointed you. Election is hidden till it is actually made known by a man receiving the office to which he has been predestined. Paul, in the recently quoted passage, after he has declared that he was separated even from his mother's womb, adds that he was created an apostle because it so pleased God. So also the Lord testifies in Jer. 1.5 that he knew Jeremiah before he was in his mother's womb, though He calls him at last to the prophetical office in His own good time. It may happen that one who is duly qualified for teaching enters into this office; nay, it is a part of Church order that none is called till he be prepared and furnished with the necessary gifts. That Christ says He is the author of both is not surprising, since it is only by Him that God acts and He acts with the Father. So then, election and ordination belong equally to both.

That ye should go. He now shows why He mentioned His grace— to make them more zealous in the work. The apostolate was not a sinecure; but they would have to contend with the greatest difficulties. Therefore Christ adds a goad, lest they should shrink from labours, annoyances and dangers. The argument is drawn from the aim. But Christ reasons from the effect when He says, *And bear fruit*, for it is hardly possible that anyone would give himself earnestly and diligently to the work, unless he hoped that his labour would be fruitful. Therefore Christ declares that their efforts will not be unsuccessful or useless so long as they are ready to obey. For He not only tells the apostles what their calling involves and demands, but also promises them success, that they may not be inactive or cold. It is almost impossible to say how important is this consolation against the numerous temptations which Christ's ministers meet with daily. So whenever we seem to be working in vain, let us remember that Christ will at last prevent our efforts from being worthless or useless. For this promise is specially opportune when no fruit appears. Our modern wits and those who seem wise to the world ridicule our efforts as unconsidered and a vain attempt to mingle Heaven and earth. For the fruit does not yet match our wishes. But since Christ, on the other hand, has promised that the reward of the work, though hidden for a while, will follow, let us labour diligently to do our duty amidst the ridiculing of the world.

It may now be asked why Christ, in saying *and your fruit should abide*, declares that this fruit will be everlasting. As the preaching of the Gospel wins souls for Christ unto eternal salvation it seems to many that it is the perpetuity of the fruit. But I extend the statement much further, as meaning that the Church will last to the very end of the world. For the labour of the apostles bears fruit even today; and our preaching is not for one age only but will increase the Church so that a new yield will show after our death.

When He says, *your fruit*, He speaks as if it had been obtained by their own industry, although Paul teaches that they who water or plant are nothing (I Cor. 3.7). And indeed the creation of the Church is too excellent a work of God for its glory to be ascribed to men. But, as the Lord displays His power by the hand of men, He is wont to transfer to them, lest they should labour in vain, what is peculiar to Himself. Yet we must remember that when He so kindly honours His disciples it is to encourage them and not puff them up.

That whatsoever ye shall ask. This clause was not put in unconnectedly, as many might think. For since the business of teaching far exceeds men's power it suffers innumerable attacks from Satan, which could never be withstood but by God's power. Therefore, that the apostles may not be discouraged, Christ prevents them with the best of help; as if He were saying, 'If the affair is too much for you and you cannot fulfil your office, my Father will not fail you. For I have appointed you to be ministers of the Gospel with the assurance that my Father will have His hand stretched out to help you whenever you pray to Him in my name to grant you help. And, indeed, the fact that the most of teachers either droop through laziness or are utterly defeated through despair happens simply because they are sluggish in the duty of prayer.

Christ's promise, therefore, urges us on to call upon God. For whoever confesses that the outcome of his work depends on God alone will offer that work to Him with fear and trembling. On the other hand, if anyone relies on his own industry and neglects God's assistance, he will be either casting away his spear and shield when he is faced with the work or he will be very busy without profit. Here we must beware of two faults, pride and distrust. As God's help is boldly neglected by those who think that they can attend to the matter themselves, so also many yield to difficulties because they do not consider that they are fighting through the power and protection of God, under whose banner they go forth to the war.

17. *These things I command you.* This also was put in opportunely, that the apostles might know that mutual love among ministers is demanded above all things, so that they may have a hearty desire to build up the Church of God. For there is no greater hindrance than when everyone works on his own and each individual does not bring his work to the common pool. Therefore, unless ministers nourish brotherly fellowship with one another they may perhaps erect some large masses, but scattered, and there will be no Church built.

18. *If the world hateth you.* After Christ has armed the apostles for the fight, He also exhorts them to patience. For the Gospel cannot be proclaimed without the world straightway going mad. Hence it will never be possible for godly teachers to avoid the world's hatred. Christ foretells this in good time. lest they should suffer the usual fate of raw recruits, who in their inexperience are daring before they have

seen the enemy but terrified when the battle is joined. But Christ not only forewarns His disciples so that nothing new and unexpected may happen to them, but at the same time confirms them by His own example. For it is not right that He should be hated by the world and that we who represent His person should have the favour of the world, which is always true to itself.

I have preferred to translate the verb γνννώσκετε in the indicative mood; but if anyone would rather have the imperative I do not object, for the meaning is unchanged. The word which follows is more difficult. For when He says that He is before the disciples it can be referred either to time or to rank. The former explanation has been the more generally received: That Christ was hated by the world earlier than the apostles were. But I prefer the second: That Christ, who is far exalted above them, was not free from the world's hatred and therefore His ministers ought not to refuse the same state. For the expression is the same as we have had twice before, in chapter 1.27 and 30. 'He that cometh after me is preferred before me; for he was before me.'

19. *If ye were of the world.* Here is another consolation—that they are hated by the world because they have been separated from it. And this is their true happiness and glory; for this is how they have been rescued from destruction.

To choose means here to separate. Now, if they were chosen out of the world, it follows that they were a part of the world and that only by God's mercy are they distinguished from the rest who perished. Again by the word *the world*, Christ in this passage designates all who have not been regenerated by God's Spirit. For, as we shall see more fully under chapter 17, He contrasts the Church with the world. But this teaching does not contradict Paul's exhortation, 'Be at peace with all men as much as lieth in you' (Rom. 12.18). For the exception which He adds is equivalent to saying that we should see what is right and proper for us, so that no one should seek to please the world and yield to its corruptions.

But yet another objection may be asked. We see that it is a common event, that wicked men who are of the world are not only hated, but accursed. It is true that in this respect the world does not love its own. I reply: Earthly men who are regulated by a fleshly outlook never have a true hatred of sin, but only so far as it affects them in regard to their own convenience or injury. Christ did not mean to deny that the world rages and storms within itself in civil strife. He only wanted to show that the world hates nothing in believers but what is of God. Hence, too, it is clear how foolishly the Anabaptists rave, who infer from this one argument that they are God's servants just because they displease the majority of men. It is easy to reply that many who are of the world favour their teaching because they are delighted at everything being in shameful confusion. Many who are out of the world hate it because they desire political order to remain sound.

20. *Remember the word.* This can also be read in the indicative mood, 'Ye remember'; but the meaning is not much different. But to my mind the imperative agrees the better. It is a confirmation of the preceding sentence, when Christ said that He was hated by the world although he was more excellent than His disciples. For it is not right that the servant's state should be better than his master's.

When he has spoken of persons, He also mentions doctrine. For nothing upsets the godly more than when they see the doctrine which is of God haughtily despised by men. For this is a horrible monstrosity and the sight of it could shake the stoutest heart. But when, on the other hand, we remember that the Son of God Himself experienced no less obstinacy, we need not be surprised that God's doctrine is so little reverenced among men. When He calls it His and their doctrine, it is a reference to the ministry. Christ is the only Teacher of the Church, but He meant His doctrine, of which He was the first Teacher, to be preached afterwards by the apostles.

21. *But all these things.* Since the fury of the world is monstrous when it so rages against the preaching of its own salvation, Christ says that this is because it is carried away by blind ignorance to its own destruction. For no man would deliberately go to war against God. Therefore, it is blindness and ignorance of God that carries the world away so that it does not scruple to make war on Christ. We must then always observe the reason for this conduct; and true consolation rests only in the testimony of a good conscience. Our minds should also be aroused to gratitude, that while the world perishes in its blindness, God has honoured us with His light. Yet we must understand that hatred of Christ comes from a stupidity of the mind, in that God is not known; for, as I often say, unbelief is blind. Not because the ungodly do not understand or know; but because the knowledge they have is confused and at once vanishes away. I have treated this subject more fully elsewhere.

If I had not come and spoken unto them, they had not had sin: but now they have no excuse for their sin. He that hateth me hateth my Father also. If I had not done among them the works which none other did, they had not had sin: but now have they both seen and hated both me and my Father. But this cometh to pass, that the word may be fulfilled that is written in their law, They hated me without a cause. But when the Comforter is come, whom I will send unto you from the Father,

*even the Spirit of truth, which proceedeth from the Father, he shall
bear witness of me: and ye also bear witness, because ye have been
with me from the beginning. (22-27)*

22. *If I had not come.* He had said that the Jews hated the Gospel
because they did not know God. Now, lest any should think that
this tended to lighten their guilt, He adds that they are maliciously
blind; just as if anyone shut his eyes lest he should be forced to see the
light. Otherwise it might have been objected against Christ, 'If they
do not know your Father, how is it that you do not cure their ignorance? Why do you not at any rate test whether they were altogether
unteachable or not?' He replies that He has performed the office of a
good and faithful teacher, but unsuccessfully, because their malice
would not let them become sound in mind. Moreover, in the person
of those men, He wanted to strike terror into all who reject God's
truth when it is offered them, or voluntarily fight against it when
known. And though God's dreadful vengeance awaits them, yet
Christ here looks rather to His own disciples to encourage them by
a sure confidence in victory, lest they should give way before the
malice of the ungodly. For when we hear that this will be the outcome, we may already triumph as in the midst of the battle.

They had not had sin. It seems as if by these words Christ was
suggesting that there is no other sin but unbelief—and indeed some
think this. Augustine speaks more cautiously, but he is nevertheless
close to that opinion. For he says that, since faith forgives and blots
out all sins, the only sin which condemns is unbelief. This is said
truly, inasmuch as unbelief not only hinders men from being delivered
from the condemnation of death, but is the fount and cause of all evils.
But all that reasoning has nothing to do with the present passage. For
the word 'sin' is not taken generally, but in respect of the subject now
under consideration. As if Christ said that their ignorance is utterly
inexcusable, because in Him they maliciously rejected God; as if we
were to call someone innocent, just and pure when we merely wanted
to acquit him of the one crime of which he had been accused. Christ's
acquittal of them is confined to one kind of sin because it takes from
the Jews the excuse of ignorance in despising and hating the Gospel.
But yet another question arises: Was not unbelief enough to condemn
men before Christ's coming? Some fanatics wrongly gather from
this passage that all who died before Christ's coming were without
faith and remained in doubt and suspense until Christ manifested
himself to them. As if there were not very many passages of Scripture
which testified that their conscience alone was sufficient to condemn
them! Paul says, 'Death reigned in the world until Moses' (Rom.

5.14). And again, 'They who have sinned without law shall also perish without law' (Rom. 2.12).

Then what does Christ mean? There is certainly a concession in these words, by which He means that the Jews have no more to offer in extenuation of their guilt, since they knowingly and wilfully rejected the life offered to them. Thus, the excuse He allows them does not completely absolve them, but only extenuates the gravity of their crime, according to the saying 'The servant which knoweth his lord's will and despiseth it, shall be flogged more severely.' For here Christ was not promising pardon to any, but convicting His enemies who had obstinately rejected the grace of God, that it might become plain that they were unworthy of all pardon and mercy.

We must observe that He is not speaking of His coming as such but as it is joined with His teaching. For the guilt of their crime would not have been so great in regard to His bodily presence only, but their contempt for His teaching made them utterly inexcusable.

23. *He that hateth me.* In this noteworthy passage we are taught that none can hate the teaching of the Gospel without showing his impiety against God. There are indeed many who pretend differently in words; for although they have an aversion from the Gospel, they want to be thought very good worshippers of God: but they are worthless, for within is hidden a contempt of God. In this way Christ uncovers the hypocrisy of many by the light of His teaching. We have spoken more fully on this subject in the passage 'Everyone that doeth ill hateth the light' (John 3.20) and again 'He that honoureth not the Son honoureth not the Father' (John 5.23).

24. *If I had not done among them the works.* To my mind He includes in the word 'works' all the instances which He gave of His divine glory; for He clearly proved by miracles and by the power of the Holy Spirit and by other examples that He was the Son of God, so that the majesty of the only begotten was plainly seen in Him, as we have it in chapter 1. It is often objected that He did not perform more or greater miracles than Moses or the prophets. The explanation is well known. Christ's miracles were more excellent in that He was not merely a minister like the rest but was properly their Author. For when He performed miracles He used His own name, His own authority and His own power. But, as I have said, He puts in this category all the testimonies of heavenly and spiritual power by which His divinity was displayed.

They have seen and hated. He concludes that His enemies cannot shuffle out of this, for they despise His power, which was clearly altogether divine; for God had openly manifested His divinity in the Son and therefore it would be in vain for them to say that they were only concerned with a mortal man. This passage warns us to consider carefully God's works, in which, by displaying His power, He wishes us to perceive and render the honour due to Him. Consequently all who obscure God's gifts, or contemptuously neglect them, are ungrateful to God and malicious.

25. *But that the word may be fulfilled.* What is contrary to nature seems incredible. But nothing is more contrary to reason than to hate God. Therefore Christ says that their minds were infected with such great malice that—amplifying their crime—they hated Him without a cause. And He quotes a passage from Psalm 35.19 which He says is now fulfilled. Not that the same thing had not already happened earlier to David, but He wishes to reprove the nation for their obstinate malice, which prevailed perpetually from age to age, being passed on from grandfathers to grandchildren endlessly. As if He had said that they were in no way better than their fathers, who had hated David without a cause.

By the word *Law* He means the Psalms. For the whole teaching of the prophets was simply a supplement to the Law, and we know Moses' ministry lasted until the time of Christ. He called it 'their Law' not to honour them, but to pierce them more sharply with a familiar title. As if He said, 'They have a Law handed down to them by hereditary right, in which they see their conduct clearly depicted.'

26. *But when the Comforter is come.* When Christ has shown the apostles that they must not think less of the Gospel because it has many adversaries, even within the Church itself, He now opposes the testimony of the Spirit to the ungodly fury of those men. And if this supports their consciences, they will never give way. As if He had said, 'The world will indeed rage against you. Some will mock and others will curse your teaching. But none of their attacks will be so violent as to break the firmness of your faith when the Holy Spirit has been given to you to establish you by His testimony.' Indeed, when the world rages on all sides, our one protection is that God's truth, sealed by the Holy Spirit in our hearts, despises all that is in the world. For if it were subject to men's judgment, our faith would be overwhelmed a hundred times a day.

We must therefore carefully note where we should stand among so many turmoils. It is because we have received, not the spirit of the world, but the Spirit which is of God, that we might know the things which are given to us by God (I Cor. 2.12). This one testimony is powerful to drive away, scatter and overturn whatever the world sets up to obscure or destroy the truth of God. Whoever is endowed with this Spirit is so far from the danger of despairing over the hatred or contempt of the world that he will be victorious over the whole world. Yet we must beware of depending on the good opinion of men; for so long as faith wanders like this, or rather, as soon as it has left God's sanctuary, it must waver miserably. It must therefore be recalled to the inward and secret testimony of the Spirit (*interius et arcanum Spiritus testimonium*), which believers know has been given to them from heaven.

Now the Spirit is said to testify of Christ because He retains and settles our faith in Him alone, that we may not seek any part of our salvation elsewhere. Again He calls Him the Paraclete, that, relying on His protection, we may never be alarmed. By this title Christ wanted to strengthen our faith, so that it might not yield to any temptations. Also, when He calls Him the Spirit of truth, it is to be applied to the matter in hand. For we must supply the antithesis, that apart from this witness men are carried about in all sorts of ways and have no firm resting-place anywhere; but wherever He speaks, He frees men's minds from all doubt and fear of deception.

When He says that *he will send him from the Father* and again that *he proceedeth from the Father*, He does so to increase the weight of His authority. For, unless we were convinced that He had proceeded from God, the testimony of the Spirit would not be sufficient against attacks so powerful and stratagems so many and fierce. Hence, it is Christ who sends the Spirit, but from the heavenly glory; that we may know that He is not a human gift but a sure pledge of divine grace. From this it is clear how idle was the subtlety of the Greeks when, on the basis of these words, they denied that the Spirit proceeds from the Son. For Christ, according to His custom, names the Father here, to raise our eyes to the contemplation of His divinity.

27. *And ye also bear witness.* Christ means that the Spirit's testimony will not be such that the apostles will have it privately, or that they alone will enjoy it, but that it will be widely spread abroad by them because they will be instruments of the Spirit, as if He spoke by their mouth. We now see how faith is by hearing and yet derives its certainty from the seal and earnest of the Spirit. Those who are not sufficiently aware of the darkness of the human mind think that faith is formed naturally by preaching alone. On the other hand, there are many fanatics who disdain outward preaching and sublimely breathe secret revelations and ἐνθουσιασμούς. But we see that Christ joins these two things together. Therefore, although there is no faith until God's Spirit enlightens our minds and seals our hearts, yet we must not seek after visions and oracles from the clouds; but the Word, which is near us, in our mouth and heart (Deut. 30.14; Rom. 10.8), must keep all our senses bound and fixed on itself, as Isaiah beautifully says, 'This is my covenant, saith the Lord: my Spirit that is upon thee, and my

words which I have put in thy mouth, shall not depart, etc.' (Isa. 59.21). This clause *ye have been with me from the beginning* was put in to tell us that the more credit is due to the apostles as eye-witnesses of what they proclaim; as John says, 'That which we have heard, that which we have seen and our hands have handled' (I John 1.1). For thus the Lord wanted us to be provided for in every way, so that nothing might be lacking for the complete confirmation of the Gospel.

CHAPTER SIXTEEN

These things have I spoken unto you, that ye should not be made to stumble. They shall put you out of the synagogues: yea, the hour cometh, that whosoever killeth you shall think that he offereth service unto God. And these things will they do, because they have not known the Father, nor Me. But these things have I spoken unto you, that when their hour is come, ye may remember them, how that I told you. And these things I said not unto you from the beginning, because I was with you. But now I go unto him that sent me; and none of you asketh me, Whither goest thou? But because I have spoken these things unto you, sorrow hath filled your heart. Nevertheless I tell you the truth; It is expedient for you that I go away: for if I go not away, the Comforter will not come unto you; but if I go, I will send him unto you. (1-7)

1. *These things have I spoken unto you.* He again says that nothing that He has spoken is unnecessary. For wars and struggles await them, and they must be provided beforehand with the right weapons. But He also means that, if they meditate deeply on this teaching, they will be ready to resist. Moreover, let us remember that what He said then to the disciples is also spoken to us. And first we should understand that Christ does not send His followers into the arena unarmed, and therefore none can fail in this warfare save through his own laziness. But we must not wait until we are in the midst of the contest, but should rather try to become accustomed to these words of Christ and let them sink in, so that we may engage in the battle when need arises. We must not doubt that victory is in our hands, so long as those admonitions of Christ are deeply fixed in our minds. For when he says, 'That ye should not be made to stumble,' He means that there is no danger that anything shall turn us aside from the right course. But how few learn this doctrine properly is plain from the fact that they who seem to have it by heart when they are out of range give way when they have to join battle, as if they were completely ignorant and uninstructed. Let us therefore adapt these weapons to our use in such a way that they may never be forgotten.

2. *They shall put you out of the synagogues.* It was no small stumbling-block to upset their minds that they were to be degraded like criminals from the assembly of the godly, or, at least, from those who boasted that they were God's people and gloried in the title of the Church. For believers are subject not only to persecutions but also to re-

proaches and ignominy, as Paul tells us (I Cor. 4. 11ff.). But Christ commands them to stand fast against this attack, because, although they may be banished from the synagogue, yet they remain within the kingdom of God. The sum of it is that we should not be crushed by the perverse judgments of men but endure boldly the reproach of Christ's cross, content with this alone, that our cause, unjustly and wickedly condemned by men, is approved by God.

Moreover, we infer from this that the ministers of the Gospel are not only ill-treated by the avowed enemies of the faith, but sometimes also endure the greatest reproaches from those who seem to be members of the Church, even its pillars. The scribes and priests who condemned the apostles boasted that they were the divinely appointed judges of the Church. And indeed, the ordinary government of the Church was in their hands and the office of judging was from God and not from men; but by their tyranny they corrupted the whole order instituted by God. Hence, the power which had been granted them for edification was nothing but a monstrous oppression of God's servants; and excommunication, which should have been a medicine to purge the Church, was directed to driving out godliness.

Since the apostles have already experienced this in their own age, we today need not be overmuch frightened by the Pope's anathemas which he thunders against us for the testimony of the Gospel. For we should not fear that they will harm us any more than those of old did the apostles. In fact, nothing is more desirable than to be estranged from that assembly from which Christ is exiled. Yet let us note that, although excommunication was so grossly abused, it did not effect the abolition of the discipline which God had appointed in His Church from the beginning. For although Satan tries his hardest to corrupt all God's ordinances, we must not yield to him by removing, because of corruptions, what God has consecrated in perpetuity. Therefore excommunication, no less than baptism and the Lord's supper, must be brought back by the corrections of its abuses to its correct and lawful use.

Yea, the hour cometh. Christ emphasizes this stumbling-block, that the enemies of the Gospel claim such authority that they think they are offering holy sacrifices to God when they slay believers. It is hard enough for the innocent to be cruelly harassed, but it is far more bitter and distressing that those injustices which the ungodly perpetrate against God's children should be regarded as just punishment and the recompense of their crimes. But we should be so established in the protection of a good conscience as to bear patiently to be oppressed for a time until Christ appears from heaven to vindicate our cause and His.

But it is surprising that the enemies of the truth, although aware of their evil, not only deceive men, but even lay claim in God's presence to praise for their unjust cruelty. I reply that hypocrites, although their conscience accuses them, always bring forward flatteries to deceive themselves. They are ambitious, cruel and proud; but they cover all these vices with the cloak of zeal, that they may indulge in them with impunity. To this is joined a certain furious drunkenness after they are steeped in the blood of martyrs.

3. *And these things will they do.* Not for nothing does Christ frequently recall the apostles to the consideration that the one reason why unbelievers so rage against them is because they do not know God. And yet this is not said to extenuate their guilt, but that the apostles may boldly despise their blind fury. For it often happens that the authority which the ungodly possess and the splendour which shines in them shake modest and godly minds. Christ, on the contrary, tells His followers to rise with holy sublimity to despise their adversaries, who are only motivated by error and blindness. For it is our strong wall, when we are surely persuaded that God stands on our side and those who oppose us are destitute of reason. Again, these words warn us what a serious evil is ignorance of God, making even parricides demand praise and applause for their crime.

4. *That when their hour is come ye may remember them.* He repeats what He had said already, that this is not an academic philosophy, but one apt for practice and use, and that He now discourses on these matters so that they may show by practice that they have not been taught in vain.

When He says *that ye may remember*, He commands them first to store in their minds what they have heard, secondly to be mindful of them when they need to be used, and finally He means that it is important that He utters predictions of things to come.

And these things I said not unto you from the beginning. Because the apostles were still delicate and weak so long as Christ lived with them in the flesh, their most good and kind Master spared them and did not let them be pressed beyond their strength. Therefore, they had no great need of confirmation while they were given leisure and freedom from persecution. Now He warns them that they must change their outlook; and as a new stage awaits them, He likewise exhorts them to prepare for a struggle.

5. *But now I go unto him.* He tempers the grief which they might conceive at His departure with the best of consolations; and this was very necessary. They who hitherto had been kept softly were called to severe and hard battles for the future. What would have become of them if they had not known that Christ, the guardian of their salvation, was in heaven? For *to go unto the Father* is nothing but to be

received into the heavenly glory, so as to possess the highest authority. Therefore, this is held out to them as a solace and remedy for grief, that Christ, absent in body, yet sits at the right hand of the Father to protect believers by His power.

Yet here He reproves the apostles for two faults: That they were too much attached to the visible presence of His flesh, and also that when this had been taken away they were overcome by grief and did not lift their eyes on high. The same thing happens to us; for we always bind Christ to our senses and then, if He does not appear according to our desire, we make it a matter for despair.

It may seem a false charge against the apostles that they did not ask where their Master was going; for earlier they had enquired of Him on this subject. But the explanation is easy. In asking, they did not lift up their minds to trust as they should above all have done. And so the meaning is, 'As soon as you hear of my departure, you become alarmed and do not consider whither or for what purpose I go away.'

7. *Nevertheless I tell you the truth.* That they may give up wanting to have Him visibly present, He declares that His absence will be useful, and uses a sort of oath. For because we are carnal, nothing is harder than to tear from our minds this foolish attitude by which we drag down Christ from heaven to us. He explains what the advantage is by saying that the Holy Spirit could not be given to them in any other way than by His leaving the world. But that presence of Christ by which He offers Himself to us through the grace and power of His Spirit is far more useful and desirable than if He were present before our eyes. And here we must now ask whether Christ could not have drawn down the Holy Spirit while He dwelt on earth. For Christ takes for granted all that the Father had decreed. And indeed, when the Lord has once indicated what He wishes to be done, it is foolish and harmful to dispute about what is possible.

And he, when he is come, will convict the world in respect of sin, and of righteousness and of judgment: of sin, because they believe not on me; of righteousness, because I go to the Father, and ye behold me no more; of judgment, because the prince of this world has been judged. I have yet many things to say unto you, but ye cannot bear them now. How-beit when he, the Spirit of truth, is come, he shall guide you into all the truth: for he shall not speak from himself; but what things soever he shall hear, these shall he speak: and he shall declare unto you the things that are to come. He shall glorify me: for he shall take of mine, and shall declare it unto you. All things whatsoever the Father have are mine: therefore said I, that he taketh of mine, and shall declare it unto you. (8-15)

8. *And he, when he is come.* I will leave out the variety of expositions produced by the obscurity of this passage and only state what seems to me to be Christ's true meaning. He had promised His Spirit to the disciples. He now commends the excellence of this gift from its effect, because the Spirit will not only rule, sustain and protect them individually but will shed His power and efficacy more widely.

He will convict the world, He says; that is, He will not remain enclosed within yourselves, but His power will be extended from you to the whole world. He therefore promises them a Spirit who will be the Judge of the world, and by whom their preaching will become so alive and effective that it will bring into order those who before ran riot in unbridled licentiousness and were restrained by no fear or reverence.

It should be observed that here Christ is not speaking of secret revelations, but of the power of the Spirit, which appears in the outward teaching of the Gospel and the voice of men. For how does it come about that a man's voice penetrates into minds, takes root there and at last yields fruit, making hearts of stone into hearts of flesh and renewing the men themselves, but because the Spirit of Christ quickens it? It would otherwise be a dead letter and an empty sound, as Paul teaches beautifully in II Cor. 3.6, where he boasts of being a minister of the Spirit in that God worked powerfully in his teaching. Therefore the meaning is that, since the apostles had been given the Spirit, they would be endued with a heavenly and divine power by which they would exercise jurisdiction over the whole world. This is ascribed to the Spirit rather than to themselves, because they will have no power of their own but will be only ministers and instruments and the Spirit alone will preside over them.

I think that under the word *world* are included both those who were to be truly converted to Christ and hypocrites and reprobates. For the Spirit convicts men in the preaching of the Gospel in two ways. Some are touched seriously and humble themselves of their own accord and assent willingly to the judgment which condemns them. Others, although they are convinced of guilt and cannot escape, do not yield in sincerity or submit themselves to the authority and control of the Holy Spirit; on the contrary, when they are subdued they groan inwardly and, although confounded, still do not cease to cherish an inward obstinacy.

We now understand how the Spirit was to convict the world through the apostles. It was because God manifested His judgment in the Gospel, by which their consciences were struck and they began to perceive their ills and the grace of God. For the verb ἐλέγχειν is here taken as 'to convict'. And not a little light will be shed on the understanding of this passage from what Paul says in I Cor. 14.24f., 'If all shall prophesy, and there come in one unbelieving or unlearned, he is convicted by all, he is judged by all; and thus the secrets of his heart are made manifest.' There Paul is speaking particularly of one kind of conviction; that is, when the Lord leads His elect to repentance by the Gospel. But this distinctly shows how God's Spirit, by the sound of a human voice, constrains men, who before were not accustomed to His yoke, to acknowledge and submit to His rule.

It may now be asked what Christ's purpose was in saying this. Some think He indicates the cause of the hatred which He had mentioned. As if He had said that they will be hated by the world because the Spirit for His part will urge the world through them. But I rather agree with those who say that Christ's purpose was different, as I hinted at the beginning. For it was very important that the apostles should know that the gift of the Spirit which was promised to them was no common thing. He therefore describes its unique excellence by saying that in this way God will set up His judgment-seat to judge the whole world.

9. *Of sin.* Now it remains to be seen what it is to convict of sin. Christ seems to make unbelief the only cause of sin; and this is twisted by commentators in various ways. But, as I have already said, I shall not refer to what individuals teach or think. First, it is to be noted that the judgment of the Spirit begins with the demonstration of sin. For the beginning of spiritual teaching is that men born in sin have in them nothing but the material of sin. Again Christ mentioned unbelief to show what man's nature is in itself. For, since faith is the bond by which He unites Himself to us, we are, until we believe in Him, outside Him and separated from Him. Therefore these words were equivalent to His saying, 'When the Spirit is come, He will show and convince you that outside Me sin reigns in the world.' Unbelief is mentioned here because it separates us from Christ, and consequently nothing is left to us but sin. In short, with these words He condemns the corruptions and depravity of human nature, lest we should think that there is even one drop of uprightness in us without Christ.

10. *Of righteousness.* We must keep to the sequence of steps which Christ sets down. He now says that the world must be convicted of righteousness; for men will never hunger and thirst after righteousness, but, on the contrary, will contemptuously reject all that is said about it if they have not been touched by a feeling of sin. We should understand of believers particularly that they cannot progress in the Gospel till first they have been humbled, and this cannot happen until they are aware of their sins. It is indeed the proper office of the Law to summon consciences to God's judgment and to wound them with

terror, but the Gospel cannot be preached aright without leading from sin to righteousness and from death to life. Therefore it is necessary to borrow from the Law that first clause of which Christ spoke.

Moreover, by 'righteousness' understand here that which is communicated to us by Christ's grace. Christ places it in His ascension to the Father; and with good reason. For just as Paul declares that He rose for our justification (Rom. 4.25), so now He sits at the Father's right hand in such a way as to exercise all the authority that is given to Him, and thus He fills all things. In short, from His heavenly glory He sheds upon the world the sweet savour of His righteousness. Now the Spirit proclaims by the Gospel that this is the only way in which we are accounted righteous. The second step after the conviction of sin is that the Spirit should convince the world what true righteousness is: That Christ by His ascension into Heaven has established the kingdom of life and now sits at the Father's right hand to confirm true righteousness.

11. *Of judgment.* Those who understand the word 'judgment' as condemnation are not unreasonable. For Christ at once adds that the prince of this world has been judged. But it seems to me that a different meaning fits in better. Now that the light of the Gospel has been kindled, the Spirit manifests that the world has been set in a good and orderly state by Christ's victory, in which he cast down the rule of Satan. As if He had said that it is the true restoration by which all things are reformed when Christ alone holds the kingdom, having triumphed over and subdued Satan. Judgment therefore is contrasted with what is confused and scattered or, if I may put it briefly, it is its antithesis (τῆς ἀταξίας), or we might say it was uprightness, a sense it often bears in Scripture. The meaning therefore is that Satan, so long as he holds the government, confuses and disturbs everything so that there is a horrible and deformed confusion in God's works. But when Christ despoils him of his tyranny the world is restored and a well-tempered order appears. Thus the Spirit convinces the world of judgment; that is, having overcome the prince of wickedness, Christ restores to order those things which formally were fallen and torn to pieces.

12. *I have yet many things.* Christ's sermon could not be so powerful with His disciples but that their ignorance still kept them puzzled about many things. Indeed, they hardly had any taste for what should have renewed them completely but for the weakness of their flesh. Therefore the consciousness of their poverty could not fail to oppress them with fear and anxiety; but Christ counters it with this consolation that, when they have received the Spirit, they will be new and very different men.

When He says that if He were to tell them more or what was more sublime they would not be equal to bearing it, He meant to encourage them with a hope of better progress, that they might not lose heart. For they ought not to estimate the grace which would be given to them by their present feelings, since they were so distant from heaven. In short, He bids them to be cheerful and courageous however weak they may be at present. Moreover as they had nothing but His teaching to rely on, Christ tells them that He had accommodated it to their capacity, yet so that they might hope soon for something loftier and richer. As if He had said 'If what you have heard from Me is not yet sufficient to confirm you, be patient for a while. For before long, when you have been taught by the Spirit as your Master, you will need nothing more. He will remove all the ignorance that now remains in you.'

Now it may be asked what those things were which the apostles were not yet able to learn. The Papists, who put forward their inventions as the oracles of God, wickedly abuse this passage. 'Christ promised the apostles new revelations,' they say, 'and therefore we must not stop at the Scripture, for He calls His disciples to something beyond.' In the first place, if they want to talk with Augustine, the solution will be easily found. For his words are, 'Since Christ is silent, which of us shall say that it was this or that? Or if he will dare to say so, whence shall he prove it? Who is so boastful and impudent, even if he says what is true, as to affirm without any divine testimony that those are the things which the Lord did not wish to say at that time?' But a surer way to refute them is given in Christ's own words which follow. The Spirit whom Christ promised to the apostles is said to be the perfect Master of Truth (*Magister veritatis*). And why was He promised but that they might hand on the wisdom which they had received from Him? There was given to them the Spirit by whose leading they discharged the office laid upon them.

That same Spirit led them *into all truth* when they committed to writing the substance of their teaching. Whoever thinks that anything ought to be added to their doctrine, as if it were imperfect and incomplete, not only accuses the apostles of dishonesty, but blasphemes against the Spirit. If the doctrine which they committed to writing had proceeded from mere learners or novices it would have needed supplementing. But, since their writings may be regarded as perpetual records (*tabulae*) of the revelation promised and given to them, nothing can be added to them without terrible injustice to the Spirit.

When they come to the matter itself, the Papists are worse than ridiculous, for they define those mysteries which the apostles were unable to bear as certain childish nursery rhymes than which nothing could be more absurd and fatuous. Did the Spirit have to come down from heaven for the apostles to learn by what ceremony cups and their altars must be consecrated, church bells baptized, holy water blessed and Mass celebrated? Whence then do fools and children learn, who understand all those things so precisely? Nothing is clearer than that the Papists mock God when they pretend that those things came from Heaven which smack as much of the mysteries of Ceres or Proserpine as they are inconsistent with the pure wisdom of the Spirit?

If we do not want to be ungrateful to God, let us rest in that teaching of which the apostles' writings declare they are the authors, since there the highest perfection of heavenly wisdom is manifested to us, which makes 'the man of God complete' (II Tim. 3.17). Let us not think it right to go beyond this. For our height and breadth and depth consist in knowing God's love which is exhibited to us in Christ. This knowledge, as Paul tells us, excels all other knowledge (Eph. 3.19); and when he declares that all the treasures of wisdom and knowledge are hidden in Christ (Col. 2.3), he does not invent some unknown Christ but one whom by his preaching he portrayed to the life, so that, as he says in Gal. 3.1, He is seen as it were crucified before our eyes. But lest there should be any ambiguity, Christ Himself later explains by His own words what the things were which the apostles were not yet able to bear.

13. *He shall declare unto you the things that are to come,* He says. Some limit this to the Spirit of prophecy. But in my opinion it signifies the future state of His spiritual kingdom, which the apostles saw soon after His resurrection but were then quite unable to comprehend. He therefore does not promise them predictions of things that would happen after their death, but only means that His kingdom would be of a different nature and its glory far greater than their minds could now conceive. Paul, in the Epistle to the Ephesians from the first to the end of the fourth chapter, explains the treasures of this hidden wisdom which even the angels in heaven learn with amazement through the Church (Eph. 3.10). Wherefore there is no need to seek them from the archives or repositories of the Pope.

For he shall not speak from himself. This is a confirmation of the clause 'he shall guide you into all the truth'. We know that God is the fountain of truth and that outside Him there is nothing sure or substantial. Therefore, so that the apostles may put their full trust in the oracles of the Spirit, Christ declares that they will be divine. As if He were saying that whatever the Spirit brings flows from God Himself. And yet the majesty of the Spirit is not lessened by these words, as if He were not God or were inferior to the Father; but they are accommodated to the grasp of our minds. For His divinity is mentioned expressly since, because of the interposing veil, we do not sufficiently understand the reverence with which we ought to receive what the Spirit reveals to us. Likewise He is elsewhere called the earnest by which God ratifies to us our salvation, and the seal by which He seals to us its certainty (Eph. 1.13f.). In short, Christ wanted to tell us that the teaching of the Spirit would not be of this world, as if it were produced in the air, but would proceed from the secret places of His heavenly sanctuary.

14. *He shall glorify me.* Christ now tells them that the Spirit will not come to set up a new kingdom, but rather to confirm the glory given to Him by the Father. For many dream that Christ taught only the elements and then sent the disciples on to a higher school. In this way they make the Gospel no more than the Law, which was called a pedagogue of the ancient people (Gal. 3.24).

This error is followed by another, no less intolerable; that having said goodbye to Christ's law, as if His reign were ended, and He now nothing at all, they substitute the Spirit in His place. From this source have flowed the sacrileges of the Papacy and Mahommedanism. For although those antichrists are dissimilar in many respects they have a common starting-point: that in the Gospel we are initiated into the true faith, but that the perfection of doctrine must be sought elsewhere, to perfect us completely. If Scripture is brought against the Pope, he denies that we should keep to it, since the Spirit has also now come and has lifted us above it by many additions. Mohammed proclaims that without his Koran men always remain children. Thus, by a false claim to the Spirit, the world has been bewitched to leave the simple purity of Christ. For as soon as the Spirit is severed from Christ's Word the door is open to all sorts of craziness and impostures. Many fanatics have tried a similar method of deception in our own age. The written teaching seems to them to be of the letter. Therefore they were pleased to make up a new theology consisting of revelations.

We now see that Christ's admonition that He would be glorified by the Spirit whom He should send is not superfluous. For it was to teach us that the role of the Holy Spirit was simply to establish Christ's kingdom and to maintain and confirm for ever all that the Father had given Him. What then is the purpose of the Spirit's teaching? Not to lead us away from the school of Christ, but rather to ratify that voice in which we are commanded to listen to Him; otherwise He would detract from Christ's glory.

The reason is given: *He shall take of mine,* says Christ. By these words He means that we receive the Spirit so that we enjoy Christ's benefits. For what does He bestow on us? To be cleansed by Christ's blood; sin to be blotted out in us by His death; our old man to be crucified; His resurrection to be efficacious in reforming us to newness of life; and, in short, to become partakers of His blessing. Therefore, the Spirit bestows on us nothing apart from Christ; but He takes from Christ what He sheds on us. We should think the same of His teaching; for He does not enlighten us to draw us away from Christ in the slightest degree, but to fulfil what Paul says, 'Christ is made unto us wisdom '(I Cor. 1.30). Similarly, to display those treasures which are hidden in Christ. In a word, the Spirit bestows on us no other riches than those of Christ, that He may bring out His glory in all things.

15. *All things whatsoever the Father hath are mine.* As Christ might seem to take away from the Father what he claimed for Himself, He acknowledges that He has from the Father all that He communicates to us by the Spirit. Again, when He says that all things belonging to the Father are His, He speaks as the Mediator, for we must draw from His fulness. He is always mindful of us, as we have said. But we see that the majority of men deceive themselves. For, by-passing Christ, they seek God by circuitous routes.

Others expound these words as what the Father has being common to the Son, inasmuch as He is the same God. But He is not so much speaking here of His hidden and so to say intrinsic power, as of that office toward us laid upon Him. In short, He declares His riches that He may invite us to enjoy them and reckons the Spirit among the gifts which we receive from the Father by His hand.

A little while, and ye behold me no more; and again a little while, and ye shall see me, because I go to the Father. Some of his disciples therefore said one to another, What is this that he saith unto us, A little while, and ye behold me not; and again a little while, and ye shall see me: and, Because I go to the Father? They said therefore, What is this that he saith, A little while? We know not what he saith. Jesus perceived that they were desirous to ask him, and he said unto them, Do ye inquire among yourselves concerning this, that I said, A little while, and ye behold me not, and again a little while, and ye shall see me? Verily, verily, I say unto you, that ye shall weep and lament, but the world shall rejoice: ye shall be sorrowful, but your sorrow shall be turned into joy. (16-20)

16. *A little while, and ye behold me no more.* Christ had often forewarned the apostles of His departure; partly that they might bear it with greater courage, and partly that they might desire more ardently the grace of the Spirit, for which they had no great desire while they had Christ present with them physically. We must therefore take care lest we get bored with reading what Christ, not without cause, insists upon. First, He says that He will in a little while be taken from

them, so that they may not cease to be of good courage when they are bereft of His presence, on which alone they relied. Next, He promises them succour in His absence; nay, He declares that He will soon be restored to them after He has gone away, but in another way, that is, by the presence of the Holy Spirit.

Some expound this second clause differently: 'You will see Me when I shall rise from the dead, but only for a little while; for I shall soon be received into Heaven.' But the words *a little while and ye behold me* do not seem to me to allow that interpretation. On the contrary, He relieves and softens their sorrow for His absence by the consolation that it will not last long. And so He commends the grace of the Spirit, by which He will be continually with them. As if He had promised that not long after, He would return and they would not be without His presence for a long time.

Nor should it be thought absurd that He says He is seen when He dwells in the disciples by the Spirit. For although He is not seen with the eye, yet His presence is known by the sure experience of faith. What Paul teaches us is indeed true, that believers, so long as they remain on earth, are absent from the Lord, because they walk by faith and not by sight (II Cor. 5.6, 7). It is, however, equally true that in the mean time they can justly glory that they have Christ dwelling in them by faith, that they are joined to Him as members to the Head, that by hope they possess Heaven along with Him. Hence, the grace of the Spirit is a mirror in which Christ wishes us to see Him; just as Paul said, 'Though we have known Christ after the flesh, yet we know him so no more. If any man is in Christ, he is a new creature' (II Cor. 5.16, 17).

Because I go to the Father. Some expound it that Christ will no longer be seen by the disciples because He will be in Heaven and they on earth. I rather refer it to the second clause, 'You will soon see me. For my death is not a destruction which will separate me from you, but a passing to the Heavenly glory, whence my divine power will be shed even to you.' And so, in my opinion, He wanted to teach what would be His state after His death, that they might be content with His spiritual presence and not regard it as a loss to them that He no longer dwelt with them as a mortal man.

19. *Jesus perceived.* Although sometimes the Lord seems to be speaking to the deaf, He at last so assists the ignorance of His disciples that His teaching may not be useless. It is for us to strive that our slowness may not be accompanied by pride or laziness, but that we show ourselves, on the contrary, humble and desirous to learn.

20. *Ye shall weep and lament.* He shows the reason why He foretold that His departure was at hand, and at the same time added a promise

about His quick return. This was that they might the better understand how necessary was the help of the Spirit. He says, 'A hard and
severe temptation awaits you. For when I am taken away from you
by death, the world will triumph over you. You will be in deepest
sorrow. The world will consider itself happy and you wretched. I
have therefore resolved to furnish you with the necessary weapons
for this warfare.' He described the time between His death and the
sending of the Spirit, for it was then that their faith lay, as it were,
overwhelmed.

Your sorrow shall be turned into joy. He means the joy with which
they would be endued when they had received the Spirit. Not that
they were afterwards free from sorrow; but that all the sorrow which
they would endure would be swallowed up by spiritual joy. We
know that the apostles, so long as they lived, fought a hard warfare,
that they endured shameful reproaches, that they had many reasons
for weeping. But, renewed by the Spirit, they put off their former
feeling of weakness, so that with lofty heroism they easily trampled
under foot all the ills that they underwent. Here their present weakness
is compared with the power of the Spirit, which was soon to be given
to them; for although they were for a time almost overwhelmed, yet
afterwards they not only fought keenly, but won a glorious victory
in the midst of their wars. Yet it should also be noted that He points
out not only the interval between Christ's resurrection and the death
of the apostles but also what followed afterwards. As if Christ said,
'You will lie, as it were, prostrate for a while; but when the Spirit
has raised you, a new joy will begin which will continually increase
until you have been received into the heavenly glory and then you
will have perfect joy.'

> *A woman when she is in travail has sorrow, because her hour is come:*
> *but when she is delivered of the child, she remembereth no more the*
> *anguish, for the joy that a man is born into the world. And ye therefore*
> *now have sorrow: but I will see you again, and your yeart shall rejoice,*
> *and your joy no one taketh away from you. And in that day ye shall*
> *ask me nothing. Verily, verily, I say unto you, If ye shall ask any-*
> *thing of the Father, he will give it you in my name. Hitherto have ye*
> *asked nothing in my name: ask, and ye shall receive, that your joy may*
> *be fulfilled.* (21-24)

21. *A woman when she is in travail.* He confirms the preceding
statement with a metaphor; or rather, He expresses His meaning
more clearly, that not only will their sorrow be turned to joy, but
also that it bears within itself the matter and ground of joy. It often
happens that when prosperity follows adversity, men forget their

earlier grief and give themselves up completely to joy, and yet the earlier grief is not the cause of the joy. But Christ means that the sorrow which they will endure for the sake of the Gospel will be fruitful. Indeed, the outcome of all sorrows cannot fail to be unhappy unless they are blessed in Christ. But since Christ's cross always bears within itself the victory, He justly compares the sorrow arising from it with the sorrow of a woman in travail, which receives its reward when she is cheered by the child's birth. The simile would not fit if sorrow did not produce joy in Christ's members when they communicate in His suffering, just as the woman's travailing is the cause of the birth. The simile must also be applied in that, although the woman's sorrow is very severe, it quickly passes away. It was no small relief to the apostles, therefore, when they heard that their sorrow would not last long.

We must now apply the use of this teaching to ourselves. Having been regenerated by Christ's Spirit, there should flourish within us such a joy as will remove all feeling of our ills. We ought, I say, to be like women in travail, for whom the mere sight of the baby is so moving that their pain hurts them no more. But as we have received only the first fruits, and these very tenuous, we experience scarcely even a few drops of that spiritual gladness which, sprinkled on our pain, soothes its bitterness. And yet that small amount clearly shows that they who contemplate Christ by faith are so far from ever being overwhelmed by sorrow that in their worse evils they rejoice gloriously.

But since the condition is laid on all creatures to travail till the final day of redemption, let us know that we also must groan until, delivered from the continual miseries of this present life, we see openly the fruit of our faith. To sum up: Believers are like women in travail, in that, born again in Christ, they have already entered into the heavenly kingdom of God and the blessed life. And they are like pregnant and travailing women, in that, being still held captive in the penitentiary (*ergastulum*) of the flesh they long for that happy state which lies hidden under hope.

22. *And your joy no one taketh away from you.* The value of the joy is greatly increased by its perpetuity. For it follows that the afflictions are light and should be calmly endured because they are momentary. By these words Christ tells us what true joy is. The world must needs be quickly deprived of its joys, which it seeks only in fading things. Therefore, we must come to Christ's resurrection, in which there is eternal stability.

By *seeing* His disciples, He refers to when He will visit them again by the grace of His Spirit, and they will continually enjoy His presence.

23. *And ye shall ask me nothing.* When Christ has promised the

disciples joy from their unconquerable courage and constancy, He proclaims another grace of the Spirit which would be given to them —such a light of understanding as would raise them even to heavenly mysteries. They were then so slow that they checked at the slightest difficulty of any kind. For, as boys learning the alphabet cannot keep at a single line without many pauses, so in almost every word of Christ there was some stumbling-block which impeded their progress. But a little later, when they had been enlightened by the Holy Spirit, they no longer suffered any delay in becoming familiar and acquainted with the wisdom of God, so as to advance amidst the mysteries of God in an unstumbling course.

Certainly the apostles did not cease to enquire at the mouth of Christ, even when they had been raised to the highest degree of wisdom. This is only a comparison between the two states. As if Christ had said that their ignorance would be corrected, so that they who halted at the least thing would penetrate easily into the sublimest mysteries. Hence the passage in Jeremiah, 'And they shall teach no more every man his neighbour saying, Know the Lord: for they shall all know me, from the least unto the greatest, saith the Lord' (Jer. 31.34). The prophet does not take away or abolish teaching, which must flourish most in the kingdom of Christ; but he says that, when all shall be taught by God, there will be no room left for the gross ignorance which holds men's minds until Christ, the Sun of righteousness, enlightens them by the rays of His Spirit. Besides, although the apostles were no different from children, nay, were more like blocks of wood than men, we know well what they suddenly became when they had been taught by the Spirit as their Master.

If ye shall ask anything of the Father. He declares whence this new faculty comes to them. They will be able to draw plentifully from God, the fountain of wisdom, as much as they need. As if He had said, 'You must not fear that you will lack the gift of understanding, for my Father will be ready with all the abundance of blessings to enrich you bountifully.' Moreover, with these words He warns them that the Spirit is not promised in such a way that those to whom He is promised may wait for Him lazily and snoring, but on the contrary, that they must be earnestly intent on seeking the grace offered. In short, He proclaims that He will then so discharge the office of Mediator that He will obtain for them from the Father liberally and beyond their prayers whatever they shall ask.

But here a difficult question arises. Was God (who could never be favourable to men otherwise than for the sake of the Mediator) first invoked in the name of Christ at that time? Christ is describing the future when the heavenly Father will give the disciples whatever they ask in His name. If this is a new and unusual favour, it would seem that we may infer that, so long as He lived on earth, He did not yet exercise the office of advocate, that through Him the prayers of believers might be acceptable to God.

24. He at once expresses this more clearly by saying: *Hitherto have ye asked nothing in my name*. The apostles probably observed the rule of prayer prescribed in the Law. But we know that the fathers were not accustomed to pray without a Mediator. For God had trained them by many exercises to such a form of prayer. They saw the high priest enter the holy place in the name of the whole people. They saw sacrifices offered daily, that the prayers of the Church might be acceptable before God. It was therefore one of the principles of faith that to call upon God would be rash and useless unless a Mediator intervened. Christ had already sufficiently declared to His disciples that He was the Mediator. But their knowledge was so obscure that they could not yet rightly fashion their prayers to His name.

Nor is it absurd to say that they prayed to God trusting in the Mediator, according to the demands of the Law, and yet did not fully and clearly understand what that meant. The veil of the Temple was still drawn across; the majesty of God was hidden under the shadow of the Cherubim; the true High Priest had not yet entered into the heavenly sanctuary to intercede for His people, nor yet had consecrated the way by His blood. It is therefore not surprising if He was not then acknowledged to be the Mediator as He is now that He appears for us in heaven before the Father, reconciling Him to us by His sacrifice, that we wretched men may dare to appear before Him with boldness. For indeed, after Christ had made expiation and was received into Heaven, He openly showed Himself to be the Mediator.

Moreover, we must observe the frequent repetition of the phrase that we must pray 'in the name of Christ'. Thus we learn that it is a wicked profanation of God's name when anyone, by-passing Him, ventures to present himself at God's judgment-seat. And if this conviction is deeply fixed in our minds, that God will willingly and bountifully give us whatever we ask in the name of His Son, we shall not call various advocates to our aid from here and there, but shall be content with Him alone who so often and so kindly offers to us His labours. We are said *to pray in the name of Christ* when we make Him our Advocate to reconcile us in favour with His Father, even though we may not expressly mention His name with our lips.

Ask. This refers to the time of His manifestation, which was to be soon afterwards. So much the less excusable are they who today obscure this part of doctrine by the pretended patronage of the saints. The ancient people had to turn their eyes to the shadowy high priest and to the sacrificed beasts whenever they wanted to pray. We are more than ungrateful if we do not keep our senses fixed on the true High Priest who is exhibited to us as our Propitiator, through whom we may have free and ready access to the throne of God's glory.

He adds, finally, *That your joy may be fulfilled.* By this He means that nothing will be wanting for the perfect abundance of all blessings, for the height of our desires and for calm contentment, provided that we ask from God whatever we need in His name.

These things have I spoken unto you in proverbs: the hour cometh, when I shall no more speak unto you in proverbs, but shall tell you plainly of the Father. In that day ye shall ask in my name: and I say not unto you, that I will pray the Father for you; for the Father himself loveth you, because ye have loved me, and have believed that I came forth from the Father. I came out from the Father, and am come into the world: again, I leave the world, and go unto the Father. (25-28)

25. *These things have I spoken unto you in proverbs.* Christ's purpose is to give His disciples courage that, with good hopes of better progress, they may not think that the instruction which they now hear is useless, even though they may not follow much in it. For they might be taken by a suspicion that Christ did not mean to be understood, and that He deliberately held them in suspense. Therefore, He declares that they will soon see the fruit of this teaching, which by its obscurity might create distaste in their minds. The Hebrew מָשָׁל sometimes means a proverb. But, as proverbs commonly contain figures and tropes, the Hebrews call מְשָׁלִים allegories or remarkable sayings, which the Greeks call *apophthegmata,* containing something ambiguous or obscure. The meaning therefore is, 'I seem to you to be speaking figuratively now and not simply and plainly; but I will soon speak to you more familiarly, that there may be nothing perplexing or difficult for you in My teaching.'

We now see what I have already mentioned. The disciples are encouraged with the hope of further progress, that they may not reject the teaching because they do not yet understand its meaning. For unless we are inflamed with the hope of making headway, our desire to learn will inevitably cool off. The fact, however, clearly shows that Christ was not speaking allegorically, but using a simple and even elementary way of speaking to His disciples; but such was their ignorance, that they hearkened to Him with astonishment. The obscurity therefore did not lie so much in the teaching as in their minds. And indeed the same thing happens to us today; for not in vain is God's Word given the commendation that it is our light. But its brightness is so beclouded by our darkness that we think we are listening to mere allegories. For as He threatens by the prophet that He will be unintelligible to unbelievers and the reprobate, as if He has a stammering tongue (Isa. 28.11), and Paul says that the Gospel is hidden from such men because Satan has blinded their minds (II Cor. 4.4), so to the weak and ignorant it mostly sounds so confused that it cannot be understood. For although their minds are not completely darkened, like those of unbelievers, yet we are enveloped as it were in mists. Thus the Lord permits us to be stupefied for a time, to humble us by a feeling of our own poverty. But those whom He enlightens by His Spirit, He causes to make such progress that His Word is familiar and known to them.

And this is the significance of the next clause: *The hour cometh;* that is, will soon come, when I shall no longer speak to you figuratively. The Holy Spirit certainly did not teach the apostles anything but what they had heard from the mouth of Christ Himself; but by shining into their hearts, He dispersed their darkness so that they heard Christ speak in a new and different way and easily grasped His meaning.

When He says that *He will tell them of the Father*, He reminds us that the aim of His teaching is to lead us to God, in whom substantial happiness lies. But another question remains: Why does He say elsewhere that it was given to the disciples to know the mysteries of the kingdom of God? For here he acknowledges that He has spoken to them allegorically. But there (i.e. Matt. 13.13) He makes the distinction between them and the rest of the people that He speaks to the people in parables. I reply: The ignorance of the apostles was not so great but that they had at any rate a weak taste of what their Master meant; and so it is not without cause that He excused them from the company of the blind. He now says that His Word has hitherto been allegorical in comparison with that clear light of understanding which He would soon give them by the grace of His Spirit. Both statements are therefore true: that they by far excelled those who had no taste for the Word of the Gospel, and yet they were still like the infants learning their A.B.C., in respect of the new wisdom which the Spirit brought them.

26. *In that day.* He repeats the reason why the heavenly treasures were to be so liberally opened up. It is because they ask in the name of Christ whatever they need. God will deny nothing asked in the name of His Son. But there seems to be a contradiction in the words. For Christ goes on to add that it will be unnecessary for Him to pray to the Father. Now what is the point of praying in His name if He does not undertake the office of Patron? Elsewhere John calls Him our

Advocate (I John 2.1). Paul also declares that Christ now intercedes for us (Rom. 3.4); and the same thing is confirmed by the author of the Epistle to the Hebrews (7.25). I reply: Christ does not directly deny in this passage that He will be Intercessor, but only means that the Father will be so inclined towards the disciples, that without any difficulty He will give freely whatever they ask. He says, 'The Father will meet you, and for His great love towards you will anticipate the Intercessor who otherwise would speak on your behalf.

Again, when Christ is said to intercede with the Father for us, let us not imagine anything fleshly about Him, as if He were on His knees before the Father offering humble supplications. But the power of His sacrifice, by which He once pacified God towards us, is always powerful and efficacious. The blood by which He atoned for our sins, the obedience which He rendered, is a continual intercession for us. This is a remarkable passage, by which we are taught that we have the heart of God as soon as we place before Him the name of His Son.

27. *Because ye have loved me.* These words tell us that the only bond of our union with God is union with Christ. To Him we are united by an unfeigned faith, which springs from the sincere attitude which He describes by the name of love. For no man believes sincerely in Christ who does not cordially embrace Him. Hence, by this word He has well expressed the power and nature of faith. But if God only begins to love us when we have loved Christ, it follows that the beginning of salvation is from ourselves, because we have anticipated the grace of God. But many testimonies of Scripture contradict this opinion. God's promise is, 'I will cause them to love me' and John says 'Not that we first loved Him' (I John 4.10). It would be superfluous to gather many passages, for nothing is surer than this doctrine, that the Lord calls the things which are not, raises the dead, joins Himself to strangers, forms hearts of flesh out of stones, manifests Himself to those who do not seek Him. I reply: God loves men in a secret way before they are called if they are among the elect. For He loves all His own before they are created. But, as they are not yet reconciled, they are justly accounted God's enemies, as Paul says in Rom. 5.10. This is why it is said that we are loved by God when we love Christ, because we have the pledge of the fatherly love of Him before whom we formerly trembled as our hostile Judge.

28. *I came out from the Father.* This expression commends to us the divine power in Christ. Our faith in Him would not be firm if it did not grasp His divine power. For His death and resurrection, the two pillars of faith, would help us little if heavenly power were not joined with them. We now understand in what way we should embrace

Christ. In such a way that our faith shall consider God's purpose and power, by whose hand He is offered to us; for we must not receive coldly the fact that He came out from God, but must also understand for what reason and purpose He came out—that He might be to us wisdom, and sanctification, and righteousness, and redemption (I Cor. 1.30).

In the second clause that follows He points out that this power is perpetual, for the disciples might have thought it a temporary blessing that He was sent into the world as Redeemer. He therefore said that He returns to the Father that they may be assured that none of the blessings which He brought is lost by His going away, since from His heavenly glory He sheds the power and effect of His death and resurrection upon the world. He therefore left the world when, laying aside our infirmities, He was received into heaven. But His grace towards us flourishes no less, for He is seated at the right hand of the Father that He may possess dominion over the whole world.

His disciples say, Lo, now speakest thou plainly, and speakest no proverb. Now know we that thou knowest all things, and needest not that any man should ask thee: by this we believe that thou camest forth from God. Jesus answered them, Do ye now believe? Behold, the hour cometh, yea, is come, that ye shall be scattered, every man to his own, and shall leave me alone: and yet I am not alone, because the Father is with me. These things have I spoken unto you, that in me ye may have peace. In the world ye have tribulation: but be of good cheer; I have overcome the world. (29-33)

29. *His disciples say.* This shows how effective was that consolation; for it suddenly raised to great cheerfulness those minds which had been cast down and broken. And yet it is certain that the disciples did not yet follow the meaning of Christ's discourse. But although they were not yet capable of this, the mere scent of it refreshed them. When they exclaim that their Master speaks plainly and not figuratively, they certainly go too far; and yet from their own point of view they say the truth, as we ourselves experience today. For he who has tasted only a little of the teaching of the Gospel is more inflamed and feels much greater energy in that small measure of faith than if he had known all Plato. Indeed, the groans that God's Spirit arouses in the hearts of the godly testify clearly that God works in a secret way beyond their grasp, for otherwise Paul would not call them 'unutterable' (Rom. 8.26).

Thus we ought to understand that the apostles felt they had made some progress, so that they could say with truth that Christ's words were not completely enigmatic. But they were deceived in that they thought they were wiser than they were. Their mistake came from not knowing what the gift of the Holy Spirit would be. They therefore rejoiced before the time; just as if someone thought himself rich with one single gold coin. From certain signs they conclude that Christ came out from God, and they glory in it as if nothing more were needed. Yet they were still far from that knowledge, so long as they did not understand what Christ would be to them in the future.

31. *Do ye now believe?* Since the disciples were too pleased with themselves, Christ warned them that they should rather remember their weakness and keep within their own small capacity. But we never really know what we lack and how far we are from the fulness of faith, until we come to some serious task; for then the event shows how weak our faith was, which we imagined to be full. Christ recalls the disciples to this and declares that soon they will forsake Him. For persecution is like a touchstone to test faith; and when the smallness of faith becomes plain, those who before were puffed up begin to tremble and draw back.

Christ's question therefore was ironical. As if He had said, 'Do you boast as if you were full of faith? The trial is at hand which will show up your emptiness.' Thus ought we to restrain our security when it becomes over-exultant. But it might seem that in the disciples there was either no faith at all, or that it was extinguished when they left Christ and were scattered abroad. I reply that, although their faith was weakened and was almost overcome, yet something was left for new branches to sprout from afterwards.

32. *Yet I am not alone.* This correction is put in to teach us that, when Christ is forsaken by men, nothing is taken from Him. For since His truth and glory are grounded on Himself and do not depend on the world's faith, if He should be forsaken by the whole world He nevertheless remains entire, because He is God and needs no outside help.

When He says that *the Father will be with him*, it is as much as to say that God will be on His side, so that He will have no need at all to borrow anything from men. Whoever meditates on this properly will stand fast, though the whole world waver, and the failure of all others will not overturn his faith. For we do not render due honour to God unless He alone is sufficient for us.

33. *These things have I spoken unto you.* He again insists how necessary those consolations are which He had used to them. And He proves it by this reason: that many distresses and tribulations await them in the world. Therefore we should notice first this warning that all the godly ought to be convinced that their life is subject to

many afflictions, so that they may be prepared for endurance. Since, therefore, the world is like a rough sea, true peace will be found nowhere but in Christ. Now we must note the manner of enjoying that peace which He describes here. He says that they will have peace if they advance in this teaching. Do we wish, then, to have calm and easy minds in the midst of afflictions? Let us be attentive to this discourse of Christ, which in itself will give us peace.

Be of good cheer. Although our sluggishness has to be corrected by various afflictions, and we must be aroused to seek a remedy for our ills, yet the Lord does not want our minds to be broken, but rather that we should fight keenly. But this is impossible unless we are sure of success. For if we had to fight while uncertain of the outcome all our enthusiasm would quickly fail. When, therefore, Christ calls us to the battle, He arms us with sure confidence in victory, although we still have to exert ourselves.

Moreover, as there is always good reason for trembling in us, He teaches us to be confident, in that He has been victorious over the world, not for Himself privately but for our sake. Thus, although we are almost overwhelmed in ourselves, if we look upon that magnificent glory to which our Head has been exalted, we may boldly despise all the evils which hang over us. If we desire to be Christians, we must not seek to be free from the cross, but must be content with this alone, that fighting under Christ's command we are out of danger even in the midst of the battle. Under the name *world* Christ here embraces everything that is opposed to the salvation of the godly and especially all the corruptions which Satan uses to lay snares for us.

CHAPTER SEVENTEEN

These things said Jesus; and lifting up his eyes to heaven, he said, Father the hour is come; glorify thy Son, that the Son may glorify thee: even as thou gavest him authority over all flesh, that whatsoever thou hast given him, to them he should give eternal life. And this is life eternal, that they should know thee the only true God, and him thou didst send, even Jesus Christ. I glorified thee on the earth, having accomplished the work which thou hadst given me to do. And now, O Father, glorify thou me with thine own self with the glory which I had with thee before the world was. (1-5)

1. *These things spake Jesus.* When the Lord had preached to the disciples about bearing the cross, He set before them the consolations, by relying on which they would persevere. After promising the coming of the Spirit, He raised them to a better hope and talked to them about the glory and splendour of His kingdom. Now He betakes Himself to prayer; and this is as it should be, for doctrine is cold unless it is given divine efficacy. He therefore shows teachers an example, that they should not only occupy themselves in sowing the Word, but by mixing their prayers with it should implore God's help, that His blessing should make their work fruitful. In short, this prayer of Christ is, as it were, the seal of the preceding teaching, both that it might be ratified in itself and that it might obtain full authority with the disciples.

When John narrates that Christ prayed *lifting up his eyes to heaven* it was a sign of unusual ardour and vehemence. By this attitude, Christ declared that in His mind's affections He was in heaven rather than upon earth, so that He left men behind Him and talked intimately with God. He looked toward heaven, not as if God (who fills also the earth) were shut up there, but because it is there chiefly that His majesty appears. Moreover, by looking towards heaven, He reminds us that God's glory is exalted far above all creatures. The elevation of His hands in prayer has the same significance, for men are indolent and slow by nature and tend downwards by their earthly spirit and need such arousing or rather carriages to raise them to God.

Yet, if we really desire to imitate God, we must take care that ceremonies do not express more than is in our minds, but that the inward feeling directs the eyes, the hands, the tongue and everything else. The publican with downcast eyes prayed aright to God (Luke

18.13) but that is not contrary to this statement. For, although he humbled himself, being confounded on account of his sins, this humbling did not prevent him from seeking pardon confidently. But it behoved Christ to pray differently, for He had nothing to be ashamed of. It is also certain that David himself prayed sometimes in different attitudes at different times as circumstances required.

Father, the hour is come. Christ asks that His kingdom may be magnified, so that He in His turn might magnify the glory of the Father. He says that the hour is come, because, although He has been manifested as the Son of God by miracles and every kind of work, yet His spiritual kingdom was still obscure, which soon after shone forth. If it be objected that nothing could be less glorious than Christ's death which was then at hand, I reply that in that death we see a boundless glory which is concealed from the ungodly. For there we know that by the expiation of sins the world has been reconciled to God, the curse blotted out and Satan vanquished.

Christ's prayer also asks that His death may, by the power of the heavenly Spirit, bear such fruit as had been decreed by the eternal purpose of God. For He says that the hour is come, not one determined by the will of men but which God had appointed. And yet the prayer is not superfluous, for Christ so depends on God's will, that He knows that He should desire what God promised would certainly take place. God will indeed do whatever He has decreed, not only though the whole world slept, but even though it opposed Him. But it is our duty to ask from Him whatever He has promised, because the purpose of promises is to urge us on to prayer.

That the Son may glorify thee. He means that the shining of His and His Father's glory is mutual. For why does Christ appear, but to lead us to the Father? It follows from this that all honour bestowed upon Christ, so far from diminishing the Father's honour, rather confirms it. We must always bear in mind under what character Christ speaks in this passage. It is not only His eternal divinity that we must think of, for He speaks as God manifest in the flesh and in His office as Mediator.

2. *Even as thou gavest him.* He again asserts that He asks nothing save what accords with the Father's will. It is a general rule of prayer not to ask more than God would willingly give; for nothing is more unreasonable than to bring before Him whatever we like.

Authority over all flesh means the authority given to Christ when the Father appointed Him King and Head. But we must note the end, which is to bestow eternal life on all His own. Christ therefore receives authority, not so much for Himself, as for our salvation. And so we should submit to Christ, not only that we may obey God, but because there is nothing more lovely than that subjection, since it is the cause of our eternal life.

Now, Christ does not say that He has been placed in command of the whole world to bestow life indiscriminately. But He restricts this grace to those given to Him. But how were they given? For the Father has also subjected to Him the reprobate. I reply: Only the elect belong to His own flock, which He guards as a shepherd. Hence, the kingdom of Christ extends to all men, but it is saving only to the elect who follow the Shepherd's voice with willing obedience. He forcibly compels others to obey Him, until at last He utterly destroys them with His iron rod.

3. *And this is life eternal.* He now describes how He gives life—when He enlightens the elect in the true knowledge of God. For here He is not dealing with the fruition of life that we hope for, but only with the way in which men arrive at life. And that this statement may be properly understood, we must first understand that we are all in death, until God, who alone is life, enlightens us. But where He has shone, we possess Him by faith and also enter into the possession of life; and this is why the knowledge of Him is truly and justly called saving. Nearly every single word is of consequence; for not any kind of knowledge is meant here, but only that which transforms us to the image of God from faith to faith. Indeed, it is the same as faith, by which we are incorporated into the body of Christ and made partakers of the divine adoption and heirs of heaven.

Because God is known only in the face of Jesus Christ, who is His living and express image, He says: *That they should know thee, and him whom thou didst send, even Christ.* That He puts the Father first does not refer to the order of faith, as if our minds descend from the knowledge of God to Christ; but the meaning is that God is known by the intervention of the Mediator.

The two adjectives are added, *true* and *only*; because in the first place it is necessary that faith shall distinguish God from the empty imaginations of men and, embracing Him with steadfast assurance, never swerve or waver; and secondly, deciding that there is nothing defective or imperfect in God, it must be content with Him alone. The explanation of some, 'That they may know thee who alone art God' is weak. The meaning is, 'That they may know thee alone to be the true God.'

But it seems that in this way Christ disclaims the right and title of divinity. If we reply that the name of God is as applicable to Christ as to the Father, the same question might be raised about the Holy Spirit. For if only the Father and the Son are one God, the Holy Spirit is excluded from that rank, which is equally absurd. The answer is easy if we heed the method of speaking which Christ keeps to throughout John's Gospel—of which I have already reminded my readers so often that they ought to be used to it by now. Christ, who appears in the form of a man, designates under the person of the Father God's power, essence and majesty. So Christ's Father is the only true God; that is, He is the God who formerly promised a Redeemer to the world. But in Christ the unity and truth of Godhead will be found, because He was humbled to raise us on high. When we have reached this point, His divine majesty shows itself and we learn that He is wholly in the Father and the Father wholly in Him. In short, whoever separates Christ from the divinity of the Father does not yet know Him who is only true God, but rather invents for himself a strange god. This is why we are told to know God, and Christ whom He sent; by whom, as it were with outstretched hand He invites us to Himself.

To some it seems unfair that men should perish merely through their ignorance of God. But this comes from their not reckoning that there is no fountain of life save in God alone and that all who are alienated from Him are deprived of life. Now, if there is no approach to God but by faith, it must be that unbelief keeps us in death. If it be objected that it is unfair to the otherwise righteous and innocent when they are condemned, the reply is obvious, that nothing right or sincere is found in men so long as they remain in their own nature. But Paul says that we are renewed in the image of God by knowledge (Col. 3.10).

It will be worthwhile now to summarize those three heads. First, the kingdom of Christ brings life and salvation. Secondly, not all receive life from Him, nor even is it Christ's office to give life to all, but only to the elect, whom the Father has committed to His care. Thirdly, this life consists in faith and Christ bestows it on those whom He enlightens in the faith of the Gospel. Hence we gather that the gift of illumination and heavenly wisdom is not common to all but peculiar to the elect. It is undoubtedly true that the Gospel is offered to all, but here Christ speaks of the secret and efficacious way of teaching by which God's children alone are drawn to faith.

4. *I glorified thee.* He said this because God had been known to the world by His teaching and miracles. And this is God's glory, when we know what He is. When He adds that He accomplished the work which was given Him, He means that He performed the whole course of His calling. For the time was now ripe for Him to be received into the heavenly glory. Nor does He speak only of the office of teaching, but embraces also the other parts of His ministry. For though there yet remained the chief part, the sacrifice of His

death by which He was to expiate the sins of us all, yet since the hour
of His death was already present, He speaks as if He had already
endured it. The sum of it is, therefore, that the Father would send
Him to possess the kingdom. For having completed His course,
nothing remained for Him to do but to display by the power of the
Spirit the fruit and efficacy of all that He had done on earth by His
Father's command—according to Paul's saying, 'he emptied himself,
taking the form of a servant. Wherefore God exalted him and gave
him a name, etc.' (Phil. 2.7, 10).

5. *The glory which I had with thee.* He desires to be glorified with
the Father; not that the Father may glorify Him in secret without any
witnesses, but that, having been received into heaven, He may show
magnificently His greatness and power, so that every knee may bow
to Him, etc. (Phil. 2.10). And so that phrase in the former clause *with
the Father,* is contrasted to earthly and fading glory; just as Paul
expresses His blessed immortality by saying that He died to sin once,
but now lives to God (Rom. 6.10).

Afterwards He declares that He desires nothing alien to Him, but
only that He may appear in the flesh such as He was before the creation
of the world. Or, if you want it more plainly, that the divine majesty
which He always had, may now shine in the person of the Mediator
and in the human flesh which He has put on. A noteworthy passage,
by which we are taught that Christ is not a novel or temporary God.
For if His glory was eternal, He also always was. Moreover, a manifest
distinction between Christ's person and the Father's is expressed here,
from which we infer that He is not only the eternal God but also the
eternal Word of God begotten of the Father before the ages.

*I manifested thy name unto the men whom thou gavest me out of the
world: thine they were, and thou gavest them to me; and they have kept
thy word. Now they know that all things whatsoever thou hast given
me are from thee: for the words which thou gavest me I have given unto
them; and they received them, and knew of a truth that I came forth
from thee, and they believe that thou didst send me. I pray for them: I
pray not for the world, but for those whom thou hast given me; for they
are thine: and all things that are mine are thine, and thine are mine:
and I am glorified in them. And I am no more in the world, and these
are in the world, and I come to thee. Holy Father, keep them in thy
name which thou hast given me, that they may be one, even as we are.*
(6-11)

6. *I manifested thy name.* Here Christ begins to pray to the Father
for His disciples; and with the same affection of love with which He
was at once to suffer death for them, He now pleads for their salvation.

The first argument for His request is that they have embraced the teaching which truly makes men children of God. Christ did not lack faithfulness and diligence in calling all men to God; but only among the elect was His labour profitable and efficacious. His preaching, which manifested the name of God, was common to all and He never ceased to assert His glory even among the obstinate. Why then does He say that He manifested it only to a few, but because the elect alone profit by the inward teaching of the Spirit? Infer therefore that not all to whom the teaching is offered are truly and efficaciously taught, but only those whose minds are enlightened. Christ ascribes the cause to the election of God; for He assigns no other difference as to why He manifested the name of the Father to some, passing over others, than because they were given to Him. From this it follows that faith flows from the eternal predestination of God, and that therefore it is not given to all indiscriminately, since not all belong to Christ.

When He adds *thine they were, and thou gavest them to me*, He first indicates the eternity of election, and then how we should think of it. Christ declares that the elect always belong to God. God therefore distinguishes them from the reprobate, not by faith, nor by any merit, but by pure grace; for while they are completely alien to Him, He yet regards them as His own in His secret counsels. The certainty consists in His committing to the guardianship of His Son all whom He has elected, that they may not perish; and it is there that we must turn our eyes if we are to be certain that we are of the number of God's children. For in itself the predestination of God is hidden; and it is manifested to us in Christ alone.

They have kept thy word. This is the third step. The first is free election, and the second the gift by which we enter under Christ's care. Received by Christ, we are gathered into the fold by faith. God's Word slips away from the reprobate, but strikes root in the elect, and so they are said to keep it.

7. *Now they know.* Here is expressed the chief thing in faith—we should so believe in Christ that our faith does not stop at the sight of His flesh but grasps His divine power. For when He says, 'They know that all things whatsoever thou hast given me are from thee,' He means that believers perceive that all they have is heavenly and divine. And, indeed, unless we lay hold on God in Christ, we must vacillate continually.

8. *And they received them.* He expresses the mode of this knowledge; for they received the doctrine which He taught them. But lest anyone should regard His doctrine as human or of earthly origin He declares that God is its Author, when He says, *The words which thou gavest me, I have given unto them.* He speaks in His usual way in the person of

the Mediator or Minister when He says that He taught only what He has received from the Father; for, since His own condition in the flesh was still lowly and His divine majesty was hidden under the form of a Servant (*sub forma servi*), it is God He refers to under the person of the Father. Yet we must keep to John's testimony at the beginning, that, inasmuch as Christ was the eternal Word of God, He was always one God with the Father. Therefore, the meaning is that Christ was a faithful witness of God to the disciples, so that their faith was grounded on nothing but the truth of God, inasmuch as the Father Himself spoke in the Son. The receiving of which He speaks came from His efficaciously manifesting to them the name of His Father through the Holy Spirit.

And knew of a truth. He now repeats in other words what He had mentioned before. That Christ came out from the Father and was sent by Him is equivalent to what precedes this, that all things which He has are from the Father. The sum of it is that faith should look directly at Christ, yet so as to know nothing earthly or contemptible about Him, but to be carried up to His divine power, so as to be firmly persuaded that in Himself He has perfectly God and all that is of God.

Note, also, that in the first clause He uses the verb *know*, and now He switches to the word *believe*. For thus He tells us that nothing can be known aright of God but by faith; but that in faith there is such certainty that it is justly called knowledge.

9. *I pray for them.* Hitherto Christ has represented what would win the disciples favour with the Father. Now He frames the prayer itself and shows that He has nothing save what accords with the Father's will. For He commends to the Father only those whom the Father Himself willingly loves. He openly declares that He does not pray for the world, for He is solicitous only for His own flock which He received from the Father's hand. But this might seem absurd; for no better rule of prayer can be found than to follow Christ as our Guide and Teacher. But we are commanded to pray for all, and Christ Himself afterwards prayed for all indiscriminately, 'Father, forgive them; for they know not what they do.' I reply, the prayers which we utter for all are still limited to God's elect. We ought to pray that this and that and every man may be saved and so embrace the whole human race, because we cannot yet distinguish the elect from the reprobate. And yet by desiring the coming of God's kingdom we pray at the same time that He may destroy His enemies. The only difference is that we pray for the salvation of all whom we know to have been created in God's image and who have the same nature as ourselves; and we leave to God's judgment those whom He knows

to be reprobate. But in the prayer related here there was a certain special reason which should not be taken as an example. Christ is not praying simply from an attitude of faith and love but enters into the sanctuary of heaven and holds before His eyes the secret judgments of the Father, which are hidden from us so long as we walk by faith.

Moreover, we gather from these words that God chooses out of the world those whom He sees fit to choose to be heirs of life, and that this distinction is not made according to men's merits, but depends on His mere good pleasure. For those who place the cause of election in men must begin with faith. But Christ expressly declares that they who are given to Him belong to the Father. It is certain that they are given that they may believe, and that faith flows from this giving. If the origin of faith is this giving, and if election precedes it in order and time, what remains but to confess that those whom God wishes to be saved out of the world are elected freely? Now, since Christ prayed only for the elect, belief in election is necessary for us if we want Him to commend our salvation to the Father. Those, therefore, who try to blot out the knowledge of election from the hearts of believers do them a grievous injury, for they deprive them of the support of Christ. These words also serve to expose the perverse stupidity of those who under the excuse of election surrender to laziness, whereas it should rather sharpen us to earnestness in prayer, as Christ teaches us by His example.

10. *And all things that are mine are thine.* The former clause suggests that the Father will certainly listen to Him. He says, 'I do not commend any to thee but those whom thou dost acknowledge as thine; for I possess nothing separate from thee and therefore I shall not suffer a rebuff.' In the second clause, He shows that He has good reason for caring for the elect; for they are His in consequence of their being the Father's. All these things are spoken to confirm our faith. We must not seek salvation elsewhere than in Christ. But we shall not be satisfied with Christ, unless we know that in Him we possess God. We must therefore believe that there is a unity between the Father and the Son, so that they have nothing separate from each other.

This agrees with the second clause, *I am glorified in the disciples.* For it follows that it is reasonable that He, for His part, should promote their salvation. And this is the best teaching for confirming our faith, that Christ will never neglect our salvation if He shall be glorified in us.

11. *And I am no more in the world.* He gives another reason why He prays so diligently for the disciples—because they were soon to be deprived of His physical presence, under which they had hitherto rested. While He lived among them He cherished them under His

wing as a hen her chickens. But now that He is about to depart, He asks the Father to cover them with His protection. And He does so for their sakes; for He provides a remedy against their fear, that they may rest on God Himself, to whom He now, as it were, hands them over. This is no little consolation to us when we hear the Son of God the more careful for the salvation of His people when He leaves them bodily; for we should infer from it that while we today labour in the world He has respect to us, that He may help us from His heavenly glory in our tribulations.

Holy Father. The object of the whole prayer is that the disciples may not lose heart, as if their state were worsened by the bodily absence of their Master. For when Christ was given by the Father to be their guardian for a time, now that He had discharged that appointment He restores them, as it were, to the hands of the Father, that henceforth they may be kept under His auspices and by His power. The sum of it, therefore, is that when the disciples were deprived of Christ's bodily presence it was no detriment to them, because God received them under His guardianship, the power of which is everlasting.

He shows the way they shall be kept: *that they may be one.* For those whom the heavenly Father has decreed to keep He collects into a holy unity of faith and the Spirit. But, because it is not enough for men to agree in general, He adds the phrase *even as we are.* Our unity will be truly happy when it bears the image of God the Father and of Christ, as the wax takes the form of the seal impressed on it. But in what way the Father and Christ are one I shall explain soon.

While I was with them in the world, I kept them in thy name. Those whom thou hast given to me I have kept, and not one of them perished, but the son of perdition; that the scripture might be fulfilled. But now I come to thee; and these things I speak in the world, that they may have my joy fulfilled in themselves. (12-13)

12. *While I was with them in the world.* Christ says that He kept them in the Father's name. He represents Himself as only a Servant, doing nothing but by the power and under the authority of God. He means, therefore, that it would be inconsistent if they should now perish; as if by His departure God's power were extinguished or dead. But it might seem absurd that Christ should surrender to God the office of keeping them; as if, after completing the course of His life, He ceased to be the guardian of His people. The reply is easy. He there speaks only of visible guardianship, ending at His death. While He dwelt on earth He had no need to borrow power from elsewhere to keep His disciples; but all this relates to the person of the Mediator, who appeared for a time under the form of a Servant. But now He

tells the disciples to raise their minds direct to heaven as soon as they begin to be deprived of the outward help. From this we conclude that Christ keeps believers today no less than before, but in a different way, because divine majesty is displayed openly in Him.

Whom thou hast given me. He uses the same argument again, that it would be all wrong if the Father ever rejected those whom His Son at His command had kept to the very end of His ministry. It was as if He had said, 'What thou didst enjoin upon Me I have faithfully executed, and I took care that nothing in My hands should perish. And when now Thou receivest what Thou didst entrust to Me, it belongs to Thee to see that it continues safe.'

He excepts Judas, and not without reason. For although he was not one of the elect, and of God's true flock, yet the dignity of his office gave him the appearance of it. Nor indeed would anyone have thought otherwise of him, so long as he held that distinguished rank. So far as grammar goes, the exception is incorrect. But if we consider the matter, it was necessary for Christ to speak like this, after the ordinary meaning of man. But lest anyone should think that God's eternal election was overthrown by Judas' destruction, He immediately added that he was the son of perdition; meaning by these words that his ruin, which before men's eyes was a sudden occurrence, had long since been known to God. For in Hebrew 'the son of perdition' is a man who is lost or appointed to destruction.

That the scripture might be fulfilled. This refers to the former clause. Judas fell that the Scripture might be fulfilled. But it would be wrong for anyone to infer from this that Judas' fall should be imputed to God rather than to himself, in that necessity was laid on him by the prophecy. For the course of events should not be ascribed to prophecies just because it was predicted in them. And indeed, the prophets only threatened what would have happened even had they not mentioned it. The cause of things must not, therefore, be sought in them. I acknowledge that nothing happens but what has been divinely ordained; but we are now only concerned with whether their being foretold and prophesied lays a necessity on men; which I have already shown to be false.

Nor was it Christ's purpose to transfer the cause of Judas' destruction to Scripture. He only wanted to remove the occasion of stumbling which might shake weak minds. Now, His argument in removing it is that God's Spirit had long ago testified that it would happen; for we are nearly always afraid of what is new and sudden. This is a very useful warning and has a wide application. For whence comes it that the majority of men today give way to offences but because they do not remember the testimonies of Scripture by which God has well armed His people and foretold beforehand all the evils and distresses which they would see?

13. *These things I speak in the world.* Here Christ shows that He was so careful in praying to the Father for His disciples, not because He was anxious about their future state, but to provide a remedy for their anxiety. We know how our minds depend on external aids; and if these offer themselves, we seize them rapaciously and do not easily let ourselves be torn from them. So Christ prays to His Father in the presence of His disciples, not because He needed words, but to remove all doubt from them. 'I speak in the world,' He says; that is, within their hearing, that their hearts may be calm. For their salvation was already safe, placed by Christ in God's hands.

He calls it His *joy*, because the disciples had to receive it from Him; or if you want it more briefly, because He is its author, cause and pledge. For in us there is nothing but fear and disquiet; in Christ alone is there peace and joyousness.

I have given them thy word; and the world hated them, because they are not of the world, even as I am not of the world. I pray not that thou shouldest take them from the world, but that thou shouldest keep them from the evil one. They are not of the world, even as I am not of the world. Sanctify them in the truth: thy word is truth. As thou didst send me into the world, even so send I them into the world. And for their sakes I sanctify myself, that they themselves also may be sanctified in truth. (14-19)

14. *I have given them thy word.* He commends the disciples to His Father in another way. They needed His help because of the world's hatred. At the same time, He says that the cause of this hatred is that they have embraced God's Word, which the world cannot bear. As if He had said, 'It is for Thee to protect those who are hated by the world because of Thy Word.' We must now bear in mind what we have just heard, that the purpose of this prayer is that Christ's joy may be fulfilled in us. Therefore, as often as the rage of the world is kindled against us, so that we seem on the brink of destruction, let us learn at once to set against it this shield, that God will never forsake those who labour for the Gospel.

He says that His disciples *are not of the world* because those whom He regenerates by His Spirit are separated from the world. God will not let His sheep wander among wolves, but will show Himself to be their Shepherd.

15. *I pray not that thou shouldest take them.* He teaches what the safety of the godly consists in. It is not that they are free from all vexations and cultivate ease and pleasure, but that in the midst of

danger they remain safe by God's help. For He does not tell the Father what is expedient, but rather has a care for their weakness, that they may, by the way which He prescribes, moderate their wishes, which mostly go too far. In short, He does not promise His disciples the grace of the Father to relieve them of all anxiety and toil, but to furnish them with unconquerable strength against their adversaries and not to let them be overwhelmed by the great number of battles which they will have to endure. If we want to be kept according to the rule which Christ laid down, we must not desire immunity from evils or pray to God to convey us straightway into blessed rest, but must remain content with the certain assurance of victory and meanwhile resist bravely all the evils from which Christ prayed to His Father that we might have a happy issue. In short, God does not take His people out of the world, because He does not want them to be soft and slothful; but He delivers them from evil that they may not be overwhelmed. For He wishes them to fight, but does not allow them to be mortally wounded.

16. *They are not of the world.* He reiterates that the whole world hates them, that the heavenly Father may more kindly help them; and at the same time He states that this hatred does not come from their fault, but because the world hates God and Christ.

17. *Sanctify them.* This sanctification comprehends God's kingdom and righteousness. That is, when God renews us by His Spirit, and confirms in us the grace of renewal and continues it to the end. Therefore, He first asks that the Father would sanctify the disciples; that is, that He would consecrate them entirely to Himself and defend them as His sacred property. Next, He describes the means of sanctification, and not without reason. For fanatics chatter emptily about sanctification but pass over God's truth, by which He consecrates us to Himself. Again, as there are others who talk a lot of nonsense about the truth and yet neglect the Word, Christ expressly says that the truth by which God sanctifies His sons exists nowhere but in the Word.

Word here means the teaching of the Gospel, which the apostles had already heard from the mouth of their Master and which they were afterwards to proclaim to others. In this sense, Paul says that 'the Church has been cleansed with the washing of water by the word of life' (Eph. 5.26). True, it is God alone who sanctifies, but as the Gospel is His power to salvation to everyone who believes (Rom. 1.16), whoever departs from it as the means must needs become more and more defiled.

Truth is here taken by way of eminence for the light of heavenly wisdom in which God manifests Himself to us that He may conform us to His image. It is true that the outward preaching of the Word does not of itself effect this, for the reprobate wickedly profane it. But let us remember that Christ is speaking of the elect, whom the Holy Spirit efficaciously regenerates by the Word. Now, as the apostles were not completely without this grace, we should infer from Christ's words that sanctification is not instantly completed in us on the first day, but that we advance in it throughout the whole course of our life until at last God puts off our flesh and fills us with His righteousness.

18. *As thou didst send me.* He confirms His prayer by another argument; namely, because He has the same calling in common with the apostles. He says, 'I now appoint them to an office which I have hitherto held by thy command. Therefore, they need to be equipped with the power of thy Spirit, that they may be equal to such a burden.'

19. *And for their sakes I sanctify myself.* By these words He explains more clearly from what source that sanctification flows which is accomplished in us by the teaching of the Gospel. It is because He consecrated Himself to the Father that His holiness might come to us. For as the blessing is spread to the whole harvest from the first-fruits, so God's Spirit cleanses us by the holiness of Christ and makes us partakers of it. And not by imputation alone, for in that respect He is said to have been made to us righteousness (I Cor. 1.30); but He is also said to have been made to us sanctification, because He has, so to say, presented us to His Father in His own person (*in sua persona*) that we may be renewed to true holiness by His Spirit. Although this sanctification belongs to the whole life of Christ (*ad totam Christi vitam*), it shone brightest in the sacrifice of His death; for then He appeared as the true High Priest who consecrated the Temple, the altar, all the vessels and the people by the power of His Spirit.

Neither for these only do I pray, but for them also that believe on me through their word; that they may all be one; even as thou, Father, art in me, and I in thee, that they also may be one in us: that the world may believe that thou didst send me. And the glory which thou hast given me I have given unto them; that they may be one, even as we are one; I in them, and thou in me, that they may be perfected into one; that the world may know that thou didst send me, and lovedst them even as thou lovedst me. (20-23)

20. *Neither for these only do I pray.* He now extends His prayer, which had hitherto embraced only the apostles, to all the disciples of the Gospel who shall be to the end of the world. Here, indeed, is a remarkable basis for confidence. For if we believe in Christ through the teaching of the Gospel, we should not doubt at all that we are

already gathered with the apostles into His faithful protection, so that not one of us shall perish. This prayer of Christ is a calm haven, and whoever retreats into it is safe from all danger of shipwreck. It is as if Christ had taken a solemn oath that our salvation will be His care and study.

He began with His apostles, that their salvation, which we know to be certain, might make us more certain of our own salvation. Therefore, whenever Satan attacks us, let us learn to oppose this shield, that it is not for nothing that the holy word of God's Son joined us to the apostles so that the salvation of all was, as it were, bound up in one bundle. There is nothing that should stimulate us more keenly to embrace the Gospel. For as it is an inestimable blessing that we are presented to God by the hand of Christ, to be kept safe from destruction, so we ought justly to put love and care for it above all other things. In this regard the madness of the world is monstrous. All desire salvation; Christ tells us the sure way of obtaining it, from which if anyone turns aside there remains for him no good hope; and yet hardly one in a hundred condescends to receive what was so kindly offered.

But the form of speech must be noticed. Christ prays *for all* who shall believe in Him. He reminds us by these words that our faith should be directed to Him, as we have said more than once already. The clause which follows, *through their word*, well expresses the power and nature of faith and at the same time is a familiar confirmation to us who know that our faith is founded on the Gospel taught by the apostles. Let the world condemn us a thousand times; this alone is sufficient, that Christ knows us to be His own and commends us to the Father. But woe to the Papists, whose faith is so far from this rule, that they are not ashamed to vomit forth this accursed blasphemy that everything in scripture is ambiguous and equivocal! The tradition of the Church is their only authority in faith. But let us remember that the Son of God, the unique Judge, approves only that faith which is conceived from the doctrine of the apostles. Moreover, the sure testimony of this will be found only in their writings.

We must also observe the saying, *to believe through the word*; which means that faith is born of hearing, because the outward preaching by men is the instrument by which God draws us to faith. Hence it follows that God is, strictly speaking, the Author of faith and men are the ministers by whom we believe, as Paul teaches in I Cor. 3.5.

21. *That they all may be one.* He again places the end of our happiness in unity, and justly. For the ruin of the human race is that, alienated from God, it is also broken and scattered in itself. Conversely, therefore, its restoration lies in its proper coalescence in one

body (*in corpus unum rite coalescat*); as Paul sees in Eph. 4.3, 16 the perfection of the Church in believers being joined together in one Spirit,
and says that apostles, prophets, evangelists and pastors are given to
restore and build up the body of Christ until it arrives at the unity of
faith. And therefore he exhorts believers to grow into Christ, who
is the Head from whom the whole body, joined together and connected by every bond of supply according to the operation in the
measure of every part, makes increase of it to edification. Wherefore,
whenever Christ speaks of unity, let us remember how foul and
horrible is the world's scattering apart from Him. Next let us learn
that the beginning of a blessed life is when we are all governed and live
by the one Spirit of Christ.

Again, we must learn that, whenever Christ declares in this chapter
that He is one with the Father, He does not speak simply of His divine
essence, but that He is called one in His person as Mediator and inasmuch as He is our Head. Many of the fathers interpreted these words
absolutely, as meaning that Christ is one with the Father because He
is the eternal God. But the Arian controversy made them seize on
detached passages and twist them to a foreign sense. But Christ's
design was very different from that of raising us to a bare speculation
on His divinity. For He reasons from the end that we ought to be one,
because otherwise the unity He has with the Father would be empty
and barren. To comprehend aright what it meant that Christ and the
Father are one, take care not to deprive Christ of His person as Mediator.
But consider Him rather as He is the Head of the Church, and join
Him to His members. Thus the connexion will best be preserved;
that, if the unity of the Son with the Father is not to be fruitless and
useless, its power must be diffused through the whole body of believers. From this, too, we infer that we are one with Christ; not
because He transfuses His substance into us, but because by the power
of His Spirit He communicates to us His life and all the blessings He
has received from the Father.

That the world may believe. Some explain *the world* as the elect who
were then still dispersed. But since the word 'world' all through this
chapter means the reprobate, I am more inclined to take a different
view. It happens that immediately afterwards He separates the same
world which He now mentions from all His people.

The verb *to believe* was imprecisely used by the Evangelist for 'to
know'; that is, when unbelievers, convicted by their own experience,
perceive the heavenly and divine glory of Christ. Hence, believing
they do not believe; for this feeling does not penetrate into the inward
attitude of the heart. And it is a just vengeance from God that the
splendour of the divine glory dazzles the eyes of the reprobate, because

they are unworthy of a genuine and clear view of it. Afterwards He uses the verb *to know* in the same sense.

22. *And the glory which thou hast given me I have given unto them.* Observe that such a pattern of perfect blessedness was expressed in Christ that He had nothing for Himself alone but rather was rich to enrich His believers. Our happiness lies in having God's image, which was blotted out by sin, restored and reformed in us. Christ is not only, as the eternal Word of God, His lively image (*imago*), but even on His human nature, which He has in common with us, the imprint (*effigies*) of the Father's glory has been engraved, that He might transform His members to it. Paul also teaches us this in II Cor. 3.18: 'We all, with unveiled face, beholding the glory of God, are transformed into the same image as from glory to glory.' Whence it follows that none is to be reckoned among Christ's disciples unless there is seen the glory of God impressed on him by the likeness (*effigie*) of Christ as by the seal of a ring. To the same purpose are the words that follow:

23. *I in them, and thou in me.* He wants to teach that in Him dwells all the fulness of blessings and that what was hidden in God is now made plain in Him, that He may pass it on to His people; as the water flowing from the fountain through various channels waters the fields everywhere.

And lovedst them. He means that this is a most brilliant sign and excellent pledge of God's love towards the godly, which the world is forced willy-nilly to feel when the heavenly Spirit dwelling in them sends forth rays of righteousness and holiness. There are innumerable other ways, indeed, in which God daily testifies to us how He loves us; but the mark of adoption rightly excells them all. He likewise adds *and lovedst them even as thou lovedst me.* By these words He wished to indicate the cause and origin of His love. For the comparative particle should be taken as causal, as if He were saying, 'Because thou lovedst me'. For the title of beloved belongs to Christ alone. But following on this, the heavenly Father has the same love for all the members as for the Head, so that He loves none but in Christ. An apparent contradiction arises here, however. For, as we have seen elsewhere, Christ declares that the infinite love of God towards the world was the reason why He gave His only-begotten Son. If the cause must precede the effect, we infer that God the Father loved men outside of Christ; that is, before He was appointed the Redeemer. I reply: In that and similar passages love means the mercy with which God was moved towards the unworthy, and even towards His enemies, before He reconciled them to Himself. It is a wonderful goodness of God and incomprehensible to the human mind, that He was benevolent

towards men whom He could not but hate and removed the cause of
the hatred that there might be no obstruction to His love. And indeed,
Paul tells us that we are loved in a double sense in Christ. First,
because the Father chose us in Him before the creation of the world
(Eph 1.4). Secondly, because in Him also God has reconciled us to
Himself and shown that He is gracious to us (Rom. 5.10). See how
we are both enemies and friends until atonement has been made for
our sins and we are restored to favour with God! But when we are
justified by faith, we begin properly to be loved by God as children
by a Father. The love by which Christ was appointed as the one in
whom we should be freely chosen before we were born and while we
were still ruined in Adam, is hidden in the bosom of God and far
exceeds the grasp of the human mind. None will ever feel that God
is favourable to him unless he understands that God is appeased in
Christ. But as all taste for God's love vanishes when Christ is taken
away, we may safely conclude that, since by faith we are engrafted
into His body, there is no danger that we shall be cut off from the
love of God; for this foundation cannot be overturned—that we are
loved because the Father has loved Him.

> *Father, those whom thou hast given me, I will that, where I am, they
> also may be with me; that they may behold my glory, which thou hast
> given me: for thou lovedst me before the foundation of the world. O
> righteous Father, the world knew thee not, but I knew thee; and these
> knew that thou didst send me; and I made known unto them thy name,
> and will make it known; that the love wherewith thou lovedst me may
> be in them, and I in them. (24-26)*

24. *I will that, where I am.* 'To will' is put for 'to desire'; for it is a
prayer, not of direction, but of request. But it may be understood in
two ways: Either, that He wishes the disciples to enjoy His external
presence; or, that God would at last take them into the heavenly
kingdom to which He goes before them.

That they may behold my glory. Some expound this as enjoying
participation in the glory which Christ has. Others explain it as
knowing by the experience of faith what Christ is and how great His
majesty is. After careful consideration, I think that Christ is speaking
of the perfect happiness of the godly; as if He said that His desire
would not be satisfied till they have been received into heaven. They
refer the beholding of the glory to the same thing. At that time they
saw Christ's glory as a man shut up in the dark obtains a feeble half-
light through small crevices. Christ now wishes that they shall go on
to enjoy the full brightness of heaven. In short, He asks that the

Father will lead them by uninterrupted progress to the full view of His glory.

For thou lovedst me. This also agrees far better with the person of the Mediator than with Christ's naked divinity. It would be harsh to say that the Father loved His Wisdom. And though we were to accept that, the context leads us in another direction. There is no doubt that Christ spoke as the Head of the Church when earlier He prayed that the apostles might be joined with Him and might see the glory of His kingdom. Now He says that the Father's love is its cause; and therefore it follows that He was beloved inasmuch as He was appointed as the Redeemer of the world. With such a love did the Father embrace Him before the creation of the world, that He might be the one in whom the Father would love His elect.

25. *O righteous Father.* He contrasts His disciples to the world so as to magnify the Father's commendation and favour of them. For it is right that they who alone know the God whom the whole world rejects should be singled out. And Christ rightly commends with a special affection those whom the world's unbelief did not prevent from acknowledging as God. By calling Him *righteous Father,* Christ triumphs over the world and its malice. It was as if He said, 'However proudly the world may despise or reject God, it takes nothing from Him and cannot prevent the honour of His righteousness from remaining sound.' He shows by these words that the faith of believers should be so founded on God that, though the whole world should attack it, it would never fail. Just as today we must condemn the Pope of unrighteousness that we may assert the praise of God.

Moreover, Christ does not simply say that God was known by the disciples, but sets up two steps: First, that He Himself has known the Father; and secondly, that the disciples knew that He was sent by the Father. But as He at once adds that He has manifested to them the name of the Father, He praises them, as I have said, for the knowledge of God which differentiates them from the rest of the world. Yet we must note the order of faith as it is described here. Properly, the Son who came from the bosom of the Father alone knows Him. Therefore, all who desire to approach God must betake themselves to Christ meeting them and must devote themselves to Him. And when He has been known by the disciples, He will at last raise them to God the Father.

26. *And I made known unto them thy name, and will make it known.* Christ indeed discharged the office of Teacher; but in order to make known the Father, He used the secret revelation of the Spirit and not only the sound of His voice. He therefore means that He taught the apostles efficaciously. Moreover, as their faith up till then was very

weak, He promises greater progress in the future and thus prepares them to hope for more abundant grace of the Spirit. Although He speaks of the apostles, we should draw from this a general exhortation to study to advance constantly and not think that we have run so well that we have not still a long journey ahead of us while we are surrounded by the flesh.

That the love wherewith, etc. That is, that Thou mayest love them in Me, or that the love with which Thou hast loved Me may be shed on them. For strictly speaking, the love with which God loves us is none other than that with which He loved His Son from the beginning, so as to make us also acceptable and lovable to Him in Christ. And indeed, as was said a little earlier, we are, so far as we are concerned and apart from Christ, hated by God and He only begins to love us when we are united to the body of His beloved Son. It is an inestimable privilege of faith that we know that Christ was loved by the Father for our sake, that we might be made partakers of the same love and that for ever.

But the phrase *and I in them* must be noted. It teaches us that we are included in that love which He mentions only by Christ dwelling in us. For as the Father cannot look upon His Son without at the same time having before His eyes His whole body, so, if we wish to be beheld in Him, we must truly be His members.

CHAPTER EIGHTEEN

When Jesus had spoken these words, he went forth with his disciples over the brook Kidron, where was a garden, into the which he entered, himself and his disciples. Now Judas also, which betrayed him, knew the place: for Jesus oft-times resorted thither with his disciples. Judas then, having received the band of soldiers, and officers from the chief priests and the Pharisees, cometh thither with lanterns and torches and weapons. Jesus therefore, knowing all the things that were coming upon him, went forth, and saith unto them, Whom seek ye? They answered him, Jesus of Nazareth. Jesus saith unto them, I am he. And Judas also, which betrayed him, was standing with them. When therefore he said unto them, I am he, they went backward, and fell to the ground. (1-6)

1. *When Jesus had spoken these words.* In this story John passes over many things which we read in the other three Evangelists; and he does so deliberately, as his purpose was to collect many things worth remembering about which they are silent. Therefore let readers learn from the other Evangelists what is lacking here.

Over the brook Kidron. In the Greek an article is prefixed to Kidron as if the brook took its name from the cedars; but this has probably crept in by error. For the valley or brook Kidron is often mentioned in Scripture. The place was so called from its darkness, for it was an overhung valley and shady. On that point, however, I do not dispute but only suggest what is more probable.

The chief thing is the Evangelist's intention in locating the place. For he wanted to show that Christ went to his death willingly. He came to a place which He knew was known to Judas. Why did He do this, but to offer Himself of His own accord to the traitor and His enemies? Nor did He make a mistake through thoughtlessness, for He foreknew all that was to happen. John afterwards adds that He went forward to meet them. He was therefore not coerced to death, but willingly bore it that He might be a voluntary sacrifice. For without obedience atonement would not have been gained for us.

Moreover, He entered the garden, not to seek a hiding-place, but to have freedom and time to pray. That He prayed three times for death to be averted is not inconsistent with that voluntary obedience which I have mentioned. For He had to fight against difficulties that

He might overcome at the last. Now that He has subdued the fear of death, He advances to death freely and willingly.

3. *Judas then.* The fact that Judas came supplied with soldiers and such a large guard is a sign of a bad conscience, which always trembles needlessly. It is certain that the band of soldiers was obtained from the Governor, who also sent a captain in command of a thousand infantry. For a garrison was stationed in the city in case of sudden mutinies, and the Governor himself kept a body-guard wherever he went. The rest were servants of the priests. But John mentions the Pharisees separately because they were more enraged, as if they cared more about religion.

4. *Jesus therefore, knowing.* The Evangelist expresses more clearly how readily Christ went down to His death, but at the same time relates the great power which He breathed with a single word, that we might learn that the ungodly had no power over Him except so far as He permitted. He replies mildly that it is He whom they seek; and yet, as if they had been struck by a violent hurricane, or rather by lightning, He prostrates them to the ground. He did not lack the power, then, to restrain their force if He wished, but He wanted to obey His Father, by whose decree He knew that He was called to die.

Again, we may infer from this how dreadful and terrifying to the ungodly Christ's voice will be when He shall ascend His tribunal to judge the world. He then stood as a lamb prepared for the sacrifice, His majesty to all appearances utterly gone; and yet at a single word His armed and determined enemies suddenly fall down. And He hurls no dread curse against them, but only replies, *I am he.* What then will it be when He shall come, not to be judged by man, but as the Judge of the living and the dead? Not in that low and contemptible state, but in heavenly glory and with His angels? He then meant to give an example of that efficacy which Isaiah ascribes to His voice (11.4). Among other mighty works of Christ, the prophet declares in chapter 11 that He will strike the earth with the rod of His mouth and will slay the wicked by the breath of His lips. True, Paul places the fulfilment of this prophecy at the end (II Thess. 2.8), but we daily see the ungodly with all their rage and pride struck down at Christ's voice; and when those men fell down who had come to bind Christ, there was exhibited a visible symbol of that fear which all the ungodly feel within themselves, will they or not, when Christ speaks by His ministers. Moreover, as this was, as it were, accidental to the voice of Christ, the property of which is to raise unhappy men who were lying in death, He will undoubtedly display towards us such power as to exalt us even to heaven.

Again therefore he asked them, Whom seek ye? And they said, Jesus of Nazareth. Jesus answered, I told you that I am he: if therefore ye seek me, let these go their way: that the word might be fulfilled which he spake, Of those whom thou hast given me I lost not one. (7-9)

7. *Again therefore he asked them.* From this it appears how strong is that blindness with which God strikes the minds of the ungodly, and how horrible is their dulness when through God's just judgment they are bewitched by Satan. Cattle and asses show some kind of feeling if they fall down, but those men, when they had seen Christ's divine power openly manifested, go on as securely as if they had not seen in Him even the shadow of a man; nay, Judas himself is unmoved. Therefore, let us learn to fear God's judgment, by which the reprobate are delivered into Satan's hand and become more stupid than the brute beasts. Nor can it be doubted that Satan carried them away with wild fury to such reckless audacity. For no madness drives a man so violently as this sort of blindness. When the ungodly have been given over to a reprobate mind, they rush against God as if they were dealing with a fly. They feel His power, but not so as to give way; for they would rather be broken a hundred times than yield. In short, their malice is a veil to stop them heeding the light of God, and their obstinacy makes them harder than stones, so that they never let themselves be tamed.

8. *I told you that I am he.* Here we see how God's Son not only submits voluntarily to death, so that He may blot out our transgressions by His obedience, but also how He discharges the office of a good Shepherd in protecting His flock. He sees the threat of the wolves and does not wait till they come at the sheep given to His care, but attacks them in good time. Whenever, then, either wicked men or devils spring upon us, let us not doubt that He is at hand to aid us in the same way. Yet by His example Christ has prescribed to shepherds a rule to follow if they want to discharge their office aright.

9. *I lost not one.* This sentence seems inappropriately quoted, since it relates to their souls rather than their bodies. For Christ did not keep the apostles safe to the last; but what He did do was that, amidst incessant dangers and even in the midst of death, He kept safe their eternal salvation. I reply: The Evangelist is not speaking merely of their bodily life but means rather that Christ, by sparing them for a time, had an eye to their eternal salvation. Let us consider how great their weakness was up to now. What do we think they would have done if they had been on trial for their life? Since, therefore, Christ did not want them to be tried beyond the strength which He had given them, He rescued them from eternal destruction. And from

this we may gather a general doctrine: Although He may try our faith by many temptations, we shall never come into the ultimate danger without Him supplying us also with strength to overcome. And indeed we see how He continually bears with our weakness when He advances to repel so many attacks of Satan and the ungodly, because He sees that we are not yet equal and ready for them. In short, He never brings His people to the battle unless they have been well trained; so that even in perishing they do not perish, because there is gain provided for them in death and in life.

Simon Peter therefore having a sword drew it, and struck the high priest's servant, and cut off his right ear. Now the servant's name was Malchus. Jesus therefore said unto Peter, Put up the sword into the sheath: the cup which the Father hath given me, shall I not drink it? So the band and the chief captain, and the officers of the Jews, seized Jesus and bound him, and led him to Annas first; for he was father in law to Caiaphas, which was high priest that year. Now Caiaphas was he which gave counsel to the Jews, that it was expedient that one man should die for the people. (10-14)

10. *Simon Peter therefore.* He now describes the foolish zeal of Peter, who tried to defend his Master unlawfully. Spiritedly and bravely, indeed, he runs great risk for Christ's sake. But as he does not consider what his calling demands and what God permits, his action is so far from deserving praise that he is severely reproved by Christ. But let us learn that, in the person of Peter, Christ condemns everything that men dare to attempt arbitrarily. This lesson is especially worth noticing, for nothing is commoner than to defend everything that we do under the cloak of zeal, as if it were unimportant whether God approved or not what men think to be right, whose whole prudence is mere vanity.

Even if we saw nothing blameworthy in Peter's zeal, we ought to be satisfied simply that Christ declares that He is displeased. But we see that it was no thanks to him that Christ was not kept from death and that His name was not a perpetual disgrace. For in offering violence to the captain and the soldiers, he acts like a footpad; for he resists the power ordained by God. Christ was already hated more than enough by the world, and this single act might have given colour to all the calumnies which His enemies falsely brought against Him. Again it was exceedingly thoughtless in Peter to try to prove his faith by the sword, while he could not do so by his tongue. When he is called to make confession, he denies; but now unbidden by his Master he raises a riot. Warned by such a striking example, let us learn to moderate our zeal. And as the wantonness of our flesh ever itches to dare more than God commands, let us learn that our zeal will turn out badly whenever we dare to undertake anything beyond God's Word. It will sometimes happen that the beginnings please us; but we shall pay for our rashness in the end. Let obedience be the basis of all that we undertake. We are also warned that those whose task it is to take up Christ's cause, do not always act so skilfully as not to slip into some fault. Therefore we should the more earnestly pray to the Lord to guide us in every action with the Spirit of prudence.

11. *Put up the sword.* By this command Christ reproves Peter's action. But we must note the reason. A private man was not permitted to rise against those invested with public authority. For this can be inferred from the other three, who relate Christ's general statement, 'he that strikes with the sword shall perish by the sword.' We must therefore beware not to repel our enemies by force or arms even when they provoke us unjustly, except so far as the laws and public rights permit. Whoever goes beyond the bounds of his calling, even should he gain the applause of the whole world, will never have his action approved by God.

The cup which the Father hath given me. This seems a special reason why Christ had to be silent; that He might be led as a lamb to the slaughter. But it serves as an example, for the same patience is demanded from all of us. Scripture compares afflictions to drinking a draught. As the master of a house distributes meat and drink to his children and servants, so God has this right over us, that He treats each one as seems good to Him; and as to whether He cheers us by prosperity or humbles us by adversity, He is said to give a sweet or bitter draught. The draught appointed to Christ was to suffer the death of the cross for the reconciliation of the world. He therefore says that He must drink the cup which His Father measured out and delivered to Him.

In the same way we ought also to be prepared for enduring the cross. And yet the fanatics should not be heeded, who assert that we must not seek remedies for sicknesses or any other kinds of affliction, lest we reject the cup which God holds out. We know that we must die once and we must be prepared for death. But because the time of our death is unknown to us, the Lord allows us to defend our life by the aids which He Himself has appointed. Diseases must be patiently borne, however grievous they be to our flesh; but while they are not yet certainly fatal we should seek alleviation of them. Only we must be careful not to attempt anything but what God's Word permits. In short, provided it remains always fixed in our hearts that the Lord's will be done, we are not failing to drink the cup which He has given us, even when we seek deliverance from the evils which press upon us.

12. *So the band and the chief captain.* It might seem absurd that Christ, who prostrated soldiers by His voice, now lets Himself be taken. For if He meant to surrender to His enemies at last, what need to perform such a miracle? But the demonstration of divine power profited in two respects. For it serves to remove the stumbling-block of our thinking that Christ yielded as if overcome through weakness; and secondly, it proves that He suffered death completely voluntarily. So far as was useful, then, He asserted His power against His enemies; but when it was necessary to obey the Father, He restrained Himself that He might become a victim. And let us remember that the body of the Son of God was bound, that our souls might be loosed from the cords of sin and Satan.

13. *And led him to Annas.* The other Evangelists omit this, since it adds little to the substance of the story; for nothing memorable was enacted there. Perhaps the convenience of the place led them to keep Christ in Annas' house till the high priest called the council.

The high priest that year. He does not mean that the office of high priest was annual, as many have wrongly thought; but that Caiaphas was high priest at that time, as Josephus plainly states. By the injunction of the Law this rank was perpetual and ended only at death; but ambition and internal revolts caused Roman governors at their own will to depose one high priest for another who could prevail by money or favour. Thus, Vitellius deposed Caiaphas and appointed Jonathan the son of Annas as his successor.

14. *Which gave counsel to the Jews.* The Evangelist repeats Caiaphas' statement, which we heard earlier. For God used the unclean mouth of a treacherous and wicked high priest to utter a prophecy (John 11.50), just as He guided Balaam's tongue contrary to his intentions, so that he was forced to bless the people whom he wanted to curse as a favour for King Balak (Num. 24.5).

And Simon Peter followed Jesus, and so did another disciple. Now that disciple was known unto the high priest, and entered in with Jesus into the court of the high priest; but Peter was standing at the door without. So the other disciple, which was known unto the high priest, went out and spake unto her that kept the door, and brought in Peter. The maid therefore that kept the door saith unto Peter, Art thou also one of this man's disciples? He saith, I am not. Now the servants and the officers were standing there, having made a fire of coals; for it was cold; and they were warming themselves: and Peter also was with them, standing and warming himself. (15-18)

15. *And another disciple.* A weak conjecture has deceived some into thinking that this disciple was John, because he is accustomed to speak

of himself anonymously. But how could John, a lowly fisherman, have been friendly with a lofty high priest? And how was it possible for him, one of Christ's household, to frequent the house of the high priest? It is more probable that this was not one of the twelve, but is called a disciple because he had embraced the teaching of the Son of God.

John is not precise in arranging the story, but is satisfied with a brief summary. For when he has related that Peter once denied Christ, he brings in other things and later returns to the other two denials. Inattentive readers were led by this to conclude that the first denial took place in the house of Annas. But the words do not say this, but express clearly that it was the high priest's maid who constrained Peter to deny Christ. We must therefore understand that when Christ was brought to the high priest, not just anyone was let in, but that the disciple who was known to him asked as a favour that Peter might be admitted. Now there is no doubt that they both followed Christ from godly zeal. But since Christ had deliberately declared that He spared Peter and the others, it would have been far better for him who was so weak to groan and pray in some dark corner than to go among men. He now greedily takes up the duty from which Christ had released him. But when it comes to the confession of faith, in which he should have stood fast, even to death, he fails. Therefore, we must always see what the Lord demands of us, that those who are weak may not undertake what is unnecessary.

17. *The maid therefore saith unto Peter.* Peter is allowed into the high priest's hall, but it costs him very dear; for even at his entry he is constrained to deny Christ. When he stumbles so disgracefully at the threshold, the emptiness of his boasting is exposed. He had boasted that he would prove an invincible fighter and triumphant unto death. Now, at the voice of one maid, and that without any threatening, he is confounded and throws down his weapons. Here is a true sample of human strength. Certainly all the strength that seems to be in men is smoke which is at once blown away by a breath. Out of the battle we are unreasonably spirited; but experience shows how foolishly and emptily we boast. Even when Satan launches no attacks, we invent empty terrors for ourselves, which disturb us before the time. The voice of a mere woman terrified Peter. And what about us? Do we not sometimes start at the sound of a leaf falling? An empty appearance of danger out of range daunted Peter, and are we not daily led away from Christ by childish absurdities? In short, our courage is such that it fails of its own accord when there is no enemy. And thus God punishes human arrogance by softening fierce minds. A man filled, not with fortitude, but wind, promises that he

will gain an easy victory over the whole world. And yet he is terrified at the shadow of a thistle. Wherefore, let us learn to be brave only in the Lord.

I am not. This does not seem an absolute denial of Christ; but since Peter is afraid to confess that he is one of His disciples, it is equivalent to denying that he has anything to do with Him. This should be carefully observed, lest anyone should think that he has escaped by acting speciously when he fails only indirectly to confess his faith.

18. *And Peter also was with them.* When the Evangelist adds that Peter was standing near the fire with the officers and servants, this helps to connect the narrative, as we shall see later. But from it appears how great was Peter's stupidity when he carelessly warmed himself with a crowd of wicked men after denying his Master. Although it is possible that he was restrained by fear lest, in leaving the high priest's house, he should fall into another similar danger.

The high priest therefore asked Jesus of his disciples, and of his teaching. Jesus answered him, I have spoken openly to the world; I ever taught in synagogues, and in the temple, where all the Jews come together; and in secret spake I nothing. Why askest thou me? ask them that have heard me, what I spake unto them: behold, these know the things which I said. And when he had said this, one of the officers standing by struck Jesus with his hand, saying, Answereth thou the high priest so? Jesus answered him, If I have spoken evil, bear witness of the evil: but if well, why smitest thou me? Annas therefore had sent him bound unto Caiaphas the high priest. (19-24)

19. *The high priest therefore asked Jesus.* The high priest interrogates Christ as if He were some trouble-maker, who had split the Church by collecting disciples; and he interrogates Him as if He were a false prophet who had tried to corrupt the purity of the faith by novel and perverse teaching. Christ had fulfilled His teaching office and does not begin a new defence; but so as not to abandon the cause of truth, He shows that He is ready to defend all that He had taught. Yet He also reproves the high priest's shamelessness in asking about what was well known as if it were doubtful. It was not enough for them to reject the offered Redeemer and the salvation promised with Him, but at the same time they condemn all the exposition of the Law.

20. *I have spoken openly to the world.* Some have fallen into the childish error of thinking that Christ's reply condemns those who expound the Word of God privately and in their own chambers when the tyranny of the ungodly forbids them to do so publicly. Christ is not discussing what is lawful or not. He only intended to refute the shameless malice of Caiaphas. This passage seems to conflict with

another saying of Christ, where He tells the disciples to proclaim on the housetops what He spoke in their ears (Matt. 10.27); and again when He declares that it is not given to all to hear the mysteries of the kingdom of God, and that therefore He confers this grace only on the twelve (Matt. 13.11). I reply: When He denies in this passage that He spoke anything in secret, it refers to the substance, which was constant, although the form of teaching was variable. For He did not speak differently among the disciples to teach them something different; nor did He act cunningly, as if He deliberately meant to hide from the people what He spoke to a few indoors. He could testify with a good conscience that He had openly declared and sincerely proclaimed the substance of His teaching.

22. *When he had said this.* This is put in to tell us how great was the rage of Christ's enemies and how tyrannical their rule; and secondly, what sort of discipline existed among the priests. They sit as judges, but they are as cruel as wild beasts. There is assembled a council, where the utmost gravity should have prevailed. And yet a mere officer is so presumptuous, in the midst of the trial and in the presence of the judges, as to strike the accused, who was not found guilty in any respect. It is not surprising, therefore, if Christ's teaching is condemned by such a barbarous assembly, from which all justice, even all humanity and decency, are banished

23. *If I have spoken evil.* That is, 'If I have sinned, accuse Me, and then when the case has been tried I can be punished according to the offence. For this procedure is not lawful; quite a different order and moderation belongs to the courts.' Christ, therefore, complains that He has been done a grievous injury if He has not sinned; and that, even if He had sinned, they ought to act lawfully and not with violence.

But Christ does not seem to observe what He elsewhere enjoins upon His followers. He does not offer the right cheek to him that struck Him on the left. I reply: In Christian patience it is not always required that he who has been struck should swallow the injury without a word; but first, he should bear it calmly, and secondly he should give up all thought of revenge and try to overcome evil with good. The spirit of Satan is already too prompt to impel the wicked to hurt without anybody provoking them. Therefore, they expound Christ's words foolishly who interpret them as commanding us to provoke those who are already too bent on mischief. He merely means that each of us should be more ready to bear a second injury than to retaliate for the first. There is nothing, therefore, to prevent a Christian man from expostulating when he has been unjustly treated, so long as his mind is free from anger and his hand clean from vindictiveness.

24. *Annas therefore had sent him bound.* This sentence is to be read

as a parenthesis. When he has said that Christ was taken to Annas' house and then, as if the meeting of the priests had been held there, gone on with his story, he now tells us that Christ was taken to the high priest's house. But as the tense of the verb has deceived many, I have preferred to translate it by the pluperfect, 'Had sent'.

Now Simon Peter was standing and warming himself. They said therefore unto him, Art thou also one of his disciples? He denied, and said, I am not. One of the servants of the high priest, being a kinsman of him whose ear Peter cut off, saith, Did not I see thee in the garden with him? Peter therefore denied again: and straightway the cock crew. (25-27)

25. *He denied.* How frightful is Peter's stupor! When he has denied his Master, he is not only untouched by any feeling of repentance, but hardens himself by his very licence in sinning. If each of them had asked him one after another, he would not have hesitated to deny a thousand times. This is how Satan carries wretched men away when he has dislodged them. We must also notice the detail narrated by the other Evangelists, that he testified with an oath that he did not know Christ. So it is with many every day. At first the fault will not be so great. Then it becomes a habit. At last conscience is put to sleep. In the end he who has accustomed himself to despise God will think nothing unlawful for him, but will dare to go to extremes. The best thing is to beware in good time, so that he who is tempted by Satan may not allow himself the slightest indulgence while he is still sound.

27. *Straightway the cock crew.* The Evangelist mentions the crowing of the cock to let us know that Peter was warned by God in the nick of time. This is why the others say that he then remembered the Lord's words; though Luke relates that the mere crowing of the cock did not move Peter until Christ looked at him. Thus, once anybody has begun to fall through the impulse of Satan, no voice, no sign, no warning will recall him until the Lord Himself casts His eyes upon him.

They lead Jesus therefore from Caiaphas into the palace: and it was early; and they themselves entered not into the palace, that they might not be defiled, but might eat the passover. Pilate therefore went out unto them, and saith, What accusation bring ye against this man? They answered and said unto him, If this man were not an evil-doer, we should not have delivered him up unto thee. Pilate therefore said unto them, Take him yourselves, and judge him according to your law. The Jews said unto him, It is not lawful for us to put any man to death:

that the word of Jesus might be fulfilled, which he spake, signifying by what manner of death he should die. (28-32)

28. *They lead Jesus therefore.* The trial which the Evangelist mentions was held before dawn. Yet there is no doubt that they had their agitators everywhere in the city to inflame the people. Thus the rage of the populace was suddenly kindled, as if with one consent they all demanded Christ's death. The trial was conducted by the priests— not that it was in their power to sentence Him, but that when they had crushed Him by their pre-judgment they might deliver Him to be judged as if everything were already known about Him. The Romans called *Praetorium* both the governor's house and the judgment-seat where he usually executed justice.

That they might not be defiled. In abstaining from all defilement that they may be purified according to the command of the Law and eat the Lord's passover, their religion is to be approved. But there are two faults, both gross: They do not consider that they bear more pollution within themselves than they can contract from entering any place, however profane; and also, they carry their care about minutiæ to excess and neglect the most important things. Paul says that to the defiled and unbelievers nothing is pure, for their minds are polluted (Titus 1.15). But these hypocrites, rich as they are in malice, ambition, deceit, cruelty and avarice, so that they well-nigh infect heaven and earth with their stench, fear only external pollutions. This is an intolerable mockery, thinking they please God so long as they do not contract defilement from contact with something unclean, though they have forgotten true purity.

Hypocrisy labours under another fault. It is careful to cultivate ceremonies, but securely neglects the most important things. For God commanded to the Jews those ceremonies contained in the Law simply that they might become accustomed to a love and zeal for true holiness. Besides, nowhere in the Law were they forbidden to enter the house of a Gentile. This was just a precaution handed down by the fathers, lest any should imprudently become unclean from an impure house. But those fine interpreters of the Law swallow a camel while they carefully strain at a gnat. It is usual with hypocrites to think it more criminal to kill a flea than a man. This fault is close to the other, of far preferring human traditions to the sacred commandments of God. They want to keep themselves pure in order to eat the passover properly. But they confine uncleanness within the walls of the governor's house, and they do not hesitate, in the sight of heaven and earth, to harry an innocent man to death. In short, they observe a shadowy passover with feigned and false reverence, but not only profane the true passover with their sacrilegious hands, but try so far as they can to overwhelm it in eternal ruin.

29. *Pilate therefore went out unto them.* An irreligious man is not unwilling to permit a superstition which he smiles at and despises. But in the main point of the case he performs the office of a good judge in ordering them to put forward their accusation if they have any. The priests, however, not having sufficient authority to condemn one whom they declare guilty, merely reply that he ought to abide by their existing judgment. For they indirectly complain of Pilate that he has not enough confidence in their integrity. They say, 'Why do you not of yourself take it as settled that he whom we prosecute is worthy of death?' This is how the ungodly, whom God has raised to a high degree of honour, are, so to say, blinded by their own splendour and permit themselves to do whatever they like. And how drunken pride is! They want Christ to be regarded as a malefactor merely on their accusation. But if we look at the facts, what evil deeds are found in Him except that He cured every kind of disease, put devils to flight out of men, made paralytics and the lame to walk, restored sight to the blind, hearing to the deaf and life to the dead? These were the facts, and they were well convinced of them. But as I said just now, nothing is harder than to arouse men drunken with pride to judge soundly and with an orderly mind.

31. *According to your law.* Without doubt, Pilate is scandalized at their barbarism and violence and reproaches them that the form of condemnation which they urged was abhorrent to the common law of all nations and humane feelings. He also censures them for boasting that they had a law handed to them by God.

Take him yourselves, he says ironically, for he would not have let them sentence a man to death. It is as if he said, 'If you had the power, he would be instantly dragged to execution unheard. Is this the equity of your law, to condemn a man without any crime?' Thus the ungodly, falsely taking God's name, subject His holy doctrine to the reproaches of enemies, and an occasion of slander is eagerly seized by the world.

It is not lawful for us. They are mistaken who think that the Jews refuse an offer Pilate made to them. Rather, knowing that he had said in mockery, 'Take him yourselves,' they expostulate, 'You would not let us. You are the judge; do your duty.'

32. *That the word of Jesus, etc.* Finally the Evangelist adds that this had to be done that Christ's prediction might be fulfilled, 'The Son of man shall be delivered into the hands of the Gentiles' (Matt. 20.19). And if we want to read the story of Christ's death with profit, the chief point is to look to God's eternal counsel. The Son of God is set

before the judgment-seat of a mortal man. If we think that this was done by men's will and do not raise our eyes to God, our faith must needs be put to shame and confounded. But when we realize that our condemnation is blotted out by Christ's, because it pleased the heavenly Father thus to reconcile mankind to Himself, we are raised on high by this alone and boldly and without shame glory even in Christ's ignominy. In each part of this narrative, let us learn to turn our eyes to God as the Author of our redemption.

Pilate therefore entered again into the palace, and called Jesus, and said unto him, Art thou the King of the Jews? Jesus answered, Sayest thou this of thyself, or did others tell it thee concerning me? Pilate answered, Am I a Jew? Thine own nation and the chief priests delivered thee unto me: what hast thou done? Jesus answered, My kingdom is not of this world: if my kingdom were of this world, then would my servants fight, that I should not be delivered to the Jews: but now is my kingdom not from hence. (33-36)

33. *Pilate therefore entered again.* Probably many things were said by both sides, about which the Evangelist is silent. And this is clear from the others. But our Evangelist here particularly insists on a single point—that Pilate carefully investigated whether Christ was brought to trial justly or not. Before the people, inflamed with sedition, everything was in an uproar. Therefore he goes into the palace. He intends to acquit Christ; but, that He may obey His Father, Christ offers Himself for condemnation. This is why He replies so briefly. With a favourable judge, who would willingly have hearkened to Him, it was not difficult for Him to plead His cause. But He considers for what purpose He came into the world and what He is now called to by the Father. He is therefore deliberately silent that He may not escape death.

Art thou the King of the Jews? Pilate would never of himself have asked about the kingdom if the Jews had not brought this charge against Christ. But Pilate takes up what was most serious so that, if he disposes of this, he may acquit the prisoner. Christ's answer suggests that there is no basis for the accusation. It thus contains an indirect refutation; as if He said, 'It is ridiculous to bring that charge against me, for not even the slightest suspicion of it falls on me.' Pilate seems to have taken it amiss that Christ asked him why he suspected Him. He therefore reproaches Him angrily that all the evil comes from His own nation. He says, 'I am sitting as judge, but it is your own country-men and not foreigners who accuse you. There is no need for you to involve me in your squabbles. I and the Romans would let you live in peace; but you make trouble among yourselves and I am reluctantly forced to take a part in them.'

36. *My kingdom is not of this world.* With these words He confesses that He is *a King*; but so far as was necessary to prove His innocence, He extenuates and excuses the slander. For He denies that there is any conflict between His kingdom and political order. As if He said, 'I am accused falsely of trying to stir up a disturbance or overturn the state. I have preached about the kingdom of God, but that is spiritual, and so you have no reason to suspect me of aspiring after a kingdom.' This was Christ's defence before Pilate; but the same doctrine is useful for all the godly to the end of the world. For if Christ's kingdom were earthly, it would be unstable and changeable, since the fashion of this world passeth away. But since it is called heavenly, we are assured of its perpetuity. Thus, if the whole world were overthrown, our consciences will, if they are directed to Christ's kingdom, remain firm not only amid shakings and convulsions but even dreadful ruin and destruction. If we are tyrannically harassed by the ungodly, our salvation nevertheless stands fast in Christ's kingdom, which is not subject to the will of men. In short, although the world is continually tossed by numberless tempests, the kingdom of Christ, in which we should seek tranquillity, is separated from them.

We are also taught the nature of this kingdom. If it made us happy after the flesh and brought us riches, luxuries and all that is to be desired for the present life, it would smack of the earth and the world. But as it is, although our state is wretched in appearance, our substantial happiness remains unimpaired. We also learn who belongs to this kingdom—those who are renewed by God's Spirit and practise the heavenly life in holiness and righteousness. Yet it must be observed that it is not denied that the kingdom of Christ is in this world. For we know that it has its seat in our souls, as Christ says elsewhere, 'The kingdom of God is within you' (Luke 17.21). But strictly speaking, although the kingdom of God dwells within us, it is a stranger to the world, since its state is completely different.

Then would my servants fight. He proves that He did not aim at an earthly kingdom, because no one is incited, no one takes up arms. For if a private man claims a kingdom, he has to gain power by means of seditious men. Nothing of this sort is seen in Christ. Therefore, it follows that He is not an earthly king.

But it is asked at this point whether it is lawful to defend Christ's kingdom by arms. For when princes are commanded to kiss the Son of God, not only are they enjoined to submit to His authority in their private position but also to use all the power they possess in defending the Church and maintaining godliness.

I reply: First, those who draw the conclusion that the teaching of the Gospel and the pure worship of God should not be defended by arms are wrong and ignorant. For Christ argues only from the facts of the present case how frivolous were the calumnies of the Jews. Secondly, although godly kings defend Christ's kingdom by the sword, it is done differently from the way in which worldly kingdoms are defended. For Christ's kingdom, which is spiritual, must be founded on the teaching and power of the Spirit. In the same way is its building effected; for neither the laws and edicts of men nor their punishments reach into consciences, yet this does not prevent princes from incidentally defending Christ's kingdom, partly by establishing external discipline and partly by lending their protection to the Church against the ungodly. But the depravity of the world causes the kingdom of Christ to be established more by the blood of martyrs than by the aid of arms.

Pilate therefore said unto him, Art thou a king then? Jesus answered, Thou sayest that I am a king. To this end have I been born, and to this end am I come into the world, that I should bear witness unto the truth. Every one that is of the truth heareth my voice. Pilate saith unto him, What is truth? And when he had said this, he went out again unto the Jews, and saith unto them, I find no crime in him. But ye have a custom, that I should release unto you one at the passover: will ye therefore that I release unto you the King of the Jews? They cried out therefore again, saying, Not this man, but Barabbas. Now Barabbas was a robber. (37-40)

37. *Thou sayest that I am a king.* Although Pilate had already learned from His former answer that Christ claimed some kind of kingdom for Himself, He now asserts the same thing more definitely; and not content with this, He makes another statement, which is a seal, as it were, of what He had said. From this we infer that the teaching about Christ's kingdom is of great importance, since He regarded it worthy of such strong protestation.

This is no doubt a general statement: *To this end have I been born, that I should bear witness unto the truth.* But it must be applied particularly to the context. The words mean that it is natural for Christ to be truthful. Moreover, He was sent to this end by the Father. Consequently, this is His peculiar office. There is no danger, then, that our trust in Him will be deceived; for it is impossible that He to whom the office of maintaining the truth has been divinely given and in whom its care is innate by nature should teach what is untrue.

Every one that is of the truth. Christ added this, not so much to exhort Pilate (for He knew that He would gain nothing by so doing),

as to defend His doctrine against the unworthy insults to which it
had been subjected. It was as if He said, 'It is imputed to me as a
crime that I have professed to be a king. And yet this is an undoubted
truth, which is received with reverence and without argument by all
who are endowed with a right judgment and a sound understanding.'
Although He says that they are of the truth, it is not that they know
the truth naturally, but inasmuch as they are ruled by the Spirit of
God.

38. *What is truth?* It seems to some that Pilate asks through curiosity,
as irreligious men are sometimes accustomed to desire eagerly to know
something new to them and yet do not know why they wish it. For
they intend only to gratify their ears. But I rather interpret it as
disdainful. For Pilate thought himself not a little insulted that Christ
should make him out to lack all knowledge of the truth. Now we
learn in Pilate a disease common among men. Although we are aware
of our ignorance, there are few who can bear to confess it. Hence it
is that the greater part reject true doctrine. Afterwards the Lord,
who is the teacher of the humble, blinds the proud and thus inflicts
on them the punishment they deserve. From the same pride is bred
the disdain of not condescending to submit to learn, because all claim
sagacity and quickness of wit. Truth is thought a common thing.
But God declares, on the contrary, that it is far higher than the grasp
of the human mind.

The same thing happens in other respects too. The principal
articles of theology are: The curse pronounced on the human race;
the corruption of nature; the mortification of the flesh; the renewal
of life; the free reconciliation through the unique sacrifice; the imputation of righteousness, by which a sinner is accepted by God; the
illumination of the Holy Spirit. Because these things are paradoxes,
they are contemptuously rejected by the common understanding of
men. Therefore few advance in the school of God, because hardly
one in ten is found who attends to the first rudiments. And why is
this, but because they measure God's secret wisdom by their own
understanding?

But that Pilate spoke in mockery is clear from the fact that he at
once goes out. In brief, he is angry with Christ for claiming to bring
forward the truth which had lain hidden in darkness. Yet his indignation shows that the ungodly never reject the teaching of the Gospel
so captiously as not to be somewhat touched by its efficacy. For
although Pilate did not get so far as to become teachable, yet he is
forced to feel some inward pricking.

39. *But ye have a custom.* Pilate was all along pondering how he
could save Christ from death. But the fury of the people was so

fierce that he kept a middle path, so as to allay their anger. For he thought it would be enough if Christ were dismissed as a malefactor and marked with perpetual disgrace. He therefore chooses out Barabbas above all others so that by comparison with him their hatred of Christ might be softened. For Barabbas was greatly detested by them all because of his atrocious crimes. For indeed, what is more detestable than a robber? But Luke relates that he was guilty of other crimes as well.

That the Jews preferred him to Christ happened only by a singular providence of God. For it would not have behoved the Son of God to have been freed from death at so unworthy a price. Yet by His death He was thrown into the deepest ignominy, so that in consequence of the release of Barabbas He was crucified between two robbers. For He had taken upon Himself the crimes of all, which could not be expiated in any other way; and the glory of His resurrection, which quickly followed, caused His death itself to be a magnificent triumph.

Now in this custom by which the Roman governor gave to the Jews at the passover one of the criminals, there was involved a gross and base abuse. It was indeed done to celebrate the sacredness of the day, but in reality it was nothing but a shameful profanation of it. For Scripture declares that he who acquits the guilty is an abomination to God (Prov. 17.15) and therefore He is far from delighting in such perverted pardon. Let us learn by this example that nothing is more perverted than to want to serve God by our own inventions. For as soon as men begin to follow their own imaginations there will be no limits until they fall into extreme madness and openly mock God. The law for the worship of God ought therefore to be sought only in His precept.

CHAPTER NINETEEN

Then Pilate therefore took Jesus, and scourged him. And the soldiers plaited a crown of thorns, and put it on his head, and arrayed him in a purple garment; and said, Hail, King of the Jews! And they struck him with their hands. And Pilate went out again, and saith unto them, Behold, I bring him out to you, that ye may know that I find no crime in him. Jesus therefore came out, wearing the crown of thorns and the purple garment. And Pilate saith unto them, Behold the man! When therefore the chief priests and the officers saw him, they cried out, saying, Crucify him, crucify him. Pilate saith unto them, Take him yourselves and crucify him: for I find no crime in him. (1-6)

1. *Then Pilate therefore took Jesus.* Pilate keeps to his purpose. But he adds yet a second ignominy, hoping that, when Christ has been scourged, the Jews will be satisfied with this lighter punishment. When he strives so earnestly and unsuccessfully, we ought to see in this the decree of heaven by which Christ was appointed to death. Yet His innocence is frequently asserted by the judge's testimony, to teach us that, free from all guilt, He was substituted as guilty for others and bore the punishment due to the sins of others. We see in Pilate also a remarkable example of a trembling conscience. Verbally, he acquits Christ, and acknowledges that there is no guilt in Him. And yet he inflicts punishment on Him as if He were guilty. Thus, those who have not so much spirit as to defend with unshaken constancy what is right, must be driven hither and thither and distracted to opposite and conflicting opinions. We all condemn Pilate, and yet, shameful to say, how many like him the world holds who scourge Christ, not only in His members, but also in His teaching. There are many who, to save from death those who are persecuted for the Gospel, constrain them to an ungodly denial of Christ. What is this but to expose Christ to ridicule, that He may lead a dishonourable life? Others select some few parts of the Gospel which they approve of and yet rend the Gospel as a whole. They think they have done wonderfully if they correct a few gross abuses. But better that the doctrine should be buried for a while than scourged like this; for it would be re-born in spite of the devil and all tyrants. But nothing is more difficult than to restore it to its purity when once it has been corrupted.

2. *And the soldiers plaited a crown.* This was undoubtedly done on

Pilate's orders, to brand the Son of God with the mark of the crime that He had made Himself a king, and that to satisfy the rage of the Jews, as if he had been convinced that they had accused Christ rightly. Yet the soldiers indulge their wickedness and insolence more freely than the judge ordered—for the ungodly eagerly seize opportunities for doing evil whenever they are offered. But what amazing cruelty of this nation, whose minds are not moved to compassion by so sad a sight! But God governs all this to reconcile the world to Himself by the death of His Son.

6. *Take him yourselves.* He did not want to give Christ up to them or abandon Him to their passion; but he declares that he will not be an executioner for them. This is plain from the reason he adds, when he says that he finds no crime in Him—as if he had said, that he will never be persuaded to shed innocent blood for their sake. That it is only the priests and officers who demand that He shall be crucified appears from the fact that there was less madness in the people, except so far as it was afterwards stirred up by the agitators.

The Jews answered him, We have a law, and by that law he ought to die, because he made himself the Son of God. When Pilate therefore heard this saying, he was the more afraid; and he entered into the palace again, and saith unto Jesus, Whence art thou? But Jesus gave him no answer. Pilate therefore saith unto him, Speakest thou not unto me? knowest thou not that I have power to release thee, and have power to crucify thee? Jesus answered him, Thou wouldest have no power against me, except it were given thee from above: therefore he that delivered me unto thee hath greater sin. (7-11)

7. *We have a law.* They mean that they are prosecuting Christ legally (*iure*), not from passion or hatred. For they saw that Pilate had indirectly reproved them. They speak as if they were in the presence of a man ignorant of the law; as if they said, 'We are allowed to live after our own manner, and our religion does not let any man pass himself off as the Son of God.' Nor was this accusation altogether without plausibility; but they erred gravely in applying it. The general doctrine was undoubtedly true, that it was not lawful for men to assume any divine dignity, and that those who ascribed to themselves what is proper to God alone deserved to be put to death. But the spring of their error lay in Christ's person, for they did not consider with what titles the Messiah is foretold in Scripture, from which they could easily have learned that He was the Son of God; nor did they even trouble to enquire whether or not Jesus was the Messiah once promised by God. So we see that from a true principle they drew a false conclusion and reasoned badly. This example warns us

to distinguish carefully between a general doctrine and its application. Many ignorant and fickle men reject even the principles of Scripture if they have been deceived by the semblance of truth, and such a licentiousness progresses too much in the world today. Therefore let us remember so to guard against falsehood that true principles may remain sound and that the authority of Scripture may not be overturned.

On the other hand we may easily refute the ungodly in this way, when they falsely and improperly allege the testimony of Scripture and the principles which they draw from it in their evil causes. Just as today the Papists, when they extol magniloquently the authority of the Church, put forward nothing but what all the children of God are agreed on. They contend that the Church is the mother of believers, the pillar of truth, that she should be heard, that she is ruled by the Holy Spirit. None of this should be denied. But when they want to appropriate to themselves all the authority due to the Church, they wickedly and with sacrilegious presumption snatch at what does not belong to them at all. For we must ponder this application, that they merit the title of Church. And here they utterly fail. Likewise, when they rage furiously against all the godly, they excuse themselves on the pretext that they have been ordained to defend the faith and peace of the Church. But when we come to the facts themselves, it is plain to see that they have nothing less in mind than to defend true doctrine, and that nothing moves them less than a care for peace and concord, but that they only fight for their own tyranny. Those who are satisfied with general principles and do not attend to details, think the Papists attack us deservedly; but the knowledge of the cause quickly disperses their smoke screen.

8. *He was the more afraid.* These words can be explained in two ways. The first is that Pilate was afraid some blame would be attached to him if there were a riot because he had not condemned Christ. The second is that, when he had heard the name 'Son of God', his mind was touched by religion. This second sense is confirmed by what follows, that he entered into the palace again and asked Christ where He came from. For it is clear from this that he was worried and anxious, because he was afraid that he would be punished for sacrilege if he laid hands on the Son of God. We must note that when he asks where Christ comes from, he is not enquiring about His country, but it is as if he had said, 'Are you an earth-born man or some god?' I interpret this passage, therefore, that Pilate was struck with the fear of the divine. For on the one hand, he saw an insurrection boiling up, but on the other, religion obliged him not to offend God for the sake of avoiding danger. This example is most note-worthy. Christ's appearance was most disfigured; yet as soon as Pilate hears God's

name a fear comes upon him of violating God's majesty in a man
worse than mean and despicable. If reverence for God prevailed so
much in an irreligious man, must not they be thrice reprobate who
today judge of divine things in sport and jest, carelessly and without
any fear? For Pilate is evidence that men have naturally an innate
sense of religion which does not allow them to rush fearlessly wherever
they like when they are concerned with divine things. This is why I
said that those who, in dealing with the teaching of Scripture, are no
more affected by God's majesty than if they had been arguing about
a trifle (*umbra asini*), are given up to a reprobate mind. Yet they will
one day feel to their destruction what veneration is due to God's
name, which they now mock so disdainfully and insultingly. It is
terrible to relate how haughtily and fiercely the Papists condemn the
clear and proven truth of God and shed innocent blood. I ask you,
where does that drunken stupor come from, but because they do not
remember that they are dealing with God?

9. *But Jesus gave him no answer.* We must not think it strange that
Christ does not reply—at least, if we bear in mind what I said before,
that He did not stand before Pilate to plead His own cause, as they do
who want to be acquitted, but rather just to undergo judgment. For
He had to be condemned when He took our place. This is why He
makes no defence. And yet Christ's silence is not inconsistent with
Paul's words in I Tim. 6.13, 'Remember that Christ made a good
confession before Pilate.' For there He sufficiently maintained the
faith of the Gospel and His death was simply the sealing of the teaching
He had delivered. Christ did not fail to make a legitimate confession,
but He did not open His mouth to beg for an acquittal. Moreover,
there was some danger that Pilate would acquit Christ as one of the
fictitious gods, just as Tiberius wanted to place Him among the gods
of the Romans. Christ therefore rightly repudiates this foolish superstition by His silence.

10. *Knowest thou not that I have power?* This shows that the dread
which suddenly moved Pilate was transitory and had no living roots.
For now he forgets his fear and breaks out into a haughty and monstrous
contempt of God. He threatens Christ as if there were no judge in
heaven. But this must always happen with the irreligious; they shake
off the fear of God and soon revert to their own character. From this
we also infer that it is with good reason that man's heart is called
deceitful (Jer. 17.9). For although a certain fear of God dwells in it,
it also boils over with impiety. Therefore, whoever is not regenerated
by God's Spirit, although for a little while he shows reverence for
the divinity, will soon betray by the contrast of his deeds that this fear
was a pretence.

Now we see in Pilate an instance of a proud man who is driven to madness by his ambition. When he wants to increase his power, he deprives himself of all praise and reputation for justice. He acknowledges that Christ is innocent, and therefore puts himself on a level with a robber who boasts that he can cut his victim's throat. Thus wicked consciences, where faith and the true knowledge of God do not reign, must needs be tempestuous, with the various affections of the flesh in conflict within them. In this way God avenges Himself strikingly on men's pride, when they go beyond their limits and claim infinite power. By condemning themselves of injustice they stamp themselves with the worst reproach and disgrace. No blindness is greater than that of pride; and it is not surprising, inasmuch as pride feels the hand of God, which it strikes against, as an avenger. Let us therefore remember that we should not indulge in thoughtless and empty boastings lest we become ridiculous; and especially that those who hold high rank should keep themselves within moderation and not be ashamed of being subject to God and liable to His laws.

11. *Thou wouldest have no power.* Some expound this generally, that nothing is done in the world save by God's permission; as if Christ said that Pilate, who thinks he can do everything, will do no more than God allows. That the world is ruled by God's will is indeed true, as also that, however much the ungodly may strive, they cannot move a finger but as God's secret power regulates. But to my mind they are better who restrict this passage to the office of the magistrate. For in these words Christ censures Pilate's foolish arrogance in praising himself as if his power had not been from God. It was as if He said, 'You claim everything for yourself, as if you had not one day to render an account to God. But it was not without His providence that you were made a judge. Consider then that His heavenly throne is far higher than yours.' Nor could a more apt admonition be found to repress the excess of those who rule over others, that they may not abuse their authority. The father thinks he can do as he likes towards his children, the husband towards his wife, the master towards his servants, the prince towards his people, unless they look to God, who wishes them to be ruled by a certain law.

Therefore he that delivered me. Some think this makes the Jews more guilty than Pilate in that, with a wicked hatred and malicious treachery, they, private persons and not endowed with lawful authority, are enraged against a righteous man. But I reckon that it makes their guilt graver and less excusable for another reason—they force a divinely appointed ruler to serve their passions. For it is a great sacrilege to abuse a holy ordinance of God to something wicked. The robber who with his own hand cuts the throat of some poor traveller, is justly abhorred; but he who under the cloak of a trial kills an innocent man is the more wicked. Yet He does not magnify their guilt to extenuate Pilate's, for He does not compare them, but rather includes them in the same guilt, because they equally pollute a holy power. The only difference is that He aims directly at the Jews and accuses Pilate indirectly who obeys their desire.

Upon this Pilate sought to release him: but the Jews cried out, saying, If thou release. this man, thou art not Caesar's friend: every one that maketh himself a king speaketh against Caesar. When Pilate therefore heard these words, he brought Jesus out, and sat down on the judgment-seat at a place called The Pavement, but in Hebrew, Gabbatha. Now it was the Preparation of the passover: it was about the sixth hour. And he saith unto the Jews, Behold, your King! They therefore cried out, Away with him, away with him, crucify him. Pilate saith unto them, Shall I crucify your King? The chief priest answered, We have no king but Caesar. Then therefore he delivered him unto them to be crucified. They took Jesus therefore, and led him away. (12-17a)

12. *Upon this Pilate sought.* Although Pilate does not act wisely, and is ruled by ambition rather than by a care for justice and therefore is wretchedly irresolute, yet his moderation is praiseworthy in that, when Christ severely reproves him, he does not fly into a passion but is the more disposed to release Him. He is judge, and yet he meekly allows the accused to be his critic. Hardly one in a hundred will be found who so calmly bears a rebuke, even from an equal.

Thou art not Caesar's friend. They extort Christ's condemnation from Pilate by threats. For they could attack him with nothing more repugnant or frightening than to make him suspect of disloyalty to Caesar. They say, 'You show that you do not care about Caesar's authority if you acquit one who has tried to overthrow everything.' This wickedness at last broke Pilate's resolution, which had so far only been shaken by their furious cries. Nor is it without good reason that the Evangelist so carefully examines and insists on these details. For it is very important for us to know that Pilate did not condemn Christ before he himself had acquitted Him three or four times, so that we may learn from it that it was not on His own account that He was condemned but for our sins. We may also learn how voluntarily He underwent death, when He refused to use the judge's favourable disposition to Him. It was this obedience that made His death a sacrifice of sweet savour for expiating all sins.

13. *And sat down on the judgment-seat.* From this appears how Pilate was pulled this way and that, as if he had been one actor playing two parts. He mounts the judgment-seat to sentence Christ to death in

the solemn form; and yet he declares openly that he does so reluctantly
and against his conscience. He calls Christ 'King' ironically, implying
that it was a trivial charge that the Jews had brought against Him; or
rather, to check their fury, he tells them it would bring disgrace on
the whole nation if a report were spread that one of that race had
been condemned for aspiring to the kingdom.

When the Evangelist says that the Hebrew name of that place was
Gabbatha, he refers to the Aramaic or Syriac language which was then
in common use. For in Hebrew *Gabah* means 'elevated'. It therefore
behoved Christ to be condemned from a high place, that He, coming
from heaven as the supreme Judge, may acquit us at the last day.

14. *About the sixth hour.* The Evangelists seem to differ and contradict one another in reckoning the time. The other three say that there
was darkness from the sixth hour while Christ was hanging on the
cross. Mark also expressly says that it was the third hour when
sentence was pronounced on Him. But it is not difficult to resolve this.
It is plain enough from other passages that the day was then divided
into four parts, as the night also had four watches. Consequently, the
Evangelists sometimes allot only four hours to a day and extend each
hour to three. At the same time they reckon the space of one hour
which was drawing to a close as belonging to the next. According to
this computation, John relates that Christ was condemned at the sixth
hour, because the time of day was drawing on to the sixth hour or the
second part. Hence we infer that Christ was crucified at the sixth
hour or thereabouts. For as he says later, the place was near the city.
The darkness began between the sixth and the ninth hours and lasted
until the ninth hour, when Christ died.

15. *We have no king but Caesar.* It shows a fearful madness that the
priests, who should have been well versed in the Law, reject the
Messiah, in whom was contained all the salvation of the people, on
whom all the promises depended and on whom the whole of their
religion was founded. Indeed, by rejecting Christ they renounced the
grace of God and all blessings. We see what madness had seized them.
Let us imagine that Christ was not the Christ. Even so they have no
excuse for acknowledging no other king but Caesar. For first, they
revolt from God's spiritual kingdom. And secondly, they prefer the
tyranny of the Roman Empire, which they abhorred, to a just government such as God had promised. Thus the ungodly fly from Christ
and not only deprive themselves of eternal life but bring down on
themselves all kinds of misery. On the other hand, the one happiness
of the godly is to be subject to the kingship of Christ whether, in the
flesh, they are set under a just and lawful government or under the
oppression of tyrants.

16. *He delivered him unto them.* Their importunity certainly forced Pilate to deliver Christ. And yet this was not done in a riot; but He was condemned in the solemn form, for there were two robbers who were tried and condemned with Him to be crucified. But John uses this word to confirm that Christ, although not convicted of any crime, was given up to the implacable cruelty of the people.

And he went out, bearing the cross for himself, unto the place called The place of a skull, which is called in Hebrew Golgotha: where they crucified him, and with him two others, on either side one, and Jesus in the midst. And Pilate wrote a title also, and put it on the cross. And there was written, JESUS OF NAZARETH, THE KING OF THE JEWS. This title therefore read many of the Jews: for the place where Jesus was crucified was nigh to the city: and it was written in Hebrew, and in Latin, and in Greek. The chief priests of the Jews therefore said to Pilate. Write not, The King of the Jews; but that he said, I am King of the Jews. Pilate answered, What I have written I have written. (17b-22)

17. *He went out . . . unto the place.* The details related here are of great value, not only for the truth of the narrative, but also to build up our faith. We must seek righteousness in the satisfaction made by Christ. To prove that He is the sacrifice for our sins, He wished both to be led out of the city and to be hanged on a tree. For, according to the command of the Law, the custom was that the sacrifices whose blood was shed for sin should be carried out of the camp; and the same Law pronounces accursed whoever is hanged on a tree (Lev. 6.30; 16.27; Deut. 21.23). Both were fulfilled in Christ, that we might be fully assured that our sins have been expiated by the sacrifice of His death, that He was made subject to the curse to redeem us from the curse of the Law (Gal. 3.13), that He was made sin that we might be the righteousness of God in Him (II Cor. 5.21), that He was led out of the city to carry with Him and take away from the midst our stains, which were laid upon Him (Heb. 13.12).

To the same purpose is what follows about the robbers. As if the savagery of the punishment were not enough of itself, He is hanged in between two robbers. It was as if He had not only deserved to be classed with others, but had been the most wicked and detestable of them all. But we must always remember that the ungodly executioners of Christ did nothing but what had been determined by God's hand and counsel. For God did not surrender His Son to their passions but wanted Him to be sacrificed as a victim of His own will and determination. And if there were the best reasons for the counsel of God in all the things which He willed His Son to suffer, we ought to consider both the dreadful weight of His wrath against sin and the immeasurable greatness of His goodness towards us. In no other way could our guilt be removed than by the Son of God becoming an outcast for us. We see Him forced to an accursed place, as if He had been polluted by a mass of all evil, that there He might appear accursed before God and men. We are assuredly too stupid if we do not see plainly in this mirror how much God abominates sin. And we are worse than stones if we do not tremble at such a judgment.

But when, on the other hand, God declares that our salvation was so dear to Him that He did not spare His only-begotten Son, what an abundance of goodness and grace do we here behold! Whoever ponders aright the causes of Christ's death, together with the fruit it yields us, will not regard the preaching of the cross as foolishness as the Greeks did, nor as an offence, like the Jews (I Cor. 1.23), but rather as an inestimable example and pledge of the divine power, wisdom, righteousness and goodness.

When John says that the name of the place was *Golgotha*, he takes it from the Aramaic or Syriac language. But the name is derived from *galgal*, which is 'to roll', because a skull is round like a ball or globe.

19. *And Pilate wrote a title also.* The Evangelist relates a memorable action of Pilate after he had passed sentence. It was perhaps the custom to affix titles when malefactors were executed, that the cause of the punishment might be known to all as an example. But what is unusual in Christ is that the title affixed to Him has no disgrace. Pilate's intention was to avenge himself indirectly on the Jews, who by their obstinacy had extorted from him the unjust execution of an innocent man, and in Christ's person to condemn the whole nation. So he does not brand Christ with the mark of any crime of His own.

But God's providence, which governed the pen of Pilate, looked far higher. It did not occur to Pilate to praise Christ as the author of salvation and the Nazarene[1] of God and the King of a chosen people. But God dictated to him this commendation of the Gospel, even though he did not understand what he wrote. By the same secret moving of the Spirit it came about that the title was proclaimed in three languages. For it is unlikely that this was the common practice; but the Lord showed by this prelude that the time was already at hand when the name of His Son should be made known everywhere.

21. *The chief priests . . . therefore said to Pilate.* They feel that they are offensively snubbed and want the title changed, so that the disgrace might rest on Christ and not on the nation. But they do not conceal the great hatred of the truth that infects them; they cannot bear the smallest spark of it. Thus Satan always stirs up his servants to try to

---

[1] Consecrated to God. (Vide *Comm. Harm. of Gosp.* on Matt. 2.23.)

extinguish, or at least to smother, by their own darkness the divine light as soon as it shines even slightly. Pilate's firmness must be ascribed to the providence of God, for there is no doubt that they attacked his resolution in various ways. Let us know, therefore, that he was divinely kept, so that he remained unbending. Pilate did not yield to the priest's prayers nor allow himself to be corrupted by them, but God testified by his mouth the firmness of His Son's kingdom. And if in the writing of Pilate Christ's kingdom was shown to be so firm that it could not be shaken by all the stratagems of its enemies, what ought we to think of the testimonies of the prophets whose mouths and hands God consecrated to Himself?

Pilate's example tells us also of our duty to be constant in defending the truth. A heathen does not retract what he has written truly about Christ, even if without understanding or intention. How great then our shame, if we are terrified by threats or perils and withdraw from the profession of His doctrine which God has sealed in our hearts by His Spirit. Moreover, we must note how detestable is the Papist tyranny, which forbids the people to read the Gospel and all the Scriptures. Pilate, a reprobate man and in other respects an instrument of Satan, was yet by a secret inspiration appointed to be a herald of the Gospel that he might proclaim a short summary of it in three languages. Where then shall we place those who, so far as they can, suppress the knowledge of it; for they show that they are worse than Pilate?

The soldiers therefore, when they had crucified Jesus, took his garments, and made four parts, to every soldier a part; and also the coat: now the coat was without seam, woven from the top throughout. They said therefore one to another, Let us not rend it, but cast lots for it, whose it shall be: that the scripture might be fulfilled, which saith, They parted my garments among them, and upon my vesture did they cast lots. These things therefore the soldiers did. (23-24)

23. *The soldiers therefore.* The other Evangelists also mention the division of Christ's garments among the soldiers. There were four soldiers, who divided among themselves the other garments. But the seamless coat could not be divided and they cast lots for it. To fix our minds on the consideration of God's purpose, the Evangelists tell us that in this respect also the Scripture was fulfilled. But the passage which they cite from Psalm 22.18 is inappropriately applied to the present subject. For although David there complains that he was a prey to his enemies, he designates his goods as a whole under the metaphor of garments. It was as if he said in one word that he had been despoiled and stripped by wicked men. When the Evangelists disregard the image, they depart from the natural meaning. But we

must understand in the first place that the Psalm should not be re-stricted to David, as is plain from many statements and especially from a clause which says, 'I will praise thy name among the Gentiles,' which must be expounded of Christ. It is not surprising therefore if that which was obscurely delineated in David is seen more distinctly in Christ, inasmuch as the truth must be clearer than its type.

Moreover, let us learn that Christ was stripped of His garments that He might clothe us with His righteousness. His naked body was exposed to the insults of men that we may appear with glory before the judgment-seat of God. As to the allegorical meaning to which some have twisted this passage, that heretics tear up Scripture; it is too far-fetched. But I would not object to the comparison that, as Christ's garments were once divided by ungodly soldiers, so today there are perverse men who mutilate with their alien inventions the whole of Scripture, with which Christ is clothed to show Himself to us. But the dishonesty of the Papists, joined to their dreadful blasphemy against God, is quite intolerable. They say that Scripture is torn in pieces by heretics but that the coat, i.e. the Church, remains entire; and thus, having rejected the authority of Scripture, they demonstrate that the unity of faith consists in the mere title of the Church, as if the unity of the Church were itself founded elsewhere than on belief in Scripture. When, therefore, they separate faith from Scripture, so that it may be attached to the Church alone, they not only despoil Christ by such a divorce but tear up His body in cruel sacrilege. And although we might grant them that the coat without seam is a symbol of the Church, they will not gain their point, for it will still need to be proved that the Church is in their power; and of this they show no sign at all.

But there were standing by the cross of Jesus his mother, and his mother's sister, Mary the wife of Clopas, and Mary Magdalene. When Jesus therefore saw his mother, and the disciple standing by, whom he loved, he saith unto his mother, Woman, behold, thy son! Then saith he to the disciple, Behold, thy mother! And from that hour the disciple took her unto his own home. (25-27)

25. *But there were standing.* The Evangelist mentions incidentally that while Christ obeyed the Father, He did not neglect His humane duty towards His mother. It is true that He was forgetful of Himself and of everything, so far as was necessary for discharging His obedience to His Father; but, that duty performed, He did not fail in what He owed to His mother. From this we learn how dutifulness towards God and men should be practised. When God calls us to anything, it often happens that our parents, wife or children call us away in a different

direction, so that we cannot satisfy all alike. If we make men equal to God, our thinking is astray. We must therefore prefer God's command, worship and honour. After this we must, so far as is lawful, give men their rights also.

And yet the commands of the first and second tables of the Law never conflict, as they seem to at first sight. But we must begin with the worship of God and then give a lower place to men. This is the significance of the statement: 'He that hateth not father or mother for my sake is not worthy of me' (Luke 14.26; Matt. 10.37). We should therefore so devote ourselves to men as not at all to hinder our worship and obedience to God. When we have obeyed God it will be right and proper to think about parents, wife and children; just as Christ cares for His mother, but from the cross to which He has been called by His Father's decree.

Yet, if we consider the details of time and place, Christ's dutifulness towards His mother was wonderful. I pass over the extreme tortures of His body. I pass over the reproaches. And although frightful blasphemies against God exhausted His mind with incredible sorrow, and although He sustained a dreadful contest against eternal death and the devil, none of this prevented His solicitude for His mother.

We may also learn from this passage the honour which God in the Law commands us to pay our parents. Christ appoints the disciple as His substitute and delivers His mother to him to support and care for. Hence it follows that the honour due to parents does not consist in mere veneration but in all necessary duties.

On the other hand, we should consider the faith of those holy women. Indeed, in following Christ to the cross, they showed no common affection; but if they had not been armed by faith they could never have been present on this stage. As for John himself, we infer that, although his faith was smothered for a little while, it was not completely extinguished. Now it is shameful if dread of the cross deters us from following Christ when the glory of His resurrection is set before our eyes, whereas the women saw nothing but its disgrace and cursing.

He calls *Mary* either the wife or the daughter of Cleophas. I prefer the latter. He says that she was the sister of Jesus' mother, according to the Hebrew idiom which calls all blood relations brothers. We see that Mary Magdalene was not delivered from seven devils for nothing, for she showed herself a faithful disciple of Christ to the end.

26. *Woman, behold, thy son!* It is as if He said, 'Hereafter I shall not dwell on the earth and be able to discharge to you My filial duties. Therefore, I set this man in My place to perform My duty.' He means the same thing when He says to John, 'Behold, thy mother!'

For by these words He commands him to regard her as a mother and care for her as his mother.

Some think that He does not call her 'mother' but only 'woman' so as not to inflict a deeper wound of sorrow on her heart. I do not reject this; but another conjecture is no less probable, that Christ wanted to show that now that He had completed the course of human life, He puts off the condition in which He had lived and enters into the heavenly kingdom where He will rule over angels and men. For we know that Christ's custom always was to recall believers from looking at the flesh. This was especially necessary at His death.

27. *The disciple took her unto his own home.* It is a sign of the reverence of the disciple for his Master that John obeys Christ's command. Hence also it appears that the apostles had families. For John could not have shown hospitality towards the mother of Christ or kept her at his own home if he had not had a house and a settled mode of life. They are therefore fools who think that the apostles left their property and came to Christ naked and empty. But they are worse than mad dreamers who place perfection in begging.

After this Jesus, knowing that all things are now finished, that the scripture might be accomplished, saith, I thirst. There was set there a vessel full of vinegar: so they put a sponge full of the vinegar around hyssop and brought it to his mouth. When Jesus therefore had received the vinegar, he said, It is finished: and he bowed his head, and gave up his spirit. (28-30)

28. *Jesus knowing.* John purposely passes over many things related by the other three. He now describes the last act, in which there was much of importance. When John says that a vessel was placed there, he speaks as if it were usual. There has been much controversy on this subject. But I agree with the view that it was a kind of drink administered to accelerate death when wretched men had been tortured long enough. But Christ does not ask for drink until all things have been accomplished; and thus He testifies His infinite love for us and His inestimable care for our salvation. No words can fully express what bitter sorrows He endured; and yet He does not desire to be free from them until He has satisfied the justice of God.

But how can He say that all things were accomplished when the chief part was still lacking, that is, His death? I reply: John includes what was soon to follow. Christ had not yet died, not yet risen again. But He saw that there was nothing to prevent Him advancing to death and resurrection. And so by His example He instructs us in perfect obedience, that it may not be hard for us to live according to His will, even though we must languish amid the worst sorrows.

That the scripture might be accomplished. It is easy to infer from the other Evangelists that the passage referred to is Psalm 69.21: 'They gave me gall for my meat, and in my thirst they gave me vinegar to drink.' It is, of course, a metaphor, by which David means not only that they denied him the help he needed, but that they cruelly multiplied his distresses. But there is nothing absurd that what had been dimly delineated in David was more clearly exhibited in Christ. For from it we perceive more fully how much the truth differs from figures, when the things which David suffered only figuratively appear openly and, as it were, in substance in Christ. To show that He was the one whom David represented, Christ chose to drink the vinegar; and that to strengthen our faith.

Those who invent an allegorical meaning for the word *thirst*, care more for ingenuity than true edification; and the Evangelist clearly refutes them when he says that Christ asked for vinegar at the point of death.

When he says that the sponge was put around hyssop, understand that they fastened it to a twig of that shrub to raise it to Christ's mouth.

30. *It is finished.* He repeats the same word that He had used before. Now this word of Christ is most memorable, for it teaches us that the whole accomplishing of our salvation and all the parts of it are contained in His death. We have already insisted that His resurrection is not separate from His death; but Christ only means to keep our faith to Himself alone, that it shall not turn aside hither and thither. The meaning therefore is that everything contributing to men's salvation is in Christ and is not to be sought elsewhere; or—what is the same thing—that the perfection of salvation is contained in Him.

But there is an implied antithesis here. Christ contrasts His death with the ancient sacrifices and all the figures; as if He said, 'Of all that was practised under the Law, there was nothing that could of itself atone for sins, appease the wrath of God and obtain justification. But now the true salvation is shown and exhibited to the world.' To this doctrine is attached the abolition of all the ceremonies of the Law. For it would be perverse to pursue shadows when we have the body in Christ.

If we assent to this Word of Christ, we should be satisfied with His death alone for salvation, and we are not free to seek help elsewhere. But the whole Papist religion aims at leading men to think up for themselves innumerable ways of seeking salvation. Hence we infer that it is full of abominable sacrileges. More especially, this Word of Christ condemns the abomination of the Mass. All the sacrifices of the Law ceased of necessity, for the salvation of men has been completed by the unique sacrifice of the death of Christ. By what right,

then, or excuse can the Papists say that they are authorized to set up
a new sacrifice to reconcile God to men? They reply that it is not a
new sacrifice but that same which Christ offered. But the refutation
is easy. In the first place, they have no mandate for offering it. Secondly, when Christ had made the one oblation He proclaimed from
the cross that all was finished. They are worse than forgers, therefore,
who treacherously corrupt and violate the testament sealed with the
holy blood of the Son of God.

And gave up his spirit. All the Evangelists carefully relate Christ's
death, and not without cause. For from it comes our trust of life and
hence, also, a secure triumphing over death, since the Son of God has
endured it in our place, and struggling with it has emerged the victor.
But we must note the phraseology which John uses, and which teaches
us that all the godly who die with Christ safely commit their souls to
the guardianship of God, who is faithful and will not suffer to perish
what He has undertaken to preserve. There is this difference between
the dying of the children of God and of the reprobate, that the reprobate breathe out their souls unthinkingly, but believers commit it as
a precious trust to God's protection, who will faithfully guard it till
the day of the resurrection. The word *spirit* is used here for the
immortal soul, as plainly appears.

*The Jews therefore, because it was the Preparation, that the bodies
should not remain on the cross upon the sabbath (for the day of that
sabbath was a high day), asked of Pilate that their legs might be broken,
and that they might be taken away. The soldiers therefore came, and
brake the legs of the first, and of the other which was crucified with him:
but when they came to Jesus, and saw that he was dead already, they
brake not his legs: howbeit one of the soldiers with a spear pierced his
side, and straight way there came out blood and water. And he that hath
seen hath borne witness, and his witness is true: and he knoweth that
he saith true, that ye also may believe. For these things came to pass,
that the scripture might be fulfilled, A bone of him shall not be broken.
And again another scripture saith, They shall look on him whom they
pierced.* (31-37)

31. *Because it was the Preparation.* This narrative also can edify our
faith, first because it shows that what had been foretold in Scripture
(Zech. 12.10) is fulfilled in the person of Christ, and secondly, because
it contains a mystery of no common value. The Evangelist says that
the Jews asked for the bodies to be taken down from the crosses. This
had certainly been enjoined by the Law of God; but the Jews, like the
hypocrites they were, attend only to minutiae and pass over the greatest
crimes without hesitation. For to celebrate their Sabbath religiously,

they are anxious about outward pollution. And yet they do not consider what a shocking crime it is to take the life of an innocent man. Thus we saw a little earlier that they did not enter into the governor's palace, lest they should be defiled—while the whole land was polluted by their wickedness. Yet by them the Lord effects what was of the greatest moment for our salvation, that by a wonderful arrangement Christ's body remains uninjured and blood and water flow from His side.

For the day of that sabbath was a high day. A reading more often received is, 'and that day was high.' But the reading I have adopted is given by many ancient and approved manuscripts. Let readers choose for themselves. If you read ἐκείνου in the genitive, sabbath must be taken as the week—as if the Evangelist said that the feast day of that week was very solemn because of the passover. Now the Evangelist speaks of the following day, which began at sunset; and they were the more scrupulous about leaving the bodies still hanging. But if we would rather read it in the nominative, 'and that sabbath day was a high day,' the meaning will be nearly the same in substance, but there would be this difference in the words, that the coming of the passover would make that sabbath more holy.

33. *But when they came to Jesus.* That they broke the legs of the two robbers and found Christ already dead and so did not touch His body is shown as an extraordinary work of the divine providence. Irreligious men will, of course, say that it happens naturally that one man dies quicker than another. But anyone who considers the story as a whole will be forced to ascribe it to the secret counsel of God that a speedier death than could have been expected saved Christ from having His legs broken.

34. *Howbeit one of the soldiers . . . with a spear.* The soldier pierced His side with a spear to see if He were dead. But God had a higher purpose, as we shall see. It was a childish invention of the Papists to manufacture Longinus out of 'lance', as a man's proper name; and, that their story should be complete, talked nonsense about this soldier having been blind but receiving his sight and being converted to the faith. And so they have put him in the active list of the saints. Since their prayers, as often as they do call upon God, are propped up on such intercessors, what, I ask you, can they ever obtain? But they who despise Christ and seek the help of the dead deserve the devil to drive them to masks and ghosts.

There came out blood and water. Some are deceived into imagining that this was a miracle. It is natural for congealed blood to lose its red colour and become like water. It is also well known that water is contained in the membranes next the heart. But they have been led astray by the Evangelist insisting so carefully that water flowed with the blood, as if he were relating something unusual and unnatural. But his intention was quite different. He wanted to adapt his narrative to the scriptural testimonies which he adds, and more especially that believers might infer from it what he says elsewhere, that Christ came with water and blood. By these words he means that Christ brought with Him the true atonement and true washing. For forgiveness of sins and righteousness and the purity of the soul were prefigured in the Law by the two symbols of sacrifices and ablutions. In sacrifices blood atoned for sins and was the price paid to appease God's wrath. Ablutions were tokens of true purity and the remedy for purging uncleanness and removing the stains of the flesh.

So that faith may no longer rest on these rudiments, John declares in the fifth chapter of his epistle that both these graces are fulfilled in Christ. Here he sets before us a visible symbol of the fact. The sacraments which Christ left to His Church have the same end. In baptism is shown to us the purgation and purity of the soul, consisting in newness of life. The Supper is the pledge of a perfect atonement. But they are very different from the ancient figures of the Law, for they set forward Christ as present, whereas the figures of the Law pointed to Him as still absent and at a distance. For this reason I do not object to Augustine writing that our sacraments have flowed from Christ's side. For when baptism and the holy Supper lead us to Christ's side, that by faith we may draw from Him as from a well what they figure, we are truly washed from our pollutions and renewed to a holy life and live before God, redeemed from death and delivered from condemnation.

36. *A bone of him shall not be broken.* This testimony is taken from Exod. 12.46 and Num. 9.12, where Moses is treating of the paschal lamb. John takes it for granted that the lamb was a symbol of the true and only sacrifice by which the Church was to be redeemed. Nor is this inconsistent with the fact that it was sacrificed as the memorial of a redemption already made. For as God wished it to celebrate that benefit, so also He promised in it the future spiritual deliverance of the Church. Therefore Paul without hesitation applies to Christ the rule which Moses lays down about eating the lamb. From this analogy or similitude faith draws no common advantage, for it beholds, in all the ceremonies of the Law, the salvation exhibited in Christ. This is also John's aim in saying that Christ was not only the pledge of our redemption but also its price, inasmuch as we see accomplished in Him what was formerly exhibited to the ancient people under the figure of the passover. By this also the Jews are warned to seek in Christ the substance of everything that the Law figured but did not actually perform.

37. *They shall look on him whom they pierced.* This passage is violently distorted by those who try to expound it literally of Christ. This is not the Evangelist's purpose in quoting it. Rather he shows that Christ is the God who had complained through Zechariah, that the Jews had pierced His heart (Zech. 12.10). Now God here speaks in a human way, meaning that He is wounded by the sins of His people, especially by their obstinate contempt of His Word, just as a mortal man receives a deadly wound when His heart is pierced. Elsewhere He says that His Spirit was exceeding sorrowful (Matt. 26.38). Now, as Christ is God manifested in the flesh, John says that in His visible flesh was openly fulfilled what His divine majesty had suffered from the Jews (so far as it was capable of suffering). Not that God is subject to outrage from men or that the reproaches cast at Him from earth ever reach Him, but because by this expression He wanted to declare the great sacrilege which the ungodliness of men is guilty of, when it rises obstinately against heaven. John justly ascribes to the Jews this action by a Roman soldier. Elsewhere they are said to have crucified the Son of God (Acts 2.36) even though they did not lay a finger on His body.

We may now ask whether God promises the Jews repentance to salvation or threatens that He will come as an avenger. When I examine the passage carefully, I myself judge that it includes both—that from a lost and desperate nation God will gather a remnant to salvation, and that by His dreadful vengeance He will show despisers whom they are dealing with. For we know that they used to mock the prophets as insolently as if they had received no commission from God and were telling them fairy stories. God says that they will not go unpunished, for He will at the last maintain His cause.

And after these things Joseph of Arimathaea, being a disciple of Jesus, but secretly for fear of the Jews, asked of Pilate that he might take away the body of Jesus: and Pilate gave him leave. He came therefore, and took away his body. And there came also Nicodemus, he who at the first came to him by night, bringing a mixture of myrrh and aloes, about a hundred pound weight. So they took the body of Jesus, and bound it in linen cloths with the spices, as the custom of the Jews is to bury. Now in the place where he was crucified there was a garden; and in the garden a new tomb wherein was never man yet laid. There then because of the Jews' Preparation (for the tomb was nigh at hand) they laid Jesus. (38-42)

38. *Joseph of Arimathaea asked of Pilate.* John now relates who buried Christ and where and with what honour. He mentions the two who committed Christ to the grave—Joseph and Nicodemus, the former of whom asked Pilate to give him the dead body which would other-

wise have been exposed to the will of the soldiers. Matthew says that he was a rich man and Luke that he was a councillor, that is of senatorial rank. As for Nicodemus, we have seen in chapter 3 that he had an honourable position among his countrymen. That he was also rich may be inferred from the great expense he went to in procuring these mixed spices.

Hitherto, their riches had prevented them from taking Christ's side, and could afterwards have hindered them no less from making a profession so hated and disgraced. The Evangelist expressly says that Joseph had earlier been held back by this fear from venturing to profess that he was Christ's disciple. Of Nicodemus he repeats what we have heard before, that he came to Jesus secretly and by night. Where do they suddenly get such heroic courage from, that in the last straits they boldly come out into the open? I pass over the evident danger they had to run; but the great thing is that they did not hesitate to take up a perpetual war against their own nation. It is therefore certain that this was done by a heavenly impulse, so that those who were afraid to give Him due honour while He was alive now hasten to His dead body as if they were new men.

They bring spices to embalm Christ's body; but they would never have done so unless they had been sprinkled and steeped with the scent of His death. This shows the truth of what Christ Himself said, 'Except a grain of wheat die, it abideth alone; but if it die, it beareth much fruit' (John 12.24). Here we have an outstanding proof that His death was even more quickening than His life. And so great was the efficacy of that sweet savour which Christ's death breathed into the minds of those two men that it easily extinguished all their carnal affections. So long as love of money and ambition reigned in them, the grace of Christ was tasteless. Now they cease to relish the whole world.

Moreover, let us learn from their example what duty we owe to Christ. Those two, in proof of their faith, not only in imminent danger took Christ down from the cross but boldly carried Him to the grave. We shall be basely and shamefully lazy if we withhold from Him our confession of faith now that He reigns in heavenly glory. The less excusable is the wickedness of those today who, although they deny Christ with treacherous hypocrisy, shelter behind Nicodemus' example. They are like him in one respect, I admit; for, so far as they can, they are careful to bury Christ. But the time for burying is past, for He has ascended to the right hand of the Father, that He may be exalted conspicuously over men and angels and that every tongue may proclaim His dominion (Phil. 2.9, 10).

Secretly for fear of the Jews. This fear was probably not blameless, for it is contrasted with the holy firmness which the Spirit of the Lord wrought in Joseph's heart. Not that all the fear by which believers safeguard themselves from tyrants and enemies of the Gospel is wrong, but because when the confession of faith is withheld from fear it shows weakness of faith. We should always think of what the Lord commands and how far He bids us go. He who stops in mid course shows that he does not trust in God; and he who values his own life more than God's command is inexcusable.

When the Evangelist gives Joseph the honour and title of disciple at a time when he was over-timid and did not dare to profess his faith before the world, we learn how kindly God acts towards His people and how He pardons their sins as a Father. And yet the pseudo-Nicodemites have no cause to flatter themselves. Not only do they keep their faith hidden inwardly, but by pretending to give their consent to ungodly superstitions, do all they can to deny they are disciples of Christ.

40. *As the custom of the Jews is.* When Christ had died in extreme ignominy on the cross, God determined that His burial should be honourable, that it might be a prelude to the glory of His resurrection. Nicodemus and Joseph spent a great deal and might be thought extravagant. But we must look to God's purpose. By His Spirit He led them to pay this honour to His Son, that by the savour of His grave He might take away our dread of the cross. But what is extraordinary should not be taken as an example.

Moreover, the Evangelist expressly states that He was buried after the custom of the Jews. By this he means that it was one of the ceremonies of the Law. For the ancient people, to whom the resurrection was not so clearly declared and who had not the proof and pledge of it in Christ, needed such aids to support them that with steadfast faith they might await the coming of the Mediator. We must therefore observe the distinction between us on whom the brightness of the Gospel has shone and the fathers, to whom the figures made up for the absence of Christ. This is why a greater pomp of ceremonies could be tolerated, which today would be blameworthy. For those who now bury the dead so expensively do not so much bury their dead as (so far as in them lies) drag down from heaven Christ Himself, the King of life, and hide Him in the tomb; for His resurrection abolished those ancient ceremonies.

There was also great carefulness and ceremony in burying the dead among the heathen, which undoubtedly originated from the fathers, as did sacrifices. But as no hope of the resurrection flourished among them, they aped rather than imitated the fathers. For God's promise and Word is like the soul which gives life to ceremonies. Take away the Word, and all the ceremonies which men observe, although apparently belonging to the worship of the godly, are nothing but decaying or silly superstition. But as for us, as we have said, we today ought to cultivate sobriety and moderation in this matter, for extravagance quenches the savour of Christ's resurrection.

41. *Now in the place where he was crucified there was a garden.* This is the third point which I have said should be noticed in the story of the burial. The Evangelist mentions the place for various reasons. First, it was no accident, nor outside the sure providence of God, that Christ's body was laid in a new sepulchre. For although He died as all other men die, yet, as He was to be the first-born from the dead and the first-fruits of them that rise, a new sepulchre was given to Him. Of course, Nicodemus and Joseph had another aim. They were concerned with the convenience of the place, since only a short time remained until sunset, when the sabbath began. But beyond their intention, God provided an unused sepulchre for His Son. These holy men are simply pleased at the nearness of the place, so that they should not break the sabbath. But God offers them what they did not seek, that He might distinguish His Son's burial by a certain sign from the usual order. This circumstance of place served also to glorify His resurrection and to throw no little light on the story which follows in the next chapter.

CHAPTER TWENTY

Now on the first day of the week[1] *cometh Mary Magdalene early, while it was yet dark, unto the tomb, and seeth the stone taken away from the tomb. She runneth therefore, and cometh to Simon Peter, and to the other disciple, whom Jesus loved, and saith unto them, They have taken away the Lord out of the tomb, and we know not where they have laid him. Peter therefore went forth, and the other disciple, and they went toward the tomb. And they ran both together: and the other disciple outran Peter, and came first to the tomb; and stooping, he seeth the linen cloths lying; yet entered he not in. Simon Peter therefore also cometh, following him, and entered into the tomb; and he beholdeth the linen cloths lying, and the napkin, that was upon his head, not lying with the linen cloths, but rolled up in a place by itself. Then entered in therefore the other disciple also, which came first to the tomb, and he saw, and believed. For as yet they knew not the scripture that he must rise again from the dead.* (1-9)

1. *Now on the first day of the week.*[1] Since the resurrection of Christ is the chief article of our faith, and without it the hope of eternal life fails, the Evangelists are the more insistent to prove it, as our author here collects much evidence to assure us that Christ is risen from the dead. But it may seem strange that he does not produce more important witnesses; for he starts with a woman. But in this way the saying is fulfilled that God chooses what is weak in the world and foolish and contemptible that He may confound the wisdom, power and glory of the flesh (I Cor. 1.27). The disciples certainly had no more earthly greatness than the women who followed Christ; but it pleased Christ to have them as the primary witnesses of His resurrection on the one ground that they are entitled to belief and are above any objections. As for the priests and scribes and the whole people, and even Pilate, nothing but gross and wilful blindness prevented them from knowing with certainty that Christ was risen. They all deserved, therefore, that seeing they should not see. But Christ revealed Himself to His little flock.

But before we go any further, it is worthwhile showing how the Evangelists agree. At first sight there seems to be some contradiction in their words. John mentions only the Magdalene, Matthew two women, Mark three and Luke does not fix the number but only

[1] *sabbatorum:* of the sabbaths.

relates that women came who had followed Christ from Galilee. But this problem is easily solved in that Matthew puts in the names of two better-known women and famous among the disciples, but John is content to name Magdalene alone, though without excluding the others. It is easy to gather from the context of his words that she was not alone, for shortly afterwards Mary says in the plural, 'we know not where they have laid him.' Therefore, although John says nothing of her companions, he does not relate anything different from the others, who mention that there were more with her.

Nor is the solution of the difference in times difficult. When John says that they came before it was light, understand that they set out during the darkness of the night; that day had dawned before they reached the tomb; and that in the evening after sunset, when the sabbath had ended, they had bought the spices. The narrative of the others must be referred to this.

There seems to be another kind of contradiction in that John says that Mary spoke only to himself and Peter, whereas Luke relates that she came to the eleven apostles and that her words were taken as madness. But this is easily explained. John deliberately passed over the rest of his colleagues, because only he and Peter came to the tomb. That Luke mentions Peter alone is for the same reason that we have just now given in regard to Mary Magdalene and the other women. Moreover, it is probable that the other nine disciples were held back by fear, lest they should be too conspicuous if they went in a body. Nor is this inconsistent with what Luke seems to hint, that they despised Mary's words, for he at once adds that Peter ran. Therefore, he simply means that when they first heard it they were as if astonished, but that at last Peter pulled himself together and followed her to see for himself.

When Luke relates that Christ appeared to Mary before she had told the disciples that the grave was empty, the order of the narrative is reversed. This is clear from the context. For he adds what, as John tells us, happened before she saw Jesus. Nor is there anything strange in this, for Hebrew writers often put first what came later in the order of time.

On the first day of the sabbaths. The Evangelists do not relate when or how Christ rose. Enough for them to explain at what time and to what people His resurrection was made known. John therefore says that Mary came on the first day of the sabbaths. Literally indeed, it is *one*; but it is common with the Hebrews to put *one* in place of *first*, because in numbering we begin with one. Now, since every sabbath day was dedicated to rest, they called the whole week a sabbath, giving this honour to the holiness of the day of naming the rest of the time from it. The women therefore, came to the tomb on the day after the sabbath, having on the same day, but after sunset, bought spices. Afterwards they went out of the city in secret and during the darkness of the night, as people do when they are afraid. Now it was the first day of the sabbaths, in respect to the following sabbath, because it was the beginning of the week of which the sabbath was the close.

3. *Peter therefore went forth.* It is surprising that when the faith of the disciples and the women was so weak and almost non-existent, they had so much zeal. And indeed it can only be that piety impelled them to seek Christ. Some seed of faith remained in their hearts, but smothered for a time, so that they were not aware of possessing what they did possess. Thus God's Spirit often works in the elect secretly. In short, we must understand that there was a hidden root from which we see the fruit coming. Although this feeling of piety which they had was confused and mingled with much superstition, yet I call it, though imprecisely, faith, because it was conceived only by the teaching of the Gospel and had Christ alone as its object. From this seed sprang at last a true and sincere faith, which left the tomb and ascended to Christ's heavenly glory. When Scripture speaks of the rudiments of faith, it says that Christ is born in us and that we in turn are born in Him. But the disciples have to be placed almost below infancy while they are ignorant of Christ's resurrection; but yet the Lord nourishes them like an unborn child in the womb. Before this they were like children and had made a little progress. But Christ's death so weakened them that they had to be begotten and formed again, as Paul says of the Galatians (Gal. 4.19).

From Peter's running slower but entering first into the tomb we may learn that many have more given to them at the end than appears in the beginning. And indeed, we sometimes see men who were most enthusiastic at the outset failing when they come to the contest, while others who were thought slow and lazy, take fresh heart when danger is nigh.

5. *And seeth the linen cloths lying.* The linen cloths were, so to say, the slough, which should produce faith in Christ's resurrection. For it was improbable that His body would be stripped to be taken elsewhere. This would have been done neither by a friend nor by a foe.

That His head was wrapped in a napkin refutes the falsehood of the Papists, who pretend that the whole body was sewn up in one linen cloth, which they show to the unhappy masses to adore. I overlook their ignorance of Latin, which led them to make the word 'napkin' (which was used to wipe sweat off the face) into a covering for the whole body. I overlook also their impudence in boasting—in five or six different localities—that they have this same napkin. But this gross falsehood is intolerable, for it openly contradicts the Gospel history. To this is added the fabulous miracle which they have invented, that the likeness of Christ's body is impressed on the linen. I ask you, if such a miracle had been performed, would the Evangelist have suppressed it, when he is so careful to relate less important things? Let us be content with this simplicity, that by laying aside the tokens of death, Christ meant to testify that He had put on a blessed and immortal life.

8. *And he saw, and believed.* It is a cold exposition which some give, that John believed what he had heard from Mary—that Christ's body had been taken away. For you will nowhere find the word 'believe' in this sense, especially when it is used simply and on its own. Nor is this inconsistent with Peter and John returning home while they are still uncertain and perplexed; for John used this expression in some places when he intended to denote the progress of faith. Moreover, Luke relates that Peter wondered at seeing the tomb in the state it was; meaning that Peter thought of something greater and higher than Mary had told him.

They had often heard from the mouth of Christ what they now saw with their own eyes, but it had slipped from their minds. Reminded now by the sight of something new, they begin to think of the divinity of Christ, though they are still far from the pure and clear knowledge of faith. John is therefore accusing himself when he confesses that he first believed when he saw the signs of Christ's resurrection.

He amplifies his own and his brethren's guilt by adding that they had not only forgotten Christ's words, but that they did not understand the Scriptures. He ascribes the deficiency in their faith to this ignorance. From this, too, we may learn a useful lesson, that we should put it down to our laziness when what we ought to know about Christ is hidden from us, because we have not profited as we ought in the Scriptures, which clearly reveal Christ's power.

To go no further for an example of this, it may seem that Christ's resurrection is indicated obscurely in them, and only under masks (*involucris*). But there are sufficiently clear testimonies for the attentive reader. In Acts 13.34 Paul proves that Christ must have risen from the dead, since God declares by the prophet Isaiah (55.3) that under His reign the mercy promised to David would be sure. Anyone unlearned might think that Paul is quoting beside the point. But they who hold the principles of faith and are well practised in the Scripture know the aptness of this argument. For if Christ is to secure to us for ever the grace of God, Christ Himself must live for ever.

There are many passages like this which it is not now necessary to collect. Let us be satisfied with just three. Psalm 16.10 says, 'Thou wilt not suffer thine holy one to see corruption.' Peter and Paul expound this prediction of Christ, and justly, for there is none of the sons of Adam who is not in himself subject to corruption. Therefore, the immortality of Christ is asserted here. It is also beyond doubt that this passage refers to Christ, 'The Lord said unto my Lord, Sit thou at my right hand, until I make thine enemies thy footstool' (Psalm 110.1). But death will not be destroyed until the last day. The kingdom is therefore assigned to Christ till the end of the world, and this kingdom cannot exist without His life. But Isaiah speaks more clearly than them all. After he has foretold the death of Christ, he at once adds, 'who shall declare his age?' (53.8). In short, we should believe that the teaching of Scripture is so full and complete in every respect that what is lacking in our faith ought rightly to be attributed to ignorance of it.

So the disciples went away again unto their own home. But Mary was standing without at the tomb weeping: so, as she wept, she stooped and looked into the tomb; and she beholdeth two angels in white sitting, one at the head, and one at the feet, where the body of Jesus had laid. And they say unto her, Woman, why weepest thou? She saith unto them, Because they have taken away my Lord, and I know not where they have laid him. When she had thus said, she turned herself back, and beholdeth Jesus standing, and knew not that it was Jesus. Jesus saith unto her, Woman, why weepest thou? whom seekest thou? She, supposing him to be the gardener, saith unto him, Sir, if thou hast borne him hence, tell me where thou hast laid him, and I will take him away. (10-15)

10. *So the disciples went away again.* It is possible that their minds were still doubtful and uncertain when they returned home. For, although John says that they believed, it was not a steady faith, but only some confused sense of the miracle, and was like a trance until they received more confirmation. And indeed, a substantial faith could not be conceived by sight alone. Besides, Christ did not show Himself to their sight until they had been more fully roused from their carnal stupor. They certainly showed a praiseworthy example of zeal in hurrying to the tomb. But Christ was hidden from them, because they sought Him too superstitiously.

11. *But Mary was standing.* The Evangelist now begins to narrate how Christ appeared both to the women and to the disciples to testify His resurrection. Although he mentions Mary only, it seems probable to me that the other women were also with her. For it is unreasonable

to suppose, as some have done, that the women fainted from fear. They wish to avoid a contradiction which I have already shown does not exist.

There is no great cause for praise that the women remained at the tomb when the disciples returned to the city. For the disciples took with them comfort and joy, but the women are filled with idle and useless weeping. In short, only a mixture of superstition and carnal feeling keeps them at the tomb.

12. *She beholdeth two angels.* A wonderful kindness of the Lord, that He overlooks so many faults in Mary and her companions! For He bestows no ordinary honour on them by sending His angels, and at last, showing Himself to them as He had not done to the apostles. Although the apostles and the women were sick of the same disease, the apostles' stupidity was the less excusable in that they had profited so little by their thorough and careful teaching. Certainly, Christ chose to reveal Himself first to the women, partly to put the apostles to shame.

Now, whether Mary knew them to be angels or thought they were men is uncertain. We know that white garments were a symbol of the heavenly glory, just as Christ was clothed in white garments when His majesty shone forth on the mountain to the three apostles. Luke tells of an angel who appeared to Cornelius. But I do not deny that Orientals wore linen clothes. But in the dress of the angels God showed something remarkable and uncommon, and, as it were, impressed marks on them to distinguish them from men. Besides, Matthew compares the appearance of the angel who spoke to the women to lightning. Yet their fear may have arisen only from their minds being struck with wonder, for it says that they stood astonished. Again, when we read that angels appeared in the visible form of men and clothed in garments, this was for men's ignorance. I have no doubt that they were sometimes clothed with true bodies. But whether there was only the appearance of bodies in these two angels I leave undetermined, because it would be superfluous to enquire. For me it is enough that the Lord gave them a human form for the women to see and hear them, while the uncommon and extraordinary dress they wore distinguished them from the rank of men and indicated something divine and heavenly.

One at the head, and one at the feet. That one angel only is mentioned by Matthew does not contradict John's story. For both angels did not address Mary at once, but only the one who was the ambassador. Augustine's allegory is weak, that the position of the angels indicated that the Gospel would be preached from East to West. It is more worth noticing that Christ initiated the glory of His kingdom by such preliminaries. For that the angels honour His tomb not only takes away the ignominy of the cross but makes Christ's heavenly majesty shine forth.

13. *Woman, why weepest thou?* From the other Evangelists it may be easily inferred that the angel said many things. But John gives a brief summary, sufficient to prove the resurrection of Christ. He speaks reproof mingled with comfort. The angel reproves Mary for her untimely weeping, but at the same time mingles joy with it when he says that there is no need to weep, since Christ is risen.

14. *And beholdeth Jesus standing.* It may be asked how Mary made the mistake of not recognizing Jesus, whom she must have known very well indeed. Some think He appeared in a different form, but I reckon that the fault lay rather in the women's eyes, as Luke says of the two disciples (24.16). We will not say, therefore, that Christ was repeatedly assuming new forms, Proteus-like, but that it is in the will of God, who gave men eyes, to weaken their keenness when He thinks good, that seeing they may not see.

In Mary we have an instance of the mistakes common to the human mind. Although Christ offers Himself to our sight, we devise various shapes for Him, so that our senses conceive anything rather than the true Christ. For the eyes of our minds are faulty in themselves and are also bewitched by the world and Satan that they may not discern the truth.

15. *Sir, if thou hast borne him hence.* She calls Him 'Sir', after the manner of her people. For the Hebrews salute peasants and other lowly men as 'Sir'. We see that Mary is concerned only with earthly things. She merely wants to obtain Christ's dead body to keep it hidden in the tomb. She leaves out the most important thing—aspiring to the divine power of His resurrection. It is not surprising therefore if such a gross attitude puts a veil before her eyes.

Jesus saith unto her, Mary. She turneth herself, and saith unto him, Rabboni; which is to say, Master. Jesus saith to her, Touch me not; for I am not yet ascended unto the Father: but go unto my brethren, and say to them, I ascend unto my Father and your Father, and my God and your God. Mary Magdalene cometh and telleth the disciples, I have seen the Lord; and how that he had said these things unto her. (16-18)

16. *Mary.* That Christ let Mary err for a little while, was useful for confirming her faith. Now, by one word, He corrects her mistake. He had spoken to her before, but His speech seemed that of an unknown man. He now assumes the character of the Master and addresses His disciple by name—as we read in chapter 10 that the Good

Shepherd calls every sheep of His flock to Him by name. And so the voice of the Shepherd penetrates Mary's mind, opens her eyes, arouses all her senses and so affects her that she forthwith entrusts herself to Christ.

Thus in Mary we have an image of our calling. For the only entrance to the true knowledge of Christ is when He first knows us and then intimately invites us to Himself, not by the ordinary voice which sounds in everyone's ears indiscriminately, but by the voice with which He especially calls the sheep whom the Father has given Him. So Paul says, 'After you have known God, or rather, have been known by him' (Gal. 4.9).

The effectiveness of the word appears from Mary immediately giving Christ the honour due to Him. For the word *Rabboni* is not only honorific, but contains a profession of obedience. Mary therefore declares that she is Christ's disciple and devotes herself to Him as her Master. This is a wonderful and secret conversion of the human mind, when God enlightens her by His Spirit and makes her clear-sighted who had been dull and indeed, altogether blind. Moreover, the example of Mary should serve as an exhortation, that all whom Christ invites to Himself should respond at once.

The word *Rabboni* is Aramaic, though they pronounce it 'Ribboni'. But words are usually changed when they are transferred to a foreign language. But it is equivalent to saying, 'My Lord' or 'Master'. In Christ's time it had become customary to use 'Rabbi or 'Rabboni' instead of Master.

17. *Touch me not*. This seems to disagree with Matthew's narrative, for he expressly writes that the women held Christ by the feet (28.9). Now, since He wished His disciples to touch Him, what reason had He for forbidding Mary to touch Him? The answer is easy, so long as we understand that the women were not repulsed from touching Christ until they touched Him overmuch. For so far as was necessary for removing doubt, He certainly did not forbid them to touch Him; but when He saw that they were too much occupied with embracing His feet, He tempered and corrected their thoughtless zeal. They fixed their attention on His bodily presence, and knew of no other way of enjoying Him than by conversing with Him on earth. And so we must infer that they were not forbidden to touch Him until Christ saw that by their foolish and unreasonable desire they wanted to keep Him in the world.

We should attend to His reason for adding, *for I am not yet ascended unto the Father*. In these words He tells the women to restrain their feelings while He was not yet received into the heavenly glory. In short, He showed the purpose of His resurrection. It was not what they had imagined, that when He had returned to life He would triumph in the world, but rather that by His ascension into heaven He should enter into possession of the kingdom promised to Him and by His Spirit should govern the Church from the Father's right hand. The words therefore mean that the state of His resurrection would not be full and complete in every respect until He had sat down in heaven at the right hand of the Father, and therefore that the women did wrong in being satisfied with having only the half of His resurrection and wanting His presence in the world. There is a twofold usefulness in this lesson. First, those who do not want to go astray in seeking Christ shall raise their minds on high. Secondly, all who try to go to Him must get rid of the earthly affections of the flesh, as Paul exhorts (Col. 3.1).

But go unto my brethren. Some limit the word brethren to Christ's relatives; but in my opinion wrongly. For why should He have sent to them rather than to the disciples? They reply, because John elsewhere declares that they were unbelievers (7.5). But I do not think it likely that Christ conferred such a great honour on those mentioned there. They must also concede that Mary obeyed Christ's command. But it follows at once that she came to the disciples. We conclude that Christ was speaking of them.

Moreover, Christ knew that the disciples, whom those men by their opinion separate, were assembled in one place. And it would have been quite absurd for Him to attend to I know not what sort of people and disregard the disciples who were assembled into one place and were agitated between hope and fear. Add to this, that Christ seems to have borrowed the expression from Psalm 22.22, where we read, 'I will declare thy name to my brethren.' For it is beyond all controversy that the fulfilment of that prophecy is related in this passage.

I therefore conclude that Mary was sent to the disciples in general, and I consider it was done as a reproach, since they had been so slow and sluggish to believe. Indeed, those whom the Son of God had so long and laboriously taught with little or no success, deserve to have as their teachers, not only women, but even oxen and asses. Yet it is a mild punishment when Christ sends His disciples to school to the women, that by their agency He may bring them back to Himself. In this also shines the inconceivable goodness of Christ in destining and appointing the women to be witnesses of His resurrection to the apostles. For the embassy given to them is the solid foundation of our salvation and contains the chief point of heavenly wisdom.

We must also notice that this was extraordinary and, as it were, accidental. They are commanded to announce to the apostles what they, exercising the office committed to them, afterwards proclaimed to the whole world. But they do not act as apostles. It is therefore wrong to draw a law out of this command of Christ, which would permit women the office of baptizing. Let us be satisfied that Christ displayed the boundless treasures of His grace in them, when He made them once the teachers of the apostles, and yet He did not want what was done by a single privilege to be taken as an example. This is especially apparent in Mary Magdalene who had been held captive by seven devils. For it was as if Christ brought her out of the deepest hell to raise her above heaven.

If any object that there was no reason for Christ to prefer the women to the apostles, since they were no less carnal and stupid; I reply that it is not for us but for the Judge to discriminate between them. But I would say that the apostles should be more sharply rebuked; because they had not only been taught more than the others, but after they had been appointed teachers of the whole world and called the light of men and the salt of the earth, they defaulted so basely. Yet it pleased the Lord to show a proof of His power in those contemptible and weak instruments.

I ascend unto my Father. By the word 'ascend' He confirms the doctrine which I have just expounded. He rose from the dead, not just to linger on earth, but that He might enter into the heavenly life and draw believers with Him. In short, with this word He forbids the apostles to stop at His resurrection in itself, and bids them go further until they come to the spiritual kingdom, to the heavenly glory, even to God Himself. There is a strong emphasis on the word *ascend*, for Christ stretches out His hand to His own that they may seek their happiness nowhere else than in heaven. For where our treasure is, there must also our heart be (Matt. 6.21). Christ states that He ascends on high. Therefore, we must ascend unless we want to be separated from Him.

When He adds that He ascends to God, He quickly dispels the sorrow and anxiety that the apostles might conceive at His departure. For He means that He will always be present with His own in His divine power. True, to ascend implies a spatial distance; but although Christ is absent in body, yet as He is with God, His power, everywhere diffused, clearly shows His spiritual presence. For what purpose did He ascend to God but that, seated at His right hand, He might reign both in heaven and on earth? In short, He wanted by this expression to commend the divine power of His kingdom, lest the disciples should take harm from His bodily absence.

The fruit and effect of that brotherly union which we have mentioned is expressed when Christ makes God the Father common to

Himself and us. He says, 'I ascend to my Father who is also your Father.' Elsewhere we hear that we are made partakers of all the blessings of Christ. But this is the foundation, that He shares with us the very fountain of blessings. Here indeed is an inestimable blessing, that believers can safely and firmly decide that He is their God who is the God of Christ, and their Father who is the Father of Christ. Nor need we fear that this confidence is guilty of rashness, for it is founded on Christ, or that it will be proud boasting, for Christ Himself has dictated it to us by His own mouth.

Now, Christ calls Him *his God*, inasmuch as by taking the form of a servant, He humbled Himself. This is therefore proper to His human nature, but it is applied to His whole person in respect of His unity, because the same one is both God and man. In the second clause there is also a difference between Him and us; for He is the Son of God by nature, we only by adoption. But so firm is the grace we obtain through Him, that it cannot be shaken by any efforts of the devil, so as to hinder us from always calling Him our Father who has adopted us in His only-begotten Son.

When therefore it was evening, on that day, the first day of the sabbath, and when the doors were shut where the disciples were, for fear of the Jews, Jesus came and stood in the midst, and saith unto them, Peace be unto you. And when he had said this, he shewed unto them his hands and his side. The disciples therefore were glad, when they saw the Lord. Jesus therefore said to them again, Peace be unto you: as the Father hath sent me, even so send I you. And when he had said this, he breathed on them, and saith unto them, Receive ye the Holy Ghost: whose soever sins ye forgive, they are forgiven unto them; whose soever sins ye retain, they are retained. (19-23)

19. *When therefore it was evening.* The Evangelist now relates that Christ's resurrection was proved to the disciples by their seeing Him. That they were all assembled in one place did not happen without the providence of God, so that its authority might be more certain and trustworthy. We must notice how gently Christ behaved to them in not keeping them in suspense longer than till evening. Moreover, He enlightened them by bringing the pledge of new life while darkness was covering the world.

It was a sign of faith, or at least of a godly attitude, that they had all assembled. We acknowledge a certain weakness in their keeping themselves hidden behind closed doors. For although at times some fear falls on even the strongest and boldest minds, it is easy to gather that the apostles were then frightened in a way that showed their lack of faith. This example is worth noticing; although they act less courageously than they should have done, they do not give way to their weakness. They certainly seek concealment to escape danger, but they pluck up enough courage to remain together; otherwise they would have been scattered and none would have dared to look at another. In this manner we too should struggle against the weakness of our flesh and not give the reins to fear, which tempts us to apostasy. Christ also blesses their zeal when He appears to them thus assembled, and Thomas is justly deprived of the grace given to all His brethren, because, like a wandering and roving soldier, he had deserted from the banner of union (*ab unitatis vexillo*). Let those who are over-timid learn to discipline and bestir themselves to correct their carnal fear. In particular, they should beware lest fear scatters them.

And while the doors were shut. This detail was deliberately added because it contains a manifest proof of Christ's divine power. For what some think—that the doors were unlocked for Him by someone and He entered in the ordinary way—is completely contrary to the Evangelist's meaning. We must understand that Christ did not enter without a miracle, to give a proof of His divinity to make His disciples more attentive. Yet I am far from admitting that what the Papists say is true, that Christ's body passed through the shut door. They maintain this to make the glorious body of Christ not only spirit-like but also infinite and not confined to any one place. But the words do not convey this meaning. The Evangelist does not say that He entered through the shut doors, but that He suddenly stood among His disciples although the doors had been shut and had not been opened to Him by any man's hand. We know that Peter went out of a prison that had been locked. Must we therefore say that he passed right through iron and beams? Away, then, with that puerile sophistry which has nothing substantial and bears in it many absurdities! Let it suffice for us that Christ wanted to confirm the authority of His resurrection for the disciples by a striking miracle.

Peace be unto you. This is the usual form of greeting among the Hebrews. By the word peace they denote all the happiness and prosperity usually desired for a happy life. The phrase is therefore equivalent to, 'May you be well and happy!' I say this because there are some who here vainly argue about peace and harmony when Christ merely intended to wish His disciples well.

20. *He shewed unto them his hands.* This confirmation needed to be added so that by all these means they might know that Christ was risen. If anyone thinks it unworthy and strange for Christ's glory that He should bear the wounds even after His resurrection, let him consider, first, that Christ rose rather for us than for Himself, and secondly, that whatever is for our salvation is glorious to Him. For when He

humbled Himself for a time it took nothing from His majesty. And since the wounds of which we are speaking serve to illuminate the authority of His resurrection, they do not derogate at all from His glory. But should anyone infer from this that Christ still has the wounded side and pierced hands it would be ridiculous, for it is certain that the use of the wounds was temporary until the apostles were fully persuaded that He was risen from the dead.

When John says that the disciples *were glad* when they saw the Lord, it means that all the grief which Christ's death had caused them was dispelled by His new life.

21. *Jesus therefore said to them again, Peace be unto you.* The only object of this second salutation seems to me that the Lord should make them listen to Him, as befitted the greatness and seriousness of what He was about to say.

As the Father hath sent me. By these words Christ, so to say, installs His apostles in the office to which He had already determined them. It is true that they had been already sent throughout Judaea, but only as heralds to command men to hear the supreme Teacher, and not as apostles to execute a perpetual office of teaching. The Lord now ordains them to be His ambassadors, to establish His kingdom in the world. Let it therefore be settled that the apostles were now for the first time appointed as ordinary ministers of the Gospel.

His words amount to His saying that hitherto He had discharged the office of Teacher, but that now that He has finished His course He commits it to them. He means that the Father made Him a Teacher of the Church on condition that He should for a time go before the rest but afterwards should substitute in His place those who would make good His absence. This is why Paul says that He gave some apostles, some evangelists, some pastors, to govern the Church till the end of the world (Eph. 4.11). Christ therefore declares first, that although He held a temporary teaching office, the preaching of the Gospel is not for a little while but is perpetual. Again, that His doctrine may not have less authority in the mouths of the apostles, He commands them to succeed to the same task (*in eandem functionem succedere*), which He had received from the Father, lays upon them the same part (*eandem personam*) and bestows on them the same authority (*idem iuris*). And it was proper that their ministry should be confirmed like this, for they were obscure and common men. Moreover, even if they had had the highest splendour and dignity, we know that anything belonging to men is far beneath faith.

It was therefore necessary that Christ should communicate to His apostles the authority which He had received from the Father, that He may declare that the preaching of the Gospel was committed to

Him, not humanly, but by God's command. But He does not set them in His place (*substituit in locum suum*) so as to give up the supreme teaching office (*summo magisterio*), which the Father willed to be in Him alone. He therefore remains and will eternally continue to be the only Teacher (*unicus Doctor*) of the Church, with the sole difference that, whereas He spoke with His mouth while He dwelt on earth, He now speaks through the apostles. The succession therefore is such that it takes nothing from Christ, but His authority remains sound and unimpaired and His glory entire. For the decree by which we are commanded to hear Him and not others is inviolable (Matt. 17.5). In short, here Christ meant to adorn, not men, but the teaching of the Gospel.

Moreover, we should note that the only subject handled here is the preaching of the Gospel. For Christ does not send His apostles to atone for the sins of the world and to procure righteousness, as He was sent by the Father. Hence, He does not refer in this passage to what is peculiar to Himself, but only appoints ministers and pastors to govern the Church; and it is on this condition that He alone keeps possession of the whole power (*ut solum ipse potestatem in solidum retineat*), whereas they claim for themselves nothing but the ministry.

22. *He breathed on them.* Because no mortal man is fit for such a difficult office (*munus*), Christ institutes the apostles by the grace of His Spirit. And indeed, to govern the Church of God, to bear the embassy of eternal salvation, to set up God's kingdom on earth and to lift men up to heaven is something far above human capacity. It is not surprising therefore that no man is found fit unless he be inspired (*adflatus*) by the Holy Spirit. For nobody can speak one word about Christ unless the Spirit governs His tongue (I Cor. 12.3), so far is it from being true that any man is sufficient to discharge faithfully and sincerely all the duties of such an excellent office (*officii*). Again, it is the glory of Christ alone to form those whom He appoints to be teachers (*doctores*) of His Church. For the fulness of the Spirit was poured out upon Him so that He might bestow it upon each one in a definite measure.

Although He remains the only Shepherd of His Church, He must needs put forth the power of His Spirit in the ministers whose work He uses. And this also He testified by an outward symbol when He breathed on the apostles; for it would be meaningless if the Spirit did not proceed from Him. So much the more hateful is the sacrilege of the Papists, who seize to themselves the honour which belongs to the Son of God. For their mitred (*cornuti*) bishops boast that in making sacrificing priests they breathe out the Spirit when they belch over them. But the fact plainly shows how different their stinking breath is from Christ's divine breathing; for all that they do is to change horses into asses. Moreover, Christ not only communicates to His disciples the Spirit whom He has received, but bestows Him as His own, as the one whom He has in common with the Father. Wherefore, all who profess to give the Spirit by breathing usurp to themselves the glory of divinity.

Now we must note that those whom Christ calls to the pastoral office (*pastorale munus*) He also adorns with the necessary gifts, that they may be equal to discharging their duty, or at least may not come to it empty and naked. And if this is true, it is easy to refute the foolish boasting of the Papists, who extol their hierarchy in high-flown laudation but cannot show the least spark of the Holy Spirit in their bishops. They want us to believe that they are the lawful pastors of the Church and the apostles and vicars of Christ, when it is clear that they are completely devoid of any grace of the Spirit. But a sure rule is here laid down for judging the calling of those who preside over God's Church—if we see the gifts of the Holy Spirit.

But Christ especially wanted to assert the dignity of the apostolic order (*apostolici ordinis*). It was reasonable that they who were chosen to be the earliest and chief preachers of the Gospel should possess unique authority. But if Christ then bestowed His Spirit on the apostles by breathing, it could seem superfluous to send the Spirit afterwards. I reply: The Spirit was given to the apostles now in such a way that they were only sprinkled with His grace and not saturated with full power. For when the Spirit appeared on them in tongues of fire, they were entirely renewed. And He did not appoint them to be heralds of His Gospel so as to send them forth immediately to the work, but ordered them to wait quietly, as we read elsewhere (Luke 24.49). And if we consider everything properly we shall conclude not that He furnishes them with the necessary gifts for the present, but that He appoints them to be the instruments of His Spirit in the future. This breathing should therefore be referred and extended especially to that magnificent sending of the Spirit which He had so often promised.

Now, although Christ could have bestowed grace on His apostles by a secret inspiration, He chose to add a visible breathing to confirm them the better. Christ took this symbol from the common way of speaking in the Scriptures, where the Spirit is often compared to wind, a comparison which we explained briefly in chapter 3. But let the reader observe that with the outward and visible symbol is also joined the Word. This is the source from which the sacraments derive their strength; not that the efficacy of the Spirit is confined within the word which sounds in the ear, but because the effect of all the things which believers receive from the sacraments depends on the testimony of the Word. Christ breathes on the apostles. They receive not only the breathing but also the Spirit. Why, save because Christ promises Him to them?

Likewise, in baptism we put on Christ, we are washed by His blood, our old man is crucified, that the righteousness of God may reign in us. In the Holy Supper we are spiritually fed on the flesh and blood of Christ. Where does such great efficacy come from, but from Christ's promise, who effects and performs by His Spirit what He testifies by His Word? Let us therefore know that any man-made sacraments are nothing but mere mockeries or frivolous games, because signs can have no truth unless the Word of the Lord is present. Now, since we never play with sacred things like this without wicked insult to God and the ruin of souls, we should be most cautious against those tricks of Satan.

If any object that the Papist bishops are not blameworthy when they consecrate their priests by breathing, because the Word of Christ is joined to the sign there, the answer is obvious. Christ did not speak to the apostles to appoint an everlasting sacrament in the Church, but wanted to declare once what we said just now—that the Spirit proceeds from Himself alone. Moreover, He never appoints men to an office without at the same time supplying strength to His ministers and furnishing them with ability. I leave out that in the Papacy the priests (*sacrifici*) are made for a far different, even a contrary, purpose; namely to sacrifice Christ to death daily; whereas they were made apostles to sacrifice men with the sword of the Gospel. We ought also to believe that Christ alone gives all the blessings which He represents and promises in outward signs. For He does not bid the apostles receive the Spirit from the outward breathing but from Himself.

23. *Whose soever sins ye forgive.* Here without doubt our Lord has briefly summed up all the Gospel. For we must not separate this power of forgiving sins from the teaching office (*a docendi officio*) with which it is connected in this passage. A little before, Christ had said, 'As the living Father hath sent me, even so send I you.' He now declares what this embassy means and demands, only He put in what was necessary, that He gave them His Holy Spirit, so that they might do nothing of themselves.

The chief end in preaching the Gospel is that men may be reconciled to God; and this is done by the free pardon of sins, as Paul also tells us when he calls the Gospel for this reason the ministry of reconciliation (II Cor. 5.18). Many other things are contained in the Gospel, but there God principally intends to receive men into grace by not imputing their sins. If therefore we want to be faithful ministers of the Gospel, we must apply ourselves most earnestly to this aspect. For the Gospel differs most from secular philosophy in that it places the salvation of men in the free forgiveness of sins. This is the source of the other blessings of God—that God enlightens and regenerates us by His Spirit, that He reforms us to His image, that He arms us with unshaken courage against the world and Satan. Thus the whole doctrine of godliness and the spiritual building of the Church rest on this foundation, that God, having acquitted us from all sins, freely adopts us as His own.

Now, when Christ gives the apostles a mandate to forgive sins, He does not at all transfer to them what is His own. It belongs to Him to forgive sins. Inasmuch as this honour is peculiar to Himself, He does not yield it to the apostles; but He commands them to declare in His name the forgiveness of sins, that He may reconcile men to God through them. In short, He alone, properly speaking, forgives sins, through His apostles.

But it may be asked why, since He appoints them to be only witnesses and heralds of this blessing and not authors of it, He extols their power so splendidly. I reply that He did so to confirm our faith. Nothing is more important for us than to be able to believe definitely that our sins do not come into remembrance before God. Zacharias in his song calls it the knowledge of salvation (Luke 1.77); and since God uses the witness of men to prove it, consciences will never be at rest unless they know God Himself speaking in their person. Hence Paul says, 'We exhort you to be reconciled to God, as if Christ besought you by us' (II Cor. 5.20).

We now see why Christ so magnificently commends and adorns that ministry which He enjoins on the apostles. He does so that believers may be fully convinced that what they hear about the forgiveness of sins is ratified, and may not think less of the reconciliation offered by men's voices than if God Himself had stretched out His hand from heaven. The Church daily receives the rich fruit of this teaching when she realizes that her pastors are divinely ordained to be sureties (*sponsores*) of eternal salvation and that the forgiveness of sins which is committed to them is not to be sought afar off. Nor should we think the less highly of this incomparable treasure because it is exhibited in earthen vessels. We have cause to thank God who has conferred on men such an honour as to represent His person (*personam sustineant*) and His Son's in declaring the forgiveness of sins.

But let us know that the fanatics who despise this embassy trample under foot the blood of Christ. On the other hand, the Papists are ridiculous in twisting this passage to fit their magical absolutions. Unless a man confesses his sin in the ear of a priest, they think that he cannot hope for forgiveness. For Christ intended sins to be forgiven through the apostles; but they cannot absolve without hearing the case; therefore confession is necessary. But they are rambling ridiculously when they neglect the most important point—that this right was granted to the apostles to maintain the authority of the Gospel which they had been commissioned to preach. Here Christ is not appointing confessors to investigate each sin in low mutters, but heralds of the Gospel, who speak up and seal on the hearts of the godly the grace of the atonement obtained through Christ. We must therefore concentrate on the mode of forgiving sins, to know what power has been granted to the apostles.

Whose soever sins ye retain. Christ adds this second clause to terrify despisers of His Gospel, that they may know that they will not escape punishment for this pride. Therefore, as the embassy of salvation and eternal life was committed to the apostles, so, on the other hand, they were armed with vengeance against all the ungodly who reject the salvation offered them, as Paul teaches in II Cor. 10.6. But this is put last because the true and genuine aim in preaching the Gospel had to be shown first. That we are reconciled to God is proper to the Gospel: that unbelievers are adjudged to eternal death is accidental (*accidentale*). This is why Paul, in the verse I have just quoted, where he threatens vengeance against unbelievers, adds, 'after that your obedience shall have been fulfilled.' He means that it is proper to the Gospel to invite all to salvation, but that it is accidental (*adventicium*) that it brings destruction on any.

We must observe, however, that whoever hears the voice of the Gospel is liable to judgment and eternal damnation unless he embraces the forgiveness of sins there promised to him. For, as it is a quickening savour to the children of God, so it is the savour of death unto death to those who are perishing. Not that the preaching of the Gospel is needed to condemn the reprobate, for by nature we are all lost, and in addition to the hereditary curse, everyone brings on himself new causes of death; but because the obstinacy of those who knowingly and willingly despise the Son of God deserve far severer punishment.

But Thomas, one of the twelve, called Didymus, was not with them when Jesus came. The other disciples therefore said unto him, We have seen the Lord. But he said unto them, Except I shall see in his hands the print of the nails, and put my finger into the print of the nails, and put my hand into his side, I will not believe. And after eight days again his disciples were within, and Thomas with them. Jesus cometh, the doors being shut, and stood in the midst, and said, Peace be unto you. Then saith he to Thomas, Reach hither thy finger, and see my hands;

and reach hither thy hand, and put it into my side: and be not faithless,
but believing. Thomas answered and said unto him, My Lord and my
God. Jesus saith unto him, Because thou hast seen me, Thomas, thou
hast believed: blessed are they that have not seen, and yet have believed.
(24-29)

24. *But Thomas.* Here is related Thomas' unbelief, that from it the
faith of the godly might be more fully confirmed. He was not merely
slow and reluctant to believe. He was downright obstinate. His
hardness was the reason why Christ again allowed them to see and
to feel Him as before. Thus a new help testifying to Christ's resurrection was given, not only to Thomas, but to us. Moreover, Thomas'
obstinacy is evidence that this wickedness is innate in almost all men,
that they hinder themselves of their own accord when the entrance
to faith is opened to them.

25. *Except I shall see, etc.* This indicates that the source of the fault
is that everyone wants to be wise from his own understanding and
flatters himself overmuch. The words have nothing in common with
faith, but are what I might call a sensual judgment. The same thing
happens with all who are so devoted to themselves that they leave no
place for God's Word. It does not matter whether you read 'the
place' or 'the shape' or 'the print' of the nails. For scribes may have
altered τύπον to τόπον, or vice versa; but it does not change the meaning. Let the reader choose as he wishes.

27. *Reach hither thy finger.* We have already spoken about Christ's
entering and His form of salutation. When He so readily yields to the
wrong request of Thomas and of His own accord invites him to feel
His hands and touch the wound in His side, we learn how earnestly
thoughtful He was for our faith and Thomas'—for it was not of
Thomas only but of us also that He was thinking, that there might be
nothing lacking to confirm our faith.

Thomas' stupidity was astonishing and monstrous. He was not
content with the mere sight of Christ, but wanted to have his hands
also as witnesses of Christ's resurrection. Thus he was not only
obstinate but also proud and insulting towards Christ. Now at least,
when he saw Christ, he should have been confounded and terrified
with shame. Yet he boldly and fearlessly stretches out his hand as if
unconscious of any wrongdoing. For it may be readily inferred from
the Evangelist's words that he did not come to his senses before he
was convinced by touching. Thus, when we render less honour to
God's Word than is its due, there overtakes us insensibly a growing
obstinacy which bears with it a contempt of the Word and shakes off
all reverence for it. The more earnestly should we labour to restrain

the wantonness of our mind, lest any of us, by going too far in contradiction and, as it were, extinguishing the sense of godliness, may shut against ourselves the gate of faith.

28. *My Lord and my God.* Tardily Thomas wakes up, and (as those out of their minds commonly do when they come to themselves) exclaims in wonder, 'My Lord and my God.' For the abruptness of the language is very vehement. Nor is it doubtful that shame made him break out into this expression to condemn his own stupidity. Besides, such a sudden exclamation shows that faith was not entirely extinguished in him, though it had been smothered. For he does not handle Christ's divinity in His side or hands, but from those signs he inferred far more than they showed. Whence is this, but because he suddenly comes to himself after forgetfulness and somnolence? It therefore shows the truth of what I have already said, that the faith which seemed to be destroyed was, so to say, hidden and buried in his heart.

This is a not uncommon event among many people. They grow wanton for a time, as if they had cast off all fear of God, and no faith is apparent in them. But as soon as God has chastised them with a rod, the wildness of their flesh is subdued and they return to their right senses. It is certain that, in itself, disease would be insufficient to teach godliness. Hence we infer that when the obstructions have been removed, the good seed, which had lain smothered, springs up. There is a remarkable instance of this in David. Given up to his lust, he riots in security, as we see. None but would have thought that faith was then completely wiped out of his mind. But by a brief warning from the prophet he is so suddenly recalled to life that it is easy to infer that some spark, though smothered, still remained in his mind and quickly burst into flame. So far as concerns the men themselves, they are as guilty as if they had renounced faith and all the grace of the Holy Spirit. But God's boundless goodness prevents the elect from rushing headlong into complete alienation. We should therefore be most careful lest we fall from faith. Yet we must believe that God keeps His elect by a secret bridle, that they may not fall to their destruction, and that He always cherishes miraculously in their hearts some sparks of faith, which He afterwards rekindles by the breath of His Spirit at the right time.

There are two clauses in this confession. Thomas confesses that Christ is his Lord, and then he goes higher and calls Him also God. We know the sense in which Scripture ascribes to Christ the name of Lord—in that the Father appointed Him to be the chief governor to hold all things under His rule, that every knee may bow before Him; in short, that He may be the Father's delegate in governing the world.

Thus, the name Lord belongs to Him properly, inasmuch as He is the Mediator manifested in the flesh and the Head of the Church. But when Thomas has acknowledged Him to be the Lord, he is at once carried on to His eternal divinity, and justly. For Christ descended to us and first was humbled and then was set at the Father's right hand and obtained dominion over heaven and earth that He might exalt us to His own divine glory and the Father's. Therefore, that our faith may arrive at the eternal divinity of Christ, we must start off from that knowledge which is nearer and easier. Thus some have justly said that by Christ-man we are led to Christ-God, because our faith progresses gradually; apprehending Christ on earth, born in a stable and hanging on a cross, it goes on to the glory of His resurrection and then at length to His eternal life and power, in which shines His divine majesty.

Yet this should be understood in the sense that we cannot know Christ aright as our Lord without the knowledge of His divinity immediately following. Nor is there any doubt that this confession should be common to all believers when we see that Christ approved it. He certainly would never have allowed honour to be taken from the Father and thoughtlessly transferred to Himself. But He plainly ratifies what Thomas said. Therefore, this one passage is abundantly sufficient for refuting the madness of Arius, for it is unlawful to imagine two Gods. The unity of person in Christ is also expressed here; for the same one is called God and Lord. He emphatically twice calls Him *his own*, showing that he speaks from a lively and earnest feeling of faith.

29. *Because thou hast seen me, Thomas.* All that Christ blames in Thomas is that he was so slow to believe that he needed to be drawn violently to faith by the experience of his senses, which is altogether inconsistent with the nature of faith. If any object that nothing is more unsuitable than to say that faith is a conviction conceived from touching and seeing, the answer is easily obtained from what I have already said. For it was not simply by touching and seeing that Thomas was brought to believe that Christ was his God; but being awakened, he remembered the teaching which had almost slipped from him. Faith cannot flow from a naked experience of things, but must have its origin in the Word of God. Christ therefore blames Thomas for honouring the Word less than he should have done and binding faith (which springs from hearing and ought to be entirely fixed to the Word) to the other senses.

Blessed are they that have not seen, and yet have believed. Here Christ commends faith on the ground that it acquiesces in the simple Word and does not depend at all on the sense and reason of the flesh. In a

short definition He therefore embraces the power and nature of faith
—that it does not stop short at the immediate sight but penetrates even
to heaven, so as to believe what is hidden from the human senses. And
indeed, we should give God the honour that His truth is αὐτόπιστος
to us.

Faith has, of course, its own sight, but it is one which does not stop
short at the world and earthly objects. This is why it is called a
demonstration of things invisible or not apparent (Heb. 11.1). Paul
contrasts it to sight (II Cor. 5.7), meaning that it does not stick at
considering the state of present things, nor look around at what
appears in the world, but depends on the mouth of God and, relying
on His Word, rises above the whole world to fix its anchor in heaven.
The sum of it is that there is no true faith but that which is founded on
the Word of God and rises to God's invisible kingdom and is superior
to all human grasp.

If any object that this saying of Christ's conflicts with another,
where He states that the eyes which behold Him present are blessed
(Matt. 13.16), I reply that Christ is there not speaking only of bodily
sight, as in this passage, but of revelation, which is common to all the
godly from the time when the Redeemer appeared in the world. He
compares the apostles with the holy kings and prophets who had been
kept under the obscure shadows of the Mosaic Law. He says that the
lot of believers is much better now, because a brighter light shines to
them, nay, because the substance and truth of the figures is exhibited
to them. There were many unbelievers then who saw Christ with the
eyes of the flesh and yet were no more blessed on that account. But
we who have never seen Christ with our eyes enjoy the blessedness
which Christ commends. It follows from this that He calls blessed
those eyes which spiritually behold in Him what is heavenly and
divine. For today we behold Christ in the Gospel no less than if He
stood with us. In this sense Paul tells the Galatians that He was crucified
before their eyes. Therefore, if we desire to see in Christ what will
make us happy and blessed, let us learn to believe where we do not
see. To these words of Christ corresponds what is said in I Pet. 1.8,
where believers are praised, who love Christ whom they have not
seen and rejoice with joy unspeakable although they do not see Him.

But the Papists' distortion of these words to prove their transubstantiation is worse than frivolous. That we may be blessed, they
tell us to believe that Christ is present in the likeness of bread (*in
specie*). But we know that nothing was farther from Christ's thoughts
than to subject faith to men's inventions. If it passes in the slightest
degree beyond the limits of the Word, it at once ceases to be faith.
If we have to believe uncritically all that we do not see, every monstrous

thing that men be pleased to invent, every fable they may babble, will hold our faith imprisoned. That this saying of Christ's applies to the case in point, we must first prove what is doubtful from the Word of God. They bring forward God's Word in support of their transubstantiation; but when the Word is properly expounded, it does not support their madness.

Many other signs did Jesus in the presence of the disciples, which are not written in this book: but these are written, that ye may believe that Jesus is the Christ, the Son of God; and that believing ye may have life in his name. (30-31)

30. *Many other signs therefore.* If this anticipation had not been added, readers might have thought that John had not left out any of the miracles that Christ performed and had given a full and complete history. John therefore declares that he has only written some things out of many; not that the others were not worth recording, but because these were sufficient to build up faith. And yet it does not follow that they were performed in vain, for they profited that age. Secondly, although today their kinds are unknown to us, we must not deduce that it is of little importance for us to know that the Gospel was sealed by a great wealth of miracles.

31. *But these are written, that ye may believe.* He means by these words that he committed to writing what should satisfy us, since it is abundantly sufficient to confirm our faith. For he wanted to meet men's empty curiosity, which is insatiable and allows itself excessive indulgence. Moreover, John was well aware of what the other Evangelists had written. And, as nothing was farther from his intention than to supersede their writings, he certainly does not separate their narrative from his own.

It may seem absurd, however, that faith is founded on miracles, when it ought to be devoted exclusively to God's promises and Word. I reply: No other use is here given to miracles than to be aids and supports of faith. They serve to prepare men's minds, so that they may give greater reverence to the Word of God. We know how cold and sluggish our attention is if we are not excited by something external. Besides, it adds no small authority to the teaching already received, when to support it He stretches out His mighty hand from heaven. Just as Mark says that the apostles taught, the Lord working with them and confirming the Word by signs following (16.20). Therefore, although faith properly rests on the Word of God, and looks to the Word as its only object, the addition of miracles is not superfluous, so long as they are also related to the Word and direct faith to it. We have explained elsewhere why miracles are called signs. It is because by them the Lord arouses men to the contemplation of His power when He exhibits anything new and unusual.

That Jesus is the Christ. He means the Christ as He had been promised in the Law and the prophets.—as the Mediator between God and men, the Father's supreme Legate, the only Restorer of the world and the Author of perfect happiness. For John did not seize on a bare and empty title to adorn the Son of God, but included under the name of Christ all the offices which the prophets ascribe to Him. We must therefore contemplate Him as He is there described. From this appears more clearly what was said before, that faith does not stick at miracles, but carries us straight to the Word. It is as if John said that what the prophets had taught by word had been proved by miracles. And indeed we see that the Evangelists themselves do not stop at relating the miracles but dwell more on doctrine, since miracles by themselves would produce nothing but a confused wonder. The words mean, therefore, that these things were written so that we might believe, so far as faith can be helped by signs.

He adds *the Son of God,* because none of the ordinary rank of men could have been found fit to perform such great things—to reconcile the Father to us, to expiate the sins of the world, to abolish death, to destroy the kingdom of Satan, to bring us true righteousness and salvation. Moreover, as the name of *Son* belongs only to Christ, it follows that He is Son by nature and not adoption. Therefore, there is contained in this name Christ's eternal divinity. And indeed, he who does not realize, through such shining proofs as are in the Gospel, that Christ is God, is not worthy to look even at the sun and the earth, for he is blind in clear light.

That believing ye may have life. This effect of faith was added to restrain men's desires, that they might not thirst to know more than is sufficient for obtaining life. For what wickedness it was to be dissatisfied with eternal salvation and want to go beyond the bounds of the heavenly kingdom! John here repeats the chief head of his teaching, that we obtain eternal life by faith, because outside Christ we are dead and we are restored to life by His grace alone. We have spoken fully enough about this subject in chapters 3 and 5.

As to his saying *the name of Christ,* rather than merely *Christ,* the reason has been explained in chapter 1.12. The reader may go to that passage, if he will, so that I may not have the trouble of repeating the same things frequently.

CHAPTER TWENTY-ONE

After these things Jesus manifested himself again to the disciples at the sea of Tiberias; and he manifested himself on this wise. There were together Simon Peter, and Thomas called Didymus, and Nathanael of Cana in Galilee, and the sons of Zebedee, and two other of his disciples. Simon Peter saith unto them, I go a fishing. They say unto him, We also come with thee. They went forth, and entered into the boat; and that night they took nothing. But when day was now breaking, Jesus stood on the beach: howbeit the disciples knew not that it was Jesus. Jesus therefore saith unto them, Children, have ye aught to eat? They answered him, No. And he said unto them, Cast the net on the right side of the boat, and ye shall find. They cast therefore, and now they were not able to draw it for the multitude of fishes. That disciple therefore whom Jesus loved saith unto Peter, It is the Lord. So when Simon Peter heard that it was the Lord, he girt his coat about him (for he was naked), and cast himself into the sea. But the other disciples came in the little boat (for they were not far from the land, but about two hundred cubits off), dragging the net full of fishes. So when they got out upon the land, they see a fire of coals there, and fish laid thereon, and bread. Jesus saith unto them, Bring of the fish which ye have now taken. Simon Peter therefore went up, and drew the net to land, full of great fishes, a hundred and fifty and three: and for all there were so many, the net was not rent. Jesus saith unto them, Come and break your fast. And none of the disciples durst inquire of him, Who art thou? knowing that it was the Lord. Jesus cometh and taketh the bread, and giveth them, and the fish likewise. This is now the third time that Jesus was manifested to the disciples, after that he was risen from the dead. (1-14)

1. *After these things Jesus manifested himself.* The Evangelist is still taking pains to prove Christ's resurrection. He relates that He appeared to seven disciples, among whom he mentions Thomas, not out of respect to him, but because his testimony is the more credible in proportion as his unbelief had been obstinate. The Evangelists account is full enough, for he carefully collects all the details which substantiate the story. We have elsewhere said that the Lake of Tiberias is called, after the Hebrew custom, a sea.

3. *I go a fishing.* That Peter was busy fishing should not be regarded as alien to his office (*officio*). By the breathing he had been ordained an apostle, as we saw earlier. But he abstained for a little while, until he

should have been clothed with new power. For he had not yet been commanded to proceed in the execution of his office of teaching (*munus docendi*) but had only been told of his future calling, so that he and the others might understand that they had not been chosen from the beginning for nothing. Meanwhile, they do what they were used to doing and what pertained to private men. It is true that, during his career as a preacher, Paul made a living by his hands, but this was for a different reason; for his time was so arranged that his manual work did not interfere with his preaching. On the other hand, Peter and his companions give themselves up unrestrictedly and entirely to fishing because they are free from public duties.

And that night they took nothing. God let them toil all night in vain to light up the credit of the miracle. For if they had caught anything, the power of Christ would not have been so clearly manifested in what followed. But when they have toiled ineffectually all night and are suddenly favoured with a huge haul, they have good reason to acknowledge the grace of the Lord. God often tries believers in this same way, that He may commend His blessing to them. If we always succeeded when we put our hand to any labour, scarcely anyone would attribute the reward of his work to God's blessing, but all would boast of their own industry and shake hands with themselves (*manus suas oscularentur*). But when sometimes they wear themselves out and torment themselves to no advantage, then, if they should succeed better, they are forced to acknowledge something extraordinary. Consequently, they begin to praise God's grace for their success.

6. *Cast the net on the right side.* Christ does not command with authority and power as Master and Lord, but advises like one of the people. And because the disciples are at a loss what to do, they readily obey this man, unknown as He is. If anything of this sort had been said to them before the first casting, they would not have obeyed so quickly. I mention this lest any should be surprised that they were so submissive, for they were already exhausted after long and useless toil. Yet it was no common proof of patience that even after daybreak they keep on at the work they had been doing all night. And indeed, if room is to be given for God's blessing, we must constantly expect it. For nothing is more unreasonable than to withdraw the hand from work at once unless it looks fruitful.

Simon Peter's nakedness is an indication that the disciples had worked hard. And yet they do not refuse to try another casting, so that they may not neglect any opportunity. Their obedience to Christ's command cannot be ascribed to faith, for they hear Him speaking as an unknown man. Now if our calling is irksome because the labour we undertake seems barren, we ought to take heart when the Lord exhorts us to steadfast perseverence. In the end we shall not lack a happy outcome; but it will be at the proper time.

And now they were not able to draw it. Christ showed His power, first, in their taking so large a draught of fishes, and secondly, when by His hidden power He preserved the net which must otherwise have been torn and burst. Other details are added: That the disciples find burning coals on the shore; that there are fishes there, and bread is also set ready. There is no lofty mystery in the number of the fishes. Augustine subtly produces the Law and the Gosepl out of the statement of the number. But if anyone examines it more closely, he will find that this is childish trifling.

7. *Therefore that disciple.* By his own example the Evangelist teaches us that we must raise our minds to God whenever we succeed beyond our expectation, for we should instantly remember that this benefit has flowed from the grace of Him who is the author of all blessings. That holy recognition of divine grace which dwelt in John's mind led him also to the knowledge of Christ. He does not recognize Christ with his eyes, but is convinced that the multitude of fishes has been given by God and so concludes that it was Christ who had guided his hands. John is the first to believe, but Peter is more zealous. He disregards danger and jumps into the lake. The rest follow in the ship. Certainly, they all come to Christ in the end, but a special zeal beyond the others seizes Peter. Whether he reached the shore by walking or swimming is uncertain. Let it suffice that his leaving the ship and going ashore was not a piece of foolhardiness, but that he went before the others in proportion to his zeal.

10. *Bring of the fish.* Although the net was filled in a moment, without hard work on their part, yet Christ ascribes the catching to the disciples. Thus we call it our bread, and yet, by asking that it may be given to us, we confess that it comes from God's blessing.

12. *And none of his disciples durst ask him.* It may be asked what hindered them—shame arising from reverence, or something else? But if Christ saw that they were uncertain, he ought to meet their doubt, as often before. I reply: Their only reason for being ashamed was that they were not certain enough that He was Christ. For we are accustomed to ask about what is doubtful and obscure. The Evangelist therefore means that the disciples did not question Christ, because they were afraid of wronging Him, so plainly did He reveal Himself by obvious signs.

14. *This is now the third time.* The number three refers to the space of time. Christ had already appeared more than seven times, but all that happened in one day is embraced under one appearance. He

therefore means that Christ had been seen by the disciples at intervals, to confirm their faith in His resurrection.

So when they had broken their fast, Jesus saith to Simon Peter, Simon, son of John, lovest thou me more than these? He saith unto him, Yea, Lord; thou knowest that I love thee. He saith unto him, Feed my lambs. He saith to him again a second time, Simon, son of John, lovest thou me? He saith unto him, Yea, Lord; thou knowest that I love thee. He saith unto him, Feed my sheep. He saith unto him the third time, Simon, son of John, lovest thou me? Peter was grieved because he said unto him the third time, Lovest thou me? And he said unto him, Lord, thou knowest all things; thou knowest that I love thee. Jesus saith unto him, Feed my sheep. Verily, verily, I say unto thee, When thou wast young, thou girdedst thyself, and walkedst whither thou wouldest: but when thou shalt be old, thou shalt stretch forth thy hands, and another shall gird thee, and carry thee whither thou wouldest not. Now this he spake, signifying by what manner of death he should glorify God. And when he had spoken this, he saith unto him, Follow me. (15-19)

15. *So when they had broken their fast.* The Evangelist now relates how Peter was restored to the rank of honour from which he had fallen. His treacherous denial, of which we have heard, made him unworthy of the apostleship, for how could he be a suitable master of the faith (*magister fidei*) who had basely revolted from it? He had been made an apostle; but so had Judas. And from the time he abandoned his post he had been deprived of the honour of apostleship. Now both the freedom and the authority to teach, which he had lost through his own fault, are restored to him. And lest the disgrace of his fall should be a hindrance to him, Christ blots out and destroys the memory of it. Such a restoration to soundness was necessary, both for Peter and his hearers—for Peter, that he might the more energetically prosecute his office, assured of the calling again laid on him; for his hearers, that the stain attaching to the man might not make them despise the Gospel. To us today it is of the greatest importance that Peter comes forth to us as a new man from whom has been wiped out the disgrace which might have been an obstacle to his position.

Simon, son of John, lovest thou me? By these words Christ means that none can faithfully serve the Church and sustain the task of feeding the flock unless he looks higher than men. In the first place, the office of feeding is in itself laborious and troublesome, for nothing is more difficult than to keep men under the yoke of God, many of whom are weak, others light and unsteady, others dull and sluggish and yet others hard and unteachable. Satan now attacks with all the stumbling-blocks he can, to break or weaken the courage of a good pastor. Add to this the ingratitude of many and other causes of weariness. Therefore he will never steadfastly persevere in this office unless the love of Christ so reigns in his heart that forgetting himself and devoting himself entirely to Him, he surmounts every obstacle. Paul states that this was his attitude, when he says, 'The love of Christ constraineth us; because we thus judge, that if one died for all, all must have been dead' (II Cor. 5.14). For although he means the love with which Christ loved us, and of which He shows us proof in His death, yet he connects with it that mutual love which springs from the feeling of such a great blessing. On the other side, wicked and false teachers who disturb the Church are branded with the mark that they do not love the Lord Jesus (I Cor. 16.22).

Those called to govern the Church should therefore remember that if they want to discharge their office truly and properly, they must start off from the love of Christ. Meanwhile, Christ testifies clearly how highly He places our salvation when He commends it so carefully to pastors. And He asserts that He will be greatly loved by them if they seriously care for it. Indeed, nothing more efficacious could have been said for encouraging ministers of the Gospel, than when they hear that the service most agreeable to Christ is that which is expended on feeding His flock. All the godly should receive no ordinary consolation when they hear that they are so dear and precious to the Son of God that He substitutes the pastors as it were in His place (*quasi in locum suum subroget*). But the same doctrine should greatly frighten false teachers, who pervert the government of the Church. For Christ declares that He is dishonoured by them and will give them a dreadful punishment.

Feed my lambs. The word 'feed' is metaphorically applied by Scripture to any kind of governing. But as the spiritual government of the Church is under discussion here, it is important to observe in what the office of pastor consists. No idle dignity is here described to us; nor does Christ bestow on a mortal man any government which he can exercise confusedly for his own pleasure. But we saw in chapter 10 that Christ is the only shepherd of the Church. We saw also why He takes this name to Himself. It is because He governs His sheep by the teaching of salvation and so feeds them, for He is the only true food of the soul. But, since He uses men's work in preaching the Gospel, He gives them also His own name, or at least, shares it with them. Therefore, they only are regarded as pastors in the sight of God who, under Christ their Head, preside over the Church by the ministry of the Word. From this we may easily infer what is the burden which

Christ lays on Peter and on what condition He appoints him to govern His flock.

By this the wickedness of the Romanists is plainly refuted. They twist this passage to support the tyranny of their Popery. They say, 'Peter, in preference to the others is told, Feed my sheep.' Why it was said to him rather than to the others we have already explained—that, free from every bad mark, he might be free to preach the Gospel. The reason why Christ thrice appoints him as pastor is to wipe out the three denials by which Peter brought everlasting shame on himself so that it shall not hinder his apostleship, as Chrysostom, Augustine and Cyril and most others have wisely observed. Moreover, in these words there was nothing given to Peter that is not common to all ministers of the Gospel.

Therefore the Papists argue in vain that he is first, since he alone is addressed in particular. And granted that some personal honour was conferred on him, I ask how they will prove from this that he has been set in the primacy. Even if he were the chief among the apostles, does it follow that he was the universal bishop of the whole world? Add that all that Peter received belongs no more to the Pope than to Mohammed. For by what right does he claim to be Peter's heir? And what sane man will admit that Christ is here bestowing on him some hereditary right? Yet he wants to be regarded as Peter's successor. Would that he were! None of us dissuades him from loving Christ and taking care to feed His flock. But to neglect the love of Christ and cast off the office of feeding, and then to boast of his succession is too absurd and silly. Now, as Christ, in committing to Peter the province of teaching, did not intend to set up a throne for an idol or for a butcher of souls, from which he might miserably oppress the Church, so He told him briefly what kind of government of the Church He approves. This takes the mask (*larva*) off all the mitred bishops, who are satisfied with a mere theatrical display and an empty title and claim for themselves episcopal authority.

16. *Feed my sheep.* Christ does not commit to Peter and the others the feeding of all indiscriminately, but only of His lambs or sheep. Elsewhere He defines whom He reckons in His flock. He says, 'My sheep hear my voice and follow me; they hear not the voice of a stranger.' Certainly, faithful teachers should try to gather all to Christ; and as they cannot distinguish between the sheep and the wild beasts, they should try by every means to tame those who are more like wolves than sheep. But after they have tried their utmost, their labour will be of avail only to the chosen sheep. For docility and faith arise from the heavenly Father delivering to obedience to His Son those whom He elected before the foundation of the world. Again,

this passage teaches us that none can be fed to salvation by the teaching of the Gospel but those who are mild and teachable, for it is not without reason that Christ compares His disciples to lambs and sheep. But it must also be observed that God's Spirit tames those who were by nature bears and lions.

17. *Peter was grieved.* Peter undoubtedly did not understand Christ's purpose in asking him the same thing so frequently. Therefore, he thinks that he is being obliquely accused, as if he had answered insincerely. But we have already shown that the repetition is not superfluous. Besides, Peter was not yet sufficiently aware how deeply the love of Christ has to be fixed in the minds of those who have to overcome innumerable difficulties. Later he learned by long experience that he had not been through such testing for nothing. And those who have to undertake the charge of governing the Church are taught in his person not to examine themselves facilely but to scrutinize thoroughly what zeal they are endowed with, lest they should shrink or faint in mid course. We are all taught that we should submit quietly and patiently if ever the Lord tests us more severely; for He has good reasons for doing so, although they are mostly unknown to us.

18. *Verily, verily, I say unto thee.* After exhorting Peter to feed His sheep, Christ arms him to undertake the impending warfare. Thus He demands from him not only faithfulness and diligence, but invincible courage in dangers and constancy in bearing the cross. In short, He tells him to be prepared to die when necessary. Now, although not all pastors are in the same position, this warning pertains to all in some measure. Many the Lord spares and refrains from shedding their blood and is satisfied simply if they devote themselves to Him sincerely through all their life. But since Satan is continually making manifold new attacks, all who undertake the office of 'feeding' must be prepared for death, for they are concerned not only with sheep but with wolves. So far as relates to Peter, Christ wanted to forewarn him of his death, that he might continually remember that the doctrine of which he was a minister would have to be ratified by his own blood in the end. Yet it seems that in these words Christ was not thinking of him alone but adorned him with the title of martyr in the presence of others, as if He said that Peter would be a very different kind of combatant from what he had shown himself to be.

When thou wast young. Old age seems to be set aside for quiet and rest, and so old men are usually retired from public duties and soldiers are released from service. Peter might therefore have looked forward to a peaceful old age. But Christ declares that the order of nature will be reversed, so that he who had lived at his own will when he was

P

young would be ruled by another when old and even undergo violent subjection.

Moreover, in Peter we have a remarkable mirror of our common lot. Many have an easy and cheerful life before Christ calls them. But as soon as they have joined His side and been received among His disciples, or at least within some time, they are drawn into hard struggles, a troublesome life, great dangers and sometimes even death itself. Although this state is hard, it must be borne cheerfully. Yet the Lord so moderates the cross by which He wishes to try His servants that He pampers them a little until their strength matures. For He knows their weakness and does not press them beyond its limits. Thus, He made allowance for Peter so long as He saw he was tender and unwarlike. Let us therefore learn to give ourselves to Him to the last breath, if only He will supply us with strength.

In this respect the base ingratitude of many appears. For the more gently the Lord deals with us, the more do we accustom ourselves to continual softness. Thus we find scarcely one in a hundred who does not grumble if, after long forbearance, he is treated more harshly. We should the rather consider God's humaneness in sparing us for a time. Thus Christ says that while He dwelt on earth He lived cheerfully with His disciples, as if He had been at a wedding, but that fasting and tears awaited them afterwards (Matt. 9.15).

Another shall gird thee. Many think that this signifies his manner of death; that he was hanged, with outstretched arms. But I interpret the word gird as simply comprehending all the external actions by which a man regulates himself and his whole life. *Thou girdedst thyself;* that is, you dressed as you liked, but the freedom to choose your dress will be taken from you. As to the kind of execution that Peter suffered, it is better to be ignorant than to trust to doubtful fables.

And carry thee whither thou wouldest not. This means that Peter did not die a natural death, but by violence and the sword. It may seem absurd for Christ to say that his death will not be voluntary. For there is no constancy and praise in martyrdom when one is hurried unwillingly to death. But this must be referred to the contest between the flesh and the spirit which believers feel within themselves. For we never obey God so freely and spontaneously but that the world and the flesh draw us as with ropes in the opposite direction. Hence Paul's complaint, 'The good which I would I do not, etc.' Besides, we must observe that the fear of death is naturally implanted in all, for it is repugnant to nature to wish to be destroyed. And so, although Christ was prepared to obey God with all His heart, He pleads against death. Moreover, Christ[1] was tormented with fears because of the

[1] Read *Christi* for *Petro*.

cruelty of men and it is not surprising if in some measure He recoiled from death. But this proved the more clearly the obedience which He rendered to God, that He would willingly have fled from death on His own account, and yet endured it voluntarily because He knew that this was the will of God. For if there had been no mental struggle, there would have been no patience.

This is a very useful lesson to know. It urges us to prayer, for we should never be able without God's special help to overcome the fear of death. Therefore, nothing remains but to offer ourselves submissively to His ruling. This serves also to sustain our minds, that we may not altogether faint if ever we waver in persecutions. Those who think that martyrs were not touched by any fear, think their own fear a reason for despair. But there is no reason why our weakness should deter us from following their example, since their experience was like ours, and they could only triumph over the enemies of truth by fighting against themselves.

19. *Signifying by what manner of death, etc.* This periphrase is very important, for although the end set before all believers ought to be to glorify God in life and in death, John wanted to adorn with a special commendation the death of those who with their blood seal Christ's Gospel and glorify His name, as Paul tells us (Phil. 1.20). It is for us now to reap the harvest which Peter's death has yielded. For our laziness is to blame if it does not confirm our faith and we do not press to the same end, that God's glory may be illuminated through us. If the Papists had considered this end in the death of the martyrs, the sacrilegious and detestable invention would never have entered their minds that it contributes to appeasing the wrath of God and paying the ransom for sins.

And when he had spoken this. Christ here explains why He had foretold a violent death. It was that Peter might be prepared to endure it. He said, 'Since you must undergo death after my example, follow your leader.' Again, that Peter may obey God more willingly when He calls him to the cross, Christ offers Himself as the leader. For this is not a general exhortation, inviting him to imitate Himself; He speaks only of the kind of death. This one consideration greatly soothes all the bitterness in death, when the Son of God presents Himself before our eyes with His blessed resurrection, which is our triumph over death.

Peter, turning about, seeth the disciple whom Jesus loved following; which also leaned back on his breast at the supper, and said, Lord, who is he that betrayeth thee? Peter therefore seeing him saith to Jesus, Lord, and what shall this man do? Jesus saith unto him, If I will that he tarry till I come, what is that to thee? follow thou me. This saying therefore went forth among the brethren, that that disciple should not die: yet Jesus said not unto him, that he should not die; but, If I will that he tarry till I come, what is that to thee? This is the disciple which beareth witness of these things, and wrote these things: and we know that his witness is true. And there are also many other things which Jesus did, the which if they should be written every one, I suppose that even the world itself would not contain the books that should be written. (20-25)

20. *Peter, turning about.* We have in Peter an instance of our not merely superfluous but even harmful curiosity, that we are drawn away from our duty by looking at others. For it is almost innate in us to examine the lives of others rather than our own, and in them to grasp at empty excuses. We willingly deceive ourselves by the semblance of excuse that others are no better than ourselves, as if their laziness absolved us. Scarcely one in a hundred considers what Paul's saying means: 'Each man shall bear his own burden' (Gal. 6.5). Therefore there is a general reproof in the person of this one man on all who look around them everywhere to see how others act and neglect what God has enjoined on themselves. Above all, they are seriously mistaken in overlooking what each man's own particular calling demands.

Out of ten God may choose one to test by heavy calamities or huge labours and leave the other nine quiet, or at least try them only lightly. Moreover, God does not treat all alike, but makes trial of every one as He thinks fit. Since there are different kinds of Christian warfare, let every one learn to keep his own position and not ask like noncombatant spectators about this or that person, for our heavenly leader urges on each of us, and we ought to be so intent on His command as to forget everything else.

Whom Jesus loved. This periphrase was put in to tell us what moved Peter to ask the question here related. He thought it strange that he alone should be called and John overlooked, whom Christ had always loved so much. Peter therefore had some pretext for asking why no mention was made of John, as if Christ's attitude to him had changed. But Christ cuts short his curiosity by telling him that it is for him to obey God's calling and that it is not for him to inquire what will happen to others.

22. *If I will that he tarry.* This sentence has commonly been shortened and the former clause read affirmatively, thus, 'I will that he tarry till I come.' But this has been done through the ignorance of transcribers, not by a translator's error. For he could not have been mistaken about the Greek word, though a single letter could easily have crept into

the Latin and altered the whole meaning.[1] The complete sentence is therefore a question and should be read as a unit. For Christ wanted to lay His hand on His disciple to keep him within the limits of his calling. He says, 'It is nothing to do with you, and you have no right to ask what will become of your colleague. Leave that to my will. You just think about yourself and get ready to follow where you are called.' Not that all anxiety about brethren is superfluous; but it should have a limit, so that it may be anxiety and not curiosity that occupies us. Let every man look to his neighbours if by any means he may succeed in drawing them along with him to Christ; but let not the offences of others hinder him.

23. *This saying therefore went forth.* The Evangelist relates that Christ's words were misunderstood and the error arose among the disciples that John would never die. He means those who were present at that conversation, that is, the apostles. Not that the name brethren belongs to them alone; but they were, so to say, the first-fruits of that holy community. It is also possible that besides the eleven He refers to others who were then with them, and by the term *went forth* he means that this error was spread in all directions. But it was probably not long-lived but existed among them until they had been enlightened by the Spirit and thought more correctly and purely about Christ's kingdom, and laid aside gross imaginations.

What John relates of the apostles happens every day, and it is not surprising. For if Christ's disciples, who were of His household circle, were so deluded, how much more are they liable to fall who have not been so familiarly taught in the school of Christ? But let us also notice where this fault arises. Christ teaches us for use and edification, and indeed, clearly. But we shade the light with the wicked inventions which we bring from our own senses. Christ did not mean to declare anything definite about John, but only to state that He had full power over his life and death. So that the lesson is simple and useful in itself, but the disciples invent and imagine more than had been said. Therefore, if we are to be freed from this danger, let us learn to be sober and wise. Such is the wantonness of the human mind that it rushes headlong into vanity. Consequently, this very error which the Evangelist had expressly warned them to be on their guard against, nevertheless spread in the world. For it was fabled that he ordered a grave to be dug for him and went into it, and the next day it was found empty. We see therefore that there will be no end to error unless we simply embrace what the Lord has delivered to us and reject all foreign inventions.

---

[1] *Sic* (thus) for *si* (if). There are, in fact, variant readings here. Some MSS and editions read *si sic*, some *sic* and at least one *si*.

24. *This is the disciple.* So far, he has spoken of himself in the third person, but now John states that it is himself, so that greater weight may be attached to an eye-witness who had fully known all that he writes about. Lest any should suspect his account, as if it had been written with partiality because Christ had loved him, he forestalls the objection, saying that he has passed over more than he had written. He does not speak of Christ's actions of every sort, but of those which relate to His public office. Nor should the hyperbole seem absurd, when we bear with what come everywhere in secular writers. Not only should we take into account the number of Christ's actions, but we must also consider their importance and magnitude. The divine majesty of Christ, which in its infinity transcended not only the senses of men but even heaven and earth, miraculously showed its brightness in these works. If the Evangelist, casting his eyes on Him, exclaims in astonishment that even the whole world could not contain a fair account, who can be surprised? Nor is he to blame if he uses a common and ordinary image to commend the excellence of Christ's works. For we know that God accommodates Himself to the ordinary way of speaking because of our ignorance, and sometimes even, so to say, stammers.

Yet we must remember what we said before, that the summary which the Evangelist committed to writing is sufficient both to establish faith and to convey salvation. Therefore, that man who has duly profited under these teachers will be wise enough. And indeed, since they were appointed by God to be witnesses to us and have faithfully discharged their duty, it is for us to depend wholly on their testimony and not to desire more than they have handed down— especially since their pens were governed by the sure providence of God, that they might not burden us with an immoderate mass of things, but, in making a selection, might deliver to us all that the only wise God, the sole fount of wisdom, knew to be expedient for us. To Him be praise and glory for ever. Amen.

The First Epistle of
JOHN

INTRODUCTION

THIS commentary originally comprised one of the commentaries on the Catholic Epistles. Calvin did not join it to that on the Gospel. It has been taken from its proper position and placed here so that his commentaries on the Johannine writings might be together (we have no commentary from him on II and III John and Revelation).

Calvin lectured on the Catholic Epistles at the Congregation in 1549[1] and printed the Commentaries (which are presumably related to the lectures) in 1551:

> *Ioannis Calvini Commentarii in epistolas canonicas. Geneva. Crispin. fol. 1551.*

The second edition followed from the same printer in 1554.

In the third edition the Catholic Epistles formed a part of what, I suppose, Calvin intended us to regard as the definitive edition of his Commentaries on the New Testament Epistles. For, not only were they all assembled here, but according to Colladon, 'in this same year Calvin revised his Commentaries on all the Epistles of St Paul and that on Hebrews and the Catholic Epistles'[2]:

> *Commentarii in omnes Pauli epistolas atque in ep. ad Hebraeos, item in canonicas. Geneva. Stephanus. fol. 1556.*

The commentary on I John appeared separately in French in 1551:

> *Commentaire sur l'epistre Canonique de S. Iean. Geneva. Girard. 8o. 1551.*

Great Ponton   T. H. L. PARKER

---

[1] C.R. xxi. 71-72. I omitted to mention in the Introduction to the Gospel that Calvin had lectured on it in 1550—C.R. xxi. 72.

[2] C.R. xxi. 82.

THE THEME

THIS Epistle is completely worthy of the spirit of the disciple whom Christ loved above the others that He might give him to us as a friend. It contains teaching mixed with exhortations. For he speaks of the eternal deity of Christ and also of the incomparable grace which He brought with Him when He was revealed to the world, and of all His benefits in general. He especially commends and extols the inestimable grace of divine adoption. From this he takes the material for exhortations. At one time he admonishes us in general to a godly and holy life; and at another he gives express directions about love. Yet he does none of this systematically, but varies teaching with exhortation. But he especially urges brotherly love. He also briefly touches on other things, such as bewaring of impostors and the like. But each particular can be noticed in its own place.

CHAPTER ONE

That which was from the beginning, that which we have heard, that which we have seen with our eyes, that which we beheld, and our hands handled, concerning the Word of life (and the life was manifested, and we have seen, and bear witness, and declare unto you the life, the eternal life, which was with the Father, and was manifested unto us). (1-2)

He first puts forward the life exhibited to us in Christ. As it is an incomparable blessing, it ought to carry us away and inflame all our senses with a wonderful desire and love for it. It is said, in a few simple words, that life is manifested. But if we consider how miserable and horrible is the state of death and also what is the kingdom and immortal glory of God, we shall see that there is something here more magnificent than can be expressed in words.

Therefore the apostle's object in setting before us the great blessing —indeed, the chief and unique beatitude—which God has conferred on us in His Son, is to raise our minds on high. But since the greatness of the subject requires the truth to be certain and fully proved, he emphasizes this aspect. For the words *that which we have seen, that which we have heard, that which we beheld, etc.*, serve to confirm our faith in the Gospel. Nor does he assert so much without cause. Our salvation rests on the Gospel, and therefore its certainty is more than necessary. And how intractable we are in believing every one of us knows too well by his own experience. What I call believing is not some easy supposition or a mere assent to what is said, but embracing something with a firm undoubting conviction, so that we dare to subscribe to the truth as definite. This is why the apostle here heaps together so many things in confirmation of the Gospel.

1. *That which was from the beginning.* The passage is abrupt and confused; to make the meaning clearer we may arrange the words thus: 'We proclaim to you the Word of life which was from the beginning and was really testified to us in many ways, that life was manifested in Him.' Or if you prefer, the meaning may be given like this: 'What we proclaim to you about the Word of life has been from the beginning and was openly shown to us, for life was manifested in Him.' But the words *That which was from the beginning* undoubtedly refer to Christ's divinity. For God was not manifested in the flesh from the beginning; but He, who always was life and the eternal Word

of God, appeared in the fulness of time as man. Again, what follows
about beholding and touching with the hands refers to His human
nature. But as the two natures constitute but one person and Christ
is one who came forth from the Father that He might put on our
flesh, the apostle rightly states in general that He had always been the
same and invisible and afterwards became visible. This refutes the
foul quibble of Servetus, that the nature and essence of deity was one
with the flesh and that the Word was transformed into flesh because
the life-giving Word was seen in the flesh.

Therefore, let us remember that the Gospel doctrine is declared,
that He who truly proved Himself to be the Son of God in the flesh
and was acknowledged to be the Son of God, was always God's
invisible Word, for he does not refer here to the beginning of the
world, but goes much further back.

That which we have heard, that which we have seen. This was not
merely hearing a rumour, which usually is not much trusted; but
John means that he taught things which he had thoroughly learnt
from his Master, so that he put forward nothing thoughtlessly. And
indeed, none will be a fit teacher in the Church who has not first
been the pupil of the Son of God and rightly taught in His school, for
His authority.should be supreme.

When he says, *we have seen with our eyes,* it is not redundant but a
fuller expression to amplify the meaning. And not content with
seeing only, he added, *we have beheld, and our hands handled.* In these
words he declares that he taught nothing but what had been made
well known to him.

But it may seem that the evidence of the senses was of little use in
this matter, for Christ's power could not be comprehended by the
eyes or hands. I reply: He is saying the same thing here as in the first
chapter of his Gospel, 'We have seen his glory, a glory worthy of the
only begotten Son of God.' He was not known as the Son of God
from His outward physical form, but by giving luminous proofs of
His divine power, so that the majesty of the Father shone forth in Him
as in a living and express image. As the words are in the plural and the
matter applies equally to all the apostles, I interpret it of them; especially as it deals with the authority of witness.

But as I said before, Servetus' wickedness is as shameful as it is
frivolous. He urges these words to prove that the Word of God
became visible and palpable. He impiously either destroys or confuses
the twofold nature of Christ. And so he invents some sort of a figment,
so deifying the humanity of Christ that he wholly removes the truth
of His human nature, at the same time denying that Christ is called
the Son of God for any other reason than that He was conceived of

234

His mother by the power of the Holy Spirit and taking away His subsistence in God. From this it follows that He was neither God nor man, although he seems to compose a confused mass from the two. But as the apostle's meaning is clear to us, let us leave that dog on one side.

Concerning the Word of life. The genitive is here used as an adjective, 'vivifying'. For, as he teaches in the first chapter of his Gospel, 'in Him was life'. But this title belongs to the Son of God on two counts: He has poured out life on all creatures; and He now restores life in us who had perished, dead (*extincta*) through Adam's sin.

Furthermore, 'Word' can be explained in two ways, either of Christ or of the teaching of the Gospel, by which salvation is brought to us. But since its substance is Christ and it contains nothing but that He who had been always with the Father was at last revealed to men, the first explanation seems to me the more simple and natural. Moreover, it is established more fully from his Gospel that the Wisdom dwelling in God is called the Word.

2. *And the life was manifested.* The copulative is explanatory, as though he said, 'We bear witness to the life-giving Word, just as the life was manifested.' But the meaning may be twofold: That Christ, who is life and the fountain of life, has been exhibited; or that life has been openly set before us in Christ. The latter necessarily follows from the former. But as to the meaning of the words, the two things differ as cause and effect. When he repeats, *We declare the eternal life,* I do not doubt that he speaks of the effect, proclaiming that we obtain life by the benefit of Christ. From this we learn that Christ cannot be preached to us without the kingdom of heaven being opened to us, so that we are raised from death and may live the life of God.

Which was with the Father. This is true, not only from the foundation of the world, but also from all eternity; for always He was God, the fountain of life. And the power and capability of giving life was in the power of His eternal Wisdom. But He did not actually exercise it before the creation of the world. But from the time when God began to set forth the Word, that power which before lay hidden was poured forth to all creatures. There had already been some manifestation; but this was not the apostle's meaning. It was, that life was only manifested in Christ when He put on our flesh and completed all the parts of redemption. For although even under the Law the fathers were associates and partakers of the same life, we know that they were shut up under the hope that was to be revealed. It was necessary for them to seek life from Christ's death and resurrection. But this event was not only far distant from their eyes but also hidden from their minds. They therefore depended on the hope of revelation, which at last followed in due time. They could not have obtained life without its being in some way manifested to them; but between us and them there is this difference, that we, as it were, hold in our hands already revealed Him whom they sought as He was obscurely promised to them in figures. But the apostle aims at removing the idea of novelty which might lessen the dignity of the Gospel. This is why he says that life had not begun only now, though it had only recently appeared, for it was always with the Father.

That which we have seen and heard declare we unto you also, that ye also may have fellowship with us: yea, and our fellowship is with the Father, and with his Son Jesus Christ: and these things we write, that your joy may be fulfilled. And this is the promise which we have heard from him, and announce unto you, that God is light, and in him is no darkness at all. If we say that we have fellowship with him, and walk in the darkness, we lie, and do not the truth: but if we walk in the light, as he is in the light, we have fellowship one with another, and the blood of Jesus Christ his Son cleanseth us from all sin. (3-7)

3. *That which we have seen.* For the third time he repeats 'seen' and 'heard', so that there may be nothing lacking to the substantial certainty of his teaching. And we must note carefully that Christ chose as heralds of the Gospel fit and faithful witnesses of everything that they were to declare. He also testifies to their motive; for he says that he was moved to write for the sole reason of inviting those he was addressing to common fellowship in an inestimable blessing. From this it appears how much he cared for their salvation. This had no little force to bring them to faith; for we must be extremely ungrateful if we refuse to hear one who wants to communicate to us part of the happiness he himself has obtained.

He also expresses the fruit received from the Gospel, that we are united to God and to His Son Christ, in whom exists the highest good. He had to add this second clause, not only to make the teaching of the Gospel precious and lovely, but also to show that he wanted them to be his companions only to lead them to God, so that they all might be one in Him. For the ungodly also have a mutual union, but it is outside God; in fact, it is to alienate themselves more and more from God, which is the worst of all evils. It is, as we have already said, our sole happiness to be received into God's favour, so that we may be really united to Him in Christ—of which John 17 speaks. In short, John says that, as the apostles were adopted by Christ as brethren who were gathered into one body to cleave to God, so he does the same with the other disciples (*collegis*). The many are made partakers of this holy and blessed unity.

4. *That your joy.* By 'full joy' he expresses better the complete and perfect felicity which we obtain from the Gospel. At the same time he tells believers where they should fix all their affections. The saying is true, 'Where our treasure is, there is our heart also' (Matt. 6.21). Whoever really grasps what fellowship with God is will be abundantly satisfied with it alone, and no longer burn with other desires. David says, 'The Lord is my cup and my heritage. The lines have fallen for me in an excellent lot' (Psalm 16.5-6). In the same way Paul declares that for him everything was dung that he might possess Christ alone (Phil. 3.8). Therefore, only he has progressed in the Gospel who reckons himself happy in communion with God and rests in that alone. He puts it before the whole world and is ready for its sake to give up everything.

5. *And this is the promise.* I do not disapprove of the rendering of the old translator, 'This is the message'; for, although ἐπαγγελία more often means a promise, yet, as John is here speaking in general of the testimony mentioned before, the context seems to demand the other sense—unless perhaps you explain it as 'The promise which we bring you includes this, or has this condition joined to it.' We should then be certain of the apostle's meaning. For he did not want to embrace the whole teaching of the Gospel, but only to show that if we desire to enjoy Christ and His blessings we must be conformed to God in righteousness and holiness. As Paul says in Titus 2, 'The saving grace of God has appeared to all, that denying ungodliness and worldly lusts, we may live soberly and righteously and holy in this world'—although here he says metaphorically that we are to walk in the light because God is light.

Now, when he calls God *light* and says that He is *in the light*, the expressions are not to be pressed too far. Why Satan is called the prince of darkness is clear enough. And when God, on the other hand, is called 'the Father of light' and 'light', we first understand that there is nothing in Him but what is clear, pure and sincere; and secondly, that He so enlightens all things by His brightness that He lets nothing vicious or perverted, no spots or filth, no hypocrisy or fraud, lie hidden. Hence the sum of it is that, since there is no agreement between light and darkness, we are separated from God so long as we walk in darkness; and that therefore the fellowship which he mentions can only exist if we also become pure and full of light (*lucidus*).

In him is no darkness at all. John very often uses this way of speaking to amplify by a contrary negation what he has affirmed. Hence the meaning is that God is light in such a way that He admits no darkness. From this it follows that He hates an evil conscience, pollution and perverse behaviour and everything that smacks of darkness.

6. *If we say.* It is an argument from contraries when he concludes that they who walk in darkness are alienated from God. But this doctrine depends on the higher principle that God sanctifies His people. For it is not a naked command that he gives, demanding holiness of life from us, but rather he shows that the grace of Christ serves to scatter darkness and to kindle in us the light of God. It is as if he said, 'God does not communicate to us an empty fiction. For the power and effect of this fellowship must needs shine forth in our life; otherwise our profession of the Gospel is false.'

That he adds *and do not the truth* is equivalent to his saying, 'We do not act truthfully. We do not cherish what is true and right.' And, as I have observed before, he frequently uses this way of speaking.

7. *But if we walk in the light.* He now says that it is a sure sign of our union with God if we are conformed to Him. Not that purity of life reconciles us to God, as the first cause. But the apostle means that our union with God is assured by the effect, when His purity shines in us. And indeed, it is true that wherever God comes, everything is so filled with His holiness that He washes away all filth. For apart from Him we have nothing but uncleanness and darkness. Hence it is evident that none lives aright unless he cleaves to God. In saying *we have fellowship one with another*, he is not referring to men, but places God on one side and us on the other.

It may however be asked who among men can so express the light of God in his life as to have this likeness which John demands. For in this way it would be necessary for him to be entirely pure and free from darkness. I reply that expressions of this sort are accommodated to the grasp of men. He is said to be like God who aspires after His likeness, however distant from it he may yet be. We need look no further than the present passage for an example. He walks in darkness who is not ruled by the fear of God and does not aim with a pure conscience at devoting himself wholly to God nor seek to promote His glory. On the other hand, he who in sincerity of heart spends every part of his life in God's fear and service and worships Him faithfully, may be regarded as walking in the light, for he keeps to the right way, even though in many things he may err and groan under the burden of the flesh. Therefore it is integrity of conscience alone that distinguishes light from darkness.

And the blood of Jesus Christ. When he has taught what is the bond of our union with God, he also shows what fruit comes from it, even that our sins are freely remitted. This is the blessedness that David describes in Psalm 32, to teach us that we are most wretched until we are born again by God's Spirit and serve Him with a pure heart. For who can be imagined more miserable than the man whom God hates and abominates and over whose head hangs God's wrath and eternal death?

This is a remarkable passage. From it we learn, first, that the expiation of Christ, effected by His death, belongs properly to us when we cultivate righteousness in unrightness of heart. For Christ is Redeemer only to those who are turned from iniquity and begin a new life. So if we want to have God propitious to us so as to forgive our sins, we should not forgive ourselves. In short, remission of sins cannot be separated from repentance, nor can the peace of God be in those consciences where the fear of God does not reign.

The passage teaches us, secondly, that the free pardon of sins is not given to us only once, but that this benefit dwells for ever in the Church and is daily offered to believers. For the apostle addresses believers here, since assuredly no man ever has been or will be who can please God otherwise, for all are held guilty before Him. For however much we may desire to act aright, we always hold to God waveringly. And half-heartedness deserves no praise from God. Meanwhile, we continually separate ourselves, so far as we can, from God's grace by new sins. Hence all the saints need daily forgiveness of sins, and this alone keeps us in God's family.

By saying *from all sin*, he means that we are guilty before God on many counts, and there is no one at all who does not labour under many faults. But he tells us that no sins prevent the godly and those who fear God from pleasing Him. He also shows how we obtain pardon, and what is the cause of our cleansing, that Christ expiated our sins by His blood. And he says that all the godly are undoubtedly partakers in this cleansing.

All this part of his teaching has been wickedly perverted by the sophists. They make out that free pardon of sins is given us only in baptism. They avow that Christ's blood avails only there; and they teach that, after baptism, God is reconciled only by satisfactions. They leave some part to Christ's blood; but when they give praise to works, even in the slightest degree, they wholly subvert what John here says on the office of expiating sins and appeasing God. For these two things can never agree: that we are cleansed by Christ's blood and that we are cleansed by works. John assigns the whole and not just the half to the blood of Christ. The sum of what we have said, then, is that believers are assured that they are accepted by God because He has been reconciled to them through the sacrifice of Christ's death. And sacrifice contains cleansing and satisfaction. Hence the power and effect of all these belong to Christ's blood alone.

By this the sacrilegious invention of the Papists about indulgences is refuted. As if Christ's blood were insufficient, they add the blood and merits of martyrs to eke it out. Yet this blasphemy extends wider among us. They say that their keys, by which they keep the remission of sins shut up, are composed partly of the blood and merits of martyrs and partly of the works of supererogation by which any sinner may redeem himself. And therefore there remains to them no remission of sins but what impairs Christ's blood. For if their doctrine holds good, Christ's blood does not cleanse us, but only comes in as, so to say, a partial help. Thus, consciences are held in suspense which the apostle here tells to rely on faith alone.

If we say that we have no sin, we deceive ourselves, and the truth is not in us. If we confess our sins, he is faithful and righteous to forgive us our sins, and to cleanse us from all unrighteousness. If we say that we have not sinned, we make him a liar, and his word is not in us. (8-10)

8. *If we say.* He now commends grace from the need for it. As none is free from sin, he means that we are all lost and hopeless unless the Lord helps us with the remedy of pardon. He emphasizes that none is innocent so that all may know the better that they need mercy to deliver them from destruction[1] and that they may therefore be the more roused to obtain the necessary blessing.

By the word *sin* is meant here, not only a depraved and vicious inclination, but the fault which actually makes us guilty before God. Moreover, as this is a universal declaration, it follows that none of the saints who now are, or have been, or shall be, are excepted from this number. Hence Augustine fitly refuted the quibble of the Pelagians by this passage. And he sagely thought that confession of sin is required, not for the sake of humility, but lest we should lie and deceive ourselves.

When he adds, *and the truth is not in us,* he confirms in his usual manner the former sentence by repetition. Yet it is not, as elsewhere, a simple repetition, but he says that they who glory in falsehood are deceived.

9. *If we confess.* He again promises to the faithful that God will be propitious to them, so long as they acknowledge that they are sinners. It is very important to be quite sure that when we have sinned there is a reconciliation with God ready and prepared for us. Otherwise we shall always carry hell about within us. Few consider how miserable and unhappy is a wavering conscience. But in fact, hell reigns where there is no peace with God. So much the more, then, should we embrace with our whole mind this promise, which offers certain pardon to all who confess their sins.

[1] Reading *exitio* for *exilio.*

240

Moreover, he teaches that this is founded on the faithfulness and righteousness of God, because God, who promises, is true and righteous. For those who think that He is called righteous because He justifies us freely, reason, as I think, too subtly. For righteousness here depends on faithfulness, and both are joined to the promise. For God could have been righteous and yet dealt with us with the utmost rigour. But as He has bound Himself to us by His Word, He did not wish to be reckoned righteous without forgiving.

Because this confession is made to God, it demands sincerity of heart. But the heart cannot speak to God without newness of life. Therefore, confession includes true repentance. God certainly forgives freely, but in such a way that the easiness of mercy does not become an enticement to sin.

And to cleanse us. The word 'cleanse' seems to be used in another sense than before. He had said that we are cleansed by Christ's blood because by His benefit sins are not imputed. But now that he has spoken of pardon, he adds that God cleanses us from unrighteousness. Thus this second clause differs from the first. Hence, he tells us that a twofold fruit comes to us from confession: That God, who is reconciled by the sacrifice of Christ, forgives us; and that He corrects and reforms us.

If anyone objects that, while we are strangers in the world, we are never cleansed from all unrighteousness so far as our reformation goes, it is quite true. But John is not telling us what God performs in us now. He says that He is faithful to cleanse us, not just today or tomorrow (for so long as we are confined in the flesh we should be in a continual progress), but what He has once begun, He continues to do daily until He at last completes it. Thus Paul says that we are chosen that we may appear unreproveable before God (Col. 1.22). And in another place, that the Church is cleansed that it may be without wrinkle or spot (Eph. 5.27). But if anyone prefers to interpret this passage as saying the same thing twice, I leave it to him.

10. *We make him a liar.* He goes still further: those who claim for themselves purity, blaspheme God. For we see that He everywhere condemns the whole human race of sin. Therefore, whoever tries to evade this accusation wars against God, as though He persecuted them without cause.

To confirm it he adds, *and his word is not in us.* As if he said that we reject this great truth which shuts up all under guilt. From this we learn that we only progress properly in the Word of the Lord when we are really humbled, so as to groan under the burden of our sins and learn to flee to God's mercy and rest only in His fatherly kindness.

CHAPTER TWO

My little children, these things write I unto you, that ye may not sin. And if any man sin, we have an Advocate with the Father, Jesus Christ the righteous: and he is the propitiation for our sins; and not for ours only, but also for the whole world. (1-2)

1. *My little children.* That we are to refrain from sin is not only the ἀνακεφαλαίωσις of the former teaching but the sum of almost all the Gospel. And yet, because we are always subject to God's judgment, we are sure that Christ so intercedes by the sacrifice of His death that the Father is propitious to us. He also anticipates any thought that he gave a licence to sin when he spoke of God's mercy, and taught that it is offered to us all. Thus he joins together the two parts of the Gospel, which perverse men, by separating, tear and mutilate. Besides, the teaching of grace has always been subject to the slanders of the ungodly. When the expiation of sins by Christ is proclaimed, they assert that a licence is given to sinning.

To forestall these slanders, the apostle declares, first, that the aim of his teaching was that men should cease to sin. For when he says, *that ye may not sin*, he only means that they should abstain from sins according to the measure of human infirmity. To the same purpose is what I have already said on fellowship with God and being conformable to Him. But he is not silent about the remission of sins; for should heaven fall and all things be confounded, this part of the truth must never be omitted. The office of Christ must be preached clearly and distinctly.

And this is what we should do today. Because the flesh is inclined to wantonness, men should be carefully warned that righteousness and salvation are obtained by Christ's death to the end that we may become God's holy possession. Yet whenever it happens that some wantonly abuse God's mercy, there are many dogs who maliciously slander us, as though we had loosed the rein to vice. We ought still to go on proclaiming the grace of Christ, in which especially shines forth God's glory and in which consists the whole salvation of men. The barkings of the ungodly should, I say, be despised, for we see that the apostles were also assailed by them.

This is why he at once adds the second clause, that when we sin we have *an Advocate*. In these words he confirms what we have already heard, that we are very far from perfect righteousness, in fact, bring upon ourselves daily new guilt, and that nevertheless there is a remedy at hand to appease God if we flee to Christ. And in this alone can consciences rest, for in it is contained the righteousness of men, on it is founded the hope of salvation.

The conditional particle *if any* should be taken as causal, for it cannot but be that we sin. In short, John means that we are not only called away from sin by the Gospel, in that God invites us to Himself and offers us the Spirit of regeneration, but that provision is made for wretched sinners, so that they may have God always propitious to them and that the sins which bind them do not stop their being righteous, for they have a Mediator to reconcile them to God. But he wants to show how we return to favour with God; and so he says that Christ is our *Advocate*. For He appears before God for the purpose of exercising towards us the power and efficacy of His sacrifice. To make this more easily understood, I will speak more bluntly. Christ's intercession is the continual application of His death to our salvation. The reason why God does not impute our sins to us is because He looks upon Christ the intercessor.

The two titles with which he afterwards designates Christ properly belong to the subject of this passage. He calls him *righteous* and *a propitiation*. He needs both these to sustain the office and person (*munus personamque*) of Advocate. For what sinner could win God's favour for us? For we are all shut off from access to Him, since none is pure and free from sin. Hence no one is fit to be the High Priest unless he is innocent and separated from sinners, as is also declared in Heb. 7.26. *Propitiation* is put in, because none is fit to be the High Priest without a sacrifice. Thus, under the Law, the priest never entered the sanctuary without blood having been shed; and according to God's appointment, it was the custom for a sacrifice to accompany prayers as the usual seal. By this symbol God wanted to show that he who procures grace for us must be furnished with a sacrifice. For when God is offended, the price of a satisfaction is required to pacify Him. From this it follows that all the saints who ever have been and who shall be, need an Advocate and that none but Christ is equal to undertaking this office. And John undoubtedly ascribed these two titles to Christ expressly to show that He is the unique Advocate.

Now we receive great consolation when we hear that Christ not only died once to reconcile us to the Father but also continually intercedes for us, so that in His name an entry to God lies open to us, that our prayers may be heard. Therefore, we should especially beware lest this honour which belongs to Him alone be transferred to another. Yet we know that under the Papacy this office is ascribed indiscriminately to the saints. Thirty years ago this outstanding article of our faith that Christ is our Advocate was almost buried. To-day they allow indeed that He is one among many, but not the only one. Those among the Papists who have a little more sense of shame, do not deny that Christ transcends the others, but they afterwards associate with Him a vast number of colleagues. But the words clearly say that he who is not a priest cannot be an advocate. But the priesthood (*sacerdotium*) belongs to Christ alone. Nevertheless, we do not take away the mutual intercessions of saints which they practise in love towards one another. But this has no reference to the dead, who have removed from their companionship with men. Nor does it refer to that patronage (*patrocinia*) which they invent for themselves that they may not be clients (*clientes*) of Christ alone.[1] For although brethren pray for brethren, they all without exception look to one advocate (*patronum*). Without doubt, then, so many advocates as the Papists devise for themselves are so many idols set up against Christ.

We must also notice, by the way, that those who imagine that Christ kneels before the Father to pray for us err very grossly. Such ideas should be put away, for they detract from Christ's heavenly glory, and the simple truth held that the fruit of His death is ever fresh and lasting for us, that by His intercession He propitiates God to us and that He sanctifies our prayers by the odour of His sacrifice and helps us by the good-will of His advocacy (*patrocinii favore*).

2. *And not for ours only.* He put this in for amplification, that believers might be convinced that the expiation made by Christ extends to all who by faith embrace the Gospel. But here the question may be asked as to how the sins of the whole world have been ex-piated. I pass over the dreams of the fanatics, who make this a reason to extend salvation to all the reprobate and even to Satan himself. Such a monstrous idea is not worth refuting. Those who want to avoid this absurdity have said that Christ suffered sufficiently for the whole world but effectively only for the elect. This solution has commonly prevailed in the schools. Although I allow the truth of this, I deny that it fits this passage. For John's purpose was only to make this blessing common to the whole Church. Therefore, under the word 'all' he does not include the reprobate, but refers to all who would believe and those who were scattered through various regions of the earth. For, as is meet, the grace of Christ is really made clear when it is declared to be the only salvation of the world.

And hereby know we that we know him, if we keep his commandments.

[1] Calvin uses *patronus* and *clientes* in their Roman sociological sense. The *cliens* is under the protection of and is dependent on his *patronus*. See above on John 14.16, p. 82.

*He that saith, I know him, and keepeth not his commandments, is a liar,
and the truth is not in him: but whoso keepeth his word, in him verily
hath the love of God been perfected. Hereby know we that we are in
him: he that saith he abideth in him ought himself also to walk even
as he walked.* (3-6)

3. *And hereby.* After he has treated the doctrine of the free remission
of sins, he comes to the exhortations joined to it and depending on it.
And first, he tells us that the knowledge of God conceived from the
Gospel is not idle but that obedience proceeds from it. He then shows
what God especially requires from us—the chief thing in life, that we
should love God. The Scripture has good reason to repeat everywhere
what we read here about the living knowledge of God. For nothing
is commoner in the world than to draw the teaching of godliness into
frigid speculations. This is how theology has been adulterated by the
sophists of the Sorbonne, so that from all their knowledge not the
slightest spark of godliness shines forth. And everywhere inquisitive
men learn enough from God's Word to let them prattle for display.
In short, the commonest evil in all ages has been an empty profession
of God's name.

John therefore assumes this principle, that the knowledge of God is
efficacious. From it he concludes that they by no means know God
who do not keep His commandments. Granted that Plato was
groping in the darkness; but he denied that the beautiful which he
imagined could be known without ravishing a man with the admira-
tion of itself—this in *Phaedrus* and elsewhere. How then is it possible
for you to know God and yet be touched by no feeling? Nor indeed
does it proceed only from God's nature that, if we know Him, we
immediately love Him. For the same Spirit who enlightens our minds
also inspires our hearts with an affection corresponding to our knowledge. And the knowledge of God leads us to fear and love Him. For
we cannot know our Lord and Father as He shows Himself without
on our side showing ourselves dutiful children and obedient servants.
In short, the teaching of the Gospel is a living mirror in which we
contemplate God's image and are transformed to it, as Paul teaches us
in II Cor. 3.18. Where the conscience is not clear, there can be only
the empty ghost of knowledge.

We must notice the order when he says, *know we that we know him.*
He means that obedience is joined to knowledge, so that the latter in
fact comes first in order, as the cause necessarily precedes the effect.

If we keep his commandments. But no one keeps them in every
particular; therefore there is no knowledge of God in the world. I
reply: The apostle is not at all inconsistent, for he has earlier established

that all are guilty before God; and thus he does not mean that those who wholly satisfy the Law keep His commandments (and no such instance can be found in the world), but those who strive, according to the capacity of human infirmity, to form their life in obedience to God. For whenever Scripture speaks of the righteousness of believers, it does not exclude the remission of sins, but on the contrary, starts out from it.

But we are not to conclude from this that faith rests on works. For although everyone has a witness to his faith from his works, it does not follow that it is founded on them, but they are a subsequent proof added as a sign. The certainty of faith dwells only in Christ's grace. But godliness and holiness of life distinguish true faith from a fictitious and dead knowledge of God. For the truth is, as Paul says, that in Christ we have put off the old man (Col. 3.9).

4. *He that saith, I know him.* How does he prove that those without godliness who boast that they have faith are liars? From its contrary. For he has already said that the knowledge of God is efficacious. For God is not known by the naked imagination, but He reveals Himself inwardly to our hearts by the Spirit. Moreover, since many hypocrites boast that they have faith, the apostle condemns all such of falsehood. For what he says would be superfluous unless many made a false and vain profession of Christianity.

5. *But whoso keepeth.* He now defines the true keeping of God's Law: To love God. To my mind this passage is expounded wrongly by those who understand it as saying that they truly please God who keep His Word. Rather take it like this: To love God in sincerity of heart is to keep His commandments. For, as I have said before, he wanted to show briefly what God requires of us and in what is set the holiness of believers. Moses said the same thing when he summarized the Law: 'Now, O Israel, what does the Lord require of thee but to fear and love Him and to walk in His precepts?' (Deut. 10.12). And again he says, in Deut. 30.19-20: 'Choose life, even to love the Lord thy God, to serve Him and to cleave to Him, etc.' For the Law, which is spiritual, does not command only external works, but especially bids us love God with our whole heart.

We should not think it unreasonable that no mention is here made of men. For brotherly love flows straight from the love of God, as we shall see later. Therefore, whoever desires that his life shall be approved by God must direct all his activities to this end. If any object that none has ever been found who loved God so perfectly, I reply that it is enough for everyone to aspire to this perfection according to the measure of grace given him. Meanwhile he lays down the definition that the perfect love of God is the proper keeping of His Word. We should progress in this just as in knowledge.

Hereby know we that we are in him. He refers to the fruit of the Gospel which he had mentioned, fellowship with the Father and His Son, and thus confirms the former sentence by its sequel. For if it is the end of the Gospel to be united with God, and there can be no communion without love, then only he really progresses in faith who heartily cleaves to God.

6. *He that saith he abideth in him.* Earlier, he had set the light of God before us as an example. Now he calls us also to Christ, to imitate Him. Yet he does not simply exhort us to the imitation of Christ, but, from the union we have with Him, proves we should be like Him. He says that a likeness in life and actions will prove that we abide in Christ. And from these words he goes on to his next clause, which concerns love to the brethren.

Brethren, no new commandment write I unto you, but an old commandment which ye had from the beginning: the old commandment is the word which ye heard from the beginning. Again, a new commandment write I unto you, which thing is true in him and in you; because the darkness is passing away, and the true light already shineth. He that saith he is in the light, and hateth his brother, is in the darkness even until now. He that loveth his brother abideth in the light, and there is none occasion of stumbling in him. But he that hateth his brother is in the darkness, and walketh in the darkness, and knoweth not whither he goeth, because the darkness hath blinded his eyes. (7-11)

7. *Brethren, no new commandment, etc.* This is an explanation of the preceding teaching, that to love God is to keep His commandments. And he is deliberately insisting on this point. First, we know that novelty is hated or suspected. Secondly, we do not easily bear an unusual yoke. Add that, when we have embraced as certain any kind of teaching, it is annoying to have anything altered or renewed in it. For these reasons John tells us that he taught nothing about love but what believers had heard from the beginning and which had become old by use.

Some explain oldness differently, that Christ now only prescribes under the Gospel the same rule of life as God had done under the Law. This is certainly most true. Nor do I deny that in this sense he afterwards calls the Word of the Gospel *the old commandment.* But I judge that he now merely means that these were the first elements of the Gospel, that they had been taught from the beginning and that there was no reason why believers should flee from them as unusual when they ought to have been imbued with them long since. For the relative seems to be put as a causative. He calls it *old,* not because it had been taught to the fathers ages before, but because it had been taught to these believers at their very entrance into religion. And it was of great use in claiming faith from them, when the readers knew that it proceeded from Christ Himself, from whom they had the Gospel.

The old commandment. The word 'old' here probably has a wider reference, for the sentence is fuller when he says *the old commandment is the word which ye heard from the beginning.* To my mind, he means that the Gospel should not be received as a recently born teaching, but as what has proceeded from God and is His eternal truth. It is as if he said, 'You must not measure the antiquity of the Gospel by the date at which it is brought to you. For in it is revealed to you the eternal will of God. Therefore, not only did God give you this rule of a holy life when first you were called to the faith of Christ, but the same has always been determined and prescribed by Him.' And without doubt, only that which has its origin from God should be regarded as antiquity and deserves faith and reverence. For men's fictions, however many years they can claim, cannot acquire such authority as to overwhelm the truth of God.

8. *Again, a new commandment.* Expositors do not seem to me to have followed the apostle's meaning. He says *new,* because God as it were daily renews it by suggesting it, so that believers may exercise themselves in it throughout their whole lives, for they can seek nothing more excellent. The elements which children learn give place later to what is higher and more substantial. But John denies that the teaching about brotherly love is like this, growing old with time, and says that it perpetually flourishes, so that it is no less the highest perfection than the elements.

But this needed to be put in, for men are always more inquisitive than they should be and a good part always seek something new. Hence there is a boredom towards simple teaching which produces innumerable monstrosities of error, everyone gaping continually after new mysteries. But when it is known that the Lord proceeds in the same even course, so that He may keep us throughout our life in what we have learnt, a bridle is put on this kind of desire. Therefore, let him who would arrive at the goal of wisdom in right living make progress in love.

Which thing is true. By this reason he proves what he had said. For in this one command to love consists, so far as our way of living is concerned, the whole truth of Christ. And what greater revelation could be expected? For Christ is indeed the end and fulfilment of all things. Hence the word 'truth' signifies that they stood as it were at the goal. For it is to be taken as a fulfilled or perfect state. He joins Christ to them as the Head to the members; as if he said that the body of the Church has no other perfection, or that they would be substantially united to Christ when holy love mutually flourished among them. Some expound it differently: 'That which is truth in Christ is also in you.' But I do not see the sense in this.

Because the darkness is passing away. The present is put here for the past. He means that, as soon as Christ shines, we have the full brightness of understanding. Not that every believer is as wise from the first day as he ought to be (for even Paul says that he laboured to apprehend what he had not understood (Phil. 3.12-13)); but because the knowledge of Christ is alone sufficient to dissipate darkness. Hence daily progress is necessary. Every man's faith has its dawn before it gets to noonday. But since God keeps on with the same teaching in which He bids us advance, the knowledge of the Gospel is justly said to be the true light, where Christ, the Sun of righteousness, shines. Thus the way is shut against the audacity of those who try to corrupt the purity of the Gospel by their own fictions; and we may safely level an anathema against the whole theology of the Pope, for it completely obscures the true light.

9. *He that saith he is in the light.* He pursues the same metaphor. He had said that love is the only true rule by which our life is to be tested; he had said that this tried law is prescribed to us in the Gospel; finally he had said that it is there like the noonday light whch we should continually keep in sight. Now, on the other hand, he concludes that all are blind and wander in darkness who are strangers to love. That before he had mentioned the love of God, but now the love of the brethren, has no more contradiction than there is between effect and cause. Moreover, these two are so interconnected that they cannot be separated.

John later says, in chapter 3, that we falsely claim to love God unless we love our neighbour, and this is very true. But now he takes love for the neighbour as a testimony by which we prove that we love God. In short, since love towards God is such that in God it embraces men there is nothing strange that the apostle in discussing love refers indiscriminately now to God and now to the brethren—as is usual in Scripture. The whole perfection of life is often placed in love for God. On the other hand Paul teaches us that he who loves his neighbour has fulfilled the whole law (Rom. 13.8); and Christ declares that the main points of the Law are righteousness, judgment and truth (Matt. 23.23). Both these are true and well agree, for the love of God prepares us to love men and in fact we also testify our dutifulness to God by loving men at His command. However this may be, it is always certain that love is the aim to which our life should be directed. And this should be the more carefully observed in that nearly all choose almost anything rather than this one commandment of God. What follows is to the same purpose, *there is none occasion of stumbling* where there is a care for love. For he who forms his life thus will never stumble.

11. *But he that hateth his brother.* He again warns us that whatever brilliant sort of virtue we show there is nothing but sinfulness if love is absent. This passage may be compared with I Cor. 13, and no longer explanation is needed. But the teaching is obscure to the world because a large part is stupefied in I know not what masks. Fictitious sanctity dazzles the eyes of almost all, whereas love is neglected or at least put in a corner.

I write unto you, my little children, because your sins are forgiven for his name's sake. I write unto you, fathers, because ye know him which is from the beginning. I write unto you, young men, because ye have overcome the evil one. I have written unto you, little children, because ye know the Father. I have written unto you, fathers, because ye know him which is from the beginning. I have written unto you, young men, because ye are strong, and the word of God abideth in you, and ye have overcome the evil one. (12-14)

12. *Little children.* This is still a general statement. He is not only addressing the young, but by *little children* he means men of all ages, as in the first verse and also hereafter. I say this because expositors have incorrectly applied the term to children. When John speaks of children he calls them παιδία, a word expressing age. But here, as a spiritual father, he calls the old as well as the young τεκνία. He will presently accommodate special statements to different ages. But they are mistaken who think that he begins to do so here. On the contrary, lest what he had just said should obscure the free remission of sins, he again drives home the doctrine which is peculiar to faith, that this foundation may always be retained—that salvation is laid up for us in the grace of Christ alone. Holiness of life should certainly be urged; the fear of God should be carefully commanded; men should be sharply goaded to repentance; and newness of life, together with its fruits, should be commended. But we must always beware lest the doctrine of faith be smothered, which teaches that Christ is the only Author of salvation and all blessings. We should indeed keep such moderation that faith may always retain its primacy. This is the law which John prescribes to us. When he has been careful to speak of good works, he anxiously recalls us to the grace of Christ, in case he seems to give them more than he should.

Your sins are forgiven you. Without this assurance there would be only a transient and sketchy sort of religion. In fact, those who pass over the free remission of sins and dwell on other things build without a foundation. But John means that nothing is more suitable to stimulate men to fear God than when they are properly taught what blessings Christ has brought them, as Paul beseeches them by the bowels of God's mercies (Phil. 2.1). From this it appears how wicked is the slander of the Papists, who pretend that we freeze the desire to do right; whereas, in fact, we extol that which alone makes us obedient children to God. For he takes as the basis of his exhortation our knowledge that God is so benevolent to us as not to impute to us our sins.

For his name's sake. He ascribes the material cause, lest we should seek other means to reconcile us to God. For it would be insufficient to know that God pardons our sins, unless we came straight to Christ and the price He paid for us on the cross. We should the more notice this, because we see that by the craft of Satan and the wicked fictions of men this path is obstructed; for foolish men try to pacify God by various satisfactions and make up innumerable kinds of expiations to redeem themselves. For the many means of deserving pardon which we push on God are so many obstacles keeping us from approaching Him. Hence John, not satisfied with teaching simply that God remits our sins, expressly adds that He is propitious to us in respect to Christ, so that he may exclude all other reasons. If we are to enjoy this blessing, we also must pass by and forget all other names and embrace only the name of Christ.

13. *I write unto you, fathers.* He now begins to enumerate different ages, to show that what he had taught was relevant to each of them. For a general address sometimes affects men less. Indeed, such is our malignity that few think that what is directed at all belongs to themselves. The old for the most part steal away as if they had exceeded the age of learning. Children refuse to hear, as if they were not yet old enough. Middle-aged men do not attend, because they are occupied with other cares. Therefore, lest any should except themselves, he accommodates the Gospel to the use of individuals. And he mentions three ages, the most common division of human life. Thus the famous Lacedaimonian chorus had three orders: the first sang, 'What ye are we shall be,' the last, 'What ye are we have been,' and the middle, 'We are what some of you have been and others will be.' Into these three degrees John divides the course of human life.

He begins with the old, and says that the Gospel is suitable to them because from it they learned to know the eternal Son of God. Peevishness is common in the old; but they are made especially unteachable because they measure wisdom by the multitude of years. Moreover, Horace in his *Ars Poetica* has justly noted in them the fault of praising the time of their youth and rejecting whatever is now done or said differently. This evil John sagely cures when he tells us that the Gospel contains not only an ancient knowledge but one that leads us to the very eternity of God. Hence it follows that there is nothing here for them to mislike. He says that Christ was from the beginning. I refer this to His divine presence, in which He is co-eternal with the Father, as well as to His power, of which the apostle speaks in Heb. 13.8, that He was yesterday what He is today—as if he said, 'If antiquity pleases you, you have Christ, who is before all antiquity. And His disciples need not be ashamed of Him who includes all ages in Himself.'

At the same time we must notice what that religion is which is really ancient; that it is the one founded on Christ. Otherwise it will avail little, however long it may have prevailed, if it originated in error.

I write unto you, young men. Although he uses a diminutive, νεανίσκοι, he undoubtedly addresses himself to all who were in their prime. We also know that that age is addicted to the vain cares of the world, so that they think little of the kingdom of God. The vigour of their minds and the strength of their bodies in a way make them drunk. Hence the apostle reminds them where true strength is placed, that they might no longer go on rejoicing in the flesh. He says, *ye are strong because ye have overcome Satan.* The copulative here is equivalent to a causal particle. And without doubt we ought to seek that strength which is spiritual. At the same time he indicates that it is received only from Christ. For he commemorates the blessings which we receive through the Gospel. He says that they had conquered who were still engaged in fighting. But our condition is very different from that of those who fight under men's banners. To them war is doubtful and the issue uncertain. But we are conquerors before we encounter the enemy; for our Head, Christ, has overcome the whole world once for all for us.

I write unto you, young children. They need another ruling; and so the apostle infers that the Gospel is well adapted to young children because there they find a Father. We now see how devilish is the tyranny of the Pope, which threatens and drives away from the teaching of the Gospel all ages, whom God's Spirit so carefully invites.

But what the apostle distributes severally is also general. We should quite slip into emptiness if our infirmity were not sustained by God's eternal truth. In us there is nothing but what is frail and fading if the Spirit of Christ does not dwell in us. We are all like orphans until we come to the grace of adoption through the Gospel. Hence, what he declares of the young is common also to the old. Yet he wanted to apply to each what was especially necessary to them, that he might show that they all without exception needed the teaching of the Gospel. The particle ὅτι can be explained in two ways, but the meaning I have given it is far the better and agrees better with the context.

14. *I have written unto you, fathers.* I regard these repetitions as superfluous. It is probable that when unlearned readers mistakenly thought that he spoke twice of young children, they thoughtlessly introduced the other two clauses. But it might be that John himself inserted for amplification the sentence about young men, for he adds that they were strong, which he had not said before, and the scribes unthinkingly decided to fill in the number.

Love not the world, neither the things that are in the world. If any man love the world, the love of the Father is not in him. For all that is in the world, the lust of the flesh, and the lust of the eyes, and the vainglory of life, is not of the Father, but is of the world. And the world passeth away, and the lust thereof: but he that doeth the will of God abideth for ever. (15-17)

15. *Love not.* He had said before that the only rule for godly living is to love God. But because we are occupied with the vain love of the world, we turn all our senses in another direction, and therefore this vanity must first be torn out of us, that the love of God may reign within us. Until our minds are cleansed, what he has said may be repeated a hundred times without profit. It would be like pouring water on to a ball; you cannot gather a drop, because there is no hollow to hold it.

By *the world* understand whatever concerns the present life when it is separated from God's kingdom and the hope of eternal life. So he comprehends in it corruptions of every kind and the abyss of all evils. In the world are pleasures, delights and all those enticements by which a man is captivated to withdraw from God. Moreover, the love of the world is severely condemned because, if we look only at the earth, we cannot help forgetting God and ourselves. Where a perverse desire of this kind rules in man and so entangles him that he does not think of the heavenly life, it is a bestial stupidity.

If any man love the world. By an argument from contraries he proves how necessary it is to cast off the love of the world if we want to please God. Afterwards he confirms this by an argument from inconsistents: the things which belong to the world are completely at variance with God. We must remember that I have already said, that this refers to an irreligious way of life which has nothing in common with God's kingdom. Men become so degenerate that they

are satisfied with the present life and think no more of the life immortal than the brute beasts. Hence, whoever enslaves himself to
earthly desires cannot be of God.

16. *The lust of the flesh.* The old translator otherwise. From one
sentence he makes two. Better the Greeks, reading it connectedly:
'Whatever is in the world is not of God,' and then introducing the
three kinds of lusts parenthetically. It was by way of explanation
that John put in these as three examples, that he might show summarily what are the cares and thoughts of men who live unto the
world. But it does not make much difference whether it is a full and
complete division; though you will find no worldly man in whom
these desires do not reign or, at any rate, one of them. It remains for
us to see what he understands by each of them.

The first clause is usually explained of all sinful passions in general;
for the flesh means the whole corrupt nature of man. Though I do
not want to argue the point, I cannot pretend that I do not prefer
another meaning. When in Rom. 13.14 Paul forbids us to make
provision for the lusts of the flesh, he seems to me the best interpreter
of this passage. What is the flesh there? The body and everything
pertaining to it. Then what is the lust of the flesh, but when worldly
men, desiring to live softly and delicately, are intent only on their own
convenience? Epicurus' threefold distinction between lusts is well
known from Cicero and others. Some he made natural and necessary;
some natural but not necessary; some neither natural nor necessary.
But John, who knew the ἀταξία of the human heart, unhesitatingly
condemns the lust of the flesh, because it always pours forth immoderately and never keeps to the means. Afterwards he comes
gradually to grosser vices.

The lust of the eyes comprehends, to my mind, lascivious looks as
well as the vanity which runs after pomps and empty splendour.

Finally follows *vainglory* or pride, to which is joined ambition,
boasting, contempt of others, blind self-love and headstrong self-
confidence.

The sum of it is that, as soon as the world offers itself, our desires
are carried away by it like unbridled beasts, because our heart is
perverse. And so various lusts, all against God, rule over us. The
Greek for *life* is βίος, that is, the way or manner of living.

17. *And the world passeth away.* All that is in the world is fading
and momentary; and so he concludes that they who place their
happiness in it make a bad and wretched provision for themselves,
especially since God calls us to the blessed glory of eternal life. It is
as if he said, 'The true happiness which God offers His children is
eternal. It is therefore unworthy for us to be entangled with the world,

which with all its good things will soon vanish away.' I interpret *lust* here metonymically as what is lusted after and what captivates men's desires. The meaning is that whatever is most precious in the world and deemed especially desirable is only a shadowy ghost.

By saying that those who do God's will shall abide *for ever* he means that they who aspire to God shall be blessed for ever. If any object that none does what God commands, the reply is obvious. He is not dealing here with the perfect keeping of the Law, but with the obedience of faith, which, although imperfect, is nevertheless approved by God. The will of God is first shown to us in the Law. But as no one satisfies the Law, no happiness can be hoped for from it. But Christ meets the despairing with a new aid, for He not only regenerates us by His Spirit so that we may obey God, but also brings it to pass that our endeavour, of whatever kind, obtains the praise of perfect righteousness.

> *Little children, it is the last hour: and as ye have heard that antichrist cometh, even now have there arisen many antichrists; whereby we know that it is the last hour. They went out from us, but they were not of us; for if they had been of us, they would have continued with us: but they went out, that they might be made manifest how that they all are not of us.* (18-19)

18. *It is the last hour.* He confirms the faithful against offences which might have disturbed them. Already various sects had arisen, which both rent the unity of the Church and also scattered the Churches. The apostle not only arms believers lest they should waver but turns it all to another end. He tells them that the last time had already come, and therefore exhorts them to greater vigilance, as if he said, 'When various errors crop up, you must be aroused, not overwhelmed. For we must infer from it that Christ is not far away. So let us look attentively for Him, lest He should suddenly take us by surprise.' We today must similarly bestir ourselves and apprehend by faith the near advent of Christ when Satan causes confusion so as to disturb the Church. For these are the signs of the last time.

But the many ages which have passed away since John's death seem to prove this prophecy false. I reply: The apostle, after the common manner which Scripture adopts, warns believers that no more remained but for Christ to appear for the redemption of the world. But he fixed no date and did not dupe the men of his age with an empty hope; nor did he mean to curtail the future course of the Church and the many successions of years during which the Church has lasted in the world. And indeed, if the eternity of God's kingdom is borne in mind, such a long time will only seem to us a moment.

We must understand the apostle's purpose in calling the last time that during which all things are being so fulfilled that nothing will remain but the final revelation of Christ.

As ye heard that antichrist. He speaks as if these things were well known. From this it is easy to conclude that believers had been taught and warned from the beginning about the future scattering of the Church; both that they might keep themselves carefully in the faith they professed and also instruct future generations to beware. For God wanted His Church to be tried in this way, in case anyone should wittingly and willingly be deceived, and so that there should be no excuse of ignorance.

But we see that almost the whole world has been miserably deceived, as if not a word had ever been said about antichrist. And what is more, under the Papacy there is nothing more well-known and common than the future coming of antichrist; and yet they are so dull that they do not see that his tyranny is exercised over them. Indeed, entirely the same thing happens to them as to the Jews, for although they hold the promises concerning the Messiah, they are further from Christ than if they had never heard His name. For the imaginary Messiah whom they have made up for themselves, turns them quite aside from the Son of God. And if anyone tries to show them Christ from the Law and the prophets he is wasting his time. The Papists have imagined an antichrist who is to harass the Church for three and a half years. All the marks by which the Spirit of God has pointed out antichrist appear clearly in the Pope; but their triennial antichrist has such a hold on the foolish Papists that seeing they do not see. Therefore, let us remember that antichrist has not only been indicated by God's Spirit, but that the marks by which he may be discerned have also been ascribed to him.

Even now have there arisen many antichrists. This may seem to have been added as a correction, as if they mistakenly thought it would be some one kingdom; but not so. Those who think that he would be just one man are dreaming. For Paul, referring to a future falling away, plainly shows that it would be a body or a kingdom (II Thess. 2.3). He first foretells a falling away that would spread throughout the whole Church, as a sort of universal evil. Then he makes the head of this apostasy the adversary of Christ, who would sit in God's temple and claim divinity and divine honours. Unless we deliberately want to err, let us learn to know antichrist from Paul's description. I have already explained that passage; it is enough now to touch on it by the way.

But how does that passage agree with John's words, when he says that there were already many antichrists? I reply that John only meant that certain sects had already arisen which were fore-runners of a future scattering. For Cerinthus, Basilides, Marcion, Valentinus, Ebion, Arius and the rest were members of that kingdom which the devil afterwards raised up against Christ. Properly speaking, antichrist was not yet in existence, but the mystery of his ungodliness was working secretly. But John uses this name that he might the more stir up the care and anxiety of the godly to repel deceits. But if the Spirit of God even then commanded believers to be on their guard when they saw only distant signs of the coming enemy, much less is it now a time for sleeping, when he holds the Church oppressed under his cruel tyranny and openly triumphs over Christ.

19. *They went out from us.* He forestalls another objection: that the Church seemed to have produced these pests and to have cherished them for a time in her bosom. For it does more to upset the weak when anyone among us who professes the true faith falls away, than when a thousand outsiders conspire against us. Therefore he confesses that they had gone out from the bosom of the Church, yet denies that they were ever of the Church. But the way to remove the objection is that the Church is always liable to this evil, so that it is forced to endure many hypocrites who, in fact, have not Christ, although with their mouth they profess His name for a time.

By saying, *they went out from us,* he means that they had hitherto held a place in the Church and were regarded as in the number of the godly. But he denies that they were of them, since they had falsely hidden behind the name of believers; just as chaff mixed with wheat on the same threshing floor cannot be called wheat.

For if they had been of us. He says plainly that those who fell away had never been members of the Church. And, without doubt, the seal of God under which He keeps His own remains firm, as Paul says (II Tim. 2.19). But here a difficulty arises; for it often happens that many who seemed to have embraced Christ fall away. I reply that there are three degrees of those who profess the Gospel. There are those who feign godliness, while a bad conscience inwardly reproves them. The hypocrisy of others is more deceptive; they not only try to keep up a pretence before men, but even dazzle their own eyes, so that they seem to themselves to be worshipping God aright. The third are those who have the living root of faith and carry a testimony of their adoption firmly fixed in their hearts. The first two degrees lack stability. John is speaking of the last when he says that it is impossible for them to be alienated from the Church. For the seal which God engraves on their consciences by His Spirit cannot be obliterated. The incorruptible seed which has struck root cannot be pulled up or destroyed. He is not speaking here of men's constancy but of God's, whose election must be confirmed. Wherefore he has good reason to say that, where God's calling is effectual, perseverance will be certain. In short, he means that those who fall away have never been thoroughly imbued with the knowledge of Christ but only had a slight and passing taste of it.

That they might be made manifest. He tells them that the trial of the Church is useful and necessary. From this it follows, on the other hand, that there is no good reason for worrying. The Church is like a threshing-floor and the chaff has to be blown away so that the pure wheat may remain. This is what God does when He casts hypocrites out of the Church, for He cleanses it from rubbish and filth.

And ye have an anointing from the Holy One, and ye know all things. I have not written unto you because ye know not the truth, but because ye know it, and because no lie is of the truth. Who is the liar but he that denieth that Jesus is the Christ? This is the antichrist, even he that denieth the Father and the Son. Whosoever denieth the Son, the same hath not the Father. (20-23)

20. *But ye have an anointing.* The apostle modestly excuses himself for having warned them so earnestly, in case they should think it was a hinted reproof that they were raw and ignorant in what they ought to have known well. In the same way, Paul allowed wisdom to the Romans, in that they were able and fit to admonish others. At the same time he showed them that they could only discharge the duty laid on them if they were reminded of it (Rom. 15.14-15). The apostles did not speak like this in flattery; but they wisely took care lest their teaching should be rejected by any kind of men; for they proclaimed what was suitable and useful, not only to the ignorant, but also to the well instructed in the Lord's school.

Experience teaches us how fastidious men's ears are. Such fastidiousness ought, of course, to be far from the godly. But a good and wise teacher will omit nothing which will gain him a hearing from all. And it is certain that we receive what is said with less attention and respect when we think the speaker is disparaging the knowledge which the Lord has given us. By his praise the apostle also stimulated his readers, since those who were endowed with the gift of knowledge had less excuse if they did not surpass others in their progress.

The sum of it is that the apostle did not teach them as if they were ignorant and elementary, but reminded them of things already known and exhorted them to stir up the sparks of the Spirit, that complete brightness might shine in them. In the next words he explained himself, saying that he did not write to them because they did not know the truth but because they had been well taught in it; for had they been quite ignorant and novices, they would not have understood his teaching.

Now, when he says that they knew *all things*, it is not to be taken generally but restricted to the present subject. When he says that they had an anointing from the Holy One, he certainly alludes to the ancient figures. The oil for anointing the priests was obtained from the sanctuary. And Daniel defines the coming of Christ as the proper time for anointing the Most Holy (Dan. 9.24). For He was anointed by the Father to pour forth a manifold abundance from His own fulness on us. From this it follows that men are not really wise in the sharpness of their own minds but only in the enlightenment of the Spirit; and further that we are only made partakers of the Spirit through Christ, who is the true sanctuary and our only High Priest.

21. *And because no lie.* He gives them a criterion to distinguish truth from falsehood. For this is not only the dialectic proposition that falsehood differs from truth (as the general rules in the schools teach) but he accommodates his words to what is practical and useful. It is as if he said that not only did they hold what was true, but also were so fortified against the deceits and fallacies of the ungodly that they wisely took heed to themselves. Moreover, he does not merely speak of one or another kind of falsehood, but says that whatever deception Satan might invent, or however he might attack them, they would be ready to distinguish between light and darkness because they had the Spirit as their guide.

22. *Who is the liar?* He does not state that only they were liars who denied that the Son of God appeared in the flesh (lest anyone in unloosing this knot should torment himself immoderately), but that they surpassed all others—as if he said that if this could not be called a lie nothing could. As we are accustomed to say, 'If treachery to God and man is not a crime, what is?'

What he had said on false prophets in general he now applies to the state of his own time. He points, as if with the finger, to those who disturbed the Church. I readily agree with the ancients, who thought that Cerinthus and Carpocrates are here referred to. But the denial of Christ extends much further; for it is not enough to confess in one word that Jesus is the Christ, but He must be acknowledged to be such as the Father offers Him to us in the Gospel. The two I mentioned gave the title of Christ to the Son of God, but imagined He was a mere man. Others followed, like Arius, who adorned Him with the name of God but despoiled Him of His eternal divinity. Marcion dreamed that He was a mere phantom. Sabellius imagined that He differed in nothing from the Father. All these denied the Son of God, for none of them really acknowledged the whole Christ, but adulterated

the truth about Him so far as they were able and made for themselves
an idol instead of Christ. Then Pelagius broke forth. He certainly
began no controversy about Christ's essence, allowing Him to be
true man and God. But he transferred to us nearly all His honour. It
indeed is to reduce Christ to nothing when His grace and power are
abolished.

Thus the Papists today, opposing free-will to the grace of the Holy
Spirit, placing part of their righteousness and salvation in the merits
of works, imagining for themselves innumerable advocates through
whom they have God favourable to them, have I know not what
fictitious Christ. But the lively and genuine image of God which
should shine in Christ they deform by their wicked inventions. They
weaken His power, obscure and pervert His office.

We now see that Christ is denied whenever the things that belong
to Him are taken from Him. And as Christ is the end of the Law and
the Gospel and has within Himself all the treasures of wisdom and
understanding, so also is He the mark at which all heretics aim and
direct their arrows. Therefore, the apostle has good reason to make
those who fight against Christ the leading liars, since the full truth is
exhibited to us in Him.

This is the antichrist. He is not speaking of that leader of defection
who was to occupy the seat of God; but he puts all who try to overthrow Christ among that wicked band. And to amplify their crime
he says that they deny the Father no less than the Son; as if he said,
'They no longer have any religion, for they utterly cast away God.'
This he afterwards confirms by adding the reason, that the Father
cannot be separated from the Son.

Now this is a remarkable statement and should be reckoned among
the first axioms of our religion. In fact, when we have confessed that
there is one God, this second article must needs be joined to it, that
He is none other than the One who is known in Christ. The apostle
is not here arguing subtly about the unity of essence. It is, of course,
certain that the Son cannot be torn from the Father, for He is ὁμοούσιος.
But here he speaks of something different; that the Father, who is
otherwise invisible, has revealed Himself in His Son alone. Hence
He is called the image of the Father (Heb. 1.3), because He represents
and exhibits to us all that is useful to be known about the Father. The
naked majesty of God would dazzle our eyes with its immense brightness. It is therefore necessary for us to look to Christ. This is coming
to the light which otherwise is justly called inaccessible.

I repeat that this is not a subtle discussion on Christ's eternal essence
which He has in common with the Father. The passage itself abundantly proves this, indeed. But John calls us to the practice of faith;

because God has given Himself to us to be enjoyed wholly in Christ, He is elsewhere sought for in vain. Or, if anyone wants it clearer, since all the fulness of divinity dwells in Christ, there is no God apart from Him. From this it follows that Turks, Jews and such like have a mere idol in place of God. For whatever titles they may give the god they worship, yet because they reject Him without whom they cannot come to God and in whom God has concretely manifested Himself to us, what have they but some creature or invention of their own? They may flatter themselves as they wish in their speculations who philosophize about divine things apart from Christ. But it is certain that they are only playing the fool, since, as Paul says, they do not hold the Head (Col. 2.19). Hence it is easy to conclude how necessary is the knowledge of Christ.

Many MSS have also the converse, 'He that confesseth the Son, etc.' But since I think that a note by some copyist has been inserted into the text, I did not hesitate to omit it. If, however, its insertion be accepted, the meaning would be that there is no lawful confession of God unless the Father is acknowledged in the Son. If anyone objects that many of the ancients thought rightly of God although Christ was unknown to them, I allow that the knowledge of Christ has not always been so clear. All the same, I contend that it has always been true that, just as the light of the sun is diffused to us by its rays, so the knowledge of God has been communicated only through Christ.

As for you, let that abide in you which ye heard from the beginning. If that which ye heard from the beginning abide in you, ye also shall abide in the Son, and in the Father. And this is the promise which he promised us, even the life eternal. These things have I written unto you concerning them that would lead you astray. And as for you, the anointing which ye received of him abideth in you, and ye need not that any one teach you; but as his anointing teacheth you concerning all things, and is true, and is no lie, and even as it taught you, abide ye in him. And now, my little children, abide in him; that, if he shall be manifested, we may have boldness, and not be ashamed before him at his coming. If ye know that he is righteous, ye know that every one also that doeth righteousness is begotten of him. (24-29)

24. *Let that abide in you.* He attaches an exhortation to his earlier teaching. And that the exhortation might be the more weighty, he shows them the fruit they would receive from obedience. Therefore he exhorts them to steadfastness in the faith, that they might keep what they had learnt fixed in their hearts.

Now when he says, 'from the beginning,' it was not that antiquity alone is sufficient to prove any doctrine. But as he had already shown that they had been correctly taught in the pure Gospel of Christ, he concludes that they should remain in it. And this order should be carefully noticed; for if we were unwilling to leave the sort of teaching we had once embraced, whatever it was, this would not be steadfastness but perverse obstinacy. Therefore we should use discrimination, so that a reason for our faith may be made clear from God's Word. Then let inflexible steadfastness follow it.

The Papists boast of a beginning in that they have imbibed their superstitions from childhood. Under colour of this they let themselves obstinately reject the plain truth. Such stubbornness is a proof that we should always start out from the certainty of the teaching.

If that which ye heard. The fruit of perseverence is that they in whom God's truth abides, abide in God. From this we gather what we are to seek in all the doctrine of godliness. He therefore makes the greatest headway who so advances as wholly to cleave to God. But he in whom the Father does not dwell through His Son is altogether vain and empty, whatever learning he may have. Moreover, it is the highest commendation of sound teaching that it unites us to God and contains whatever belongs to the true enjoying of God.

Finally, he tells us that it is substantial happiness when God dwells in us. The expression is ambiguous. Either, 'This is the promise in which he has promised us eternal life'; or, in apposition, 'This is the promise which he gave us, even eternal life.' But the choice is open, for whichever way you take it the meaning is the same. The sum of it is that we can only live if we nourish to the end the seed of life conceived in our minds. John greatly emphasizes this point, that in Christ is placed not only the beginning of the blessed life but also its perfection. But this can never be repeated too much; for it is well known that it has always been a source of ruin to men that, not content with Christ, they have delighted in wandering outside the simple teaching of the Gospel.

26. *These things have I written unto you.* The apostle again apologizes for admonishing those who were well equipped with understanding and judgment. But he did so, that they might look to the judgment of the Spirit, lest his exhortation should be useless. It is as if he said, 'I do my part; but it is necessary for the Spirit of God to direct you in all things. For my voice will sound in your ears in vain, or rather beat on the air, unless He speaks within you.'

When we hear what he wrote about seducers, we must always observe that it is the duty of a good and diligent pastor not only to gather the flock but also to drive away wolves. For what is the use of proclaiming the pure Gospel if we connive at the open impostures of Satan? And so no one can faithfully teach the Church unless he is set

on banishing errors wherever he finds them spread by seducers. When
he says *the anointing which ye received of him,* I refer it to Christ.

27. *And ye need not.* As I have already said, John would have been
ridiculous if he had given useless teaching. Therefore he did not
ascribe to them so much wisdom as to suggest that they were not the
pupils of Christ. He only means that they were not so ignorant that
they needed to be taught what was unknown, and that he did not set
before them anything that the Spirit of God might not Himself supply.
Fanatical men wickedly snatch at this testimony to exclude from the
Church the use of the external ministry. He says that believers, taught
by the Spirit, already understood what he delivered to them, so that
they did not need to learn things as if they were unknown. He said
this to gain more authority for his teaching, when each one found in
his heart a subscription to it engraven by God's finger. But as every
man understood according to the measure of his faith, and as in some
faith was small, in others middling and in none perfect, it follows that
none knew so much that he did not need to progress.

This doctrine is useful in yet another way. When men really understand what is necessary for them, we have still to admonish and rouse
them that they may be the more established. For when John declares
that they were taught all things by the Spirit, it should not be taken
generally, but restricted to the contents of this passage. In short, all
he had in view was to strengthen their faith when he recalled them to
the trial of the Spirit, who is the only fit critic and approver of doctrine
and seals it in our hearts; so that we may assuredly know that God
speaks. For since faith must look to God, He alone can be a witness to
Himself, to convince our hearts that what our ears receive has come
from Him.

And these words mean the same thing: *As his anointing teacheth you
concerning all things, and is true.* That is, the Spirit is like a seal, by which
the truth of God is testified to us. When he adds, *and is no lie,* he
indicates another office of the Spirit; that He rules us with judgment
and discernment lest we should be deceived by falsehood, should
hesitate and be perplexed and waver as in things doubtful.

Even as it taught you, abide in him. He had said that the Spirit abides
in them. Now he exhorts them to abide in His revelation, specifying
the revelation. He says, 'Abide in Christ, as the Spirit has taught you.'
I know that another exposition is common: 'Abide in it,' referring to
the anointing. But as the immediately following repetition can only
apply to Christ, I do not doubt that here also he speaks of Christ.
And the context demands this, too; for the apostle dwells on the point
that believers should keep the pure knowledge of Christ and should
not try to reach God by any other way.

At the same time he clearly shows that the children of God are enlightened by the Spirit simply so that they may know Christ. So long as they did not turn aside from Christ, he promised them the fruit of perseverence, even that they should have boldness and not be ashamed at His presence. For faith is not a naked and frigid apprehension of Christ, but a living and real sense of His power which begets confidence. In fact, faith cannot stand when it is daily tossed by so many waves unless it looks to Christ's coming and is supported by His power to give calmness to the conscience. But the nature of confidence is best expressed when he says that it can boldly bear the presence of Christ. For those who securely indulge in their vices turn their backs, so to say, on God. And they can only find peace by forgetting Him. This is the security of the flesh, which stupefies men, so that they turn away from God and neither dread sin nor fear death. Meanwhile they fly from the judgment-seat of Christ. But a godly confidence rests on the sight of God alone. This is why the godly calmly wait for Christ and do not dread His presence.

29. *If ye know that he is righteous.* Again he passes over to exhortations, as he mingles them continually with the teaching throughout the Epistle. But by many arguments he proves that faith is necessarily joined to a holy and pure life. The first is that we are spiritually begotten in the likeness of Christ. From this it follows that no one is born of Christ save he who lives righteously. It is, however, uncertain whether he means Christ or God when he says that they who are born of Him do righteousness. It is certainly a manner of speaking used in Scripture that we are born of God in Christ. But there is nothing absurd in the other, that they are born of Christ who are renewed by His Spirit.

CHAPTER THREE

Behold what manner of love the Father hath bestowed upon us, that we should be called children of God. For this cause the world knoweth us not, because it knew him not. Beloved, now are we children of God, and it doth not yet appear what we shall be. We know that, when he shall be manifested, we shall be like him; for we shall see him even as he is. And every one that hath this hope set on him purifieth himself, even as he is pure. (1-3)

1. *Behold, etc.* The second argument is from the dignity and excellence of our calling. It was no common honour, he says, that the heavenly Father bestowed on us in adopting us as His children. This great favour should kindle in us a desire for purity, so that we may be conformed to Him. Nor can he who acknowledges himself to be one of God's children fail to purify himself. To strengthen his exhortation he magnifies God's grace. For when he says that love has been bestowed, he means that it is from mere liberality that God regards us as His children. For whence does such an honour come to us but from the love of God? Therefore, love is here declared to be free. There is, indeed, an imprecision in the language. But the apostle preferred imprecision to not declaring what needed to be known. In short, he means that the more abundantly God's goodness has been poured out upon us, the more are we bound to Him. Just as Paul besought the Romans by the mercies of God to present themselves as pure sacrifices to Him (12.1). At the same time we are taught, as I have said, that the adoption of all the godly is free and does not depend on any regard to works.

The sophists' statement that God foresees those who will be worthy to be adopted, is clearly refuted by these words; for in this way the gift would not be free. It is especially worthwhile to understand this doctrine; for since the only cause of our salvation is adoption, and the apostle testifies that this flows only from the mere love of God, no place is left for our worthiness or the merits of works. How are we sons? Because God began to love us freely when we deserved hatred rather than love. It follows that, as the Spirit is the pledge of our adoption, if there is any good in us, it should not be set up in opposition to God's grace, but on the contrary ascribed to Him.

When he says that we are *called*, the term is not meaningless, for it is God who with His own mouth declares us to be sons; just as He gave a significant name to Abraham.

For this cause the world. This trial grievously assaults our faith, that we are not regarded as God's children, or that no mark of so great an excellency appears in us, but on the contrary almost the whole world holds us in derision. Hence it can hardly be inferred from our present state that God is our Father, for the devil so manages everything that he obscures this benefit. He circumvents the offence by saying that we now are not yet acknowledged to be what we are, because the world does not know God; and so it is not surprising if the children of the world despise us. A remarkable mirror of this very thing is in Isaac and Jacob. Although they were both chosen by God, Ishmael persecuted Isaac with laughter and mockery, and Esau persecuted Jacob with threats and the sword. Therefore, however much we may seem to be oppressed in the world, our salvation stands and is firm.

2. *Now are we children of God.* He comes now to every man's own feeling. Although the ungodly may not entice us to give up hope, our present state is far short of the glory of God's children. Physically, we are dust and a shadow, and death is always before our eyes. We are exposed to a thousand miseries and our souls to innumerable evils, so that we always find a hell within us. The more necessary is it that our senses should be withdrawn from the view of present things, lest the miseries by which we are on every side surrounded and almost overwhelmed should shake our trust in that happiness which as yet is hidden. For the apostle means that we act wrongly in estimating by the present state of things what God has bestowed on us, when we ought with undoubting faith to hold to what does not yet appear.

We know that when he shall be manifested. The conditional should be rendered as a temporal adverb, 'when'. But the verb *manifested* is to be taken in a different sense from before. The apostle has just said, 'it doth not yet appear what we shall be', because the fruit of our adoption is as yet hidden, for our felicity is in heaven, and we are now far away, strangers on earth. For this transient life, constantly exposed to a thousand deaths, is far different from that eternal life which belongs to the children of God. We are shut up in the slaves' penitentiary (*ergastulum*) of our flesh and are far distant from the freedman's domain of heaven and earth. But the verb now refers to Christ's being manifested. For he teaches the same thing as Paul in Col. 3.3-4, where he says, 'Your life is hid with Christ. When Christ, who is your life, shall appear, then shall ye also appear with him in glory.' For our faith can only stand if it looks to the coming of Christ. The reason why God defers the manifestation of our glory is because Christ is not manifested in the power of His kingdom. This, I say, is the only way to sustain our faith, so that we may patiently wait for the promised life. As soon as anyone turns away in the slightest degree from Christ, he cannot help failing.

The word *to know* implies the certainty of faith, to distinguish it from opinion. Neither simple nor universal knowledge is meant here, but that which each man should apply to himself, that he may be sure that he will some time be like Christ. Therefore, although the exhibiting of our glory depends on Christ's coming, the knowledge of it is well founded.

Like him. He does not mean that we shall be equal to Him. For there must be a difference between the Head and the members. But we shall be like Him in that He will conform our lowly body to His glorious body, as also Paul teaches us in Phil. 3.21. For the apostle wanted to show us briefly that the ultimate aim of our adoption is that what has, in order, come first in Christ, shall at last be completed in us. But the reason which is added may seem weak. For if Christ makes us like Himself, we shall have the sight of this in common with the ungodly, for they shall see Him too. I reply that this is a familiar seeing, but it will fill the ungodly with fear; nay, they will flee from the sight in terror. His glory will so dazzle their eyes that they will be confounded and stupefied. For we see how Adam, conscious of his wrong, dreaded God's presence. And God declared this in general by Moses to men, 'No man shall see me and live' (Exod. 33.20). For it cannot be otherwise but that God's majesty, like a consuming fire, will burn us up like stubble, because of the weakness of our flesh. But inasmuch as the image of God is renewed in us, we have eyes prepared for the sight of God. And now, indeed, God begins to restore His image in us; but in what a small measure! Therefore, unless we are stripped of all the corruption of the flesh, we shall not be able to behold God face to face.

This is also expressed by the term *even as he is*. He does not take from us all seeing of God now; but, as Paul says, 'We now see through a glass darkly' (I Cor. 13.12). But he afterwards distinguishes this life from the seeing of the eye. In short, God presents Himself to be seen by us now, not as He is, but as our little capacity can grasp. Thus Moses' words are fulfilled that we only see, as it were, His back (Exod. 33.23), for His face is too bright.

We must also notice that the manner which the apostle mentions is taken from the effect, not the cause. For he does not tell us that we shall be like Him because we shall enjoy the sight of Him, but proves that we shall be partakers of the divine glory because, unless our nature were spiritual and endued with a heavenly and blessed immortality, it could never come so near to God. Yet the perfection of glory will not be so great in us that our seeing will comprehend God totally, for the diversity of proportion (*longa distantia proportionis*) between us and Him will even then be very great. But when the apostle says that we shall see Him as He is, he refers to a new and ineffable mode of vision, which we have not now. For Paul teaches us that as long as we walk by faith we are absent from Him. And when He granted the fathers to see Him, He was always seen, not in His own essence, but under symbols. Hence the majesty of God, now hidden, will only then be seen in itself when the veil of this mortal and corruptible nature is removed.

I pass over subtle arguments. For we see how Augustine tormented himself with them and never freed himself, whether in his letters to Paulus and Fortunatus, or in his *Civitas Dei* (ii.2) or elsewhere. But what he says is worth noticing, that in this enquiry our mode of living is of more importance than our mode of speaking, and we must beware not to lose that peace and holiness without which none shall see God, by arguing as to the manner in which He can be seen.

3. *And every one that hath this hope.* He now infers that our desire for holiness should not grow cold because our happiness has not yet appeared, for the hope is sufficient. And we know that what is hoped for is hidden. Therefore the meaning is that, although yet we have not Christ present before our eyes, it cannot but be that if we hope, it will stir and stimulate us to the pursuit of purity, for it leads us straight to Christ, who, as we know, is the perfect pattern of purity.

Every one that doeth sin doeth also lawlessness: and sin is lawlessness. And ye know that he was manifested to take away sins; and in him is no sin. Whosoever abideth in him sinneth not: whosoever sinneth hath not seen him, neither knoweth him. (4-6)

4. *Every one that doeth sin.* The apostle has already shown how ungrateful we are towards God if we minimize the honour of adoption, in which, of His own good will, He prevents us, and if we do not at least render Him mutual love. He also put in this admonition so that our affection should not be lessened by the deferment of the promised happiness. Now, as men are accustomed to flatter themselves in evils more than they should, he corrects this perverse indulgence and declares that all who sin are unrighteous and transgressors of the Law. For there were probably at that time those who extenuated their vices by this flattery, 'It is not surprising if we sin; we are only men. And there is a big difference between sin and iniquity.'

The apostle now destroys this flippant excuse by defining sin as the transgression of the divine Law. His object was to produce a hatred and horror of sin. To some the word sin seems light; but iniquity or transgression of the Law cannot be so easily overlooked. Yet the apostle does not make sins equal by accusing of iniquity all who sin; but he simply wants to teach us that sin comes from contempt of God and that by sinning the righteousness of the Law is violated. Hence John's concept has nothing in common with the crazy paradoxes of the Stoics.

Moreover, to sin does not here mean to offend in some action; nor is the word *sin* to be taken for every single fault. But he calls it sin when men whole-heartedly rush into evil. And he means that only those men sin who are devoted to sin. For believers, who still labour under the lusts of the flesh, are not to be regarded as unrighteous, although they are not pure or free from sin. But since sin does not reign in them, John says that they do not sin, as I shall soon explain more fully.

The sum of the passage is that the perverse life of those who indulge themselves in the licence of sinning is hateful to God and is unendurable to Him because it is against His Law. It does not follow from this, nor can it be inferred, that believers are unrighteous. For they want to submit to God and they abhor their own vices even in individual offences, and they also compose their life so far as they can to the obedience of the Law. But when there is a deliberate will to sin, or a continued course, the Law is transgressed.

5. *And ye know that he was manifested.* He shows by another argument how far sin and faith differ from one another. For it is Christ's office to take away sins, and this is why He was sent by the Father. And it is by faith that we are aware of Christ's power. Therefore, he who believes in Christ is necessarily cleansed from his sins. But elsewhere it is said that Christ takes away sins because He atoned for them by the sacrifice of His death, that they may not be imputed to us before God (John 1.29). In this place John means that Christ really and actually (as they say) takes away sins, because through Him our old man is crucified and His Spirit through repentance mortifies our flesh with all its depraved desires. For the context does not permit us to expound this of the forgiveness of sins. As I said, he reasons thus, 'Those who do not cease to sin make void the benefit of Christ, since He came to abolish the reign of sin.' This is to be referred to the sanctification of the Spirit.

And in him is no sin. He is not speaking of Christ individually but of His whole body. He states that wherever Christ pours out His strength no room is left for sin. He therefore at once infers that those who abide in Christ do not sin. For if He dwells in us by faith, He performs His own work of cleansing us from sins. From this it appears what it is *to sin*. For Christ by His Spirit does not renew us

entirely in a day or a moment, but continues the partially begun renewing throughout our life. Therefore, believers cannot help being
exposed to sin so long as they live in the world. But inasmuch as
Christ's kingdom flourishes in them, sin is abolished. Meanwhile
they are reckoned according to the chief part; that is, they are said to
be righteous and to live righteously because they sincerely aspire to
righteousness.

They are said not to sin because, although they labour under the
infirmity of the flesh, they do not consent to sin, but in fact struggle
and groan, so that they can truly testify with Paul that they do the evil
they would not. He says that believers *abide* in Christ because we are
by faith engrafted in Him and united with Him.

6. *Whosoever sinneth hath not seen him.* In his usual way he added
the opposite clause, that we may know that the faith and knowledge
of Christ are a vain pretence without newness of life. For Christ is
never at leisure where He reigns, but the Spirit puts forth His power.
And it may properly be said of Him that He puts sin to flight, as the
sun dispels darkness by its brightness. But here we are again taught
how lively and efficacious is the knowledge of Christ; for it transforms us into His image. So by seeing[1] and knowing we are simply
to understand faith.

*My little children, let no man lead you astray: he that doeth righteous-
ness is righteous, even as he is righteous: he that doeth sin is of the devil;
for the devil sinneth from the beginning. To this end was the Son of
God manifested, that he might destroy the works of the devil. Whosoever is begotten of God doeth no sin, because his seed abideth in him:
and he cannot sin, because he is begotten of God. In this the children
of God are manifest, and the children of the devil.* (7–10a)

7. *He that doeth righteousness.* The apostle here teaches that newness
of life is shown by good works. And that likeness between Christ
and His members of which he spoke only exists if it brings forth fruit.
It is as if he said, 'Since we must be conformed to Christ, the truth
and testimony of this must be present in our life.' It is the same exhortation as that of Paul in Gal. 5.25, 'If ye live in the Spirit, also walk
by the Spirit.' For many would like to persuade themselves that they
have this righteousness buried in their hearts while iniquity openly
occupies their feet, hands, tongue and eyes.

8. *He that doeth sin.* This word *to do* refers to external actions, so
that it means that the life of God and Christ is not present where men
act perversely and wickedly. On the contrary, such are the slaves of
the devil. By this way of speaking he better expresses how they

---

[1] Reading *aspectum* for *affectum*.

differ from Christ. For as he had set up Christ as the fount of all righteousness, he now defines the devil as the head of sin. He denied that any belongs to Christ save he who is righteous and shows himself so by his actions. He now banishes all the others to the fellowship of the devil and puts them under his government, so that we may know that there is no middle course, but that Satan exercises his tyranny where Christ's righteousness is not supreme.

We are not, however, to imagine two adverse principles, like the Manichees. For we know that the devil is not evil by nature or by origin of creation, but by the vice of his own fall. We also know that he is not equal to God, so as to contend with Him in equal terms, but that he is constrained unwillingly and can do nothing but by the permission and will of his Creator. In the last verse, where he said that some were born of God and some of the devil, John did not imagine a transfer such as the Manichees dreamed. He means that the former are governed by the Spirit of Christ and that the others are carried away by Satan, as God grants him this power against the unbelieving.

For the devil sinneth from the beginning. As he did not speak only of Christ individually when he said that He is righteous, but set Him forth as the fountain and cause of righteousness; so now, when he says that the devil sins, he comprehends his whole body, that is, all the reprobate. It is as if he said, 'It belongs to the devil to move men to sin.' From this it follows that his members and all who are ruled by him are given up to sin. But the beginning the apostle mentions is not in eternity, as when he says that the Word is from the beginning. For there is a wide difference (*diversa ratio*) between God and creatures. In God, beginning has no time. Since, then, the Word was always with God, you can find no point of time in which He began to be, but must necessarily come to His eternity. But here John only meant that the devil had been an apostate from the creation of the world, and that since then he had never ceased to scatter his poison among men.

To this end was the Son of God manifested. He repeats in other words what he had said before—that Christ came to take away sins. From this, two conclusions are to be drawn: That those in whom sin reigns cannot be reckoned among the members of Christ, nor by any means belong to His body. For wherever Christ puts forth His strength, He overthrows the devil as well as sin. And John immediately adds this; for the next sentence, where he says that those who do not sin are born of God, is a conclusion from what has gone before. As I have already said, it is an argument drawn from what is inconsistent; for Christ's kingdom, which necessarily brings righteousness with it, cannot stand with sin. I have already mentioned above what 'not to sin' means. He does not represent the children of God as wholly free from all vice, but denies that anyone can really claim this title save those who heartily strive to form their lives in obedience to God.

The Pelagians and the Cathari abused this passage when they imagined that believers are in this world endowed with angelic purity. In our age some of the Anabaptists have renewed this madness. But all who dream of such a perfection show clearly what dull consciences they have. So far from countenancing their error, the apostle's words are sufficient to confute it.

He says that they who are begotten of God *sin not*. Now we must see whether God regenerates us in a moment, or whether regeneration is so begun in us that the remnants of the old man stay in us till death. If regeneration is not yet full and complete, it only frees us from the bondage of sin within its own limits. From this it appears that God's children must needs labour under faults and sin daily; that is, inasmuch as they still have some remnants of their old nature. Nevertheless, the apostle's contention stands firm that the end of regeneration is to destroy sin and that all who are begotten of God live righteously and godly because God's Spirit corrects the lusting of sin.

The apostle understands the same thing by *the seed* of God. God's Spirit so forms the hearts of the godly to upright affections that the flesh and its lusts do not prevail, but are tamed and as it were yoked, so that they are checked. In short, the apostle ascribes the superiority in the elect to the Spirit, who suppresses sin by His power and does not let it flourish.

9. *And he cannot sin.* The apostle mounts higher and plainly declares that the hearts of the godly are so effectually governed by God's Spirit that they follow His leading inflexibly. This is far from the teaching of the Papists. It is true that the Sorbonnists confess that man's will cannot desire what is right unless assisted by God's Spirit. But they imagine such a movement of the Spirit as leaves us the free choice of good and evil. From this they derive merits in that we willingly obey the grace of the Spirit which it is in our power to resist. In short, they define the grace of the Spirit to be only that we can choose aright if we will. John speaks very differently here. He not only tells us that we cannot sin, but also that the moving of the Spirit is so effectual that it necessarily keeps us in continual obedience to righteousness. And this is not the only passage of Scripture which teaches us that the will is so formed that it cannot be otherwise than right. For God declares that He gives His children a new heart; and He promises to do this so that they may walk in His commandments. Moreover, John not only shows how efficaciously God works once in man, but clearly says that the Spirit follows up His grace in us to the end, so that to newness

of life is added inflexible perseverance. So let us not, like the Sorbonnists, imagine some neutral moving which makes men free either to follow or to reject; but let us know that our hearts are so ruled by God's Spirit that they constantly cleave to righteousness.

Moreover, the absurdity which the Sophists object is easily refuted. They say that in this way the will is taken away from man. But they are wrong; for the will is from nature. But since the corruption of nature brings forth only depraved inclinations, it is necessary that the Spirit of God shall reform it that it may begin to be good. And then because men would immediately fall away from the good, it is necessary that the same Spirit should carry through to the end what He has begun. As to merit, the answer is easy; for it cannot be regarded as absurd that men merit nothing. And yet they do not cease to regard good works as good, which flow from the grace of the Spirit, because they are voluntary. They also have the reward of being freely ascribed to men as if they were their own.

But a question arises here: Whether the fear and reverence of God can be extinguished in anyone who has been regenerated by God's Spirit. For this seems to be the consequence of the apostle's words. Those who think differently cite David as an example. For a time he was overcome by a brutish stupor, and no spark appeared in him. What is more, in Psalm 51 he prays that the Spirit may be restored to him. From this it follows that he had been deprived of Him. But I do not doubt that the seed by which God regenerates His elect is both incorruptible and keeps its power for ever. I grant that it may sometimes be stifled, as in David; but yet when all godliness seemed to be extinct in him, a live coal was hidden under the ashes. Satan strives to root out whatever is from God in the elect. But when the utmost is allowed him, there always remains a hidden root which afterwards sprouts. But John is not here speaking of one act (as they call it) but the continued course of life.

Some fanatics dream of I do not know what eternal seed in the elect, which they always bring with them from their mother's womb. But they violently twist John's words to this end; for he is not discussing eternal election, but starts out from regeneration. There are also those who are twice as frantic and want everything to be lawful to believers, under the pretence that John says they cannot sin. They therefore want us indiscriminately to follow wherever our inclinations lead. So they take licence to commit adultery, steal and murder, because where God's Spirit rules there can be no sin. The apostle's meaning is very different. The reason why he denies that believers sin is because God has engraven His Law on their hearts, according to the saying of the prophet (Jer. 31.33).

10. *In this the children of God are manifest.* In a few words he infers that those who do not prove they are God's children by their godly and holy life, claim such a position and name in vain. For it is by this mark that they show they differ from the children of the devil. But he does not mean that they are so manifested that they can be openly recognized by the whole world, but simply that the fruit and effect of divine adoption always appear in the life.

Whosoever doeth not righteousness is not of God, neither he that loveth not his brother. For this is the message which ye heard from the beginning, that we should love one another: not as Cain was of the evil one, and slew his brother. And wherefore slew he him? Because his works were evil, and his brother's righteous. Marvel not, brethren, if the world hateth you. (10b-13)

10. *Whosoever doeth not righteousness.* Here to do righteousness and to do sin are opposed to one another. To do righteousness is simply to fear God sincerely and (so far as human weakness permits) to walk in His commandments. For although, precisely speaking, righteousness is nothing but the perfect observance of the Law, from which believers are always distant, yet because God does not impute their offences and failings to them, the semi-obedience which they render to God is called righteousness. But John says that all who do not live righteously are not of God; for God regenerates by His Spirit all whom He calls. Hence newness of life is a perpetual testimony of the divine adoption.

Neither he that loveth not his brother. He accommodates a general doctrine to his purpose. Hitherto he had exhorted believers to brotherly love. Now he turns the sum of true righteousness to the same end. Thus, this clause is added as explanation. But I have already said why the whole of righteousness is comprehended in brotherly love. The love of God has the first place, of course; but since on this depends love among men, it is often, by synecdoche, included in it, as well as vice versa. He then declares that everyone who is endued with beneficence and humaneness is, and is to be regarded, righteous, because love is the fulfilling of the Law. He confirms this statement by saying that believers were so taught from the beginning, signifying that his definition should not have seemed new to them.

12. *Not as Cain.* Another confirmation, drawn from contraries. In the lives of the reprobate and the children of the devil hatred reigns and, as it were, holds the dominion. He sets forward Cain as a mirror. This served meanwhile for the consolation of believers, for he concluded *Marvel not, if the world hateth you.* This explanation should be carefully noticed, for men are always deceived about the way of

living; placing holiness in fabricated works and tormenting themselves about trifles, they think they are doubly acceptable to God. Like the monks, who proudly call their way of life a state of perfection. And the worship of God under the Papacy can only be regarded as the offscourings of superstitions. But the apostle declares that the only righteousness that God approves is when we love one another; and what is more, that where hatred, dissimulation, envy and enmity prevail, the devil reigns. But at the same time we must also remember that, because brotherly love comes from the love of God as effect from cause, it is not separate from it, but on the contrary, the very reason why John praises it is because it is evidence of our reverence for God.

By saying that *Cain* was driven to slay his brother because his works were evil, he tells us that where ungodliness rules, hatred occupies all the parts of life. He reminds us of Abel's works so that we may learn to bear it patiently when the world hates us gratuitously and without just provocation.

We know that we have passed out of death into life, because we love the brethren. He that loveth not abideth in death. Whosoever hateth his brother is a murderer: and ye know that no murderer hath eternal life abiding in him. Hereby know we love, because he laid down his life for us: and we ought to lay down our lives for the brethren. But whoso hath the world's goods, and beholdeth his brother in need, and shutteth up his compassion from him, how doth the love of God abide in him? My little children, let us not love in word, neither with the tongue; but in deed and truth. (14-18)

14. *We know*. He commends love to us by a remarkable saying, that it is testimony of our transition from death to life. From this it follows that we are blessed if we love the brethren but wretched if we hate them. There is none but desires to be freed and delivered from death. Therefore those who, by cherishing hatred voluntarily give themselves up to death, must be dull in the extreme. But when the apostle says that love makes it known that we have passed into life, he does not mean that man is his own deliverer, as if by loving the brethren he could rescue himself from death and procure life for himself. For here he is not discussing the cause of salvation. But as love is the special fruit of the Spirit, it is also a sure symbol of regeneration. Therefore, the apostle argues from the sign and not from the cause. For, since none sincerely loves his brethren unless he is born again by God's Spirit, he rightly concludes that this same Spirit of God, who is life, dwells in all who love the brethren. But it would be perverse for anyone to infer from this that life is obtained from love, inasmuch as love is the prior in order.

A more plausible argument would be that love makes us more certain of our life, and therefore confidence of salvation rests on works. But the answer to this is easy. Although faith is confirmed by all the aids of the graces of God, it does not cease to have its foundation only in the mercy of God. For example, when we enjoy the light, we are sure the sun is shining. If the sun actually shines on the place where we are, we see it more clearly. But even when the visible rays do not reach us, we are satisfied that the sun diffuses the benefit of its brightness to us. So when faith has been founded on Christ, some things can happen to help it; but yet it rests on Christ's grace alone.

15. *Is a murderer*. To stimulate us the more to love, he shows how detestable hatred is in God's sight. Everyone is horrified at a murder; we all execrate the very name. But the apostle declares that all who hate their brethren are murderers. He could have said nothing more harsh. Nor is this hyperbolical, for we wish him to perish whom we hate. It is not the point that a man may keep his hands from mischief; for the mere desire to hurt is condemned in the sight of God no less than the attempt. In fact, when we do not even desire to do harm but yet want an evil to befall our brother from elsewhere, we are murderers.

Therefore, the apostle portrays the thing in its true colours when he calls hatred murder. This exposes men's foolishness in abominating the name but making nothing of the crime itself. What is the cause of this? That the external appearance of things engrosses all our senses; but before God it is the inward feeling that is taken into account. That none may any more extenuate so grievous an evil, let us learn to recall our judgments to God's tribunal.

16. *Hereby know we*. He now shows what true love is. It would not have been enough to praise it unless its power were understood. As the perfect rule of love, he sets before us the example of Christ; for He testified how much He loved us by not sparing His own life. This is the goal which he tells us to aim at. The sum of it is that our love is approved when we transfer the love of ourselves to our brethren, so that each one, forgetting himself in a way, consults the good of others.

Of course, it is certain that we are far from equality with Christ. But the apostle commends to us the imitation of Him; for although we do not overtake Him, we must yet follow His steps, even if at a distance. No doubt, since it was the apostle's object to drive out the empty boasting of hypocrites who claimed that they had faith in Christ, though in fact they had no brotherly love, he signified by these words that, unless this desire flourishes in our minds, we have nothing in common with Christ. But, as I have said, he does not so set before us the love of Christ as to require us to be equal with Him. For what would this be but to drive us every one to despair? But he means that our feelings should be so formed that we may desire to devote our life and our death first to God and then to our neighbours.

Another difference between us and Christ is that our death cannot have the same power. For God's wrath is not appeased by our blood, nor is life procured by our death, nor the punishment due to others paid. But in this comparison the apostle was not looking at the end or effect of Christ's death, but meant only that our life should be formed to His example.

17. *But whoso hath the world's goods.* He speaks now of the common duties of love which flow from that highest spring. It is when we are prepared to spend ourselves for our neighbours even to death. Yet he seems to reason from the greater to the less; for he who refuses to alleviate his brother's need from his own abundance while his life is safe and secure, will far less expose his life for him. Therefore, he denies that there is love in us if we defraud our neighbours of help. But he so commends this outward kindness that at the same time he best expresses the true way of doing good and the sort of attitude that should rule in us.

Therefore let the first proposition be, that only he truly loves his brother who testifies as much by the actuality whenever an opportunity occurs. The second is, that anyone is bound to help his brethren to the extent of his means; for in this way the Lord supplies us with the opportunity to exercise love. The third is, that the necessity of every man should be looked to. For inasmuch as anyone needs food and drink or other things of which we have abundance, so he entreats our aid. The fourth is that no kindness pleases God unless it is joined with τῇ συμπαθείᾳ. There are many apparently liberal men who are yet not at all touched by their brethren's miseries. But the Apostle says that our heart must be opened; and this is done when we put on the same feeling, so that we feel the ills of others as if they were our own.

The love of God. He is here speaking of loving the brethren. Why then does he mention the love of God? Because the principle is to be held that the love of God cannot fail to beget in us love for the brethren. And God tests our love when He tells us to love men from regard to Himself; as Psalm 16.2 says, 'My goodness extendeth not to thee, but to the saints that are in the earth is my will and my care.'

18. *Let us not love in word.* This first clause contains a concession. For we are not able to love with the tongue only. But since many falsely claim this, the apostle allows, as is often done, the name of the thing to their pretence. But in the second clause he reproves their

vanity by denying that it truly exists save in action. The words
should be explained thus: Let us not profess by the tongue that we
love but prove it by action, for this is the only true way of loving.

*Hereby shall we know that we are of the truth, and shall assure our
heart before him. For if our heart condemn us, God is greater than our
heart, and knoweth all things. Beloved, if our heart condemn us not,
we have boldness toward God; and whatsoever we ask, we receive of
him, because we keep his commandments, and do the things that are
pleasing in his sight.* (19-22)

19. *Hereby shall we know.* He now takes the word *truth* in a different
sense, but with an elegant *prosonomasia* (name-giving). If we truly
love our neighbours it is a testimony to us that we are born of God,
who is the truth, or that the truth of God dwells in us. But we must
always remember that we do not receive the knowledge which the
apostle mentions from love, as if we had to seek from it the certainty
of salvation. And indeed, we only know that we are God's children
by His sealing His free adoption on our hearts by His Spirit and by
our receiving by faith the sure pledge of it offered in Christ. Therefore,
love is an accessory or inferior aid, a prop to our faith, not the foundation on which it rests.

Why then does the apostle say that *we shall assure our heart before God?*
In these words he tells us that faith does not exist apart from a good
conscience. Not that assurance comes from it or depends on it; but
because we are truly, and not falsely, assured of our union with God
only when He manifests Himself in our love by the efficacy of His
Holy Spirit. For we must always consider what the apostle is dealing
with. Since he condemns a feigned and false profession of faith, he
says that there can be no genuine assurance before God unless His
Spirit produces in us the fruit of love. All the same, although a good
conscience cannot be separated from faith, none should conclude from
this that we must look to our works for our assurance to be firm.

20. *For if our heart condemn us.* From the contrary he proves that
those who have not the testimony of a good conscience bear the name
and appearance of Christians in vain. For if anyone is conscious of
guilt and is condemned by the feeling of his own mind, far less can
he escape God's judgment. Therefore it follows that faith is overturned by the disquiet of an evil conscience.

He calls *God greater than our heart* with reference to judgment,
inasmuch as He sees far more keenly than we do and investigates more
searchingly and judges more severely. This is why Paul says that
although he was not conscious of guilt in himself, he was not thereby
justified (I Cor. 4.4). For he knew that, however attentive he was to

his duty, he erred in many things and through thoughtlessness was ignorant of mistakes which God saw. Therefore, what the apostle means is that he who is pressed and straitened by his conscience cannot escape God's judgment.

This is also the import of what follows, that God seeth all things. For how can those things be hidden from Him which even we, who beside Him are dull and blind, are forced to see? Therefore explain it like this: 'Since God sees everything, He is far superior to our heart.' It is quite common to take a copulative as a causal particle. The meaning is now clear. Since God's knowledge penetrates deeper than the perceptions of our conscience, none can stand before Him unless the integrity of his conscience sustains him.

But here a question may be objected. It is certain that the reprobate are sometimes plunged by Satan into such stupor that they no longer feel their own evils and without sorrow or fear rush headlong to their perdition, as Paul says. It is also certain that hypocrites are accustomed to flatter themselves and arrogantly despise God's judgment. They are drunken with a false opinion of their righteousness and are untouched by their sins. The reply is easy. Hypocrites are deceived because they flee from the light, and the reprobate feel nothing because they depart from God. Indeed, the only security for an evil conscience lies in concealment. But the apostle is here speaking of consciences which God drags out into the light, forces to His judgment seat and disturbs with an awareness of His judgment. Yet it is also true in general that the only calm peace we can have is that which God's Spirit gives to purified hearts. For as we have said, those who are stupefied often feel secret prickings, and in their lethargy torment themselves.

21. *If our heart condemn us not.* I have already explained that this does not refer to hypocrites or gross despisers of God. For however pleased with their lives the reprobate may be, the Lord weigheth the hearts, as Solomon says (Prov. 16.2). God's scales prevent anyone from being able to boast in His investigation that he has a clean heart. Hence the meaning of the apostle's words is that we come into God's presence with calm confidence only when we bring with us the testimony of a heart conscious of what is right and good. Paul's saying is certainly true, that by the faith which relies on the grace of Christ a confident access to God is opened to us (Eph. 3.12). And again, that peace is given us through faith, so that our consciences may stand in peace before God (Rom. 5.1). But there is no difference between these statements: Paul shows the cause of confidence; but John mentions only an inseparable result, which, although not the cause, is yet necessarily joined with it.

A greater difficulty arises here, however, which seems to leave no confidence in all the world. For who can be found whose heart reproves him in nothing? I reply: The godly are accused like this so that they may at the same time be absolved. For they need to be seriously pierced inwardly by their sins, that terror may train them in humility and self-hatred; but presently they flee to Christ's sacrifice where they have sure peace. Yet from another angle the apostle says that they are not accused, because although they may acknowledge that they fail in many respects, they are still sustained by this testimony of conscience, that they truly and sincerely fear God and desire to submit to His righteousness. All who are endowed with this godly feeling and also know that all their endeavours, however far from perfection, please God, are justly said to have a calm or peaceful heart, because there is no inward pricking to disturb their calm cheerfulness.

22. *And whatsoever we ask.* Because these are connected—confidence and calling upon God. Just as earlier he had shown that an evil conscience is incompatible with confidence, so now he declares that none can really call upon God save those who fear and worship Him aright with a pure heart. The latter follows from the former. It is a general principle of Scripture that the ungodly are not heard by God, but that their sacrifices and prayers are, on the contrary, an abomination to Him. Therefore the door is here shut against hypocrites, lest in contempt they should break into His presence.

He does not, however, mean that we have to bring a good conscience, as if it obtained favour for our prayers. Woe to us if we look to works, which contain nothing but a cause for trembling! Therefore believers only aspire to God's tribunal by relying on Christ the Mediator. But as the love of God is always joined with faith, the apostle, to reprove hypocrites the more severely, deprives them of the unique privilege with which God honours His children, so that they may not think that their prayers have access to God.

When he says *because we keep his commandments*, he does not mean that confidence in prayer is founded on our works. He is only teaching that godliness and the sincere worship of God cannot be separated from faith. Nor should it seem absurd that he uses a causal particle when not discussing a cause, for an inseparable addition is sometimes mentioned as a cause, as when someone says, 'Because the sun shines over us at noon there is more heat then,' although it does not follow that heat comes from light.

And this is his commandment, that we should believe in the name of his Son Jesus Christ, and love one another, even as he gave us commandment. And he that keepeth his commandments abideth in him, and he

*in him. And hereby we know that he abideth in us, by the Spirit
which he gave us.* (23-24)

23. *And this is his commandment.* He again adapts a general idea to
his own purpose. The sum of it is that such is the discord between us
and God that we are debarred from access to Him unless we are united
by brotherly love to one another. Here he does not commend love
alone, as before, but joins it to faith as a companion and handmaid.

The Sophists distort these words with their inventions, as if we
obtained liberty to pray, partly by faith and partly by works. When
John requires for the genuine way of prayer that we keep God's
commandments and then teaches us that this observance consists in
faith and love, they conclude that we ought to derive confidence in
prayer from these two things. But I have already said several times
that he is not dealing with how or by what means men may prepare
themselves to dare to pray to God. For here he is not concerned with
cause or worthiness. John only shows that God grants none the
favour and privilege of intercourse with Himself but His own children,
even those who have been regenerated by His Spirit. Therefore the
import of this passage is that, where fear and reverence for God do
not reign, God will not hear us.

But if we intend to obey His commandments, let us see what he
commands. He does not separate faith from love, but demands of us
that both as it were mutually embrace one another. This is why he
puts the word commandment in the singular. But this is a remarkable
passage, for he defines clearly and briefly what the complete perfection of a holy life consists in. There is therefore nothing to cause
us any difficulty, since God does not at all lead us round about through
long labyrinths, but simply and briefly sets before us what is right
and what pleases Him. What is more, there is no obscurity in this
brevity; for He shows us clearly the beginning and the end of living
aright. But the reason why he here mentions only brotherly love and
omits the love of God is, as we have said elsewhere, that brotherly
love flows from the love of God and thus is a sure and true proof
of it.

In the name of his Son. 'Name' refers to preaching—a reference which
should be noticed, for few understand what it is to believe in Christ.
But we can easily gather from this manner of speaking that the only
right faith is that which embraces Christ as He is preached in the
Gospel. Hence also, as Paul tells us in Rom. 10.14, there is no faith
without teaching. We must also observe that the apostle places faith
within the knowledge of Christ, for He is the living image of the
Father and in Him are hidden all the treasures of wisdom and know-

ledge. Therefore, as soon as we turn aside from Him, we can do nothing but wander in error.

24. *He that keepeth his commandments.* He confirms, as I have already said, that the union we have with God is manifested when we mutually love. Not that our union starts out from this, but that it cannot be idle or fruitless whenever it begins to exist. He proves this by giving a reason: God does not abide in us unless His Spirit dwells in us. But wherever His Spirit is, He necessarily displays His power and efficacy. From this we readily conclude that only they who keep His commandments abide in God and are united to Him.

When therefore he says *and hereby we know*, the copulative *and*, since it is put causally, is equivalent to 'for' or 'because'. But the details of the present reason should be considered, for although the statement verbally agrees with Paul's, when he says that the Spirit testifies to our hearts that we are God's children and through Him cry to God, 'Abba, Father', yet there is some difference in the sense. Paul is speaking of the certainty of free adoption which the Spirit of God seals on our hearts. But John is here looking at the effects that the Spirit, dwelling in us, produces. As also Paul when he says that they are the sons of God who are led by God's Spirit. For he also is dealing with the mortification of the flesh and newness of life. The sum of it is that it appears from this that we are God's children, when His Spirit rules and governs our life. At the same time, John teaches us that whatever good works there are in us proceed from the grace of the Spirit and that the Spirit is not obtained by our righteousness, but given to us freely.

CHAPTER FOUR

Beloved, believe not every spirit, but prove the spirits, whether they are of God: because many false prophets are gone out into the world. Hereby know ye the Spirit of God: every spirit which confesseth that Jesus Christ is come in the flesh is of God: and every spirit that confesseth not that Jesus Christ is come in the flesh is not of God: and this is the spirit of the antichrist, whereof ye have heard that it cometh; and now it is in the world already. (1-3)

He returns to the former doctrine, which he had touched on in Chapter Two. For (as is usual with something new) many misused Christ's name to sow their own errors. Some made a semi-profession of Christ; but when they had a place among His intimates they had more power to hurt. It was especially in Christ Himself that Satan seized the opportunity to disturb the Church; for He is the stone of offence, against whom all must stumble who do not keep to the right way which God has shown us.

Now, the apostle's teaching here consists of three parts. First, he shows an evil dangerous to believers, and therefore tells them to beware. He tells them how to beware—by distinguishing between the spirits; and this is the second part. In the third place, he points to a particular error, which was most dangerous to them. He forbids them to listen to those who denied that the Son of God was manifested in the flesh. We will now consider each in turn.

Although in the passage the reason is put in afterwards, that many false prophets had gone forth into the world, it is convenient to begin with it. This statement contains a useful warning; for if Satan had already moved many to broadcast their impostures under the name of Christ, similar examples of this today should not dismay us. For it is the perpetual state of the Gospel that Satan strives to infect and corrupt its purity by all sorts of errors. Our age has produced some horrible and monstrous sects, and many stand aghast at this; and not knowing where to turn to, give up every interest in religion, finding no better way to extricate themselves from the danger of error. They are utterly foolish; for simply by fleeing the light of truth they cast themselves into the darkness of error. Therefore, let this be firmly fixed in our minds, that from the time the Gospel began to be proclaimed, false prophets appeared. This teaching will fortify us against that offence.

Many are, so to say, bound by the antiquity of errors and dare not break from them. But John here points out an inward evil of the Church. Now, if there were impostors mixed up with the apostles and other faithful teachers, what wonder is it if, with the teaching of the Gospel long since oppressed, many corruptions have spread through the world? There is no reason why antiquity should prevent us from distinguishing between truth and falsehood.

1. *Believe not every spirit.* As we have said, when the Church is harassed by controversies and contentions many are frightened away from the Gospel. But the Spirit lays down a very different remedy for us. Believers should not receive any doctrine thoughtlessly and uncritically. So we should beware lest, out of offence at the variety of opinions, we wish to bid farewell to teachers and with them the Word of God. It is enough to be moderate and say that all are not to be heard indiscriminately.

I take the word *spirit* metonymically, as signifying one who claims to be endowed with the gift of the Spirit to perform a prophet's office. For since none was permitted to speak in his own name, and credit was only given to speakers inasmuch as they were the organs of the Holy Spirit, God adorned prophets with this title, that they might have more authority, as if He singled them out from mankind in general. Hence, they were called spirits who, by giving their tongues to the oracles of the Holy Spirit, in a way represented His person. They supplied nothing from their own senses, nor did they come forward in their own name. But the purpose of their honourable title was that God's Word should not lose reverence from contempt for the minister. For God wanted His Word to be always received from the mouth of men no less than as if He had Himself openly appeared from heaven.

At this point Satan interposed, and when he had substituted false teachers to adulterate God's Word, he also gave them the name that they might deceive the more easily. Thus false prophets have always superciliously and boastingly claimed whatever honour God bestowed on His own servants. But the apostle deliberately used this name, lest they who falsely claim God's name should deceive us with their masks. Just as today we see many who are so stupefied by the mere title of 'the Church' that they would rather cleave to the Pope, to their eternal ruin, than deny him the least part of his authority.

We ought to notice the concession. The apostle could have said that not every sort of man should be believed. But since false teachers claimed the title of the Spirit, he left it to them, at the same time telling them that what they professed was frivolous and worthless unless they exhibited the reality; and that they were foolish who were so astounded at the mere name of this honourable title that they dared not enquire into it.

Prove the spirits. Since not all were false prophets, the apostle here declares that they should be brought to trial. And he addresses not only the whole Church as a body, but each individual believer. But it might be asked where we get this discernment from. Those who reply that God's Word is the rule by which everything that men put forward should be tried, say something but not everything. I grant that doctrines should be tested by God's Word. But unless the Spirit of wisdom is present, there is little or no profit in having God's Word in our hands, for its meaning will not be certain to us. Gold, for example, is tested by fire or touchstone, but this can only be done by those who understand the art, for neither touchstone nor fire is of any use to the unlearned. If, then, we are to be fit critics, we must be endowed with and directed by the Spirit of discernment. But, since the apostle would have been commanding this in vain if the faculty of criticism were not supplied, we may assuredly conclude that the godly will never be left destitute of the Spirit of wisdom as to what is necessary, provided they ask for Him from the Lord. But the Spirit will only guide us to a true discrimination if we subject all our thoughts to the Word. For, as I have said, it is like a touchstone; nay, it should be regarded as far more necessary to us, for only that which is drawn from it should be regarded as true doctrine.

But a difficult question arises here. If everyone has the right and liberty to judge, nothing will ever be settled as certain and the whole of religion will waver. I reply: There is a twofold trial of doctrine, private and public. The private is that by which each one settles his own faith and safely rests in that doctrine which he knows has come from God. For consciences will never find a safe and quiet harbour elsewhere than in God. The public trial relates to the common consent and πολιτεία of the Church. For since there is the danger of fanatical men arising and presumptuously claiming that they are endued with the Spirit of God, it is a necessary remedy that believers shall meet together and seek a way of godly and pure agreement. But the old proverb is true, So many heads, so many viewpoints; and therefore it is a remarkable work of God when He tames our obstinacy and makes us think alike and agree in a pure unity of faith.

But when under this pretext the Papists want everything that was ever decreed in the councils to be regarded as certain oracles because the Church has once tested them as being from God, is too frivolous. For although the ordinary way of seeking consent is to gather a godly and holy council, where controversies may be decided from God's Word, yet God has never bound Himself to the decrees of any council.

T

Nor does it necessarily follow that, as soon as a hundred or so bishops meet together somewhere, they have duly called on God and enquired at His mouth what is true. In fact, nothing is clearer than that they have often departed from the pure Word of God. Therefore, here also the testing which the apostle prescribes must take place, so that the spirits may be proved.

2. *Hereby know ye.* He establishes a special mark by which they may more easily distinguish true prophets from the false. But he only repeats what we have heard before; that, just as Christ is the object at which true faith aims, so He is the stumbling-block on which all heretics stumble. We are safe, then, so long as we abide in Christ. But when we depart from Him, faith is lost and all truth made void.

But let us remember what this confession contains. When the apostle says that *Christ* came, we infer that He was before with the Father. By this His eternal divinity is shown. By saying that He came in the flesh, he means that by putting on flesh, He became a real man, of the same nature with us, that He became our brother—except that He was free from all sin and corruption. And finally, by saying that He came, we must note the cause of His coming; for the Father did not send Him for nothing. Christ's office and power depend on this.

Therefore, as the ancient heretics departed from this faith, partly by denying Christ's divine nature, partly His human, so the Papists today. Granted that they confess Christ to be both God and man, yet they certainly do not retain the confession which the apostle demands, for they rob Christ of His power. For where free-will, merits of works, invented worship, satisfactions and the advocacy of saints is set up, how very little remains for Christ! Hence the apostle meant that, since the knowledge of Christ includes the sum of the doctrine of godliness, our eyes should always be directed and fixed on that, so that we may not be deceived. And indeed, Christ is the end of the Law and the prophets; and from the Gospel we learn nothing but His power and grace.

3. *And this is the spirit of the antichrist.* The apostle put this in to make the impostures which lead us away from Christ the more detestable. We have already said that the doctrines of the kingdom of the antichrist was notorious and well-known, and that believers had been warned of the future scattering of the Church, that they might be very careful. They justly dreaded that name as something wicked and ominous. The apostle now says that all who detract from Christ are members of that kingdom.

He also says that the spirit of antichrist *will come* and that *it is already* in the world; but in a different sense. He means that it was already in the world, because it performed the mystery of its iniquity. But since the truth of God had not yet been overwhelmed with false and spurious teaching; since superstition had not yet succeeded in corrupting the worship of God; since the world had not yet treacherously departed from Christ; and since the tyranny opposed to the kingdom of Christ had not yet openly exalted itself, he says that it would come.

Ye are of God, my little children, and have overcome them: because greater is he that is in you than he that is in the world. They are of the world: therefore speak they as of the world, and the world heareth them. We are of God: he that knoweth God heareth us; he who is not of God heareth us not. But this we know the spirit of truth, and the spirit of error. (4-6)

4. *Ye are of God.* He had spoken of one antichrist; now he mentions many. But the plural refers to false prophets who had already come forth before their head appeared. The apostle's aim was to encourage believers to resist impostors bravely and undauntedly. For keenness falters when the outcome of the battle is doubtful. Besides, it might have made the good afraid when they saw that hardly had the kingdom of Christ arisen than enemies lined up to suppress it. Therefore, although they have to fight, he says that they had conquered because they would be successful. It is as if he said that in the midst of the battle they were already out of danger, for they would be victorious.

But this doctrine should be extended further. Whatever contests we may have against the world and the flesh, certain victory accompanies them. Indeed, hard and fierce struggles await us one after another; but as we fight by Christ's power and are armed with God's weapons in fighting and striving, we are victorious. As to the general tenor of this passage, it is a great comfort that, with whatever tricks Satan may attack us, we shall stand in the truth of God.

But we must notice the reason immediately given: because *greater,* i.e. stronger, is he who is in you than he who is in the world. For such is our weakness that we succumb before we engage the enemy. We are so entangled in ignorance that we are open to all kinds of falsehoods and Satan is a wonderful master in the art of deceiving. Even if we held out for one day, doubt might creep into our minds as to what will happen tomorrow, and we should be in continual anxiety. Therefore the apostle tells us that we are strong, not by our own power, but by God's. From this he concludes that we can no more be conquered than can God Himself, who has armed us with His own power to the end of the world. But all through this spiritual warfare the thought should stay in our hearts that it would be all up with us if we were to fight in our own strength; whereas victory is certain, for God repels our enemies while we are quiet.

5. *They are of the world.* It is no small consolation that those who dare to attack God in us are armed only with the help of the world. And the apostle means the world, inasmuch as Satan is its prince. He gives another consolation when he says that the world embraces in the false prophets what it acknowledges as its own. We see the great propensity to vanity in men. Hence, false doctrines easily get in and spread everywhere. The apostle says that there is no reason why this should disturb us, for it is nothing new or unusual if the world, which is wholly false, should readily listen to falsehood.

6. *We are of God.* Although this really applies to all the godly, it refers strictly to the faithful ministers of the Gospel. For the apostle, from the confidence of the Spirit, here glories that he and his fellow-ministers served God in sincerity and received from Him whatever they taught. False prophets claim the same thing, for they are accustomed to deceive under the mask of God. But faithful teachers are very different from them, in that they declare nothing of themselves in word but what they manifest in deed.

We should, however, always bear in mind the subject that he is dealing with here. The number of the godly was small, and unbelief prevailed almost everywhere. There were few real adherents of the Gospel; the most part was rushing into error. This gave occasion of stumbling. To forestall this, John tells us to be satisfied with the fewness of the believers because all God's children honoured Him and submitted to His teaching. And he at once opposes the contrary clause: *they who are not of God* do not hear the pure teaching of the Gospel. By these words he means that the vast multitude to whom the Gospel is not acceptable do not hear God's honest and true servants, because they are alienated from God Himself. Hence it is no lessening of the authority of the Gospel that many reject it.

But a useful admonition is joined to this doctrine. We prove ourselves to be God's by the obedience of faith. Nothing is easier than to claim that we are God's; and so nothing is commoner among men. Just as today the Papists proudly vaunt that they are worshippers of God, and yet no less proudly reject God's Word. They may pretend to believe God's Word, but when it comes to the test, they shut their ears. But to revere God's Word is the only testimony that we fear Him. Nor is there any room for the excuse which many make, that they flee from the teaching of the Gospel when it is set before them because they are not fit to judge. For it cannot be but that everyone who sincerely fears and obeys God knows Him in His Word.

If any object that many of the elect do not attain faith immediately, but may even stubbornly resist, I reply that they are not at that time to be regarded as God's children, by our way of thinking. But it is a sign of a reprobate man when he stubbornly rejects the truth. And it must be observed in passing that the hearing mentioned by the apostle is to be understood of the inward and sincere hearing of the heart, which happens by faith.

By this we know. The relative to *by this* is included in the two preceding clauses; as if he said, 'The truth is to be distinguished from falsehood in that some speak from God, others from the world.'

But by *the spirit of truth and of error,* some think that hearers are meant; as if he had said that those who surrender themselves to the deceits of impostors were born to error and had the seed of falsehood in themselves, whereas those who consent to the Word of God show themselves ipso facto to be true. I do not accept this. For the apostle takes spirits here μετωνυμικῶς for teachers or prophets, and I think he means simply that the testing of doctrine must be referred to these two, to see whether it be from God or the world.

In speaking like this, however, he seems in fact to say nothing. For all are ready to object that they only speak from God. So today the Papists boast with professorial superciliousness that all their inventions are the oracles of the Spirit. Mohammed, too, asserts that he has drawn his dreams only from heaven. In olden times the Egyptians lied that the mad absurdities with which they bewitched themselves and others had been divinely revealed. But I reply that we have the Word of the Lord, which should be consulted first. Hence, when false spirits claim the name of God, we must enquire from the Scriptures whether it is as they say. So long as we use godly care, with humility and modesty, the Spirit of discernment will be with us and as a faithful interpreter will expound what He Himself speaks in Scripture.

Beloved, let us love one another: for love is of God; and everyone that loveth is begotten of God, and knoweth God. He that loveth not knoweth not God; for God is love. Herein was the love of God manifested in us, that God hath sent his only begotten Son into the world, that we might live through him. Herein is love, not that we loved God, but that he loved us, and sent his Son to be the propitiation for our sins. (7-10)

7. *Beloved.* He returns to the exhortation which he pursues in nearly the whole epistle. We have said that he mingles the teaching of faith with exhortation to love. He so dwells on these two points that he continually passes from one to the other. When he commends love to one another he does not mean that we do this duty when we in our turn love our friends because they love us. But because he addresses believers in common, he could not have said anything else

than that they were to love one another. This statement he confirms
by the reason he had already often put forward, that none can prove
himself the son of God unless he loves his neighbours, and that the
true knowledge of God of necessity begets love for God in us.

In his usual way he also opposes to this the contrary clause, that
there is no knowledge of God where love does not thrive. And he
takes it as an axiom that God is love; that is, that His nature is to love
men. I know that many reason more subtly and that the ancients
especially have misused this passage to prove the divinity of the Spirit.
But the apostle simply means that as God is the fountain of love, this
affection flows from Him and is poured out wherever there is knowledge of Him—just as he had at first called Him light in that there is
no darkness in him, but rather He enlightens all things by His brightness. So he is not speaking here of the essence of God, but only shows
what we experience Him to be.

But we must notice two things in the apostle's words: That the
true knowledge of God is that which regenerates and reconstructs us,
so that we become new creatures; and therefore, that it must be that
it conforms to God. Away then, with that foolish invention of
fides informata. For if anyone separates faith from love it is as if he
were trying to take away heat from the sun.

9. *Herein was the love of God manifested.* The love of God is testified
to us by many other proofs as well. For if it is asked why the world
was created, why we have been put in it to have dominion over the
earth, why we are preserved in this life to enjoy innumerable blessings
and are endowed with light and understanding, no reason can be
given but the free love of God towards us. But here the apostle
chooses the chief example, which transcends everything else. For it
was not only the infinite love of God which did not spare His own
Son, that by His death He might restore us to life, but it was a more
than wonderful goodness which ought to ravish our minds with
amazement. Christ is such a shining and remarkable proof of the
divine love toward us that, whenever we look to Him, He clearly
confirms to us the doctrine that God is love.

He calls Him *the only begotten* as an amplification. For He showed
His unique love to us in that He exposed His only Son to death for our
sakes. Moreover, He who is by nature His only Son, makes many so
by grace and adoption; that is, all who by faith are ingrafted into His
body. He expresses the purpose for which God sent Christ—that we
may live through Him. For apart from Him we are all dead; but in
His coming He brought life to us, and unless our unbelief prevents it
we feel in ourselves the effect of His grace.

10. *Herein is love.* He brings out God's love by another reason, that

He gave us His Son when we were enemies—as also Paul teaches in Rom. 5.8—but here he uses different words: God, moved by no love of men, loved them of His own accord. In these words he wanted to teach us that God's love towards us was free. And although it was the apostle's object to set forth God for us to imitate, yet the teaching of faith which he puts in must not be overlooked. God freely loved us. Why? Because He loved us before we were born. Therefore because in that depravity of nature our hearts were turned away from Him and not at all leaning towards upright and godly feelings.

If we gave place to the sophistries of the Papists, that God chooses each one as He foresees him to be worthy of love, this doctrine that He first loved us would no longer stand. For then our love to God would be prior in order, even though in time posterior. But the apostle assumes it as an axiom of Scripture, of which these profane sophists are ignorant, that we are born so corrupt and depraved that there is in us, as it were, an inborn hatred of God so that we desire nothing but what is displeasing to Him, and every affection of our flesh wages continual war against His righteousness.

And sent his Son. Therefore, it was from God's mere goodness, as from a fountain, that Christ flowed to us with all His blessings. And just as it is necessary to know that we have salvation in Christ because our heavenly Father has loved us of His own accord, so when we are seeking a solid and complete certainty of the divine love, we must look to none other than to Christ. Hence, all who leave out Christ and enquire into their determination in God's secret counsel are mad to their own ruin.

He again shows the cause of Christ's coming and His office when he says that He was sent to be the propitiation for sins. And first, these words teach us that we have all been alienated from God through sin and that this discord remains until Christ intervenes to reconcile us. Secondly, we are taught that our life begins when God, appeased by the death of His Son, receives us into favour. For propitiation strictly refers to the sacrifice of His death. Hence we see that to Christ alone belongs this honour of expiating for the sins of the world and taking away the enmity between God and us.

But here it seems as if there is an inconsistency. For if God loved us before Christ offered Himself to death for us, what need was there for another reconciliation? Hence the death of Christ might seem superfluous. I reply that when Christ is said to have reconciled the Father to us, it is to be referred to our feeling; for as we are conscious of sin, we can only conceive of God as angry and hostile until Christ absolves us from guilt. For whenever sin appears, God wants His wrath and the judgment of eternal death to be felt. From this it follows that we cannot fail to be terrified by the present sight of death until Christ abolishes sin by His death and delivers us from death by His own blood. Moreover, God's love demands righteousness. Therefore, to be convinced that we are loved, we must needs come to Christ, in whom alone is righteousness.

We now see that the variety of expressions occurring in Scripture and corresponding to the different aspects, is most appropriate and useful for faith. God interposed His Son to reconcile Himself to us (*ad se nobis reconciliandum*) because He loved us. For we were yet enemies to God, continually provoking His wrath. What is more, the fear and terror of a bad conscience deprived us of all relish for life. Therefore, as to the feeling of our faith, God began to love us in Christ. And although the apostle is here dealing with the first reconciliation, let us know that it is a perpetual benefit of Christ to propitiate God to us by expiating sins. The Papists also concede this in part. But then they go on to weaken and almost annihilate this grace by introducing their fictitious satisfactions. But if men redeem themselves by their works, Christ cannot be the unique propitiation, as He is called here.

> *Beloved, if God so loved us, we also ought to love one another. No man hath beheld God at any time: if we love one another, God abideth in us, and his love is perfected in us: hereby know we that we abide in him, and he in us, because he hath given us of his Spirit. And we have beheld and bear witness that the Father hath sent the Son to be the Saviour of the world. Whosoever shall confess that Jesus is the Son of God, God abideth in him, and he in God. And we know and have believed the love which God hath in us. God is love; and he that abideth in love abideth in God, and God abideth in him.* (11-16)

11. *Beloved.* The apostle now accommodates to his purpose what he has just taught about the love of God, and exhorts us by God's example to brotherly love. In the same way Paul sets before us Christ, who offered Himself to the Father as a sacrifice of a sweet odour, that every one of us might devote himself to his neighbour (Eph. 5.2). And John tells us that our love should not be mercenary, when he bids us love our neighbours as God has loved us. For we must remember that we have been loved freely. And without doubt, when we look to our own convenience or return friends like for like, it is self-love and not love of others.

12. *No man hath beheld God.* The same words occur in the first chapter of the Gospel. But John[1] had not the same end in view there, for he meant that God could only be known as He has revealed

---

[1] *Joannes Baptista.* Plainly an error either of Calvin, scribe or printer.

Himself in Christ. Here the apostle extends the same truth further, that we comprehend the power of God by faith and love so that we know that we are His children and He abides in us.

First, however, he speaks of love when he says that *God abideth in us* if we love one another; for then His love is perfected, i.e. truly proved to be, in us. It is as if he said that God shows Himself as present when by His Spirit He forms our hearts to brotherly love. In the same sense he repeats what he had already said, 'That we know that he abides in us by the Spirit which He gave us.' For this is confirmation of the previous sentence, since love is the effect of the Spirit.

The sum of it is that, since love comes from the Spirit of God, we cannot love the brethren truly and with a sincere heart unless the Spirit displays His power. In this way He testifies that He abides in us. But by His Spirit God abides in us. Therefore, by love we prove that we have God abiding in us. On the other hand, whoever claims to have God and does not love the brethren, shows his emptiness by this alone, for he separates God from himself.

When he says *and his love is perfected*, the conjunction is put for a causative particle. And here love may be explained in two ways: either that with which we love God, or that which He breathes into us. That God has given us His Spirit or of His Spirit are the same thing, for we know that in a measure the Spirit is given to each individual.

14. *And we have beheld.* He now explains the other part of the knowledge of God which we have touched upon, that He communicates Himself to us, and offers Himself to be enjoyed, in His Son. From this it follows that we receive Him by faith. For the apostle's aim is to show that God is so united to us by faith and love that He truly abides in us and in a way makes Himself visible by the effect of His power, when otherwise He could not be seen.

When the apostle says, *We have beheld and bear witness*, he means himself and the others. And he does not mean any sort of seeing, but what is joined to faith and by which they recognized the glory of God in Christ; for it goes on that *he was sent to be the Saviour of the world*, and this knowledge flows from the illumination of the Spirit.

15. *Whosoever shall confess.* He repeats the principle that we are united to God by Christ and that we can only be joined to Christ if God abides in us. Faith and confession are here put indiscriminately in the same sense. For although hypocrites may falsely claim faith, the apostle only acknowledges in the order of confessors those who truly and sincerely believe. When he says that Jesus is the Son of God, he puts the whole sum of faith in a word or two, for there is

nothing necessary for salvation which faith does not find in Christ.

When he has said in general that men are so engrafted into Christ by faith that Christ joins them to God, he adds the argument, that they themselves had beheld, accommodating a general statement to his readers. Then follows the exhortation that they should love others as they were loved of God. Therefore, the order and connexion of his discourse is this: Faith in Christ brings it to pass that God abides in men, and we are partakers of this grace. Moreover, as God is love, none can abide in Him unless he loves his brethren. Therefore, love should reign in us, since God joins Himself to us.

16. *And we know and have believed.* This is equivalent to his saying, 'We have known by believing'; for such knowledge is only perceived by faith. But we gather from this how far an undecided or doubtful opinion is from faith. Moreover, although, as I have said already, he here wanted to accommodate the final sentence to his readers, he defines the substance of faith in different ways. Before, he had said that it is to confess that Jesus is the Son of God. Now he says that by faith we know God's love towards us. From this it appears that the fatherly love of God is apprehended in Christ and that nothing certain is known of Christ save by those who know themselves to be God's children by His grace. For the Father daily sets His Son before us to adopt us in Him.

God is love. This is, so to say, the minor proposition in the syllogism. For he reasons from faith to love like this: By faith God dwells within us. But God is love. Therefore, wherever God abides, love must also flourish. From this it follows that love is of necessity joined to faith.

Herein is love made perfect with us, that we may have boldness in the day of judgment; because as he is, even so are we in this world. There is no fear in love: but perfect love casteth out fear, because fear hath torment; and he that feareth is not made perfect in love. (17-18)

17. *Herein is love made perfect.* There are two clauses in this sentence: that we are partakers of the divine adoption when we resemble God as children their father; and secondly, that this confidence is an incomparable blessing, for without it we are most miserable. So in the first place he shows God's purpose in embracing us in His love and how we enjoy the grace exhibited to us in Christ. Therefore, God's love toward us is to be understood here. He says it is *perfected*, because it is abundantly poured forth and really bestowed and is complete in every respect. But he affirms that only they are partakers of this blessing who prove themselves to be God's children by being conformed to Him. It is therefore an argument from things connected.

That we may have boldness. He now begins to show the fruit of the divine love toward us, although later he does so more clearly from the contrary. But it is an inestimable blessing that we may boldly dare to stand before God. For by nature we dread the presence of God, and justly, for since He is the Judge of the world and our sins keep us guilty, death and hell must come to our thoughts along with God. From this comes the dread I have mentioned, so that men flee from God so far as they can. But John says that believers are not afraid when they are told of the last judgment, but on the contrary approach God's judgment-seat confidently and cheerfully, because they are convinced of His Fatherly love. Therefore, everyone has advanced so far in faith as he is well prepared in his mind to look forward to the day of judgment.

As he is. By these words, as has already been said, he means that we in our turn are required to resemble the image of God. Therefore, what God is in heaven, He bids us be in this world, that we may be reckoned His children. For when God's image appears in us, it is, as it were, the seal of His adoption.

But in this way he seems to place part of our confidence in works. So the Papists get puffed up here, as if John denied that by relying on God's grace alone we can have a sure confidence of salvation without the co-operation of works. But they are deceived in this; for they do not consider that the apostle is here not arguing from the cause but from what is joined to it. We willingly allow that none is reconciled to God through Christ without also being reformed to God's image, and that the one cannot be separated from the other. Therefore the apostle rightly excludes from confidence of grace all in whom no likeness of God is seen. For it is certain that such are completely foreign to the Spirit of God and Christ. We also do not deny that newness of life, as the effect of divine adoption, serves to confirm confidence; but as a secondary support, whereas we must be founded on grace alone. Otherwise, indeed, John's teaching is inconsistent; for experience shows, and even the Papists are forced to confess, that in regard to works there is always occasion for trembling. Hence, none comes to God's judgment-seat with a calm mind unless he is sure that he is freely loved.

But we need not be surprised that none of these things please the Papists, for the only faith that they, poor wretches, know, is one entangled with doubts. Moreover, hypocrisy spreads a darkness over them, so that they do not seriously consider how formidable God's judgment is when Christ is not present as Mediator. Others neglect the resurrection of the dead as being a fable. But we must keep our faith fixed on His grace alone if we are to go forth to meet Christ cheerfully and joyfully.

18. *There is no fear.* He now commends the excellency of this blessing from its contrary, saying that we are always tormented until God frees us from that wretched torture by the remedy of His love for us. The sum of it is that there is nothing worse than being worried by continual disquiet, and we arrive at a calm rest outside fear by being aware of God's love towards us. From this appears what a singular blessing of God it is that we should be favoured with His love. From this teaching he will soon draw an exhortation; but before he exhorts us to our duty he commends to us this gift of God which by faith removes our fear.

I know that many expound this passage in a different sense. But I am thinking of what the apostle meant, not what others think. They say there is no fear in love in that, when we love God voluntarily, we are not constrained by force and fear to serve Him. According to them, therefore, servile fear is here opposed to voluntary reverence. From this has grown up the distinction between servile and filial fear. I grant it is true that when we freely love God as a Father, we are no longer constrained by the fear of punishment. But this has nothing to do with this passage, in which the apostle is only teaching that, when by faith we see and know the love of God, peace is given to our consciences that they may no longer be disturbed.

But it may be asked, When does perfect love cast out fear? For we are endued with only a taste of the divine love for us, and therefore can never be wholly freed from fear. I reply: Although fear is not completely shaken off, yet, when we flee to God as a quiet harbour, safe and free from all danger of ship-wreck and tempest, fear really is cast out, for it gives place to faith. Therefore, fear is not cast out in such a way that it does not assault our minds; but it is so cast out that it does not disturb us or hamper the peace that we obtain by faith.

Fear hath torment. Here the apostle magnifies the grace of which he speaks. For, as it is most wretched to suffer continual torments, there is nothing more desirable than to present ourselves before God with a calm conscience and composed mind. That, as some say, servants fear because they have before their eyes punishment and the rod, and that they only do their work because they have to, has nothing to do with the apostle's meaning, as we said before. So when they expound the next clause as that he who fears is not perfect in love because he does not submit willingly to God, but would rather be quit of his service, it does not at all agree with the context. On the contrary, the apostle is telling us that when anyone fears (that is, has a disturbed mind) it is the fault of unbelief. For when the love of God is properly known, it calms the mind.

We love him, because he first loved us. If a man say, I love God, and hateth his brother, he is a liar: for he that loveth not his brother whom he hath seen, cannot love God whom he hath not seen. And this commandment have we from him, that he who loveth God love his brother also. (19-21)

19. *We love him.* The verb ἀγαπῶμεν can be read either as indicative or imperative, but the former agrees far better with the sense. For, to my mind, the apostle repeats the proceeding sentence, that as God has prevented us by His free love, we should in return render to Him His due—as he at once adds that He ought to be loved in men, or that our love for Him should be testified towards men. But if the imperative is preferred, the meaning would be the same: that as God has freely loved us we also should now love Him.

But this love can only exist if it begets brotherly love among us. Therefore he says that they who boast that they love God while hating their neighbours are liars. But the reason he gives does not seem sufficiently firm, being a comparison between the minor and the major. He says that if we do not love our neighbours with whom we live, much less can we love the invisible God. Now two contradictions are plain here. For the love which we have for God flows from faith and not sight, as we read in I Pet. 1.8. Secondly, the basis in regard to God is very different from that in regard to men. Whereas God ravishes us to love Him for His infinite goodness, men often deserve hatred. I reply that the apostle takes for granted what should undoubtedly be sure among us, that God offers Himself to us in men who bear engraved in them His image, and that He requires us to perform to them the duties which He Himself does not need. Just as we read in Psalm 16.2, 'My benefits reach not to thee, O Lord; towards the saints who are on the earth is my love.' And certainly, fellowship in the same nature, the use of so many things and mutual intercourse, must draw us to love unless we are like iron. But John only meant that it is a false boast when anyone says that he loves God but neglects His image which is before his eyes.

21. *And this commandment.* This is a stronger argument from Christ's authority and teaching. For He not only commanded the bare love of God, but bade us also love our brethren. We must therefore so start out from God as to cross over to men at the same time.

CHAPTER FIVE

Whosoever believeth that Jesus is the Christ is begotten of God: and whosoever loveth him that begat loveth him also that is begotten of him. Hereby we know that we love the children of God, when we love God and do his commandments. For this is the love of God, that we keep his commandments: and his commandments are not grievous. For whatsoever is begotten of God overcometh the world: and this is the victory that hath overcome the world, even our faith. And who is he that overcometh the world, but he that believeth that Jesus is the Son of God? (1-5)

1. *Whosoever believeth.* He confirms the union of faith and brotherly love by another reason. For since God regenerates us by faith, He must needs be loved by us as a Father. But this love embraces all His children. Therefore faith cannot be separated from love.

The first statement is that all who are born of God believe that Jesus is the Christ. Here again you see Christ alone set forth as the object of faith, since it finds in Him righteousness, life and every desirable blessing and the whole God. Hence the only true way to believe is when we direct our minds to Him. Moreover, to believe that He is the Christ is to hope from Him everything that has been promised about the Messiah. And it is no empty title of Christ that is here ascribed to Him. Rather, it designates the office to which He was appointed by the Father. As in the Law, the full restoration of all things, righteousness and happiness were promised through the Messiah, so today all this is more clearly expressed in the Gospel. Therefore, Jesus can only be received as Christ if salvation is sought from Him, since this is why He was sent by the Father and is daily offered to us.

For this reason the Apostle justly declares that all who really believe have been born of God. For faith is far above the grasp of the human mind and we have to be drawn to Christ by our heavenly Father, since none of us can ever ascend to Him by his own efforts. And this is what the apostle says in his Gospel, that those who believe in the name of the Only begotten were not born of blood or of the flesh (1.13). And Paul says that we are not endued with the spirit of this world, but with the Spirit who is from God, that we may know the things that He has given us (I Cor. 2.12). For eye has not seen, nor ear heard, nor the mind conceived, the reward laid up for those who love God. The Spirit alone arrives at this mystery. Again, inasmuch as Christ is given to us for sanctification and brings with Him the Spirit of regeneration, in short, as He engrafts us into His body, this is another reason why none can have faith unless he is born of God.

Loveth him also that is begotten of him. Augustine and other older writers applied this to Christ, but incorrectly. For under the singular the apostle signifies all believers, and the context plainly shows that his only purpose was to derive mutual love from faith as a fountain. This is an argument drawn from the common order of nature, but what is seen among men is transferred to God. But we must notice that the apostle is not speaking only of believers and passing over those who are without, as if only the former are to be loved and we should have no care or thought for the rest. But by this elementary lesson, so to say, he teaches us to love all without exception when he bids us make a beginning with the godly.

2. *Hereby we know.* In these words he briefly shows what true love is—that which is referred to God. Hitherto he has said that true love to God exists only where we also love our neighbours. For this is always its effect. But he now teaches that men are loved rightly and duly when God stands first. And this definition is necessary, for it often happens that we love men apart from God, as when unholy and carnal friendships think only of private advantage or some other vanishing object. Therefore, as he had first urged the effect, so now the cause. For he wants to show that mutual love should be so culti-vated among us that God may be put first.

To the love of God he joins the observance of the Law; and justly, for when we love God as our Father and Lord, reverence must of necessity be joined with love. Moreover, God cannot be separated from Himself. Since therefore, He is the fountain of all righteousness and uprightness, he who loves Him must necessarily have his mind set to the obedience of righteousness. The love of God is no idle thing. From this passage we also infer what true observance of the Law is. For if we obey God by keeping His commandments only from the constraint of fear, we are very far from true obedience. Therefore the first thing is to devote our hearts to God in willing reverence, and then to form our life to the rule of the Law. This is what Moses meant when he summarized the Law by saying, 'Israel, what doth the Lord thy God require of thee, but to love him and obey him?' (Deut. 10.12).

3. *His commandments are not grievous.* He put this in, lest difficulties should break or lessen our enthusiasm, as often happens. For some who have followed a godly and holy life with a cheerful mind and great enthusiasm, afterwards grow weary, finding their strength

inadequate. Therefore, to stir up our efforts, John says that God's commandments are not grievous. But on the other hand it may be objected that we have experienced something very different and that even Scripture declares that the yoke of the Law is unbearable (Acts 15.10). The reason is also clear, for since self-denial is a sort of prelude to keeping the Law, can we say that it is easy for a man to deny himself? No indeed! For since the Law is spiritual, as Paul teaches in Rom. 7.14, and we are only flesh, there must be a great difference between us and God's Law. I reply, that this difficulty does not arise from the nature of the Law but from the vice of our flesh. And Paul expressly declares this; for, after he has said that it was impossible for the Law to give us righteousness, he immediately puts the blame on our flesh.

This explanation quite reconciles the statements of Paul and David, which are apparently very contradictory. Paul makes the Law the minister of death, declares that it works nothing but the wrath of God, that it was given to increase sin, that it lives that it may kill us (II Cor. 3.7; Rom. 4.15). David, on the contrary, says that it is sweeter than honey and more to be desired than gold, and among other commendations, he says that it cheers hearts, converts to the Lord and quickens. But Paul is comparing the Law with man's corrupt nature, and this is where the conflict arises. But David shows how they are affected whom God begets again by His Spirit. Hence the sweetness and delight for which the flesh has no relish. And John has included this difference, for he confines these words, *God's commandments are not grievous*, to God's children, lest anyone should take them generally. Thus he suggests that it is through the power of the Spirit that it is not grievous or vexatious for us to obey God.

But the question does not seem to be fully resolved yet. For, although believers are ruled by the Spirit of God, they wage a hard contest against their own flesh. And however hard they struggle, they perform hardly the half of their duty; nay, they almost fail under their burden, as if they lay between the anvil and the hammer, as we say.[1] We see how Paul groaned like a prisoner and cried out that he was wretched because he could not freely serve God. I reply that the Law is called easy in so far as we are endowed with heavenly power and overcome the lusts of the flesh. For however much the flesh may wanton, believers feel that there is no delight save in following God.

We must also observe that John is not speaking of the bare Law, which contains only commands, but joins with it the fatherly kindness of God, by which the rigour of the Law is softened. When we know

---

[1] *quasi inter sacrum et saxum constituti*—as if placed between the victim and the stone. A proverb from Plautus.

that we are graciously forgiven by the Lord if our works do not
satisfy the Law, it makes us far quicker to obey; as it is said in Psalm
130.4, 'But there is forgiveness with thee, that thou mayest be feared.'
It is therefore easy to keep the Law in that believers, sustained by
forgiveness, do not despond when they fall short. Meanwhile, the
apostle tells us that we must fight if we are to serve the Lord. For the
whole world hinders us from going where God calls us. Therefore,
only he keeps the Law who courageously resists the world.

4. *This is the victory*. He had said that all who are begotten of God
overcome the world; and now he also expresses the way to overcome.
For it might still be asked where this victory comes from. He places
the victory over the whole world in faith.

A remarkable passage. For although Satan continually launches
his hard and dreadful assaults, the Spirit of God declares that we are
out of danger, and so takes away our fear and animates us to fight
bravely. The past tense is stronger than the present or the future. He
says, *that hath overcome*, that we might feel certain, as if the enemy had
already been put to flight. It is, of course, true that our warfare lasts
all through our life, that our conflicts are daily, that new and manifold
battles are every moment begun against us by the enemy from every
side. But as God does not arm us for one day alone, and as faith is not
of a day's duration but is the perpetual work of the Holy Spirit, we
are already partakers of victory, as if we had already finished the war.

But this confidence does not induce sluggishness, but we are always
anxiously intent on the fight. For the Lord tells His people to be
assured; but He does not want them to be secure. On the contrary,
He declares that they have already overcome, that they may fight
more spiritedly and strenuously.

The term *world* has a wide meaning here, comprehending whatever
is against God's Spirit. Thus, the depravity of our nature is a part of
the world; all lusts, all the stratagems of Satan; in short, whatever
leads us away from God. A heavy weight of war lies on us among
such·manifold forces of men, and we should have been vanquished
before the battle had not God promised us the victory. But this
promise both arms us always with the unconquerable power of God,
and also, on the other hand, annihilates all the strength of men. For
the apostle is not telling us that God merely lends us His aid, so that,
helped by Him, we may be equal to resisting. But he places victory
in faith alone. But faith receives from another that by which it overcomes. Therefore, they take from God what is His own who ascribe
the triumph to their own power.

5. *Who is he that overcometh the world?* This is a reason from the
foregoing sentence. We conquer by faith because we borrow strength

from Christ. As also Paul says, 'I can do all things in him that strength-
eneth me' (Phil. 4.13). Only he is superior to Satan and the world
and does not give way to his own flesh, who distrusts himself and rests
on Christ's power alone. For by the word faith he means a living
apprehension of Christ which applies to us His strength and office.

> *This is he that came by water and blood, even Jesus Christ; not with the
> water only, but with the water and with the blood. And it is the
> Spirit that beareth witness, because the Spirit is the truth. For there
> are three that bear witness in heaven, the Father, the Word, and the
> holy Ghost: and these three are one. And there are three that bear
> witness in earth, the Spirit, and the water, and the blood: and these
> three agree in one. If we receive the witness of men, the witness of God
> is greater: for the witness of God is this, that he hath borne witness
> concerning his Son. (6-10)*

6. *This is he that came.* That our faith may rest safely on Christ, he
says that the concrete substance of the shadows of the Law appears in
Him. I do not doubt that by the words 'water and blood' he refers to
the ancient rites of the Law. The purpose of the comparison, moreover, is not only that we shall know that the Mosaic Law was abolished
by Christ's coming, but also that we shall seek in Him the fulfilment
of what the ceremonies formerly figured. They were of many kinds;
but under these two the apostle comprehends the whole perfection of
holiness and righteousness. By water all filth was washed away, so
that men might come to God only pure and clean. And by blood
there was expiation and a pledge of full reconciliation with God. But
the Law only sketched out in external symbols what was to be substantially and really performed by the Messiah. John therefore aptly
proves that Jesus is the once promised Christ of the Lord, because He
brought with Him that by which He sanctifies us wholly.

There is no ambiguity about the blood by which Christ reconciled
God; but how He came by water may be queried. It is improbable
that it refers to baptism. I think that John here expresses the fruit and
effect of what he related in the Gospel history. For when he says there
that water and blood flowed from Christ's side it is without doubt to
be regarded as a miracle. I know that such a thing does happen
naturally to the dead. But it came to pass through God's sure purpose
that Christ's side was a fountain of blood and water, so that believers
might know that the true cleansing, of which the ancient baptisms
were figures, is in Him, and that they might also know that then
was fulfilled what all the sprinklings of blood formerly promised.
Therefore, this brief division is the best, because it shows summarily
in what direction the ancient ceremonies chiefly pointed—that men

should be cleansed from their stains and liberated by all the sacrifices, so that they should have God favourable to them and be consecrated to Him. Also, the truth was exhibited in Christ, because the Law had nothing but visible figures. On this subject we have spoken more fully in Hebrews 9 and 10.

And it is the Spirit that beareth witness. In this clause he teaches how believers feel the power of Christ—because God's Spirit makes them certain. And, that their faith might not waver, he adds that the testimony of the Spirit establishes a full and real firmness. He calls the Spirit 'truth' because His authority is indubitable and should be abundantly sufficient for us.

7. *There are three that bear witness in heaven.* Some omit the whole of this verse. Jerome thinks it happened through malice rather than error, and that only among the Latins. But, since even the Greek MSS do not agree, I hardly dare assert anything. But because the passage reads better with the clause added and as I see that it is found in the best and most approved copies (*codicibus*), I also readily embrace it. And the meaning would then be that God, to confirm our faith in Christ most abundantly, testifies in a threefold way that we should rest in Him. For, as our faith acknowledges three persons in the one divine essence, so in the same three ways it is called to Christ to rest on Him.

When he says, 'these three are one', he is not referring to essence but rather to agreement. It is as if he said that the Father and His eternal Word and Spirit harmoniously approve the same thing about Christ. Hence some MSS (*codices*) have εἰς ἕν. But even if you read ἕν εἰσιν, as in other MSS (*exemplaribus*), there is no doubt that the Father, the Word and the Spirits are called one in the same sense as afterwards the blood, the water and the Spirit are.

But it seems a meaningless repetition for the Spirit, who is one witness, to be mentioned twice. I reply: Since He bears witness of Christ in different ways, a twofold testimony is fitly ascribed to Him. For the Father, together with His eternal Wisdom and Spirit, declares from heaven, as it were authoritatively, that Jesus is the Christ. Therefore, we are to consider the single majesty of the Divinity. But as the Spirit dwelling in our hearts is an earnest, pledge and seal to confirm that decree, He again speaks on earth by His grace. Yet inasmuch as not all accept this reading, I will expound what follows as though the apostle referred only to the witnesses on earth.

8. *There are three.* He accommodates the statement about water and blood to his own purpose, that they who reject Christ may be inexcusable. For He proves Himself to be the one formerly promised, by abundantly strong and clear testimonies. For, since water and blood

are the pledges and effects of the salvation He brought, they truly testify that He was sent by God. He adds a third witness, the Holy Spirit, who in fact holds the first place, for otherwise the water and the blood would have flowed in vain. He it is who seals in our hearts the testimony of the water and the blood. He it is who by His power makes the fruit of Christ's death come to us, who makes the blood shed for our redemption penetrate our souls. In a word, He makes Christ with all His blessings become ours. Thus, when Paul has said, in Rom. 1.4, that by the power of His resurrection Christ showed Himself to be the Son of God, he at once adds, 'through the sancti-fication of the Spirit'. For whatever signs of divine glory may shine forth in Christ, they would be obscure to us and we should overlook them, unless the Spirit opens for us the eyes of faith.

Readers may now understand that John cited the Spirit as a witness along with the water and the blood, because it is the peculiar office of the Spirit to cleanse our consciences by the blood of Christ, that the cleansing He brought might be efficacious to us. On this subject some remarks are made at the beginning of the previous epistle, where Peter uses nearly the same expression, that the Holy Spirit cleanses our souls by the sprinkling of the blood of Christ.

But we may infer from these words that faith does not apprehend a bare or empty Christ, but that also His power is quickening. For why was Christ sent to the earth, save to reconcile God by the sacrifice of His death and because the office of washing had been appointed to Him by the Father?

But it may be objected that this distinction is superfluous, because Christ cleansed us by expiating our sins. Therefore the apostle men-tions the same thing twice. I allow that cleansing is included in expiation, and that is why I did not distinguish between the water and the blood. Yet if anyone considers his own weakness, he will soon be aware that it is not in vain or thoughtlessly that the blood is distinguished from the water. Moreover, the apostle (as we have already said) is alluding to the rites of the Law. But for the sake of human weakness, God had formerly appointed washings as well as sacrifices. And the apostle wanted to express clearly that the truth of both has been exhibited in Christ. This is why he had said earlier, 'Not by water only.' For he means that not only is a part of our salvation found in Christ, but, so to say, the whole of it entire, so that nothing has to be sought elsewhere.

9. *If we receive the witness of men.* He reasons from the minor to the major, how ungrateful men are if they reject Christ, who has been divinely approved, as he said before. For if in worldly affairs we trust to the word of men who may lie and deceive, how reasonable that we

should give less credence to God when He is sitting as it were in His own court as supreme judge. It is only depravity that stops us receiving Christ, for He provides authority for His power by genuine proof.

Moreover, he calls the testimony of God not only that which the Spirit declares in our hearts, but also that which we have from the water and the blood. For that power of cleansing and expiating was not earthly but heavenly. Hence the blood of Christ is not to be estimated after the ordinary human manner. Rather we must look to God's design, who ordained it for blotting out our sins, and also to the divine power flowing from it.

For the witness of God is this, that he hath borne witness concerning his Son. He that believeth on the Son of God hath the witness in him: he that believeth not God hath made him a liar; because he hath not believed in the witness that God hath borne concerning his Son. And the witness is this, that God gave unto us eternal life, and this life is in his Son. He that hath the Son hath the life; he that hath not the Son of God hath not the life. (9b-12)

9. *For the witness of God is this.* The particle ὅτι does not here mean the cause, but is to be taken as explanatory. For when the apostle has told us that God deserves far more credence than men, he now adds that we can have no faith in God save by believing in Christ, for God sets Him alone before us and makes us stand in Him. From this he infers that we believe in Christ safely and with calm minds, because God by His authority claims our faith. He does not say that God speaks outwardly, but that everyone of the godly feels inwardly that God is the author of his faith. From this it appears how much that transient opinion which is dependent on something else differs from faith.

10. *He that believeth not.* As believers possess the benefit of knowing that they are out of danger of erring because they are founded on God, so he makes the ungodly guilty of extreme blasphemy, because they charge God with falsehood. There is undoubtedly nothing more precious to God than His truth. Therefore, no more atrocious injury can be done to Him than to despoil Him of this honour. Next, to stir us up to believe, he takes an argument from the contrary. For, if to make God a liar is a horrible and execrable impiety, because then that which is peculiar to Him is taken away, who would not fear to withhold faith from the Gospel, in which God wishes to be regarded as uniquely true and faithful? This should be carefully noted.

Some wonder why God commends faith so much, and why unbelief is so severely condemned. The highest glory of God turns on this. Since He wanted to show a special example of His truth in the

Gospel, those who reject the Christ there offered to them leave Him nothing. Therefore, although we may grant that a man in other parts of his life is angelic, yet his holiness is devilish so long as he rejects Christ. Thus, we see some in the Papacy much pleased with I know not what mask of sanctity while they go on obstinately resisting the Gospel. Let us understand that the beginning of godliness is to embrace this teaching obediently which He has so solemnly confirmed by His testimony.

11. *That God gave unto us eternal life.* Now that he has set forth the result, he invites us to believe. The respect is due to God that whatever He declares to us is forthwith beyond controversy. But when He freely offers us life, our ingratitude will be intolerable unless with prompt faith we receive such lovely and sweet teaching. And, indeed, the apostle's words are meant to show that we should not only obey the Gospel reverently lest we insult God, but that we should love it because it brings us eternal life. From this we also infer what is to be especially sought in the Gospel—the free gift of salvation. For the fact that God there exhorts us to repentance and fear should not be separated from the grace of Christ.

The apostle, to keep us entirely in Christ, once more repeats that life is contained in Him; as if he said that this is the only way that God the Father has appointed for us to obtain life. And the apostle here briefly includes three points. That we are all given over to death until God in His free goodness restores us to life. For he plainly states that life is given by God, and from this it follows that we are destitute of it and that it cannot be acquired by merits. Secondly, he teaches us that this life is conferred on us by the Gospel, since there the goodness and fatherly love of God towards us is revealed. Finally, he says that we can only become partakers of this life by being engrafted into Christ by faith.

12. *He that hath not the Son.* This is confirmation of the previous sentence. It should have been sufficient that God placed life in Christ alone, from whom it should be sought. But in case anyone should turn away to another, he excludes from the hope of life all who do not seek it in Christ. We know what it is to have Christ, for He is possessed by faith. So he deprives of life all who are outside the body of Christ.

But this seems irrational, for the histories tell of great men who were endued with heroic virtues and yet were complete strangers to Christ; and it seems absurd that such excellent men had no honour. I reply that we are greatly mistaken if we think that everything that is excellent in our eyes is also approved by God. Indeed, it is said in Luke 16.15, 'that which is exalted among men is an abomination in the sight of God.' For we are satisfied with external appearances, because the filthiness of the heart is hidden from us. But God sees that underneath lies the foulest filth. And so it is not surprising if apparent virtues, flowing from an impure heart and tending to no right end, stink to Him. Besides, where, apart from the Spirit of Christ, does purity of heart come from or a true concern for godliness? There is, therefore, nothing praiseworthy save in Christ.

A further reason removes all doubt. The righteousness of men is placed in the forgiveness of sins. If you take this away, the certain curse of God and eternal death awaits us all. It is Christ alone who reconciles the Father to us, as He has once appeased Him by the sacrifices of His death. From this it follows that God is propitious only in Christ and that only in Him is there righteousness.

If any object the case of Cornelius, whom Luke said was accepted by God before he was called to the faith of the Gospel (Acts 10.2), I reply briefly that God sometimes deals with us in such a way that the seed of faith does not come up on the very first day. Cornelius had no clear and distinct knowledge of Christ; but as he was endowed with some feeling of God's mercy, he must also have understood something about the Mediator. But God has hidden and wonderful ways of acting. Therefore let us disregard those unprofitable speculations and keep only to that plain way of salvation which He has shown us.

These things have I written unto you, that ye may know that ye have eternal life, even unto you that believe on the name of the Son of God. And this is the boldness which we have toward him, that, if we ask anything, according to his will, he heareth us: and if we know that he heareth us whatsoever we ask, we know that we have the petitions which we have asked of him. (13-15)

13. *These things have I written unto you.* There should be daily progress in faith; and so he says that he was writing to those who already believed, so that they might believe more firmly and certainly, and thus enjoy a full confidence of eternal life. Hence, the use of teaching is both to initiate the ignorant in Christ and also to confirm more and more those who know Him. Therefore we must pay heed to our duty of learning, that our faith may increase throughout the whole of our life. For there are still many remnants of unbelief in us, and our faith is so weak that what we believe is not yet really believed without more confirmation.

Moreover, it is noteworthy how faith is confirmed—when Christ's office and power are explained. For the apostle says that he wrote these things (that eternal life is to be sought in Christ alone) in order

307

that they who were already believers might believe—i.e. make progress in believing. It is therefore the duty of the godly teacher, that he may confirm disciples in faith, to extol the grace of Christ as much as possible, so that we may be satisfied with that and desire nothing more.

By obscuring and weakening this truth in every way, the Papists show clearly enough that they care for nothing less than the right teaching of faith. For this same reason their schools should be shunned more than all the Scyllas and Charybdises, for a man can hardly enter them without certain shipwreck to his faith.

The apostle teaches further in this passage that Christ is the proper object of faith and that confidence of salvation is joined to the faith we have in His name. For the end of believing is to be the children and heirs of God.

14. *And this is the boldness.* He commends the faith he mentioned by its fruit; or he shows in what our confidence is chiefly placed; that is, that the godly dare to call on God undauntedly. As also Paul says in Eph. 3.12, that by faith we have access to God with boldness; and also in Rom. 8.15, that the Spirit opens our mouth so that we do not hesitate to cry, Abba, Father. And indeed, if we were driven away from approaching God, nothing could be worse for us. But so long as this refuge is open to us, we should be happy in all ills. Nay, this one thing makes our troubles blessed, because we know with certainty that God will be our deliverer, and relying on His fatherly love towards us, we flee to Him.

Therefore, let us hold fast this statement of the apostle's, that the chief trial of our faith is calling upon God, and that we do not rightly and faithfully call upon Him unless we are completely convinced that our prayers will not be in vain. For the apostle denies that they are endued with faith who are doubtful and waver. From this it appears that the teaching of faith is buried and almost extinct in the Papacy. They certainly mutter a lot of prayers and gabble a great deal about calling on God. But they pray and tell us to pray, with doubtful and wavering hearts and even condemn this boldness which the apostle requires as necessary.

According to his will. By this phrase he wanted to tell us in passing that the right rule of praying is when men subject their wishes to God. For although God has promised to do whatever His people ask, He does not permit them the unbridled liberty of asking whatever comes into their heads, but has laid down for them a law of proper prayer. And, indeed, nothing is more useful for us than this bridle. For if each of us were allowed to ask what he liked, and if God indulged our wishes, it would be in our worst interests. For we do not know what is for the best. Nay, we seethe with depraved and harmful desires. But God supplies a twofold remedy, lest we should pray outside the command of His will. He teaches us in His Word what He wants us to ask, and He has also set over us His Spirit as our leader and ruler to restrain our affections, that we may not let them stray beyond due bounds. For, as Paul says, we do not know what or how to pray, but the Spirit helps our infirmities and excites in us unutterable groans (Rom. 8.26). We should also ask the mouth of the Lord to direct our prayers. For, as has been said, God has appointed for us in His promises the legitimate way of praying.

15. *And if we know.* This is no superfluous repetition, as it seems to be. What the apostle has said in general about the success of prayer, he now affirms in particular. The godly desire or ask for nothing from God that they do not obtain. But when he says that all the wishes of believers are heard, he is speaking of sound and modest wishes which are composed to the rule of obedience. For believers do not run away with the bit between their teeth or indulge themselves in anything, but always in their prayers look to what God commands.

Therefore, this is an application of the general doctrine to the special and individual use of each person, lest believers should doubt that God is favourable to every and each prayer, and that they may wait with quiet minds while the Lord executes what they have prayed for, and that, relieved from all trouble and anxiety, they may cast their cares on God. But this peace and security ought not to damp down our zeal in prayer, for he who is sure of a happy outcome should not cease to pray to God. For the assurance of faith certainly does not beget sloth. The apostle only meant that everyone should be quiet amid his needs when he has placed his sighings in the bosom of God.

If any man see his brother sinning a sin not unto death, he shall ask, and God will give him life for that sin not unto death. There is a sin unto death: not concerning this do I say that he should make request. All unrighteousness is sin: and there is a sin not unto death. We know that whosoever is begotten of God sinneth not; but he that was begotten of God keepeth himself, and the evil one toucheth him not. (16-18)

16. *If any man.* The apostle broadens even further the fruit of the faith which he has referred to, that our prayers may also avail for our brethren. It is a great thing that God kindly invites us to Himself and is ready to help us as soon as we are in difficulty. But that He undertakes to listen when we ask for others also, is no small confirmation to our faith, to assure us completely that we shall never meet with a rebuff in our own cause.

Now the apostle exhorts us to be mutually careful for the salvation of one another. He also wants the failures of the brethren to stir us to prayer. And surely it is an iron hardness not to feel pity when we see souls, redeemed by Christ's blood, going to ruin. But he shows that a remedy is at hand for brethren to help brethren. He says that he who prays for the perishing will restore life to him, though the words 'he shall give' can refer to God, as if it were said that God will grant to your prayers the life of a brother. Yet the sense will stay the same, that the prayers of believers will avail even to rescuing a brother from death. If we understand it of man, that he may give life to a brother, the expression is hyperbolical, but contains nothing absurd. For what is granted us by the free goodness of God we are said to give to others. Such a great benefit should greatly stimulate us to ask for our brethren the forgiveness of sins. And when the apostle commends to us συμπάθεια, he tells us at the same time how much we should beware of the cruelty of condemning our brethren or of over great rigour in despairing of their salvation.

A sin not unto death. So that we may not cast away all hope of the salvation of those who sin, he shows that God does not punish their failures so grievously as to reject them. From this it follows that we should regard them as brethren, since the Lord keeps them in the number of His children. But he denies that the sins are unto death, not only in which the saints daily offend, but even when they grievously provoke God's wrath. For so long as room for pardon remains, death does not yet entirely occupy the throne.

The apostle is not, however, here distinguishing between mortal and venial sin, as afterwards became common. For the distinction which prevails in the Papacy is completely foolish. The Sorbonnists avow that mortal sin hardly exists, apart from the grossest wickedness, which is, so to say, palpable. Thus, in venial sins they think there may be the greatest filth hidden in the soul. In short, they think that all the fruits of original sin, so long as they do not break out externally, are washed away by a light sprinkling of holy water. And what wonder, when they do not regard as blasphemous sins, doubts about God's grace or any lusts or evil desires if they are not consented to? If a man's mind be upset by unbelief, if impatience tempts him to rage against God, whatever monstrous lusts may titillate him, the Papists regard as too light to be regarded as sins, at least after baptism. It is therefore not surprising that they make the worst crimes into venial offences, for they weigh them in their own balances and not in God's. But among believers it should be an indubitable principle that whatever wars against God's Law is sin and by its nature mortal. For where there is transgression of the Law there is sin and death.

Then what does the apostle mean? He says that sins are not mortal which, although deserving death, are yet not punished so severely by God. He is therefore not considering sins in themselves, but forming a judgment on them from the fatherly goodness of God, which overlooks the sin where yet there was blame. In short, God does not give over to death those whom He has restored to life, although it is no thanks to them that they are not alienated from life.

There is a sin unto death. I have already said that this refers to the sin for which there is no hope of forgiveness left. But it may be asked what this is, for it must be very atrocious, when God punishes it so severely. From the context we may infer that it is not what they call a partial fall, or the transgression of a single commandment, but apostasy, men alienating themselves completely from God. For the apostle adds afterwards that God's children do not sin, that is, they do not forsake God and give themselves wholly to Satan as his slaves. It is not surprising if such a defection is mortal. For God never so deprives His own of the grace of the Spirit but that they keep some spark of godliness. Therefore, they must be reprobate and given up to destruction who so fall away as to reject all fear of God.

If anyone asks whether the door of salvation is shut against their repentance, the answer is plain. As they are given over to a reprobate mind and are destitute of the Holy Spirit, they can do nothing but with obstinate minds rush always to the worse, adding sins to sins. Moreover, as the sin or blasphemy against the Spirit always brings such a defection with it, there is no doubt but this is indicated here.

But again it may be asked by what indications we know that a man's fall is fatal. For unless we could know this certainly, there would have been no point in the apostle making the exception that they were not to pray for a sin of this sort. Therefore, it is right sometimes to determine whether the fallen is without hope or whether there is still room for the remedy. That indeed, I allow to be true, and it is evident beyond controversy from this passage. But as this very rarely happens, and as God commends to us the infinite riches of His grace and bids us follow His example in being merciful, the judgment of eternal death must not be rashly levelled against anyone. On the contrary, love should dispose us to hope well. Yet if the ungodliness of some does not seem otherwise than hopeless to us, as if the Lord had pointed it out with His finger, we should not contend against the just judgment of God or seek to be more merciful than He is.

17. *All unrighteousness.* This passage can be expounded variously. If you take it in apposition, the sense would not be inapt: 'Though all unrighteousness is sin, every sin is not unto death.' Another meaning

is equally suitable: 'Because sin is all unrighteousness, it follows that any one sin is not unto death.' Some take all unrighteousness as 'complete unrighteousness', as if the apostle had said that the sin of which he spoke was the accumulation of unrighteousness. But I would rather embrace the first or second explanation; and as it comes to the same thing, I leave it to the judgment of readers to determine which is the more appropriate.

18. *We know that whosoever is begotten of God.* If you imagine God's children to be completely pure and free from sin, as the fanatics contend, the apostle is inconsistent, for he would be taking away the mutual duty of prayer among brethren. Therefore, he says that he who does not wholly fall away from the grace of God sinneth not. Hence he wants prayer to be made for all God's children, because they do not sin unto death. He adds a proof: Whoever is born of God keeps himself, that is holds himself within the fear of God and does not let himself so be led away as to extinguish all sense of godliness and to surrender himself completely to the devil and the flesh.

For when he says that *the evil one toucheth him not,* he refers to a deadly wound. For the children of God do not remain untouched by the wounds of Satan, but ward off his blows with the shield of faith, so that they do not penetrate into their hearts. Therefore spiritual life is never extinguished in them. This is *not to sin,* when believers labour under the infirmity of the flesh, but groan under the burden of sin, are displeased with themselves and do not cease to fear God.

Keepeth himself. He transfers to us what belongs to God. For were any of us the keeper of his own salvation, it would be a wretched protection. Therefore, Christ asks the Father to keep us (John 17.11) signifying that this is not by our own help. The advocates of free-will lay hold of this expression to prove from it that we are kept from sin partly by God's grace and partly by our own power. But they fail to see that believers do not possess of themselves the custodianship of which the apostle speaks. And, indeed, he does not speak of their power here, as if they could defend themselves by their own strength, but only shows that they should resist Satan, that they may never be wounded by his weapons. And we know that we fight armed only with the weapons of God. Therefore, believers keep themselves from sin inasmuch as they are kept by God.

And we know that we are of God, and the whole world lieth in the evil one. And we know that the Son of God is come, and hath given us an understanding, that we may know him that is true, and we are in him that is true, even in his Son Jesus Christ. This is the true God, and eternal life. My little children, guard yourselves from idols. (19-21)

19. *We are of God.* He takes the substance of this exhortation from his previous teaching. For what he had declared of the children of God in common, he now applies to those he was writing to. And he did this to stir them up to beware of sin and to encourage them to repel the assaults of Satan. Let readers note that it is only true faith that, so to say, applies to us God's grace. For the apostle acknowledges as believers only those who gather themselves into the order of God's children. Nor does he put probable conjecture (as the Sophists say) for confidence. For he says we know. The substance of it is that, as we have been begotten of God, we should strive to prove by our separation from the world and from the holiness of our life that we have not been called in vain to such a great honour.

Now this admonition is very necessary for all the godly; for wherever they look, Satan has his enticements ready, by which he seeks to draw them away from God. It would therefore be difficult for them to keep on in their true course were not their calling more to them than all the hindrances of the world. Therefore, if we are to be well-armed for the contest, these two things must be held, that the world is wicked and that our calling is from God.

Under the word *world* the apostle undoubtedly embraces the whole of mankind. By saying that it lieth in the wicked one, he places it under the dominion of Satan. There is therefore no reason why we should hesitate to flee the world which, by contempt of God, gives itself up to the bondage of Satan. And there is no reason for us to fear its enmity, for it is alienated from God. In short, since corruption fills all nature, believers should study self-denial. And since nothing is seen in the world but malice and depravity, they must needs say farewell to flesh and blood if they are to follow God. The other side should also be added; that it is God who has called them, that they may oppose His protection against all the machinations of the world and Satan.

20. *And we know that the Son of God is come.* Since God's children are assailed on every side, he (as we have said) encourages and exhorts them to constancy in resistance, and for this cause, that they fight under God's banner and know assuredly that they are ruled by His Spirit. And now he tells them where this knowledge is especially to be sought. He says that God is so revealed to us in Christ, that now there is no reason to waver. The apostle is not thoughtless to dwell on this, for, unless our faith is really founded on God, we shall never stand firm in the battle. This is why the apostle teaches us that we have obtained by the benefit of Christ a sure knowledge of the true God, so that we may not fluctuate in uncertainty.

By *true* God he means, not the veracious but the truly God, to distinguish Him from all idols. Thus true is opposed to the fictitious, for it is ἀληθινός, and not ἀληθής; just as in John 17.3, 'This is life eternal, to know thee, the true God, and Jesus Christ whom thou hast sent.' And he justly ascribes to Christ this office of enlightening our minds in the knowledge of God. For, as He is the unique image of the invisible God, as He is the only interpreter of the Father, as He is the only guide of life, indeed, as He is the life, the light of the world and the truth, we necessarily vanish away into our own inventions so soon as we depart from Him.

And it is said that Christ *hath given us an understanding*, not only because He shows us in the teaching of the Gospel of what kind is the true God and also enlightens us by His Spirit, but because in Christ Himself we have God manifested in the flesh; since, as Paul says, in Him dwells all the fulness of the God-head and are hid all the treasures of knowledge and wisdom (Col. 2.3, 9). Thus it is that, in a sense, the face of God shines to us in Christ. Not that there was no knowledge or only a doubtful knowledge of God before Christ's coming, but because He now reveals Himself more fully and clearly. And this is what Paul says in II Cor. 4.6, that God, who formerly commanded light to shine out of darkness in the creation of the world, has now shone in our hearts by the brightness of the knowledge of His glory in the face of Christ.

And we must note that this gift is peculiar to the elect. Christ certainly kindles for all indiscriminately the torch of His Gospel, but not all have eyes in their minds to see it. On the contrary, Satan spreads a veil of blindness over many. Therefore the apostle means the light which Christ kindles inwardly in the hearts of His people, and which once kindled is never extinguished, although it may for a time be smothered.

We are in him that is true. By these words he tells us how efficacious is the knowledge he mentions; for by it we are engrafted into Christ and are made one with God. For it has a living root deeply fixed in the heart, so that God lives in us and we in Him. Since he omits the copulative in saying, we are *in him that is true, in his Son,* he seems to express the manner of our unity with God, as if he said that we are in God through Christ.

This is the true God. Although the Arians have tried to get round this passage and some today agree with them, we have here a remarkable title to the divinity of Christ. The Arians transfer this passage to the Father, as if the apostle again declares that He is the true God. But this repetition is too frigid. He has already twice declared that the true God is He who has been made known to us in Christ. Why add at once, *This is the true God?* It belongs most suitably to Christ.

For when he has taught us that Christ is the leader by whose hand we are guided to God, he now, in amplification, affirms that Christ is that God, lest we should think we have to seek further. And this he confirms by adding, *and eternal life*. It is doubtless the one and the same who is said to be the true God and eternal life. I pass over the fact that the relative οὗτος is usually restricted to the last person mentioned. Therefore, I say that Christ is properly called eternal life; and that this way of speaking is frequent in John none can deny.

The sum of it is that, when we have Christ, we enjoy the true and eternal God, for He is to be sought nowhere else. And secondly, we become partakers of eternal life because it, hidden in the Father, is offered to us in Christ. The Father is the origin of life, but the fountain from which we must draw it is Christ.

21. *Guard yourselves from idols.* Although this is a separate sentence, it is, so to say, an appendix to the preceding teaching. For the life-giving light of the Gospel should scatter and put to flight, not only darkness, but also all mists, from the minds of the godly. The apostle not only condemns idolatry, but commands us to beware of all images. By this he signifies that the worship of God can not be kept sound and pure when men begin to desire images. For superstition is so inborn in us that the least occasion will infect us with its contagion. Dry wood laid on coal will burn less easily than idolatry will seize and over-run men's minds when a chance is given them. Who cannot see that images are the sparks? Sparks, do I say? Rather torches, which will set the whole world on fire.

Yet the apostle is not only speaking of statues, but also of altars, and comprehends all the instruments of superstitions. And the Papists are ridiculous to twist this passage to the statues of Jupiter and Mercury and the like, as if the apostle were not teaching in general that godliness is corrupted whenever a corporeal figure is ascribed to God, or whenever statues and pictures are set up for worship. Let us therefore remember that we should be so careful to remain in the spiritual worship of God as to banish far from us everything that may turn us aside to gross and carnal superstitions.

INDEX OF SCRIPTURE REFERENCES

INDEX OF SCRIPTURE REFERENCES

INDEX OF NAMES

GENERAL INDEX

adoption, i. 74, 81, 223; ii. 136, 266f, 294f
adultery, i. 208f
accidental judgment, blindness, i. 75f, 173, 254f
angels, i. 23, 44, 118, 275; ii. 3, 196
antichrist, ii. 256f, 260, 286f
apostacy, i. 177f; ii. 257f
apostle, i. 96, 107, 233; ii. 80, 114, 116, 129, 146, 204f

Baptism, i. 29f, 64f, 78f, 88; ii. 186, 200, 206, 239
Bible, i. 99, 139, 149, 168f; ii. 4, 36, 88, 121, 172, 180, 190, 194, 195, 213f, 225, 226, 285, 289

calling, i. 14, 35, 39, 162; ii. 4, 98, 139, 146, 198, 224
cleansing, ii. 58ff, 186, 241, 304
Church
    authority, ii. 64
    apostolate, ii. 102ff, 203, 205ff, 218
    body and Head, i. 126, 268; ii. 83f, 148, 151, 248f
    calling, i. 14, 34, 141, 179; ii. 102f
    discipline, i. 248f, 253; ii. 50, 113
    government, i. 27, 81f, 202f, 258f, 263ff; ii. 21f, 203, 204, 219f
    keys, ii. 206f
    ministry, ii. 203f, 207, 215f, 218f, 220, 263
    ministry of women, ii. 199, 200
    ordination, ii. 204f
    perpetuity, ii. 103
    purity, i. 2, 51ff; ii. 65f, 241, 262f, 269f
    schism, i. 200f, 245, 246, 270; ii. 255f
    tradition, i. 95ff, 226, 261; ii. 147
    unity, i. 267f, ii. 22, 104, 142, 147f, 180, 236

Church (cont.)
    worship, i. 48f, 95, 97f, 99ff; ii. 27f, 36, 134f, 169
    communion with God, ii. 236, 237, 238, 247, 262, 282
    confession of faith, i. 104, 246, 250, 265; ii. 3, 20, 49, 50, 188, 223, 293f
    confession of sin, ii. 207f, 240ff
    councils, ii. 285f

death, i. 129f; ii. 157, 184
devil, i. 188f, 227ff; ii. 56, 91, 271

election, i. 162ff, 273; ii. 61f, 101f, 135ff, 145f, 149f
Eucharist, i. 34, 169ff; ii. 183f, 186, 206, 212
everlasting life, i. 74f, 178, 232, 263; ii. 8ff, 37f, 55f, 118, 136, 233, 235

faith, i. 17ff, 50, 58, 74, 75, 85f, 103f, 109, 114, 121, 129, 146, 155f, 159f, 162, 164, 166, 176f, 179, 193f, 198, 220, 253f; ii. 6, 7ff, 15, 33, 45, 51, 73f, 77ff, 83f, 123, 130f, 132, 136, 137, 139, 141, 147, 148f, 193, 195, 211f, 213, 233, 246, 250, 264, 276, 279, 281, 290, 293f, 298, 301f, 305, 307f
forgiveness, i. 32f, 129, 132f; ii. 58, 189, 207, 239, 241, 301
free-will, i. 17, 77, 130, 164, 165, 222f; ii. 272f, 312

Gentiles, i. 16f, 266f
God
    Creator, i. 10, 131
    glory, i. 25, 187; ii. 2, 134, 135, 149